JOHN DOBLE, *Justice of the Peace*
At his office on Soldier's Gulch, Volcano

John Doble's
JOURNAL AND LETTERS FROM THE MINES

Volcano, Mokelumne Hill, Jackson and San Francisco

1851-1865

Edited by
CHARLES L. CAMP

VOLCANO
· PRESS ·

Volcano Press, Inc.
Volcano, Amador Co., California

Paperback edition published by Volcano Press, Inc. 1999

ISBN 1-884244-18-1

Library of Congress Cataloging-in-Publication Data

Doble, John, 1828-1866.
    [Journal and letters from the mines]
    John Doble's journal and letters from the mines : Mokelumne Hill, Jackson, Volcano, and San Francisco, 1851-1865 / edited by Charles L. Camp.
    cm.
    Originally published: Denver: Old West Pub. Co., c 1962.
    Includes index.
    ISBN 1-8844244-18-1 (pbk.)
    1. Doble, John, 1828-1866--Diaries. 2. Doble, John, 1828-1866--Correspondence. 3. Gold miners--California--Diaries. 4. Gold miners--California--Correspondence. 5. California--Gold discoveries. 6. San Francisco (Calif.)--Biography. 7. Volcano (Calif.)--Biography. 8. Mokelumne Hill (Calif.)--Biography. 9. Jackson (Calif.)--Biography. I. Camp, Charles Lewis, 1893-   . II. Title. III. Title: Journal and letters from the mines.
    F865.D6   1999
    979.4' 04' 092' dc21   98-46963
                                           CIP

Volcano Press, Inc.
P.O. Box 270
Volcano, California 95689-0270

Cover design by Terry Grillo
Cover photograph provided courtesy of the
Bancroft Library, University of California, Berkeley

HYPERLINK http://www.volcanopress.com
E-mail HYPERLINK mail to: sales@volcanopress.com
Telephone: 800/879-9636
Fax: 209/296-4995

Printed in the Unites States of America

PUBLISHER'S PREFACE

One evening in 1952 my friend Charles Camp was visiting me in Denver, and I handed him an old manuscript diary to examine. I had purchased this diary in 1928, in Cincinnati, and recognized its value as a remarkable record of a California miner in the 1850's. He wrote legibly, and gave intimate details of his daily life, but had failed to reveal his identity.

Dr. Camp was greatly impressed by what he read. I asked if he thought it good enough to edit and publish. His reply was enthusiastically affirmative. The diarist recorded a particularly interesting vigilante meeting in the Gold Rush town of Jackson, the wealth of day-to-day detail about placer mining, business, and gold-camp housekeeping.

Dr. Camp's interest in the diary remained constant, and in the course of time I took the diary to California, leaving it with him for further evaluation. A thorough reading reinforced his first impression, and through internal evidence revealed the name of the diarist—John Doble.

Doble's diary, published here, is the final result of Dr. Camp's interest and the informed scholarship he has brought to bear upon it. As edited, it is an important and in many ways unique contribution to our knowledge of the California Gold Rush. In a period in which there was no newspaper to record the daily life of the busy towns of Volcano and Jackson, Doble recorded much of value. He was a man whose mind was concerned with details. Because he did not know what to leave out, he put everything in, bringing his times vividly to life for readers of later times. He wrote with charm, recording his feelings as few of his contemporary Californians had time or inclination to do. You as the reader have the illusion of being part of the story. You are happy when John makes a rich strike; you are grieved with him when his partner Jim dies.

The discovery of the letters from John Doble to Lizzie E. Lucas was a remarkable and timely coincidence. Dr. Camp was attracted by a name John Doble in the Berkeley telephone directory, who turned out to be a grand-nephew of our John Doble. This visit revealed another amazing coincidence. Only a few weeks before, the Berkeley John Doble had received a surprising visit from a descendant of the original John's Lizzie, a James R. Little of Columbia, Missouri, who possessed a sheaf of actual letters from John to Lizzie who, in the end, did not marry John after all.

The letters form an extremely interesting addition to the diary, for in them Doble describes, in an impressive literary style, life in the mines and in San Francisco. They also cover a later period than the diary. It is our hope that publication of this book will somehow bring to light subsequent diaries which Doble must have kept.

In his diary John Doble records much about little-known places in the Mother Lode. Inspired by this aspect of the work, Dr. Camp has prepared three remarkable maps which locate many places that have never before been mapped and that have long since disappeared from the land. Working over a span of nearly four years, he talked to many people and consulted numerous manuscripts and printed sources, as he indicates in "The Map and the Acknowledgements." Beyond that he worked over most of the area in the footsteps of John Doble and his fellow miners. As a result, Charles Camp's maps form a contribution to our knowledge of the Calaveras mines in the 1850's comparable to John Doble's own diary.

FRED A. ROSENSTOCK

ACKNOWLEDGMENTS

The cover was designed by Volcano resident Terry Grillo. Mr. Grillo's family has lived in Volcano for five generations, beginning with his great-grandfather, a miner and rancher in the area who arrived from Liguria, Italy in 1856. He walked from San Francisco to Volcano, much like Mr. Doble, and lived in Volcano while the Journal was written.

John Doble's signature is used on the cover and the title page. It was reproduced from an original document which is illustrated on the page facing page 50. The document has been in the possession of the Grillo family for many years.

The cover daguerreotype of the four miners was brought to Mr. Grillo's attention by the Amador County Archives in Jackson, California. It is provided courtesy of the Bancroft Library, University of California, Berkeley. Bancroft records list the exposure as being made in 1855; it may be the earliest known photographic record of Volcano. It remains an amazing record of Volcano before the valley was ripped almost inside out by unmanaged logging and placer mining, and finally, by hydraulic mining.

It is also a snapshot of the real wild West. The legends of the West come from places like Volcano in 1855...men were shot or knifed over honor or villainy, fortunes were lost and won on poker tables, and generally, people lived hard and fast. It was nearly gone, civilized, structured and buttoned up, less than 20 years later.

Heartfelt thanks to C. Penny Hancock-Callmeyer and Dixie Robertson of Bertelsmann Industry Services, Inc. for their invaluable assistance in creating and producing this paperback edition. Dixie is no longer with us; her last days were spent working on the layout and pagination of this book.

John Doble's *Journal and Letters from the Mines* was originally published in 1962 by The Old West Publishing Company of Denver. One thousand copies were printed. So last, but not least, our thanks to The Old West Publishing Company for granting permission to reissue the *Journal* in 1999, the sesquicentennial anniversary of the California Gold Rush.

Volcano Press
Volcano, California

TABLE OF CONTENTS

ILLUSTRATIONS AND MAPS

INTRODUCTION TO
JOHN DOBLE'S JOURNAL

The whole civilized world, as well as parts not so civilized, was inflamed by the fever of the gold discoveries of '48 and '49. It was quite normal and usual that a young man, unmarried and with no settled plans, should have left his home in Indiana and cast himself into the maelstrom of the Gold Rush. It was somewhat unusual that he should have remained in California for so many years. It was nothing less than astonishing that during this time and particularly during the days of his toil as a pick-and-shovel miner he should have had the zeal and perseverance to keep up a lengthy, detailed and observant journal, reflecting his thoughts, feelings and experiences. Here is an honest and reliable narrative, boyishly and sometimes almost painfully naïve, and candid. Doble's life is a sample of what many a young miner endured in his struggles to succeed in the placers of California.

His powers of observation enable us to re-picture those fervid scenes from the viewpoint of a gold digger; for this is a genuine grass-roots diary, giving more intimate details than could ever have been told by those who simply tramped through the mines without soaking their hands and feet in mud and cold water.

John Doble writes as he may have talked, fluently and easily. He fills his pages with the life whirling about him. We meet the restless miners as they come and go—his partners and friends, and those who try to fleece him; his traveling companions Cap. Reid, Doc. Belles, Major Coleman, Bill Ryal, and Tom Baldwin the fiddler; his associates on the Mokelumne, Doc. Tickett, Dan Curry, Joe Wallace, Billy Spencer, Mad Jack Nelson, Black Jack the sailor, Capt. Van Allen and old Eby Hollis; at Jackson, Sam Watson the vigilante; and at Volcano, many more.

Society at Volcano had become a mobile and turbulent mixture of many races, nationalities and factions: Chinese, Chileans, Sonorans, Spanish-Californians, French, German, Dutch, English, Irish, Scottish, Swedish, Turkish, Kanakas, Negroes and American Indians, to say nothing of the Americans—Yankees and Southerners; emigrant families, old-timers and greenhorns, rascals, mountebanks, dancing girls and murderers; living side-by-side with the most admirable and gentle souls like Doble himself, who would sit up nights with the sick, take up collections for the unfortunates, start circulating libraries, conduct theatricals and debating lyceums, organize temperance parades and camp meetings.

The town, tucked away in the mountains, inaccessible during storms, became an almost self-sufficient unit. There were bakeries, breweries, lumber mills, a sash-and-door factory, a general store and express office, hotels, saloons, a theatre and churches, a newspaper, lawyers, a doctor or two, a dentist, ministers and a priest, local wags, and George Horn the spoofing frontier philosopher. Neighboring ranches supplied meat and vegetables, milk and eggs. The population rose to 5,000 where only 100 or so live today.

Doble describes the arrival of the overland trains, with wives and daughters, to the huge delight of the lonely miners who go out along the road to greet them. Kit Carson comes through with his great flocks of sheep and his Mexican drovers. Flint and Bixby establish headquarters nearby for their sheep and cattle from across the Plains. Rod Stowell the Texas gunman projects himself into the second of his killings and barely escapes a lynching party.

We meet Smith and Slater, keepers of the Spring Saloon and bath house. Smith sells the mortgaged establishment to Doble and absconds. And this isn't the first or last time that our gentle journalist is taken in by conniving partners.

Doble and Doc. Carpenter, the pioneer, build a house in town. There he attends the death of his best friend and afterwards invites an English couple to help with the housekeeping.

The burning of the Eureka Hotel and Duke's store along with it, the marriages and balls, the peculiar methods of handling the refractory clay in Soldier's Gulch, exploration of the caves along South Branch, Pike Hill and Indiana Gulch—these are vividly described.

The slow approach of starvation when the village is cut off by floods, the day-by-day rise in food prices, the deaths by drowning and cave-ins, when the coffins are washed out of the graveyard and the bridges are carried away—Doble makes all this a part of his story.

He prospects at Latimer's Store, Alabama Gulch, the forks of the Mokelumne, Ballard's Humbug, Clapboard Gulch, Jackass Gulch, and Indian Flat. He recalls the excitement of the rich strike and the discouragement of hard times when claims don't pay wages. His earnings run from 12 cents to more than forty dollars a day. He mildly succeeds after years of hard, back-breaking, hand-blistering toil.

He wanders about as all the prospectors did, visiting the camps and towns within two-day's travel: Dutchmans Gulch, Rich Gulch, Big Bar, White's Bar, Watkin's Bar, Kohlberg's Humbug, Nigger Gulch, Indian Gulch, Mosquito Gulch, Independence, the Woodhouse Quartz Mill, Butte City, French Camp, Secreta, Clinton, Indian Diggins, and far away Chickamasee or Grizzly Flats. Some of those ephemeral tent and cabin camps are now gone from the face of the land and even their locations have been forgotten.

This, then, is the journal of John Doble, from which are printed extracts written in the years 1851-1854. Much of it is a daily diary, contained in one large notebook of some 357 pages. The period from November 22, 1851, in Nicaragua, until February 8, 1852, near Mokelumne Hill, was written at Volcano, from memory. He had kept a memorandum which he lost. The period between February 8 and November 16 was copied from a second pocket diary. From then until the end, February 11, 1854, the entries were made directly into the present large book.

There are scores, perhaps hundreds of diaries and reminiscences of overland journeys by gold hunters. There may be almost as many records of voyages around the Horn and across Central America and Mexico by various routes. Most of these narratives end abruptly upon arrival in the mines. When the going got rough the diaries were laid aside. It was difficult for a weary digger, stiff and sore, with blistered and chapped hands, to keep up his writing by candle light or on Sundays when so many diversions were proffered in the saloons and dance halls. Nevertheless this is exactly what John Doble managed to do, with a determination that evokes our interest and gratitude.

The gold excitement attracted traveling writers such as Bayard Taylor and J. Ross Browne, artists of the caliber of J. M. Letts and J. D. Borthwick, humorists and chroniclers of the stamp of James H. Carson, Leonard Kip, and Alonzo Delano, to say nothing of the tender memories of Bret Harte and the puckish humor of Mark Twain. In all this rich array of talent we find scarcely anything quite so expressive of the feelings and fortunes of the long-tom sluicer and hopeful prospector as this narrative of John Doble's. One tale that does this job adequately, the Canfield "Diary of a '49er," is made up from background knowledge and bar-room gossip, in a remarkable way, but it is not a genuine diary, and the plot is laid in the Northern Mines. Doble's adventures were farther south, and like Canfield's "Jackson," Doble's remarks extend beyond localities and incidents to the relations between men, peculiar men such as only the mines attracted and produced. And we have here the diarist's own feelings, his reactions to the strange environment as well as the image of that environment.

Besides the placers and the primitive quartz mills, there were ranches near the mines, cattle ranges, sheep and goat and pig farms, vegetable plots, saw mills and tanneries. The crude roads and trails were lined with pack mules and burros, freight wagons and stages. The population of the Mother Lode counties in the early '50's exceeded that of all the rest of California.

John Doble's journal is followed by a long correspondence in the early '60's from Volcano, Jackson and San Francisco. John had heard of Miss Lucas of Pennsylvania whom he had never met. They wrote to each other for three years and broke off only after she married another man.

All this should be of more than personal interest. The changes in Doble's life and character while he remained so long a bachelor in Volcano may be typical of what was happening to some of those old-time prospectors who lived out their lives in serene isolation, in the mountains and deserts of the West.

BIOGRAPHICAL NOTE

John Doble was born February 7, 1828, on his father's farm in Sugar Creek Township, Shelby County, Indiana. He was the fifth child in a family of eight children, being the eldest son of William A. and Catherine Huffman Doble, who were married in Kentucky, October 30, 1821. John's father, William A. Doble, was the son of Joseph and Barbara (Estes) Doble of Pennsylvania and Virginia respectively. They were of English ancestry. William A. was born in Virginia on August 25, 1798. After the death of his first wife, the mother of eight of his children, William married Margaret Jane Nickel (or Nichols), on July 1, 1834. They had four children.

William A. Doble died on August 23, 1852, in Indiana. His son Henry, born on September 18, 1831, became an enterprising hardware merchant at Shelbyville.[34] William's second son, Abner, born June 15, 1829, sailed for California on November 28, 1849, on the ship *Rowena*, Captain Swain. He landed at San Francisco on June 25, 1850,[35] went to Humboldt Bay the same year and was one of the first settlers there.[36] Abner returned to San Francisco where he became prominent in public affairs. He continued in the blacksmithing and iron working business and was the proprietor of extensive ranch properties.[37] His iron foundry, in charge of his son William A., was still in operation on the corner of Fremont and Howard streets, near the Shot Tower, up to the time of the fire. He ran for Mayor of San Francisco in 1863 and was defeated.[38]

Abner married Margaret ("Maggie") McFarland on March 26, 1856. He died in San Francisco on December 22, 1904, following the death of his wife on February 14 of the same year. Their children: Lizzie May (who became Mrs. Francis Ferrier), Robert M., Mary Virginia (Mrs. Albert E. Hill) and William A. of San Francisco. Robert McFarland Doble was the father of John Doble of Berkeley, of Henry Doble of Sausalito, of Robert, Jr., and of Margaret and Alice Doble.[39]

John Doble's letter of August 27, 1860, to Elizabeth Lucas briefly mentions nearly all that is known of his early life. He had a "common school education," was trained as a blacksmith, "quit that to learn the mercantile business," was employed as a bookkeeper, volunteered in 1846 for service in the war with Mexico, served for a year in the

xiii

3d Regiment of Indiana Volunteers under Col. James Henry Lane. He fought in the battle of Buena Vista.

As his diary indicates, he returned to Indiana and left from there for California in 1851. He describes himself in 1860 as 5 feet 9 inches tall, weight 147 pounds, blue eyes (one with a squint), dark hair and sunburnt whiskers.

He died in San Francisco on the night of October 8-9, 1866. As reported in the *Daily Morning Call*, October 10, 1866: "Yesterday morning, a blacksmith named John Doble, residing on Pine Street opposite the Academy of Music, was found dead in his bed. When the deceased was discovered he had a pipe in his mouth, showing that he had fallen asleep while smoking. A post mortem examination developed the fact that the deceased came to his death from apoplexy . . ."

He apparently had two funerals: one by Mission Lodge No. 169 of the Masons at 9:30 on October 10, and another at noon on the same day. He was buried at the Laurel Hill Cemetery. When occupation of that site was terminated, his remains were removed to Cypress Lawn, July 24, 1940, and interred there on September 22, of the same year.

John Doble's library of some "200 volumes" was preserved by his brother, Abner. When Abner and Margaret went to Berkeley in later years to live with their daughter Lizzie and her husband, Francis Ferrier, the library went with them and was kept intact in its large walnut case until 1929. Some of the books are still treasured by Mr. and Mrs. Victor H. Doyle of Berkeley. Several bear John Doble's bookplate as well as labels of bookstores in Volcano, Jackson and San Francisco, where they were purchased.

John's taste in literature ranged through the classics: Milton, Pope, Dante, Boswell, Gibbon, and Cowper, into such curiously genteel works as: John T. Watson's "Poetical Quotations and elegant extracts," Hugh Blair's "Lectures on Rhetoric and Belles Lettres"; and H. G. Adams' "Language and Poetry of Flowers" with hand painted illustrations. There is also an 1845 edition of Hoyle's "Games."

The library was loaned out freely among John's friends. It must have seemed strangely out-of-place in that dingy, one-roomed bachelor's den, and amid the crude surroundings of a mountain gold camp. Possibly it actually was the "circulating library," among the first of its kind, that has been credited to Volcano in those early days.

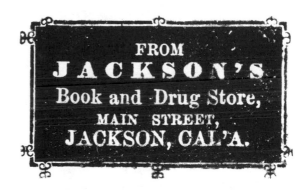

Bookplate and dealers' labels
From John Dobles' Library

INDIANA TO NICARAGUA

Shelbyville   Shelby Co   Indiana

Oct. 27 1851   Just Returned from a visit to my Relatives on Buck Creek   Father handed me two letters from J W Reid at Indianapolis which informed me that he had determined on a trip to California and wished my company   I answered him immediately that I would try and make ready to go and forthwith commenced preparations   went to Knightstown settled with Ballard   thence to Carthage and collected & discounted notes until I got $206   then returned to Shelby & Packed my trunk & received another letter from J W Reid which informed that Dr Belles was going to accompany us ...

Nov. 13th 1851   Snowed & rained all night last night   this morning cold & unpleasant   arrived at Buffalo after daylight in time for the 8 o-clock train to Albany   Paid at Buffalo for Cakes & Apples   .10
Took the train for Albany   Paid at Attica for Freshments   .15
and at Canandagua for refreshments   .10
" " Syracuse   " Tobacco   .15
Arrived at Albany sometime after dark and took the Splendid Steamer Isac Newton for New York   Paid on the Steamer for Berth   .50
for Refreshments   .38

Nov. 14   Arrived at New York this morning about ½ past seven & after looking round sometime put up at the Northern Hotel   went out in town   called at Cammann & Whitehouses & presented the draft

1

that I got from Father & received for it a draft on New York State Bank
then visited the Brother Johnathan & Nicaragua line of Steamers
offices at the Nicargua office   they ask $180 Dollars for Steerage pas-
sage   at the other $135 transportation across the Isthmus not included
Went up Broadway to the Astor place down Nassau etc   & then to
supper   After Supper went to Barnums and with Reid saw the Mysterious Stranger or the Happy family played   the play was interesting
Paid out to day
For Buttons for Overcoat   .10
For Seeing Museum   .25

*   *   *

Nov. 17 This morning cloudy & has been raining during the night
The Daniel Webster arrived last night about 600 passengers   went
and looked through her   liked her arrangements verry well   I was at
the office of the Vanderbilt line but did not see the clerk   we all went
up to the Whitney line office but have not yet made any arrangements
find a great many going etc   met with a yankee who said he was
going   the boys Suspicion him for a runner   don't know whether he
is or not
    Treated him on Ale for which I paid   12½
Visited the office of the Nicaragua line again with Belles & another
man who is going in our company but the clerk of the office is so crusty
we could not get anything out of him   Reid tried Whitney & says he
offered to make some reduction etc   tried my strength on a machine
and pulled up 4.50 lbs for which I paid one cent   .01
Evening clear & pleasantly cool
Visited Hinman Lodge IOOF in Odd fellows Hall
    paid for Omnibus ride   .06

Tuesday, November 18th 1851

    Started this morning with the Doc from our Boarding house to go
to the medical College, we went up Courtland St eastward to Broad
way then North on Broadway to Grand St then East on Grand St to
Crosby St then North on Crosby to the Medicall College on New York
University & College of Phyicians & Surgeons which is situated on
Crosby one Door South of Spring   went all through the building first
in the College Hall then to the Anatomical Museum   looked through
that and then went to the Anatomical Lecture Room   Listened to a
part of the Lecture and then I left Doc and walked up to Broadway and
seen the Fulton Guards pass   a verry good looking company they

were too   then returned to the College and went into the Materia Medica Room & talked with the Janitor awhile when I again went to the Lecture room again   the Lecture soon ceased   we then went to the dissecting room in which there was four subjects and several pieces the smell was not verry bad   we then returned to the Lecture Room when the lecture again begun over a subject which was on the table stayed only to see the subject uncovered when I left and the Doc pretty soon followed   we went on Spring St west to Green Street then South on Green to Canal then west on Canal to West Broadway then south on west Broadway through College place to Barclay then west on Bar- clay to Greenwich then South on Greenwich to Courtland then west on Courtland home   arrived at home by half past 12 just in time for dinner   after dinner I went down to the office of the Vanderbilt line asked for Allen the agent but could not learn where he was (he being not in)   came back to the Hotel and went up to the west Street Market   went all through it and it is the best market I have ever saw (I must here say the book keeper who is in the Vanderbilt office is a verry unsociable fellow therefore I asked for Allen the agent)   after Supper Reid & I went to the Broadway theater with D. H. Cole the man who has joined us to go with us   Cut round there considerable and from there went to 77 Grant Street   I came home and I left Reid with a *friend* & started back to hunt him and met him on the way

Paid out to day For Ale	.31
For Oysters	.06
" Ale	.18
" Theatre	.50
" Contingents	3.45

*   *   *

New York City   Wednesday Nov 19th 1851 . . .

Started down to hunt Reid and met him on the way   then Reid Belles & I went up and went on board the Georgia   liked her verry well   concluded to purchase our tickets at the Law line (i e the Panama line)   could not find Cole so we came down to dinner at ½ past 12   Reid had been trying Whitney to get him to make a reduction in the fare and thought he could get a reduction of ten dollars on the passenger . . .

After supper Reid & one of the returned Californians & I went up onto Broadway to a Gun & Pistol Store and after I looked at the Pistols I Bought one of Colts ReVolvers for which I Paid 18.00   Then came home and went to bed

New York City, Thursday, November 20th 1851

Morning cloudy foggy & cool   after Breakfast I went down to Vanderbilts office and found nobody in but the Servant   asked for Allen but could not get any satisfactory answers   pretty soon Doc Bellous came in and the Cap & Major was looking at the Vessel so we went out on the Pier and found them looking around at the sights etc. after looking round at the vessels etc. & the manner of lifting Coal from the barges we all repaired to the office   found quite a crowd there so Cap Reid and I went down the Battery and went into Castle Garden For which we paid a piece   .12½

Castle Garden is a large building of about 150 feet Diameter—circular and contains within a Theatre with one circle & the pit built on Spiles about 2.00 feet from shore opposite the Battery   after looking round we returned to the office and found Doc Belles and Major Coleman still there (I must here say that yesterday we settled on the names that we should each be known and called by)   after we had been in the office a few minutes we concluded to get the tickets so Reid went up on Wall St to get exchange (he having nothing [but] Indiana & Ohio money) and Doc and I went on board the Webster and picked out the berths we would occupy   we chose the berths alongside the gangway which we got   I got 139 Coleman 140 Belle 141 Read 142

We then all came up home and then Doc Belles went to the Medical College and Reid Coleman and I went to the Brokers at 29 wall St and got $5.00 each in dimes for this reason we learn that on the Isthmus dimes counts 12½ cents   we paid 4 per ct for the Exchange which made it cost me   .20

I forgot to say before we left the office that we bought our tickets through to San Francisco which cost us each   180.00

*   *   *

Friday, November 21st 1851 . . .

(Just befor dinner the Cap & I went down to the Vanderbilt office to see about what time we should go on board the Webster   we were told to go on board about Eleven o-clock tomorrow   we then went on her and looked at her awhile & then came home to dinner)

And Doc & I went up Courtland and made some enquiry   as we were coming back we met the Cap & Major so we all went up Washington St to the corner of Warren and bought 20 lbs crackers the Cap having bought some beef & Ham when he was out   we then came back to the Hotel and sit about til supper . . .

Nov. 22   This morning is cloudy cool and windy   we packed up our trunks and took them on board about 10-o-clock then came back and payed our bills ... Then took our Carpet Bags and went on board the Vessel   it not being ready to start Doc & I went up to the Hotel again and stayed a few minutes and then went back to the Vessel where we found the Captain he having been over on East St to get some letters of Introduction etc which he got &c   Sailed Exactly at three wind strong & cool from the west   2 Steamers went out just before us   we were detained a short time waiting for a couple of men who did not get to the pier in time so they came off to us in a small boat after we had got some half mile from land   when we got into the sound the officers Examined the passengers tickets and found four boys who had no tickets   they were immediately ordered into the small boat

Volcano   Caliveras Co   California   Oct 11th 1852

The Vessel rocked & shook so & the wind blew across the decks & I had nor could get no place to write except on the Ice box in front of the Cabin so I had to stop writing in this & take notes in a pocket memorandum with the purpose that at some future time I would copy it into this book

On the 5th of February last I had the bad luck to lose my memorandom so from this stop to that time I will have to write altogather from memory   I left my trunk in the City which I only got a few days ago therefore I have not written any in this book til now   I intend to keep a note still & write this up by spells when I can find time now to go back to the place of stopping   the boys that were put into the small boat were transfered from thence to the pilot boat and were landed from that on sandy Hook point   at least that was thier reported destination   the officers did not find all the stowaways as those were called who had concealed themselves on board in order to get their passage free   there were two others found the next day who had to do work about Decks the rest of the passage

Passage from New York

We had a verry pleasant trip down to San Juan De Nicaragua or as it is now called Grey-Town on the Bay called San Juan Del Norte in Central America   the 2nd & 3rd days out from N York we had high winds & heavy seas   the ships officers said it was while we were off Cape Hatteras & in the Gulf Stream   we passed the Northern Coast of Hayti on a beautiful Calm Clear morning & it was a great curiosity to see the hundreds of Fishing Boats out in the sea but near land loaded

with ½ naked & Jet Black Natives following their Avocation of fishing   we also passed in sight of several of the uninhabited Ilands of the
Bahama Group also one high Iland in the Caribbean sea that was also
uninhabited   The passengers were generally well pleased with their
passage and living while on the Webster but a few who had never been
beyond their own Fathers farm away down in Maine were verry much
displeased because their fare was not as good as the Cabin passengers
Doct Belles was verry sick all the way down with sea sickness   D H
Coleman was sick for a day or two   Cap Reid & myself escaped without any sickness whatever our only trouble was in trying to get the
Doctor to pick up courage enough to stir around the decks & thereby
regain his health but all our exertions were unavailing he would not
stir round any at all scarcely & so he was sick till we got onto fresh
water again   The steerage was verry much crowded so it was verry
disagreeable sleeping below decks so most of the passengers slept on
the upper Decks which was verry pleasant as after a couple of days
sailing we got into a warner Climate   it was verry cool the two first
days out & the wind steady from the west   the balance of the trip
was quite pleasant and nearly calm   The Vessel made land on the
10th day out & sailed down the coast ½ a day & found they were wrong
& tacked & stood up the coast and found they had made land some 30
miles south of the Bay   we dropped anchor in the Bay just after
dark   there were several Vessels in the Bay which we found next
morning were an English Cutter an English Steamer & several schooners sloops Bungoes & small craft besides 2 small Steamers that looked
at a distance like 2 Canal Boats with a wheel stuck on the Stern whose

Passage from New York, Trip Across Central America, Grey Town

Legitimate business we found was to Convey the passengers by the
Vanderbilt line up the Nicaragua River[1]   we here understood that
Vanderbilts Steam Ship Prometheus had a day or two previous been
fired into by the English Cutter for the offence of not having paid the
Port Charges   there were a good many stories afloat so I will not
mention any of them   The coast around the Bay looked verry beautiful being covered with a heavy growth of vegetation through low and
sandy & looked like it was nearly on a level with the water though I
suppose the Tide was in   the Bay is several Miles in extend & protected from the sea by a natural Breakwater which is a long low point
of land extending out between the Bay & sea & appears to be verry
narrow   some places the surf rolled over it   Grey Town situate on

the Back of the Bay and at the Mouth of the San Juan River or one
of its Mouths consisted of several frame houses covered with shingles
& dignified with the names of famed Hotels and a few Native huts
thatched with straw & Minosa leaves that looked as if they had been
built since Noahs flood   The Population consisted of the English
Consul and a few Yankees among which were the Hotel keepers & one
store and Grocry keeper a goodly number of Boatman of all Nations
& a pretty considerable sprinkling of Native Guatimalians who are a
cross between the Spaniard & Negro & Whiteman & Indian & Generally
go naked or with nought but a breech clout & look more like wild beast
than human and are famed for Ignorance & superstitution & their
natural fear of wild beasts & poisonous reptiles in which their country
abounds and their Indolence & filth and love for the rich & delicious
fruits which their country affords a plentiful supply   as to dress
however a few are supplied with red flannel shirts & a verry few with
the cast off Clothing of the Americans & other who pass through
their Country

Up the Rio San Juan to Nicargua

We were not allowed to land here at all   about 9 in the Morning
after we had dropped anchor one of the little boats came alongside and
took off the steerage Passengers with all their luggage   but before we
left the Webster our baggage was all weighed (except such as we could
carry in our hands) (such as Carpet sacks knapsacks &c &c) and we
were charged 15¢ pr lb for whatever the Company had to transport
across for us   as soon as we were on board a verry great impatience
was manifest to get off up the River   we swung away from the side
of the Webster & after passing under the Guns of the English Frighet
we stood away for the River

We Entered one of the outlets of the River near the Town   this
outlet is verry narrow in fact so narrow that the boat rubbed the brush
on the sides   the banks were invisible being so thickly covered with
the Mimosa Trumpet wood & different kinds of grapes Vines & trees
we were much amused by the antics of the Monkeys and cries of the
Parrots & Parrokeets which were disturbed by the passage of our boat
and the shooting of the Alligators which occasionally showed themselves above water   the river seems to have spread in every direction
through the country near the coast   the Islands were verry numerous
and without exception coverd as the banks with a heavy or thick
growth of vegetation   the first place we saw the ground after leaving
the bay was at a natives Ranch about 40 miles from the Bay   this

consisted of 2 huts built of Reeds & one shed covered with the Mimosa
& near them a large patch of Plantain & a small spot of Indian corn
just in Tassel   Towards evening we passed several such Ranches   all
looked verry much as if they were gone down or going down with age—
during the day the passengers were so much interested with the
appearance of the country &c &c that nothing else was thought of but
towards evening Where will we stop—   will we run all night   How
will we live & How will we sleep were questions presently asked   To
the first question and the second an answer was soon had as the
Captain informed us we would stop for the night just below the first
Rapids which are known as the Muchachos Rapids & that we (or he)
would stop at Castillio or Main Rapids   the 3rd question was not so
easily answerd   a Majority of the passengers had brought some victuals with them from New York but those that had not were obliged to
buy from those that had or do without as there was nothing to eat on
the boat except a few green Oranges which sold rapidly at a Dime
apiece   some bid high for provision & were supplied at enormous
prices by those who had to spare   some begged & some with a des-
perate determination resolved to do without until they got to the
stopping [place]   we reched the anchorage about 9 in the evening &
anchored in the middle of the River   it was a beautiful Moonlight
night and all nature seemed Calmed to rest   The 4th and last question was answered with I don't know.   The boat was verry verry

Arriba El Rio San Juan de Nicaragua

small so there was not Room for all to sleep without lieing in the
Gangways which was not admissible so a considerabl number had to
content them selves with [a] seat or to walk the Deck to keep from
falling asleep and thereby falling overboard   to pass away the time
& amuse them selves some sung while others applauded or listened
some shouted while others tried to imitate them   some & a verry few
slept while others yawned & wished to do the same   for my part I
amused myself awhile looking at & listening to the rest & for the rest of
the night either slept on my seat or walked the Deck nearly over
powered with sleep   *Up the River*

   Day was looked for [with] considerable anxiety by many after the
singing & hooping was stopped   at length the Day began to dawn &
with it commenced the howling of Babboons the Chattering of Monkeys the squeaking & squalling of Parrots & other Tropical Birds the

grunting & blowing of Alligators the occasional Roar of a Lion & scream of the Panther which rung out on the morning air with a fearful and Ominious Distinctness   The Morning was calm as the night had been beautiful & all these sounds togather made a horrid noise   the Verdure being all green & so thick that the eye could not penetrate even to the Earth from which it grew that any & all of these beasts & birds might & many did come even to the waters edge   we did not see but could distinguish that they were so near by the fearful distinctness of their cry or the shaking of the Brush   The River had for the last few miles been more in a body & the Ilands had become fewer & here all its water was collected in one body which was some 400 yards wide & looked a beautiful Rver though a Rapid Current & boiling & muddy water did not add to its beauty any

about sun up the Anchor was heaved up & the boat again got under weigh   we passed up over the rapids without any difficulty as the water was high though the boatmen said they had a deal of difficulty when the River was low

Again this morning we took a Lunch of raw Ham & soda crackers which we had brought from N York with us & the others of the passengers who had victuals eat it   those who had now either bought begged or done without   Ham sold as high as 50 cents per lb & other things in proportion   after eating we passed the time in watching our progress & occasionally we would pass a bungoe loaded with goods etc for San Carlos or Virgin Bay   these bungoes are a Canoe shaped vessel of various sizes some being (i e the largest) large enough to hold 100 persons when well crowded   most of them were manned with ½ naked Natives & a few with enterprising yankees going up on the line for the purpose of selling food & notions to hungry & needy California bound bipeds   previous to the time of the Establishment of the Nicaragua Tranit Company the Transit was made by the assistance of these bungoes and ships boats which are purchased or hired at the Bay by the passengers and then rowed up the river & across the lake & then left or sold at Virgin Bay   the passage up the River in this manner is verry tedious & fatiguing as the current is verry strong & the distance considerable & the weather generally verry hot   the vegetation being so thick along the banks the air is generally still on the river & [in?] parts of the year clear without cloud or rain so the sun shines with a greater power making it verry hot & disagreeable to a Northerner

Up the Nicaragua River

As I before said the Coast was low at & near the Bay but to the North and south of the Bay there is several high points of land   also about 40 miles up the River & to the North is two or 3 high sharp Hills or Mountains which are visible from the River   these hills like the balance of the country in view are thickly covered with verdure   we landed at the foot of the Castilios Rapids about 9 in the Morning Many were glad to get where there was some chance of getting something to eat as they had eaten nothing since leaving the Webster The River here made a considerable turn   a high ridge of hills here run directly across the River & stretch away to the N & S   the Rapids are about 300 yards long   the bed of the stream is verry rocky & over the rocks the [river] runs with considerable rapidity there being about 8 feet fall in the 300 yards   it looks as if at some time long since the River had washed it[s] way through the ridge & the stone that was in it had formed the rapids   we landed in the curve at the foot of the Rapids where the rushing of the water over the falls forms an Eddy & walked up round the point some 300 yards to where the next steamer lay that was to take us forward on our trip   our baggage was put in a boat & huled round up over the falls by the Men of the boats with the assistance of some 50 of the passengers   The Boat above the falls was called the Director was but verry little larger than those below only her wheels were on the side and were two instead of one though I did not think that of much advantage.

Castillio Rapids On the River Nicaragua

After looking round the boat & seeing our baggage stowed away we took a look round the falls to see how maters stood & things arranged below the point & some 200 yards below the Boat landing was two old pole huts roofed with palm leaves   at the landing was a small plank pen & above the falls was four canvass houses all of which had Liquors & provisions   the plank pen at the lower landing was the commencement of a Hotel the stoves for which came up on our Boat   the prices here were verry high   Bread pr lb $1.00   Coffee pr cup 10 cents Ham pr lb 50 cents   Drinks of all kinds except water 25 cents pr Drink   Bananas & Plantains 10 cents a piece   Oranges & Lemons 10 cents & one Dollar a Meal at all the shanties   we walked round the point again to see if the other Boat with the Cabin Passengers was in sight but it was not so we went up on the hill (On the south side of the River where we were) to see what was said to be an old Fort & found some Vine covered & Moss grown stone walls that were crumbling away very much in some places nearly on a level with the surrounding Earth   it had the appearance of once having been a strong fortress there appeared to have been a building of 4 stories & several underground Dungeons which were yet perfect on the East & west & on a level with the upper floor were two flat spaces surrounded by a strong Breastwork on the corners of which were yet standing sentry Boxes yet perfect a deep ditch on the outside of the breast (walled) walled up some 20 feet & 10 feet wide   this went round the back side &

The Castle[2]

so formed a barrier round the three sides of the works   The front appeared to have been defended by the walls only as the ground was low making the wall some 40 feet high   the floors doors windows &c were all gone but the holes in the walls denoted where they once had been on the west side   & in the wall of the house was a large stone covered with an inscription in spanish which I copied but having lost my book I cannot now recollect it   The Stone of which it was built were said to have been brough from the Mountains beyond the Lake it was a species of granite or Marble & appeared of a fine quality   the River making a bend round the hill gave a view from the fort of several Miles up & down   the point of the hill seemed to have been filled out to the water by the fragments from the buildings   they were digging a road round the point & found all the way round nothing but broken & small pieces of stone   The Natives say that it was built by some Pirates many years ago who were driven out by the Spanish Government   Report said that it was believed that a great Treasure had been left by the Pirates & many had spent some time picking about the old walls in the hope to discover the hidden Treasure but none have yet discovered it   about 5 in the evening the other Boat arrived but the Capt of the Director would not start out til next morning (one of the Ladies got a fall in passing to the shore & was slightly hurt here Doc Belles got his first case since leaving home   the Lady was a Daughter of a Mr. Latimer who lives on the Caliveras not far from San Andres) so we had to look out for a place to sleep as there was no room on the Boat for more than ½ the passengers[7]   I lost sight of the Cap Doc & Maj Coleman about dark so I crawled in between a couple of Trunks on the Boat rapped up in my Over Coat & managed to sleep part of the night & for the balance lied & tried to sleep   next morning I found the other boys had slept at one of the shanties on the floor (which was the ground smoothed off) on stick couches & Hammocks for the moderate sum of 50¢ a piece   stick couches are made of 2 poles for side rails & sticks or pieces of cane nailed or tied with raw hide crosswise for bed cord & palm or plantain leaves for a bed   those who slept on the floor were furnished 1 Blanket pr Man   those in Hammocks or on couches had nothing but whatever clothes they had   The Ladies were accommodated with the after part of the Boat where they slept some on Benches some in Hammocks & some on the floor   The morning was cloudy & we had a light shower of rain but not enough to wet & it was lucky it was so for there was not shelter enough for ½ the passengers if it had rained hard   About nine o clock we got started again   the Boat made verry poor Headway   The River widened a little above the falls & there were no more Islands & the water was clear but the current was still strong

Stowaways
Up the River and On the Lake

At each change of Boats an exertion was made to detect any who had no Tickets but none could be found although there was two boys of 18 who had managed to get along so far without being detected until it was too late to leave them   they were discovered on the Webster 2 Days out and on the Boats below the falls   they were not discovered but on this Boat they were pointed out to the Officers by a Man who had not bought a through Ticket at the start & he had to pay a large price for a Ticket here   so while he was in a bad humor he pointed out the stowaways but they were permitted to proceed by becoming waiters & drudgery boys on the different Vessels   On the Pacific side the Captain took them as Cabin Waiters.

We stopped to [get] wood about 5 miles from Castilio Rapids   could not get to land for the brush & vines on the bank but run out a plank which reached the shore through the walls of Vegetation by a hole cut through   we got up to the Toro Rapids about 1- of the clock where we found the Lake Boat Central America waiting for us   The Toro Rapids are 9 miles from Castillio   we passed from our Boat to the other the Director having come over the falls which are so shallow that the Lake Boat cant go over them with safety though the current is not very rapid   here another ridge seems to have once crossed the River as at Castillio   as soon as we had changed Boats we pushed off and arrived at the outlet in to the lake about 5 in the evening

Lake Nicaragua

The upper part of the River from Toro Rapids is about ½ a mile wide and clear water the banks low up to the Lake except the North side at the Lake where a high ridge comes down the Lake shore and stops at the mouth or head of the River   on this point is an old spanish & Native Town with some 50 Huts   it is called San Carlos   several Foreign Traders have established themselves here though since the Steamers have got to running no passengers stop here   some Men came off to us in a small boat but we stopped but a few minutes when we came into the lake   I was struck with its Remarkable beauty   to our left lay a beautiful circular Bay some two miles across & [in] front the lake & to the North the same dotted here & there with beautiful little Islands   to the West lay the Ridge of Mountains known as the Coast Range & To the North was seen two high and Isolated peaks which we learned stood about the Middle of the Lake on two Circular Islands some 20 Miles in diameter   The slopes of these Mountains were said to be rich in the productions of the Country   The water was quite calm when we came into the Lake and to the eye appeared as a sheet of silver when looking towards the sun but by dark we had got out into the lake & a good breeze was blowing which made a short chopping sea and verry rough for our small boat though it was larger than any of the others we had been on since leaving the Webster   We all lay down wherever we could find a place & rapped in whatever we had coat or blanket   there was room enough on this boat to sleep without being much crowded   for my part I slept but little   the air was cool & my Coat was not sufficient to keep me warm so I passed the most of the time in walking a round the boat   about 2-o clock we landed on the south side of the South Mountain Island for wood & from that to daylight lay there taking in wood   at daylight shoved off & by 10 got into Virgin Bay the wind still blowing strong from the East   The Anchor was dropped about ¼ of a Mile from shore & Dragged some so when the Boat came to a stand we were about 300 yards from the landing   The wind was so high that a boat larger than a yawl could not be Managed with oars so the Boats yawl went ashore with a line which was made fast to a tree standing in the edge of the water & the other end to the Steamer   by this line a large Bungoe was brought out   by the time the (the) Bungoe got along side nearly all of the passengers had collected on the guard which brought [it] nearly to the water   the Bungoe got along side & was made fast with some difficulty as the water was so rough that it was a hard matter even for those who were used to it to stand without holding on   as soon as it was made fast all those on the outside threw in their baggage such as Carpet sacks & knapsacks &c   and watching the rise and fall of the boats when ever they were even jumped in after the baggage   in ½

Landing at Virgin Bay

an hours time the Bungoe was filled under the seats & on the seats with men & baggage promiscuously   for my part I got in about the last so I got on the top   about 3/5 of [the] passengers got in at this time which pressed the Bungoe verry low in the water   it was about 60 feet long and 8 feet wide   had seats crosswise & near the Top every 3 ft leaving a space below the seats about 6 ft deep   we left the side of the Steamer as soon as all were in & by the aid of the line pulled toward shore   there was 8 Natives in [it] who were the workers of the Bungoe hired I suppose for the occasion   we got along verry well with an occasional shower of water thrown over us whenever a large wave struck the side until we got within some 5 yards of the shore when the Bungoe struck bottom   the wind being so high it had been driven some distance out of the way notwithstanding the line to pull by   as soon as she struck all the Natives on board jumped out into the water and put theirselves to work to shove off   when we were on the bottom the water broke over us frequently so we all got wet   after ½ an hours pulling & shoving we got the bow of the Bungoe against the shore   then all were in a hurry to get ashore   some ran over the bow   some were carried by the Natives & some who thought they could not get any wetter jumped over the side and waded ashore   The shore was crowded with Natives with fruit fish fowls & meat to sell & many with trinkets peculiar to the country such as beads gourds shells &c with any quantity of catholic crosses attached to long strings of beads & many other jewels made of Lead brass & copper & some few of silver   Our first care was to eat something and then watch the progress of the landing of the rest   Cap Reid was yet on the Boat so Doc Major & I took a lunch & then seated our selves near the shore to watch the others land

Th Natives here as before were ½ naked though a few were well dressed   The Bungoe got in good time 4 this time there was more care in getting into it   as a majority of the passengers left were women & children they all got in without any serious accident though many were somewhat bruised as they had to be dropped or thrown from the Boat into the Bungoe & run the chance of being caught in the arms of the Man in waiting for them   they came ashore much the same as we did only the ladies Modesty was some what shocked by having to ride ashore on the backs of Naked Natives   however that was not of much consequence as it was soon over   A large Iron life Boat was now taken out for the baggage which by night landed all

the baggage safe   Our next care was to dry ourselves & see where we
could find a place to lodge or whether we would start for the Pacific
this evening   many of the passengers started on with the intention
of stopping on the way for the night   My partners & my self concluded to stay here and go on in the morning   The Ladies & some of
the men found places to lodge at some of the Hotels here   we lay in
the Mule yard behind the Agency office where we would not be in the
wind that was blowing   before going to rest which we did about 12
o clock at night we took an observation of the Town Country around
&c &c   The Town as others previous consisted of 15 or 20 pole & palm
huts with some 12 or 15 canvas house Dignified with the names of
famed Hotels & provision Stores   The Most of the inhabitants were
Natives   the rest were of all Nations or many Nations & as is usual
several yankees   there were a goodly number of females all of easy
virtue & all Natives   I heard of nor seen but one woman of any other
Country and she was from Scotland   herself & husband had gone out
3 miles on the Road and built a pole house covered with canvas for
the purpose of trading with the passengers but their calculations were
prematurely and sadly put an end to   the night before we got to
Virgin Bay three Natives had procured admission into the house for
the purpose as they said before entering of obtaining water as they
were lost & thirsty   it being a wild Country & but few houses the
plea was reasonable so the husband got up and opened the Door but
as soon as they obtained admission they attacked him with their large
knives (which most of the Natives carry at their side) and in a few
minutes dispatched him   the wife seized an Allens revolver which lay
under the pillow and commenced snapping it at them which so frightened them that they run away   however not before one of the villians
had cut two severe gashes across her arms one on each & several slight
wounds on her wrists hands & breast   when they left she fainted and
did not regain her senses for some time so report said   The Bay is an
open arm of the lake being nothing but a circle or bend in the Lake
shore   directly East & in front of the Bay stand the two Lake Mountains of which a pretty view is had from the shore   the tops are most
of the time at this season enveloped in clouds as also the higher peaks
of the Coast range   the country around the Bay is beautifully undu-
lating & verry rich being covered with a heavy growth of Vegetation
we slept as I before said very comfortable in [a] mule yard on the west
side of the Agency office being protected by it from the East wind
which blows steadily at this Season   in the Morning as soon as we

had breakfasted we looked around to see how we were to get across
the land   about 8 o-clock the Native Buccaros & Rancheros begin
to come in with their Mules which they hired to the Transit company
or passengers for $5.00 the trip paid in Dimes 8 to the $1.00   The
Agent allowed each passenger a mule or gave him the price of a mule
for his Ticket (this being the last stage we four (i e Doc Belles Cap
Reid & D H or Major Coleman & myself) concluded for two of us to
sell our Tickets & the other two take mules and change on the way   I
& Doc took the first walk   The Ladies most of them Donned the
unmentionables & Boots & seated astride of a mule or horse performed

Across the Land

the journey in this way   though to some of them it was too great a
shock to their Modesty so they preferred trying the trip in the common
way but ere they had performed ½ the journey they wished they had
followed the example set by those of More courage   by ½ past nine
we got started   I stopped at the house of the Murdered Man & saw
the woman   she was slow & sick from the effects of her wounds and
fright   she said she was well attended to by the folks of another ranch
a few miles ahead   the Marks of the fray were yet visible in splotches
of blood on the sides & floor (which was the ground) of the house   she
commenced telling me the circumstances but I could not stay to listen
to her as my company was gone on   after going some 4 miles we
began to ascend the mountain slopes   the Roads branched in every
direction while on the level but here they were collected togather   my
party got seperated after leaving the house of the Murdered Man but
we came togather at a house 6 miles from the Bay   here we changed
& Doc & I took the Mules   The roads were verry bad the Mud having
been deep & the top dry enough to walk on but not enough to support
a Mule so I soon found I could have got along better without the Mule
but I got seperated from the boys verry soon after taking the Mule so
had to keep it   we stopped awhile to rest at the summit of the pass
which is not verry high here   some enterprising yankees & spanish
have built a canvas house here & you procure Refreshments at the
following prices Drinks 25 cents a piece Coffee 10 cents a cup Bread &
meat 1.00 pr lb & Meals $1.50 pr Meal   In going down the west side
I had to lead or drive my mule most of the way as the road was narrow
& in many places steep and the Mud stiff & deep so it could not carry
me as well as I could walk   as we approached the Coast the Timber
which on each slope of the Mountains was verry scattering and in
many places none at all began to grow heavier & thicker and the mud

to get softer & deeper   about 3 miles from the Coast the roads fork one going in some distance to the North of the town & at the upper side of the Bay   I took with Many others the upper Road but verry soon fell behind the Company I started with & while winding about through the brush & vines trying to get along without going directly in the Road in which the Mud was verry deep   I heard a verry sharp scream which somewhat frightened me as I was alone in a Dense forest in a country infested by wild Beasts & the scream resembling those I had heard on the River   I knew if any animals was near me I could not escape as my mule could hardly get along alone so pulled out my revolver determined to fight it out if need be but while I was looking and listening the scram was repeated and this time being on the watch I knew it to be human   so I hastened back to the place from whence came the noise and after some search found it to proceed from an old Lady who like myself had got lost from her(e) crowd   she & her horse had got so entangled in the vines & brush that I had to use my knife pretty freely to extricate her from her dilema   after freeing her(e) she asked me many questions about the rest & she was in much fear that we were entirely lost but I reassured her to the best of my ability & promised to take good care of her til I again conducted her to her company   she then seemed content & being a verry voluble Lady she amused me with incidents of her life until we came up with the company again which was at the Mouth of a small creek some 2 miles above the town   the Tide being in this creek was swimming   she informed me her husband was in California & she was going to him under the escort of an acquaintance   she was about 40 years of age when we got to the Mouth of the creek we found some 80 or a hundred men some with their clothes off swimming mules & men across & some on the banks assisting in different manners   several ladies came up & swam across on their mules & some were assisted across by the men in the water   my protegee thought she would cross on a mans back but when she was getting off her horse on to the back of a naked man (who was Major Coleman) her notion took a turn and she rode her mule across   by an hour by sun we had all got across and to the Town where we found the most of the passengers

The Timber along the coast of the Lake & pacific was the Trumpet wood Mimosa & various other kinds with an innumberable variety of Vines covered generally with flowers some of which I gathered & have since sent home to my sister   on the slopes of the Mountain the Timber varies some   The Gourd Tree & the Cow Harm thorn which

bears a thorn the shapes & appearance of a cows head & horns in Miniature   the Gourds of the Gourd Tree are made verry useful by the
natives which they use for drinking cups & various other things   the
cane & Willow is frequently met with wherever there is a moiist soil
grass & the flag is not scarce   in cutting off a bush I got several red
ants on my hand   they stung me severely   on noticeing them I saw
them in every direction as thick as the Black ant in Mexico   their
sting is verry severe though not dangerous   my hand was swollen
for several hours from the effects of the stings   Cultivation of the
soil is verry little followed here the Native population being mostly
herdsmen   I saw but one field of corn & that was back of Del Sud
which was about knee high and looked verry beautiful   I heard it
belonged to an American   however the Natives do cultivate the corn
in considerable quantities in some part of the country   also most of
the small grains with pepper & Tobacco in abundance

San Juan Del Sud

When we got into the Town of Del Sud we found in waiting for us
the Steamer Gold Hunter (we met the homeward bound passengers at
Virgin Bay) which had come down for us in place of the Independence
which was out of order & was in Dock for repairs   the Captain was on
shore & seemed a verry clever fine man   he made good promises of
good food & fare on our upward trip   we looked round at the Town
& country and stopped for lodging & feed at one of the men boarding
houses we having got tired of our New York provisions

The Bay is the most Romantic & beautiful one I ever saw but not a
verry safe one when the western winds prevail as it is all open in front
it is about 4 miles long and 2 wide   the mouth or connection with
the ocean being about 1½ miles wide   the upper and lower on North
& south side is bounded by high Mountains the sides of which are next
or toward the water bare rock and the tops covered with heavy Timber
the western Boundary is the Boundless Pacific & on the East a low
sandy beach which gradually rises until it form a beautiful & fertile
Valley of 6 or 8 miles in extent on the south side & on the Bay is built
the Town directly on the sandy Beach   it consists of 50 or 60 Native
houses or huts some of which are covered with Potters Tiles   the
rest as usual   one large frame house which is an Hotel built from
dismantled Vessels   some 20 or 30 canvas houses which are grocries &
feeding houses known as Hotels or Provision stores

The Government has made this military post and have built a house which can neither be called Garrison or barracks but only a pole potters tile covered shanty in which some 60 or 70 ragged Native soldiers are quartered commanded by a spanish officer   they are verry ragged and dirty & look any thing else but the soldier   The Town is improving rapidly although one half of the Foreign inhabitants are sick with chills & fever which is verry prevalent at this time There are several staunch frame houses going up at the south end of the Town which are intended for business houses   It is verry disagreeable to go about as the town is built on the sand & the wind continually blowing the sand always moving in the are [air] so it is verry difficult to keep one eyes from being filled with it   or when the wind is not blowing the sun is so hot a person is in danger of being sun struck   we went to our lodging house at dark but could not get to lay down until the business was over for the day so we took a walk into the woods back of town to consult with Doctor Belles how he should proceed in regard to an offer he had which was the Ships Doctor on the Gold Hunter offered him his Berth for 100 Dollars & we advised him to take it which he did next morning   he sold his Steerage Ticket for 100 so he got Cabin passage & a chance to make more by being a Doctor

San Juan Del Sud and the Gold Hunter

Next Morning we expected to go on board but our baggage had not arrived yet so we had to wait for it   the roads are so bad the mules that are lead get along with difficulty so that some of them take two days to get across the land which is only 12 miles across   I saw several while coming across that were mired & one that had fell in a Ravine & had to be lifted out & several men were thrown in the mud by their mules giving out   also a great many mules gave out & were left on the road for their owners on their Buccaros to find as they might or could   we passed this day in loafing and looking round at what we might see & I sold my revolver for $25.00 & 7 Bullets for it for 12½ cents a piece making .97   I then went down round the south end of the Bay & picked up some shells rocks & coral &c &c which I preserved & brought with me   the cliffs looked higher & more grand when looking up at them from the base

The shipping in port was but little being one or two ships 4 or 5 schooners & several smaller craft with the usual number of small boats & other Port craft

Towards evening our Trunks came and we went down to go on board as it was getting dark   all the others having got their baggage

& were on board we had to pay for getting on board $1.00 for our trunks 20 cents I had some 3 cent pieces in my pocket book with some gold dollars & through a mistake gave only 3 cents for getting on board

Volcano Oct 20th 1852

I have written the foregoing by odd spells up to this time & will now continue to write whenever I have time until I get it all wrote as I have began I intended to have mad this a journal of all I made & lost or spent & all I received & payed out until I returned home again but as I have lost my book I must let that go & I will only write whatever happens to my mind while writing without pretending to make a correct a/c of what I receive & expend &c so now I will return to where I left off & that I believe is where I was going on the Steamer at Del Sud

We were carried by the Boatman through the water to their boats as the waves run up so high on the beach the boat could not come close enough for the passengers wading some steps or being carried as I was to the boat & when all were in we shoved off to the Steamer which lay some ½ mile from shore they took some Cattle on board in the evening by tieing them to a small boat and drawing them through the water to the Steamer & then hitching a rope to their horns & with block & Tickle draw them up on deck we found all ready for to start the Captain only being on shore he came on board about 8 & by nine we were again on the mighty Oceans wave the weather being verry warm we slept on Deck as indeed I did all the way up to San Francisco there being no Chance to sleep below

Realajo New Grenada

By daylight next morning I was up & stiring round the Decks to see what kind of craft I was on board of but as daylight begin lighten up the coast & the rough & rugged & high mountain peaks begin to loom up in the growing light my attention was attracted to the coast from which I hardly took it during the day only when I went to my meals we were sailing or steaming at the rates of 5 mile an hour at a distance of about 6 miles from the Coast which was a high Barren Rough & Sterile ridge of Mountains the base of which is here iternally washed by the unceasing Motion of the Great Pacific this Range of Mountains is in sight or immediately on the Coast all the way up to San Francisco & I suppose they continue up some distance into Oregon in Mexico there is several Volcanos in it one of which we saw as we came up

We reached the Anchorage of Realajo about 5-o-clock in the evening

& stopped for Coal & provision   Realajo is about one hundred miles from Del Sud & is a small Town situate on a small River of the same name which empties in a beautiful Bay some 20 miles long and on an average 4 miles wide of same name as the Town on River   the Anchorage is about 3 miles from the Bay & the Town about 4 miles from the Anchorage   at the Town it is nothing but a narrow & shallow creek & the only reason it is called River is that Vessels can go up at all tides about 5 miles from the Bay   the spot of ground that is above high tide where we stopped to Coal contains about 2 acres   all the rest around is covered with a low growth of Timber so thick that nothing but serpents & such *ilk* can get through it & at high tide is covered some feet with water   a small pier was built out about 60 feet for carrying coal onto the Vessels at which when we came in was lieing the Propeller McKim

Realajo Guatimala

We dropped Anchor about 6-o-clock about 20 or 60 yards from shore & in 10 minutes our vessel was crowded all round with canoes of the Natives with something to sell and until it got too dark they sold rapidly to the passengers as our fare was not so good on the Gold Hunter as we expected   they sold Oranges at 1 for a Dime Chickens 65c a piece Coaco Nuts 10c Mangoes 5c Cocos 5c Limes & Lemons from 10 to 20c per Dozen Lime juice 60c pr Bottle Lemon juice the same Plantains & Bananas 5c a piece sugar about 4c pr lb being in cakes of about 2 lbs each   bread was scarce among them & the passengers did not want it nor was there any flesh of any kind to sell among them   but parrots and Monkeys were plenty at from 5 to 10 Dollars a piece   these prices are made so high by the Americans being there & teaching them how to charge   after dark awhile all the canoes vamosed to the shore   before dark a good number of the passengers went on shore myself among the rest for which we had to pay a dime to the Master of the canoe we went ashore in   there was but one small frame house on this piece of dry ground and that was occupied by a number of Natives who were females of easy Virtue —   on the ground however were Many Natives who slept and stayed in the open air or in their Canoes   there was two large piles of coal one of which the McKim was fast lessening   there was about 200 passengers on the McKim a Number of which were sick and 5 of them had died since leaving Panama from where she had been 14 days coming and it is only 600 miles   the passengers were verry angry that they had been fooled into coming on board of her   after dark awhile I went back to the vessel where I took a comfortable sleep til morning   however I

watched the Natives on shore awhile around their fires   they were
dancing and singing with great glee some were playing on the Guitar
while others tripped the light Fantastic toe to the soul stiring strains
drown from the wire stringed instrument called the Guitar   though
being almost out of hearing it did not amuse me much   during the
night the McKim dropped down from the Pier & anchored some 50
yards below so that next morning our Vessel drew up to the Pier and
commenced taking in Coal   in the morning I had a good look at the
McKim   she had been in a hard storm the day before she got in here
and had her Main Mast torn away leaving only a stump about 15 feet
high also the Bow sprit was torn away like[wise] stays Boom & all   she
remained here (here) repairing until a few hours before we left when
she started out which was the last we saw of her   however I heard she
had landed at San Francisco about a month after we did with some 50
of her passengers dead & a Majority of the rest sick and unable to
Move about   The passengers looked bad at Realajo & two of them
died while we were there and one died the day before we got there   a
runner came round about sun up wanting passengers for the town of
Realajo so I with some 8 others went up in a ships Boat for the sum of
75c a piece   the Town is built on the south side of the creek or River
as it is called and consists of about 100 houses built in the Mexican
fashion of Mud & sticks of stone & of Adobes   a custom house [of]

Realajo The Town

Adobes plastered outside & in covered with potters tiles also a quaint
old Catholick Church built of Stone & looking verry much as if it had
been built in the beginning of the Christian Era   it stands in the
Centre of a square or Plaza of some two acres around which the town
is built   it is furnished as all Catholick Churches are in this country
with a Steeple surmounted with a cross and a chime of Bells to fore-
warn poor Sinners that their end is approaching & it is time to Make
their peace with heaven by paying the Priest a certain sum for saying
a certain number of Prayers and burning a certain number of waxen
Tapers for him

The doors were closed while I was in Town so I did not get to see the
inside but suppose the out side was a sample of what was to be seen
within   the walls were filled with Niches containing Linages of different Saints & on each corner of the square was placed a large wooden
cross   also at the corner of each Street the same in order that the
devout might have frequent opportunities of showing their devoted-

ness to the prevailing Religion by puling off their Sombreros & going down on their knees whenever they passed one of these & noticed the Steeple was not large enough to hold all the bells so 3 or 4 were placed on square wooden frames around the church 10 or 12 feet from the ground In this place I observed a peculiar kind of Cactus I never before seen it was used for hedging it grew to the height of 20 feet without limb leaaf or knot it was as large at top as bottom come out of the ground straight & showed no roots was 8 square & fluted with beautiful regularity on the ridges of the flutes grew little tufts of thorns like on the prickly pear but showed no signs of flours fruit or leaves Coler was vegetable green. Thorns yellow

Goes Back to the Steamer

We took dinner at a Mexican Restaurant and got a verry good dinner for the moderate sum of 1.00 a lot of Ladies & Gentlemen who came up before us took dinner at an American Hotel the only one in the place I stopped at the store of an American who had concluded to remain in the country some two years previous & had married a wife & had taken the usual oath of alligience which was to support the prevailing Government at the time & before he could marry the oath taken was to never leave the country he was verry tired of his oath an the country wife oath & all & countemplated leaving the country his wife was a good looking Native of a tawny coler & straight black hair jet Black Eyes form tall straight & Elastic & features regular &c &c I had bought a pistol at Del Sud which was a revolver of the Colt patent but of a different make however I should have said an infringement on the Colt patent at the Cafe where we took dinner I offered to sell it I had only paid 7 Dollars for it to a Native & the bar keeper offered me 12 Dollars for it I agreed to take it and he went out & said he would come back in a few minutes & pay me & he did not come so I threatened to shoot all the bar keepers about the house if he did not come back which scared them verry much I had been drinking wine very freely which in this country is verry fiery so was somewhat excited though we soon left the Cafe & I sold my pistol for the sum of $10.00 to a spaniard as I left the Town we found the boat all ready & by sundown we were on the Gold Hunter again

Realajo Anchorage

In the Morning after a good nights sleep I felt verry well the fumes of the wine being all evaporated our Vessel was still taking in Coal & the McKim repairing as the day before also there was 3 other

Vessels in port 2 British Brigs and one American ship which were in when we came in   a large number of the passengers went up to day to the Town of Realajo but I did not want to go again   I did not mention about the Ditch in the River but I will now   about one mile below the Town the River made a bend of some 3 miles in the shape of a horse shoe & in the middle of the horse shoe was some high rocks which prevented Vessels from going up to the town so the Government thought to cut a ditch across the neck which was some 30 yards & thereby permit vessels to come up   so the ditch was cut to low tide about 12 feet wide but they found all rock to go through there being only about 18 inches of dirt on the rock so the ditch was given up   at high tide small boats go through the ditch but at low tide it is dry this shows the Government had no perseverance nor ambition   the Dich may or might have been cut with no verry great expense as the rock is a verry soft kind but they wanted men that had some knowledge & perseverance to do the work therefore it remains of no benefit to the country   however if the ditch was cut there is no anchorage at the town as the water is verry shallow there

Anchorage in Realajo River

There was several Spaniards & Americans cume to our Captain wanting passage out of the country as there had been an insurection in the country & they in hopes of gaining by it had joined the Revolutionists   but they had been defeated so they were now trying to get out of the country   but our Vessel being already crowded our Captain could not or would not take any more passengers   I believe he would not for at Acapulco he took on several who had plenty of money to pay &c   Our Captain promised to get plenty of good provisions here so he bought of the British Vessels some flour beef & bread to do to Acapulco and by 5 in the evening was ready to start out   after laying 2 days & 2 nights here we dropped down the River some ½ mile to another spot of dry ground on which there was a cabin & took on some beeves which were brought to the Vessel by being tied to the stern of a boat & drawed through the water & were hoisted on board as before

NICARAGUA TO CALIFORNIA

I here noticed the phosphorescent Glare of the water more than at any other time   the boat that brought the cattle out left a long streak of flam behind & the struggles of the cattle in the water made light enough to be distinctly seen from the Deck of the vessel   and the fish darting through the water made light enough for us to see the fish   & in every direction were flashes of light from the fish moving through the water   about 10-o-clock the beeves were got on board

Pacific Ocean

and we were again on our way up the Coast of Central America   I stayed up til 12-o-clock watching the flashes & streaks of light made in the water by the fishes moving about & the Vessel   running behind the vessel was a broad glare of light for some hundred yards or so

We arrived at Acapulco about the 16th of Dec   the date I dont recollect but we stopped there for two days taking in Coal & provision & then again stopped at San Diajo for about 8 hours & took in provision & was a going to take in water but the Steamer Northerner came in and our Captain wanted to beat it into Francisco so he put out about 8-o-clock in the evening and left the water Casks with 2 men to be picked up when the Vessel returned   we arrived at San Francisco on the 2nd Day of Jan/52 just 8 hours after the Northerner   I must here go back to speak of our trip up the Coast   after leaving Realajo we found one Cask of the bread which was Brown Liverpool sea Bread

was mouldy & was filled with worms & wevil   this raised considerable
commotion among the passengers & about one half of the cask was
thrown over board that was as it came within the power of the Steerage
passengers   The Store Room was aft so the Steerage passengers had
no access to it   however the food was so bad they one day sent a
Committee aft to see the Captain but he with fair words and promises
of doing better put them off a while longer   & another source of

Trip Up the Coast

irritation to the passengers was the Decks around the boilers caught
fire every day or two & caused considerable alarm   one or two nights
while I was sleeping close to the smoke stack the fire caught enough to
blaze several feet above the Deck which caused considerable alarm
one night in particular all the passengers were asleep or appeared to
be and every thing about the Decks was still   no noise disturbed the
quiet of the scene except the occasional footstips of the watch & the
working of the Machinery when about midnight some wakeful passenger discovered the Mid deck was on fire   he immediately waked
up all those sleeping around the smoke pipe myself among the rest &
then many cried *fire fire* aloud so all the passengers were aroused and
the Deck was soon crowded and for a short time confusion reigned
supreme but by the prompt exertions of the 2nd Mate assisted by
many of the passengers the fire was extinguished without doing much
damage   however it was not quite put out for the next day it again
broke out so a committee was appointed by the passengers to see that
watches were always on duty around the place of the fire and that day
the seat of the fire was discovered which was in the beams supporting
the Decks around the furnace & they appeared to have been burning
for a long time   the fire was then entirely extinguished by the assistance of some of the passengers   the water was taken in at the wheels &
passd forward to the Hatchway in the middle Deck & down that to the
Orlop Deck then through a small square hole in the petition around
the boilers thence up on the boilers & there throwed on the fire   after
this was done we were no more alarmed by the cry of fire although we
kept up the watch until we arrived at the City

Before we arrived at the City of Acapulco the Bread that was
bought at Realajo was entirely consumed so that the last day we had
nothing but meat   this created a great excitement on board and the
passengers appointed a committee to see if anything was in the Store-
room   but the committee did not act so the matter was dropped so far

as any actual action was concerned   yet the fire only slumbered
which was manifest by the supressed grumblings which were hourly
heard on board   We arrived at Acapulco in the evening & passed in
between the headlands of the Bay & Anchored about an hour by sun
The Bay of Acapulco is the most beautiful I ever saw   the entrance
from the sea is about ½ a Mile wide & on both sides of this entrance
the land rises to the height of thousands of feet presenting to the
passenger nothing but bare rocks & white capped waves   the neck of
the Bay or passage in is about 1 mile long so that when once in the
Bay all sight or communication with the sea is entirely cut off only

Acapulco, Mexico

by this passage   the Bay lays parallel with the coast & is about 2½
miles long and about 1 mile wide with several high points of land
running from inland far into the Bay on the lower most or farthest
south of these points   & on the flat lieing North of this point is built
the City of Acapulco   On the Point & facing the Entrance to the Bay
is built a strong Spanish Fortriss or Rectangular fort built of a gray
looking stone which is abundant here   the point is about 100 feet
above high tide & is mostly a solid Rock surrounded with high piles
of loose & large Boulders which look like Granite   On some of these
rocks and in the water I found several of the sea spiders or porcupine
[urchins] which were about 3 inches in Diameter & were of the shape
of a half Globe surrounded with long quills which were hard & verry
sharp   I took one off (it was hard to pull loose from the rocks) & was
going to preserve it but could get nothing suitable to put it in so I
pulled off some of the quills & kept them & threw the other away   we
lay here two days so I was all round the town   it is quite a town as
the hoosier says but of its size I have no definite information more
than the appearance so could not form an idea of its size   like all
Mexican Towns it had its Catholic Church & Nunnery & as usual they
looked of ancient structure

The Market place was an open space in front of the Church & on the
shores about the Centre of the Town   here was a low sandy Beach
in front of the Town and being daly washed by the tides was a most
beautiful place to walk on at low tide   every street & Garden had its
rows of the Majestic Cocoa nut tree and on most all of them clusters
of the Cocoanut which to a hungry man looked verry tempting   I
took a walk out back of the town to a creek that puts into the Bay
below the town & took a thorough wash along with a number of the

passengers　　the water was warm as the climate and was most pleasant　　we passed the Grave yard which was enclosed with a low brush
fence & had hundreds of Crosses stuck up over it　　wherever a grave
was made a cross was planted　　on returning to the town I went into
two or 3 of the Blacksmiths shops & was much amused looking at their
work　　their Anvill was either a rough uneven shaped piece of Iron
Cast in a hole in the ground & to work on was laid on a block loose　　or
was a round piec some 6 or 8 inches long & stuck in a block planted in
the ground & for belouses they had 2 small circular things set on posts
high enough for the forge & from each a wooden pipe run to the fire
these wer worked by a man who drew them one at a time & pushed
the same to keep up a constant blast which was verry weak　　I find

City of Acapulco

the Mexicans are verry far behind the age in improvements　　the
wood workers were equally as rude in their work & their tools

　　I was on shore very late the last night　　I stayed in the City & next
morning we started out about 9-o-clock　　in passing out we saw 3
small whales playing in the water　　There was a vessel in here that
was homeward bound that had a hole in her hull & was sunk on shore
or in shallow water that is at low tide　　her bow was high & dry ashore
at high tide she was nearly buried in water　　she had on board when
she run in here 250 passengers who were now waiting for them to
raise the Vessel which they were trying to do　　I exchanged 50 Dollars
with one of them & gave him American or United States Coin for California Gold for which I got $2.50　　California Gold was 5 pr ¢ discount
at all the Ports along the Coast but as I was coming to California it
was as good as any for me　　There was in Port several sailing Vessels
besides one Steamer which was stopped here by the hands for their pay
& the Vessel was sold to pay charges &c &c

　　Our trip from Acapulco to San Diego was verry pleasant as we had
no high winds except as we crossed the Gulf of California　　the only
place we were out of sight of land on the whole trip　　however I must
except the Grumbling and swearing of the passengers about their fare
which was hard indeed though there was enough such as it was but
damn the *sort*

Up the Coast and San Diego

　　We passed close under the land at Capes St Lucus & San Blas　　those
rugged and Iron bound shores were quite a curiosity to us North men
San Blas is not so high as St Lucus but is more rugged and the rocks
stuck up in sharper peaks than any I ever saw　　another source of

amusement to the passengers was to watch the gyrations of the Many thousands of birds that flock to this coast in the winter season and pick up a living by fishing in the mighty deep   I have frequently seen them disappear beneath the waves for minutes & return to the surface with fish in their beaks   we saw several Whales & many thousands of porpoises and other fish but only 2 or 3 sharks   as we passed into the Bay at San Diego we saw from the Decks the monument which designates the line between Mexico and the United States   we took in coal here from an old hulk that is used as a store ship   & the water casks were sent to a creek several Miles off for water with two men in a boat   but the North America came in which was a Steamer of the Panama Line so our Captain in order to beat her to Francisco left his water casks men & boat & put out just as the North America came in which was at dark   The Town of San Diego Lies about 6 miles above the mouth of the Bay   I[t] was not at where we took in coal was some two miles from the mouth & here they have some 10 or 11 houses all new & lately built by the americans & some 8 or 10 tents

San Diego and San Francisco

occupied by a company of Sodiers   the Bay is seperated from the Sea by a high ridge that is nearly barren of Vegetation   in the bay there is a beautiful low small Island that is owned by a man who got a grant of it from the Mexican Government a short time before it fell into the hands of the Americans   On our passage from here to Francisco our water was short but we were not much inconvenienced by that as the weather was cool & one day it rained a heavy shower   my sleeping place was rather uncomfortable but I made out to weather it through although a severe cold was the consequence.

We landed at the Pacific Wharf on the 2nd day of January 1852 about 10 of the clock in the morning   our first care was to find a house to get dinner which we did on the Wharf where we left our trunks   we then went & got shaved (i e Cap & me) and our hair cut for which we paid for shaving   .25
& cutting hair   .50
I then went to hunt my Brother Abner who I had not seen for better than two years I found him at work in his shop in the City on California Street between Kearny and Montgomery   I will leave to those similarly situated to imagine or describe our joy at again meeting each other for I cant describe it   after we had conversed awhile we went to supper at the Philadelphi house which was near by   after supper we took a walk over the City and visited all the gaming houses a long

commercial & clay Streets   we spent the time til late in this way &
went home to bed and tried to sleep but for my part I slept but little
as the vermin were too abundant to let me

San Francisco

Next Morning Cap Reid & I took a look at the City—however I am
a head of my story   the evening we landed Doc Belles & Maj Coleman went up the River to Stockton   I helped them off & then went
back to try to recover Colemans watch which he had dropped in the
2nd story of the privey at the Union Hotel which is over the Bay the
water being about 12 feet deep   I could not get it   the Boatman
fished for it some time but could not find it   it was a Gold Lever
worth about $65.00   I then went & took my trunk to my Brothers
shop and in shouldering it at the Hotel I knocked off a lamp Globe &
chimney which cost me to replace it   3.50
We looked round awhile & found so many houses to let we concluded
it would not do to attempt to go into business here so we concluded
we would go up to Stockton the next day   so I then went to the shop
& he went to deliver some letters he had   I had delivered my letters
to [S - - ? - -] from Newark with out any result   it being Sunday
Abner & me went round to see the town from the hills   we first went &
looked at a lot he has bought over beyond happy Valley near the Bay
Mission or Mission Bay which is an arm of the San Francisco Bay
that puts out towards the Mission Dolores   we then walked round on
the hills back of the City & got home by dinner   our conversation
was of home of which we could scarcely ever tire   spent the evening
as before only we visited all the Dance houses on Pacific Street which
were all crowded   Next day Cap & I prepared to go to Stockton   I
prepared myself for the Mines by purchasing a pair of blankets & 2
heavy woolen shirts one of which [I] put on & with a leathern belt to
which hung a knife in a leathern scabbard and in my carpet sack a
change of coarse clothes with other little necessaries   the Boat was
to start at 4 so at that time we were at long Wharf the place of starting   the Steam was up the Bells rung & we started but before we got
to the end of the Wharf a flue burst but being a small flued boat it
done no damage so we had to return to the City & wait another day
it being now night we again walked round the City to see what we
could see   we visited several Auction Rooms among them the Chinese
Auction Room in which was sold all kinds of chinese wares & curiosities
& valuables which I can not enumerate   Next day having to stay til
4-o clock P.M. Cap & I took a look among the Auction & other stores

Goods appeared plenty and sales dull   I noticed some sales made at a
verry low figure such as English cheese 17c pr lb Bottled Ale $2,50 pr
Dozen potatoes 1¾c pr lb flour $1,50 pr quarter sack Ham 11½c pr
lb Heavy Double Souled knee Boots $2,50 pr pair   these sales were
at a verry low figure & the City seemed filled with goods   I bought
a hat & pair of shoes & paid for both $3,00 which was as cheap as I ever
bought them in the States

San Francisco and San Joaquin River

At 4 we were again at the Boat and this time nothing happened so
we got off   we passed out among the shipping which appeared as
thick as it did at New York & passed to the right of the Island [Alcatraz]
in front of the City on which there was one solitary house   the Island
is a high hill so there is no Room for many buildings   by dark the
City was out of sight

The darkness prevented me from seeing the Bay as I would have
liked to   when daylight again appeared we were in the San Joaquin
River which is a River to be remembered when once seen   the
country as far as the eye could reach was low level & mostly covered
with water in which was growing long grass [tules] so thick you could
not see into it 10 steps no more [than] 3 feet in many places & in many
places were large ponds on the waters of which were sporting & feeding
thousands of water fowl of all descriptions   through this Italy of
Lagunes & Grass wound the Rio San Joaquin a narrow verry croked
and deep & muddy stream   on each bank was a ridge of 2 or 3 feet
in hight which seemed to be the only dry ground visible in many places
the River is seen ahead in 2 or 3 places when to get to these places a
circuit of several miles is made and the crooks are so short that the
boats rub the banks frequently in turning but this makes not much
difference as there is no timber nor rock the banks being altogather
formed of a loose loam and sand thrown up by the current which is

Stockton

verry strong   there were several sail Vessels such as sloops & schooners
in the River some of which our boat rubbed in passing   the River
being so narrow it was unavoidable   we landed at Stockton about
nine of the clock (I had traded my cloth coat for a watch at the City
so I had the time) & put up at the Galt House which is a Large
New House just started[3]   I here Met with J M Woolen who I was
acquainted with in Shelbyville   he treated me verry friendly

Stockton is built on a Neck of land formed by a bayou running into
the San Joaquin at the head of tidewater and seems to be a flourishing

Town   the Wharf is on the Bayou as the River Bank is not so good a
landing   after Breakfast we looked round Town a little thinking if we
could find a house suitable to start a Cigar & Tobacco Store but not
finding any that suited us we concluded to let it go and I shouldered
my carpet sack & started for the Mines   I left the Cap at Stockton
he expected to go to Sacramento   Stockton is built as low down the
River as the Ground will admit it being only 1 mile from the Lagunes
or as they are here called the Tulares   when I was in the Town it was
with difficulty that a person could get along the streets they were so
muddy   the side walks were almost impossible & in the streets the
Mud was hub deep & verry hard to get through   they asked for the
rent of a house 12 by 24 feet square $120.00 pr Month & at San Fran-
cisco 300 Dollars & larger houses in proportion   The Auction Sales
were a little better here than at the City and business seemed brisker
than at the city   *San Joaquin & Caliveras*

I walked out 6 Miles & put up for the night at the Semmins[4] or 6
mile house where several waggons had stopped   I tried to make a
bargain with them to haul me as the walk of 6 miles had tired me verry
much but their prices were more than I wished to give so I kept on as
before   next morning my bill for supper Breakfast & Bed was $1,75c
I walked on to the 15 mile house which is kept by a man who has his
family with him so he has a good custom   I stopped awhile here & the
waggons came up & I put my carpet sack & blankets on one of them
we [went] to dinner at a house by the way side for which we paid a
dollar (every house is a tavern & most all have bars)   we crossed the
caliveras at the upper Bridge which has lately been built by a company
in opposition to bridge lower down which charged verry high for crossing so they thought to stop them from imposing on the public so   as
the Caliveras all through the Vally lays verry deep in the ground &
the banks are of a loose loamy formation so that it is next to impossible
to cross for any length of time in one place especially where there is
much travel   after passing the Bridge about 2 miles we turned into the
hills   all the way from Stockton here we came through a level open
country thinly covered with large & low oak timber   this is called the
San Joaquin Vally as that is the Main River running through it

At Latimers' on the Caliveras

We stopped for the night at the Tremont house which is a Canvas
house situate in a narrow Vally on a beautiful Mountain Stream about
35 miles from Stockton   next day we arrived at the Double springs

about 3-o clock not having left the Tremont til late & here at the
Tremont I played my [first?] game of poker at which I lost during the
game[5]   1.50
at the double springs I took dinner and here I parted from the waggons
they going on to Campo Seco on the Mokelumne & I going to Latimers
on the Caliveras   I paid them for hauling my carpet sack   1.37

The Double Springs are situate in a small Vally at the head of the
Creek that the Tremont is on & take their name from a small spot of
springy ground out of which pour two large streams of spring water
say 2 inches of water in each[6]   I passed over several deep Canons on
my way to Latimers which were branches of the Caliveras & arrived
there at about 5 in the evening   I found the Major & Doc were about
Major was at work some 2 miles from here & Doctor Belles was gone
on a prospecting tower   Latimers is situate on a deep broad Gulch
about one miles from its junction with the Caliveras & ½ a mile below
the forks of the River and 3 miles below San Andres[7]   the Major
came to Latimers in the evening (where he was boarding) & gave me
the following account of their proceedings so far   he intended to go to
Sonora but Doc persuaded him to come up the Caliveras & they had
formed a company with 5 others who were T W Baldwin Wm Ryal
who were also passengers on the Gold Hunter & were from New York
but were Englishmen Originally from London and a Mr Holbrook Chas
Anderson and Solomon whose other name I forget   these 3 were old
Miners and were used to Mining though they had been for the last
year other wise engaged   Holbrook it was that was gone with Doc
prospecting & the others were working on Indian Gulch until they
should Return   The next day after I arrived the Men all went to
their work & I bough some tools which were an Iron shovel for   2.00
    A small pick with handle   2.50
    1 Tin pan for washing Gold   1.50
and I went to work sinking a hole on a small flat below Latimers   I
worked all day but could get nothing but small specks which I did not
save   I worked verry slow as I knew nothing about it & the ground
was hard to dig being full of stones   by night I got a hole about 3 feet
square & 4 feet deep & was verry tired at that   the next day being
Sunday Major & I went & sunk the hole to the ledge but found nothing
more   the Ledge or Bed rock is found almost everywhere among the
hills at a few feet below the surface   an that is where most of the
Gulch Gold is found   after we had quit the hole we went down on
the River & washed several pans of dirt but got nothing more than the

color & that in verry small specks   The River here runs through a
narrow Canon   on each side the rocks rise almost perpendicular for
several hundred feet   we soon returned to the house tired of prospecting   Latimer keeps a Store & boarding house & being on the Road a

Latimer and the Buckeye Store

Tavern also and on this day [it] is crowded with Customers as on
Sunday but few work but all trade so the store was crowded as also
was another store a few hundred yards below latimers   we loafed
round the store til after dinner and then walked up the Gulch & up
on the hill to a quartz lead that had been dug for some 30 feet bedded
in slate & Granite which came to the tops of the ground on a high hill
the Gold is generally distributed through the Quartz but in such fine
particles that it is not visible with the naked eye   as we came back
to the store we met the Doctor & Holbrook just returning   they
reported good prospects over on the Divide between the North Fork
of the Caliveras & the Moqualumne but on the Moqualume slope
which is to the North & west of the Caliveras   so on their report we
bundled up and started the next morning for Angiers that being the
place of destination & near the prospected ground   We arrived at the
Buckeye Store after a hard walk over high hills & deep Ravines & Rich
flats   we crossed the Chilean flat [Chili Gulch] in our way which is a
verry rich flat & is all laid off and most of the dirt thrown up ready for
the rain which is now expected daily   when we arrived at the Buckeye
Store a Council was called of the 7 who were in the Company before I
came whether they should take me in or not & whether they should
take Lumber from here to build Toms with as here there was a Mill &
the nearest place lumber could be had it being yet 6 miles to Angiers

Buckeye Store Moquolumne River

There was some objection to my coming into the Company which
I think came from Doc Belles but he kept it carefully concealed   Major
Coleman was determined I should be one of the company and the rest
were easy about it   after some time talking about that & the Lumber
I was considered one of them & then the question of the Lumber was
discussed   the time spent came verry good to me to rest for I was
verry tired having carried my carpet sack & blankets pick shovel &
pan   altogether they weighed 48 lbs which was no light load over the
road we came   we concluded at last to get the lumber & adjourned to
the Mill to look at the lumber   the Mill was built in the same Gulch
the Store was on & was called the Buckeye Mill & Gulch same name[8]

The Mill was built against an Oak tree & was long enough to saw plank 12 feet   was run by steam made by a boiler of 6 feet in length & 3 feet in diameter with a 4 inch Cylinder   there was no piece of timber in the mill frame over 6 inches square yet they sawed logs 16 inches in diameter   we picked out lumber enough for a Tom for which we paid 16c a foot and hired a donkey & left Charley Anderson to bring it up with the Donkey   we went on to Angiers   on the Road we passed in sight of the Moquolumne River which was about 1800 feet below us we passed along the side of the Mountain next the River which looked from that height like a large serpent winding along among the Mountains   we arrived at Angiers at dark & Charley with the Donkey did not get up til about 10- o clock & then we had to go with lights to help him cross the Gulch which was verry deep & steep banks   the Donkey

At Angiers on Alabama Gulch[9]

got tangled in the brush at the bottom of the Gulch but when we got to him with our lights we soon extricated him   the plank were 12 feet long and 16 *in* wide & were packed two on each side of the Donkey so they went forward past his head & as far back as possible   they charged us for the Donkey 3 Dollars   we used him ½ a day

Next morning Dock & Holbrook went to work at making the Tom which is a trough the length of the plank & wi[d]th of one plank & about 6 inches deep with a short sheet Iron ridelle at one end slightly turned up through which the fine gravel water & gold falls in to a box beneath placed to receive it   the gold being the heaviest sinks to the bottom & the gravel & dirt is washed away   the rest of the company after buying some tools went to clearing away a place to work in the Alabama Gulch just below Angiers house

Angiers house is situate on the East & North side of the Alabama Gulch which runs into the Moqualumne about 3 miles below the first fork   his house is a small frame with a dirt floor the posts mortised in the ground & weather boarded and covered with fine clapboards   his store & sleeping rooms (he keeps as is usual in California boarding house store & Tavern with a Bar) are built in the same manner   his beds is the dirt floor with 2 blankets one to sleep on & one under or as the sleeper pleases   his store nor house is never closed the doors being about 8 feet wide & for a shutter a sheet of canvas which is rolled up during the day and at night let down to keep out the night air—he keeps a Butcher also who kills daily one beef & sometimes 2 or 3 all of which readily sells to the Miners &c   by night we had a place cleared away for to go to work & they had the Tom ready   so in the morning

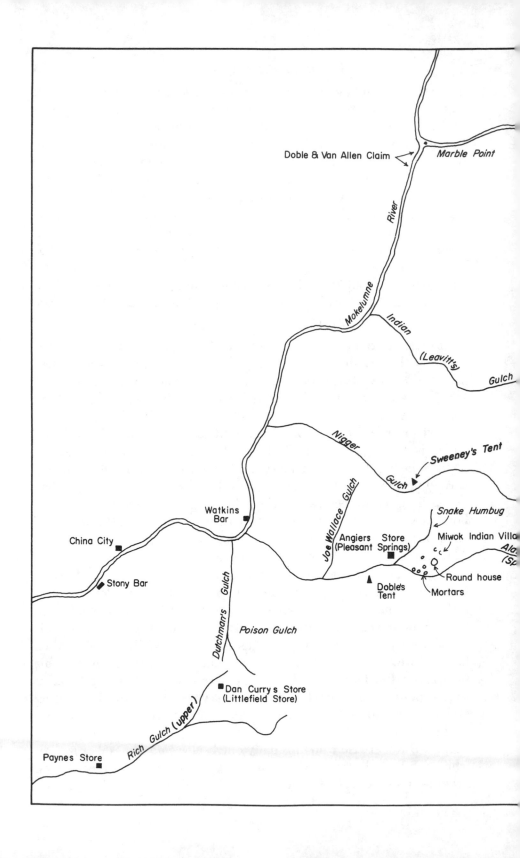

Doble & Van Allen Claim → • Marble Point

Mokelumne River

Indian (Leavitt's) Gulch

Nigger Gulch

Sweeney's Tent ▲

Joe Wallace Gulch

Watkins Bar ■

China City ■

Snake Humbug ↘
Miwok Indian Villa[ge]

Angiers Store
(Pleasant Springs) ■

Ala[...]
(S[...]

Round house ↗
Mortars ↗

◆ Stony Bar

▲ Doble's Tent

Dutchman's Gulch

Poison Gulch

Dan Curry's Store ■
(Littlefield Store)

Rich Gulch (upper)

Paynes Store ■

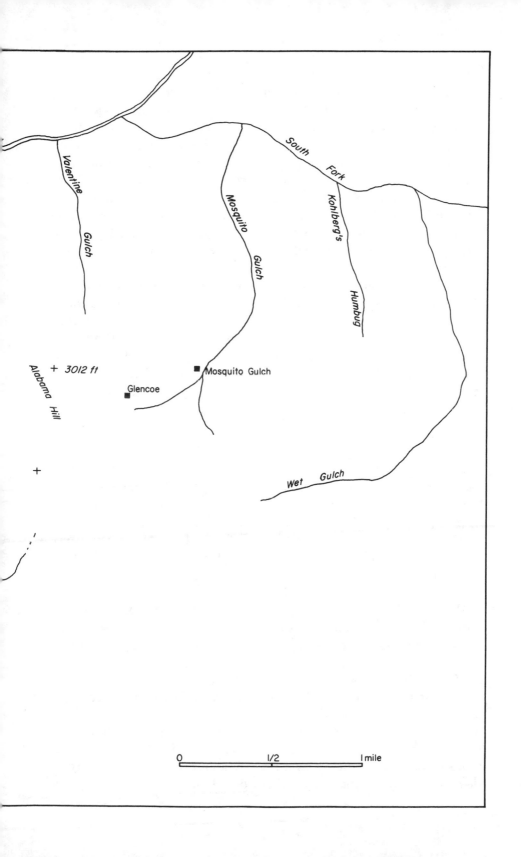

we put it in the Gulch & doc Holbrook & I went & chopped out long troughs to lead the water to the Tom   I had bought an axe & gave 3.50 for an axe & handle   after we had got troughs for the one Tom we found that 8 could not work to advantage with one Tom so Holbrook went down to the Buckeye & got plank & Doc & him made another Tom while Doc & I cleared a place lower down the Gulch to work it in   we [had] the 2nd Tom to work on Friday evening & we made that evening 20c which I kept it being the first gold I had dug & saturday we made one dollar which I also kept & the other 4 who had been washing since wednesday morning had made near 20 dollars so we were not yet discourged

On Sunday several of us took pick pan & shovel & went down the Gulch to the River   Major & [I] went together one way and Ryal & Baldwin went another   we went down Alabama Gulch   they went down a Gulch to the West of that   Angiers Store is near the top of the ridge on a small flat   the Gulch runs nearly level for ½ a mile & starts down to the River over one continuous fall til it reaches the river   these falls are about ½ a mile long & frequently the water falls

The Country Around Angiers

40 feet over a smooth Granite rocks & all the way down every bench or uneven place is filled with large boulders of the granite stone   we went down over these falls sometimes sliding a distance & sometimes letting ourselves down by the bushes which grew in abundance along the side & in the crevices of the rock   we reached the River about noon & found several tents at the Mouth of the Gulch most of them deserted   but one was occupied by a company of Miners who were staying here watching a claim they had in the River which they dug a race round & partly worked the last year & the water raised and they had to quit til next summer   they were working in the bars & banks of the river—   we went up the River some ½ a mile & prospected some of the bars but found nothing except at one place where some-body had a claim   I washed 5 pans & got 20c which with [what] I had before I have yet   The River Gold is finer smother & thinner than the Gulch Gold though all I have seen of both were fine no piece being larger than 6c   We returned by the trail which the Miners have made in passing up to the store & back   we being Novices in climbing Mountains it made us verry tired   when we arrived at Angiers it was supper time & I was so tired I did not feel like eating anything   The Store was crowded when we returned & about dark a good many of them were tolerable tight or in other words ½ drunk & after dark they

got to singing sailor songs & playing games &c and got us all up & Tom Baldwin played the fiddle for them & they danced & sung till near

Angiers Store

morning not letting us sleep any   Angiers has his wife here with him & she was grealty distrubed by the noise & obscene Language used such is California   wherever women is not there reigns vice & immorality   Monday Morning Baldwin was not able to go to work he had drinked too much the night previous   the rest of us started to work when Charley informed us he had met with an old sailor friend (Charley was a sailor) of his who lived on Muquito Gulch & wanted him to come and live with him so he withdrew from the Company then shortly Doc & Holbrook said they could not work any more as they had not made any thing so they left us & went to the Moquolumne Hill which is a Town below this place & is the County Seat of this (Caliverus) County   so the remaining five went to work again & worked two days & did not make board   Holbrook & Doc returned & they wanted to get what they had paid on the tools & said they were going to the City again so we divided the tools & then Maj Coleman & Solomon was discouraged & they left too so there was none but Baldwin Ryal & myself left   I was going back to the City to get money to live on while I tried to make something but Angier told me he would let us have any thing we wanted so I stayed and went in debt for food &c   I paid my board which was 10.00 a week   Bill & Tom hat no money to pay thiers   and after the others left we three went to work again together   *At Angiers Caliverus County Cal*

We worked for one week & Angier then told us he could not board us more than another week so we began to make preparation to camp & board ourselves   during these two weeks we did not make enough to pay our board and we were in debt for some of the tools although I had paid for all I had got & had some money left but I would not pay when the other boys could not as I might get out of money and be in the fix they were   We were working in the Gulch about 200 yards below the Store & here the Gulch was a canon & that is steep sides & narrow at the bottom   here the hills rose abruptly on both sides & the bottom where the branch run was 7 or 8 feet wide   in the bottom of this canon we dig for the Oro or Gold   we turn the water which here is not much into a small ditch to one side of the Gulch & set our Tom one side & let the water run through it & take up the gravel dirt & grass roots from the bottom of the Gulch & mash them in the Tom &

at night take what is in the ripple box (i e the box under the end of the Tom) wash it in the pan & thus get the gold   we wash all the dirt in the bottom of the Gulch to the Ledge which is here about 3 feet on an average though some places it is bare   the Ledge here is a gray Granite rock which is verry hard   we find the most gold in the little cracks & crevices in the rock & sometimes wedged in so hard that it is dug or picked out with difficulty although we find some mixed with the loose dirt and grass roots on the top   the grass roots are verry thick & hard to dig in places also the brush roots are with difficulty dig up

We three worked along for two weeks togather & did not make enough to pay board and at the end of that time moved into a tent which we had borrowed from a sailor living here by name Jo Wallace we placed this tent within the banks where an old Cabine had been burned & the dirt that was thrown up around was yet standing so it made a good defense against the cold & winds   we bought a lot of things to keep house which I yet have the bill   I will Copy it here with several other bills of provision   I find by the bill it was about the 25th of January when we went to boarding ourselves   well now to the Bill

Messrs J Doble & Co

Bot of D L Angier & Cos

This pick was bought	Jany 23	1 pick & Handle	5.00
when we wore out what	" 25	3 Tincups @ 25	.75
we had before—	" "	3 " plates @ 25	.75
This Oven was a com-	" "	1 Dutch Oven (cast Iron)	4.50
mon flat bottomed Iron	" "	1 Camp Kettle (2 gallon)	2.00
vessel	" "	1 Box pepper	.25
	" "	1 lb candles (Stearine)	.75
	" "	1 Frying pan	2.00
	" "	1 lb. Ground coffee	.50
	" 26	16 " cheese English @ 37½	6.00
	" "	16 " Butter @ 87½	13.60
	" "	50 " Flour " 12	6.00
This fry pan was a com-	" "	5 " sugar brown	1.00
mon handled fry pan	" "	9 " Ham @ 30c	2.70
This a/c [account] is all	" "	½ lb Saleratus @ 75	.37
what we got from the	" "	1 Beefs heart	1.50
time we went to board-	" "	7 lb Beef for quarter @ 20	1.40
ing ourselves until we	" "	1 lb coffee	.50
made money enough to			49.57

Operations at Angiers

pay for what we had	Feb	1	5 lb sugar @ 25	1.25
got which was on the	"	2	5 " Beef " "	1.25
21st of Feb as the Bill	"	"	2 " Pork salt @ 20	.40
shows this being a fac	"	"	2 " Nails " 25	.50
simila of Angiers Bill up	"	"	1 " Candles (stor) @ 75	.75
to that time the 21st	"	"	8 " Beef " 20	1.60
of Feb was some time	"	"	1 Paper Tacks	.50
after I lost my book so	"	"	9 lb Beef @ 25	2.25
I have notes from the	"	"	7 " Pork " 20	1.40
5th of Feb which will	"	"	3 spoons (Iron) @ 25	.75
show the payment of	"	"	10 lbs Beef @ 25	2.50
this Bill in another	"	"	4 " Potatoes @ 12½	.50
place hereafter though	"	"	50 " Flour @ 12	6.00
I have just given this to	"	"	8 " Potatoes @ 12½	1.00
show what we had to	"	8	6 " sugar @ 20	1.20
pay for provisions in	"	"	½ " Tallow Candles	.13
the Mines & that before	"	"	14 " Beef @ 20	3.20
we had a chance or did	"	"	2 Boxes Matches @ 12½	.25
make anything we	"	11	1 box pepper	.25
were in the Mines for	"	"	10 lb Beef @ 25	2.50
nearly two months be-	"	"	1 " Coffee (ground)	.50
fore we made enough to	"	13	19 " Beef @ 25	4.75
pay expenses	"	"	1 Plug Tobacco (½ lb)	.50
	"	"	1 Paper Tobacco (fine cut)	.50
	"	14	1 " " "	.50

Feb 1st By cash   43 15
" 21 Recd Payt   40 35

D L Angier
pr
Joel Angier

At Angiers Known as The Pleasant Springs or Angiers Store

I purposed writing or copying several of the bills now that I have in my possession but as I have a memorandum from the 5th of February I will give them as they occur

Angier had placed in large letters painted on canvass over his store door "Pleasant Springs" Taking this as the name of his place the name was taken from the numerous springs gushing forth to the surface along Alabama Gulch on which he was situated & from this the Gulch was sometimes called Spring Gulch Where Angiers store stands is on a flat about ½ a mile wide & the store is at the foot of the hill towards the top of the ridge or Mountain   it is about a mile to the top   between the store and the falls puts into Spring Gulch several small gulches 2 of which forms the flat where they head   & our [place] from the other side forms a flat also. Our tent stands on the side of the hill about 50 yards above the bottom of the Gulch under a large Oak tree from which the water when it rains falls in large drop & splatters through the tent & makes every thing very damp we cook in a large fire place that once belonged to the cabin the tent is placed with the front pole against one jam so the fire keeps the tent warm   we have no fastenings to the tent so the dogs have several times come into the Tent & have taken out whatever Meats &c they could find   I tried several times to get to shoot them but could not catch them[10]

I have Noticed the population of the Mines are very unsettled   in coming up here we met every day persons going to the city from the Mines and now that I am here men are passing daily up & down   some come here and work a short time & then leave for some other part of the Mines   I have met with men here frequently who have been from the Extreme known southern Mines to the Extreme known Northern Mines and are now worth nothing   I have got acquainted with men here who have been here in this neighborhood for 2 & 3 years and known every thing that man can know of the Mines yet these men are nearly worthless   some of them were at the opening of the rich lead in Rich Gulch of the Caliverus (which heads ½ a mile from here) & they had claims from which they took as high as 2 lb a day yet these men are worth nothing   as soon as they get a little ahead they go to drinking and keep it up until the money is out and go back to digging again until they get another start when again the same course is pursued   these men are mostly sailors though some of them are good men or appear to have once been   so now & then there is one who is a landsman but such are scarce among the reckless & disipated   when one is found to be a reckless dissipated man he is most sure to be a man of some information & talent   one there is here who appears to have on[c]e been a valuable man but strong drink has ruined him &c

Pleasant Springs February 8th 1852

I have now written from memory all that I think of [from] the time I communced a memorandan in my pocket book & have come to where I have a memorandom again so from that I now write   Yesterday

being the 7th was my 24th Birth Day & as some times happens the
Boys made me treat pretty freely & consequently we were all last night
rather Elevated or in other words somewhat corned as in this country
where Liquors are to be had of every description & but little that is
made of corn we were at least ½ drunk & to day a heavyness in the
brain with a curious singing in the Ears & an apparent propensity in
every thing visible for a rotary motion is a part of the consequences

We have quit work some days ago in the place we first commenced
& have moved down to the head of the falls   we are are now working
just where the first fall commences   the bottom of the Gulch here is
about 20 feet wide filled up from two to 8 feet with large loose stone
which we designate by the name of Boulders   these stone we have to
move before we can get to the Ledge at the bottom though on both
sides of us it rises nearly perpendicular high above us forming a verry
beautiful & Romantic situation as through the opening over the falls
the River is visible about ½ a mile of it which at this height & distance
(which is ¾ of a mile looks like a white & blue Ribbon of a wide kind
wherever the stone sticks up in it or it falls   the breaks in the water
look white & in other places blue.

The River is generally about 50 yards wide

Spring Gulch Feb 8th 1852

We are now working on a rotton Granite Ledge which looks verry
much like sandstone it being so soft that for several inches we can
pick it up with ease   we have worked 3 or 4 days & not found any
thing worth naming   just above us has been a company working all
winter & they have taken out several lumps   one a few days ago
which weighed 108/00 [dollars]   I was at the hole they were working
in when they found it & they gave 3 cheers heartily when they found
it   they had found that day (this was late in the evening) several
pieces enough to make 3 ounces in pieces from one to 10 Dollars but
the big lump so excited them they cheered heartily

The Timber on the hills & flats here (however the flats scarcely ever
have any timber on them) is principally pine Oak Live Oak and Buckeye   the undergrowth is redwood Greasewood Arrowwood & a kind
of bush nearly resembling black Oak with a mixture of some rare kinds
of wood that I dont know & any quantity of Vines & creeping things
that resemble wood   also there is a kind of wood which is called
poison Oak which effects a person like the poison vines in Indiana
the Oak is low red backed wood which much resembles the ivy in the

States only it is not a vine but a small bunchy wood   this wood when rubbed or the leaves are mashed on the skin it soon breaks out like the small pox—inflamed sores which remain in a putrid state for several weeks & are difficult to heal   Also another plant that grows in great abundance in all low & damp places called the soap plant   this plant has some of the properties of the common soap   it is a bulbous root of some 4 inches in length enclosed in a thick covering of longitudinal

Alabama Gulch Feb 8th 1852

placed fibres which are much the same as sea grass   these fibres seem to be a thrown off coating from the plant as the outer portion are generally rotten while the inner are strong & apparently fresh   I used the plant for some time instead of soap but I found it irritated the skin therefore I discontinued the use of it   The Indians use it altogather for washing   speaking of Indians There is a large Camp of them about ¼ mile up the Gulch on a flat at the foot of the summit ridge of this Divide   This camp when I first came here consisted of 3 huts & a round or council house   the 3 huts are made by setting up sticks or poles in a circle of from 6 to 10 feet in diameter & leaning the tops togather & covering with bark skins brush cloth or anything that comes their way   a hole is left on one side for an entrance   in these the Indians with their dogs lie promiscuously & when the weather is cool they build a little fire in the door of their huts over which they pass to & fro or in & out   The Council house is built by digging a hole about 3 feet deep & 20 feet in diameter   then in the centre is set 4 forks in a square of 4 feet then from this edge of the hole to sticks laid on the 4 forks are laid poles which support a roof   the roof is made by laying sticks across the poles & sometimes skins & bark are used then on this covering putting 2 or 3 inches of dirt   a hole is left in the centre for the smoke to ascend & the door is a ditch dug under one side 2 feet deep   to get in they all go on their hands & knees

Sunday February 8th 1852

We have made with last weeks work 22.95 which when we have it all togather looks big   I have always heard that Gold glitters but none that we have will glitter at all   it is a dull yellow coler that is all that is smooth   there is some that is rough that has a bright coler but it does not glitter & I am informed that gold never glitters   This is the beginning of my cook week as I have to cook bread for tomorrow   it is my first cooking since I left Mexico & it goes verry awkward yet I got a pretty good loaf Baked   Our tent having no fastening at the bottom in front the dogs have several times got in & taken our meat & turned things over so to day I loaded Tom Baldwins shot gun on purpose that if any dogs came round to shoot them   while we were eating dinner 2 Indian dogs came directly to the tent as if they would come in but when they saw us they turned & run   I catched the gun & fired after them but they were so far off that the shot only hit one in the hind parts & crippled him   he dragged himself down into the branch or at the water of the gulch & there lay til a man killed him with a stone to ease him of his misery   towards evening I learned he belonged to an Indian Doctor and near night the Doctors squaw or Mohala came round with 4 or 5 children after her & one on her back hunting him   when they found him they took a cry over him & left him without shroud or burial

I find the Indians think a great deal of thir dogs in fact almost as much as they do of thier children

Monday February 9th 1852

This Morning when we went to work we felt verry much discouraged with our claim & concluded to look round for another place so Tom went down to the River to see if we could not get a claim down there he returned about one & reported the chance had & he was so much fatigued with his walk that he did not work this evening   Bill & [I] made in the days work only   2.50 but we had struck in the evening a verry pretty crevice which we thought we would yet find something in   we will continue to work it awhile yet anyhow   The Indians have made several threats to Angier against him for letting us kill their dog   it seems the whole camp is interested in the dog   The Indian dress if dress it can be called is verry much varied   the most of them dress in the cast off clothing of the Americans   though some few of them have bought good clothes of the Americans and others here   many of them however wear nothing but a shirt & some only a blanket   & verry few wear the breechclout   the squaws never wear pants but any other article of clothing they can get hold of they wear   they are all squaws & men verry fond of beads & seashells & mostly hang short strings of beads with a piece of shell at the ends of the strings all about their persons & I have seen one man with 20 yards of beads around his neck or one squaw with as much round her waist   they have been visiting at this camp from Moquolumne Hill & last night after moon up they started home whooping and yelling so they waked us all up &c

Tuesday Feb 10th 1852

Tom was verry much scared   he thought they were going to attack us for killing the dog & so he got his gun & revolver ready and called to me to get my revolver so to meet them as they came   I did not want to get up but he would have me do so so I got off my back & made ready for them but they did not come so all the good I done was to spoil a pot of coffee by sticking my foot in it as I got up   The Moon was shining clear and bright   The weather the last day or two has been clear pleasant & beautiful

Feb. 10   We went to work in our crevice & followed it about a foot & found nothing but in another just above that one we found 4 ounces mostly in small pieces but two pieces weighed $20.00   it was mostly wedged under a thin layer of the rotton Granite & some of it verry hard to pick out without breaking the stone   this put us again in good spirits so we will probably work the claim out   about midnight last night we were awakened by the coyotes or wolves howling round Angiers Correl   I got up & went over to the store   two of the men at the store went out to try to shoot them but could not find them as they quit their noise as soon as the men went out

Feb. 11   Worked hard to day   followed a verry pretty triangular crevice all day & got only $5.00   this crevice was in the solid granite & smooth so that if gold was in & water ever run through it it would wash it out   this crevice lay diagonally across the Gulch and ended where the Ledge rose at the sides   some of the Gold we found is nearly black & the dirt looked as if it might have been burned   the weather is most beautiful clear & pleasant &c

Thursday February 12th 1852

Worked as usual   Ledge looks like gold   the dirt & gravel about the same as before but no gold scarcely only got little better than a dollar to day   the news of our *Strike* of 4 ounces has brought many Miners round to see where we found it

Many different views & opinions among them about the Gold   some thinks it washed into the Gulches out of the hills others think it thrown at some time long since all over the country by Volcanic action & Others that it is a natural formation & has always been where we find it   I incline to the opinion that it is a natural formation formed near where we find it & that at one time was generally distributed over the country but the heavy rains removing so much dirt off the hills into the Gulches would naturally carry with it all the Gold in it consequently it is the plentiest in the Gulches   we had several verry heavy rocks to move so I strained my back a little which hurts me badly   weather cloudy but quite pleasant   looks like rain &c

Feb. 13   Worked to day up the centre of the Gulch   the Ledge is again changed to rotten Granite   we washed out soon after dinner & had near an ounce   we then washed for an hour or so & picked out one lump that weighed $10,00 & had in the ripple box about $5 00 we thought that would do for one day as we were all tired & my back hurt so we knocked off for the day   Rained some during the night & was raining in the morning   the day was cloudy & some drizzling rain but warm & pleasant

Feb. 14   Worked as usual only a little harder and got to work a little earlier & worked a little later in hopes of striking some thing big but did not   only made during the day about ½ an ounce   after

Saturday February 14th 1852

supper we went over to Angiers & settled up our bill (which I have previously copied into this book) which we have not been able to do before since we have been here   we then divided the dust remaining & each one share was 12.37   (I find I have lost the bill but I recollect the amount the most of it for my Birth day treat 7.75   4 Dollars for Liquors & the balance for shot powder & Led & tobacco   I then redeemed Maj Colemans pistol (a colts revolver) which he had pawned to get money to leave here with when he got so badly discouraged the amt was 20.00   I had previously sold my watch after having the misfortune to break the Chrystal to Angiers Butcher by name Jacob Strain for the sum of 20.00   & had paid my board and all but the a/c of $7.75 so I had some money left when all was settled   but the other Boys (Tom & Bill) could not pay their private a/c at all nor had they any money left scarcely when the bill was paid   I got and kept the two lumps that weighed 20 00 [dollars] I also bought a ½ lb bar of lead   paid for it .37

The Indians are going to have a big Fandango here   about 500 came in from other places to this camp to day   they came in in companies of from 20 to 50   they come in Indian file the Men carrying their bows & arrows and the squaws the luggage in their conical shaped baskets suspended on their backs by a strap round over the forepart of their heads and them that had children carried them in the basket with the balance of the Luggage apparently promiscuously &c

Sunday February 15th 1852

Went over to Angiers after Breakfast and got some shot which cost 50c pr lb   The Store & yard was crowded with Indians of all sexes &

sizes dressed in all manners of way from a shirt above to a full and
fine cloth dress with calf boots & high top beaver with a belt & revolver
The Indians that were dressed were from near the Vally   those
undressed & half dressed were from the Mountains   some that [had]
the finest cloth had it all decked off with beads & shells which con-
stitute the principle of Indian Ornament   They were buying large
quantities of beef & Cognac which most of them are fond of that is the
Cognac   and all are fond of the beef   they seemed to have plenty of
the dust & payed for all they got   some of them were getting pretty
drunk   came back to the tent & run some balls for the pistol & took it
and the shot gun & started out to shoot birds or anything that was
Bueno for Chumuck (i e good to eat)   I went down Rich Gulch   it
is the first time I have seen it   there is tents strung all along it and
it is now dug up for 50 feet wide for 3 miles and better   the hills are
low on both sides and the Gulch wide   There has been several fortunes taken out of this Gulch   The Man that built and lived in the
cabin that stood where our tent stands went home with 57 lbs or
upwards of Eleven thousand Dollars & the Gulch is yet paying well   I
returned homeward by way of the flat at the head of the Gulch & in
crossing the flat I found a single red flower the only one I have yet
seen   it is of a kind nearly resembling in shape the Lambs tongue   I
preserved it pressing it in paper as it is the first I have seen and being
all alone in a large flat where nothing but grass and weeds were to be
sen & scarcely yet above the ground   I found nothing worth shooting
at so came home as I went only I had a few Quartz Chrystal specimens & the flower which I preserved   After supper an old sailor or
Portugee came over (he lived at Angiers) & wanted us to go up to the
Indian Camp with him so Bill & I went with him   we looked round
the camp awhile & then returned   this is the first time I have been
there since the first Sunday I came here & the camp has increased from
3 to about 200 huts with a great many brush shades which answer the
purpose of huts

Stewart being Amorously inclined came again after us to go to the
camp   I did not want to go so bill & him went & took some brandy
with them to treat the Indians but they being more virtuous than
Stewart calculated they run him & Bill off but not til they were pretty
tight & Stewart & Bill not much better   Capt Van Allen came to us
this evening & proposed going in company & taking a River claim   we
agreed & tomorrow will go & see it &c   weather clear & pleasant &c

Feb. 16   There were several Drunken Indians passing about during the night yelling & hooping & *making night hidious* with their drunken clatter so we did not sleep much during the night   After Breakfast we three in company of Van Allen and sweeney another Miner that lives here started to go down to the River   we went up the ridge about 2 miles   passed an old Indian camp on the way consisting of a round house & several huts   we started down the hill near the top of the highest ridge of Mountains between the coast Range & the summit ridge of the Siera Nevada   from the top we had a view of the country from one to the other which was very beautiful   it took us good two hours to reach the River   we got to it about one mile below where the south fork puts into the north   on both sides the hills are verry high   the River is about 50 yards across that is the space between the hills   the water only covers about ½ this space the balance being bare slate ledge or where the Ledge is low large & small rock gravel & sand & black sand in abundance   we passed up the River til within ¼ mile of the Forks where our claim was to be   the most of the distance over bars of stone gravel and sand though in many places the [banks] rose high & bare confining the water to verry narrow limits   at one of these places a log had been put across on which 3 of [us] crossed   the water running beneath & close to us in a roaring surging torrent which deafened our voices so we could not hear each other holloo   The other two were taken across in canoe below where the water was more calm & wide   We put up notices that we intended to work about 50 yards as soon as the water would permit   we then all picked about in the crevices of the Ledge with our knives and got about 25c in verry fine scaly Gold & then started home   we were about 4 hours getting up the hill again   we arrived at home about 3 of the clock very tired of our trip   in coming up the Mountain I found several small light blue flowers & some red which I preserved as before   when on the top of the hill we stopped to rest I noticed the North & East sides of the hills were all thickly covered with timber & underbrush and the south & west sides only covered with thin growth of oak & pine   the cause I did not look for

March Feb 16th 1852

The River as I before said was about 50 yards wide that is the level space between the Mountains   but the water at this time does not fill more than ½ that distance   the channel runs from side to side forming bars on each side   in every bend there is a bar sometimes wide & sometimes narrow   sometimes these bars are nothing but bare ledge & in this case but verry little Gold is found   but the most of

them are covered from nothing to 20 feet with large Boulders small *do*
sand & Gravel   in these bars is found the greatest quantity of Gold
& Generally found under the (the) loose matter above in the crevices
of the Ledge   but frequently found generally distributed among the
stones & in the sand wherever there is loose dirt rotton stone sand &
Gravel or small cracks or crevices in the Ledge there is found Gold
along the river   Where we went down was about one mile from the
forks   our claim was about 400 yards below the fork   between that
& the forks had been worked out last year but had not paid much
just in the forks where the two streams come togather is a pile of
square stone some 60 feet high or I might say a square pile of stone
the stone are of various sizes & it appears as if it had been built by
hands looks like a square tower from a short distance below   just
below this tower & in the main River is a narrow Ledge Island some
150 yards long   but I did not go to see it only as I looked from
our claim

After we got home & I had eaten some dinner we concluded to not
go to work til tomorrow so Bill & Tom went over to Angiers & I took
the gun & pistol and took a stroll over the hills   I found no game
worth shooting so I returned by way of the Indian camp which now
consists of about 400 huts & brush shelters   as I approached the camp
I passed a ½ dozen or so of squaws pounding acorns & on a nearer
approach I was greeted with the howling & barking of some 50 or 60
dogs which all came out at me as if they would take me whether or no
but I knew their nature so I advanced to the camp & the dogs surrounded me but kept at a respectful distance

In coming up the Gulch or in crossing the Gulch I passed some ½
Dozen squaws pounding Acorns & I stopped & looked at them awhile &
while I was in the camp I noticed their manner of cooking &c which I
will now try to describe   The season is past for Oak mast & there is
none in the woods that I have seen except what is stored away by the
birds in the bark of the pine trees   so I suppose they have them stored
away somewhere however the squaws were pounding the Acorns   I
have frequently seen large stones with flat surfaces laying on the top
of the ground & all the flat surface filled with small round holes in the
shape of a physicians Morter which I did not know how they came
there or how they were made or what they were made for but now a

The Digger Indians, Their Cooking, Etc.

solution of the Enigma was before me   The ½ dozen squaws that I
stopped to look at were all seated flat on the Ledge of rock in the

bottom of the Gulch which was bare for several yards & smooth & level & each had between her legs & in a small round hole in the rock a small pile of Acorns on which they were pounding with an Oval shaped stone about 8 inches long with all their power at least from the way they seemed to exert themselves it appeared they were using all their power They thus begin to pound their acorns on the smoth surface of the rock but the continual pounding soon wears a hole which gradually deepens until it becomes too deep for use   it is then deserted and another one begun[11]   They had a shade over them of bushes stuck in the ground in a Circular form & the tops brought togather over the rock to protect them from the heat of the sun   the pounding seemed verry laborious as each and all of them were purspiring profusely some of them sweating so profusely as to wet the rock for several inches around them or where they sat   The Acorns after being hulled that is the shell or hard covering taken off are thus ground to a fine meal in this manner   it is then taken to their fires which are generally built on a flat place near water where they scoop a hole in the ground of a circular form about 3 inches deep & into this hole put the meal spreading it over the bottom about 2 inches deep   They then take from the fire small stones which have been heating & plunge them in to a basket of water at hand until it (the water) is boiling   They then pour the water on the meal in the hole until the hole is full this sets the meal all afloat   the flour of the Acorn then settles to the bottom while the husk or redish covering which is next to the shell settles on the top while this is settling I will tell what the baskets are   they are made of willow & so tightly woven as to hold water & when they become covered with dirt & well worn they look like an earthen pot that was well worn & are equally as good to hold water   When the water has all settled into the earth leaving the Acorn meal in the hole—they then with their hands (for they have no other utensils for the purpose) scrape off the top which is of a redish color & throw it in another basket & thin it with boiling water into a thick soup   this leaves in the hole a layer of beautifully white looking meal   this they scrape out as near the bottom as they can without getting any of the dirt with it & form into oblong cakes of about a pound each   they then scrape out the bottom of the hole which is generaly ½ dirt & make it into soup like the top only thinner so the dirt settles to the bottom   the soup is made in small baskets & then a part is carried to the camp and given to the men & boys & part is kept at the fire for the squaws Girls & papooses   the part taken to the men is the cakes and top soup & the part kept for the cooks or squaws [is] the bottom with the dirt in it

The scalding process they say takes the bitter belonging to the acorn off though I cant say for I never tasted any of it after it was cooked though I have frequently tried to eat the acorn which is verry bitter more so than in the states   There is a small berry grows here that they dry & pound in the same manner as the Acorn which they eat with their soup in its powdered state without any preparation   this they call panola [pinole]   They eat their soup by dipping their fingers in it & then licking it off their fingers sometimes making a spoon of the 4 fingers of the hand and dipping the soup with this natural spoon and in a peculiar & comical (comical to me but I suppose natural to them) manner pouring it into the mouth & from thence I will leave it to phisiologists and physicians to tell what becomes of it   while passing about the camp I noticed hundreds eating in this way while many were roasting meat by laying it on the fires in pieces of all sizes up to 50 lbs or thereabouts & eating it as soon as cooked or half burned with out seasoning of any kind   The squaws as is usual among Indians do all the work while the Men look on & see that it is well done   They carry their children whil young bound to a board made of sticks on their backs   I will try to describe   the board is made by first bend-ing a stick of ½ an inch in diameter in the shape of a magnet or ox bow & then binding with strips of deer skin or sinews small sticks crosswise and as near togather as possible until they get a board of 2½ feet in length with the bow at the top   on this they bind the child from its feet to its neck leaving only its face & head uncovered & there keep it until it can stand or walk   though I suppose thy some-times take them off the board yet I never saw one off that couldnt

The Indians and Their Customs &c

walk   when moving about this board is either hung on their backs by a string over the forehead or laid in the basket which they generally carry in the same manner   this basket which nearly every squaw has one is in shape like a candle extinguisher & generally holds about 1½ bushels — and is made of willow as the others but is not watertight this basket answers the purpose of waggon cart wheelbarrow & every thing else to carry luggage about though they sometimes pack on horses when they have them   one more thing of the children   in hot weather they fix to the bow at the top of the board a shade for the childs head made of willow tightly woven & in shape something near a ladies feather fan the edges generally hung with short strings of beads tipped with small pieces of the pearl Oyster shell   in cool or rainy

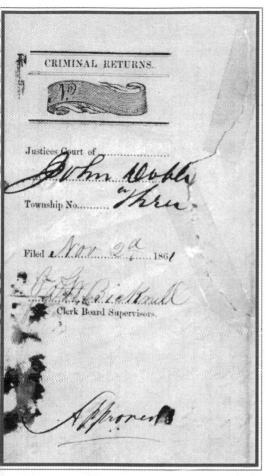

CRIMINAL RETURNS.

Justices Court of ....

John Doble

Township No......... *Three*

Filed *Nov 22* 186*1*

....

Clerk Board Supervisors.

CRIMINAL RETURNS, TOWNSHIP NO. 3
A document from John Doble's Justice Court

On October 21, 1861, a defendant whose name is unreadable on this document, was brought before John Doble, Justice of the the Peace for Township No. Three, Amador County, California, on a complaint by Jacob Bernhard. The charge was intention to do a bodily injury.

The defendent was "held in Bonds to keep the Peace & fined the Costs of suit which were paid."

The cover and title page of this edition of *Journal and Letters from the Mines* uses John Doble's signature. It was taken from this document.

Township No. .... *Three*

I ..... *John Doble* ..... the Justice of the Peace the said proceedings were had, do certify that on the ..*21*.. day of ....*Oct*....
the above named Defendant *was* accused before me by the complaint of *Jacob B.*
of the public offence of .... *Intention to do a B.*
Injury

That afterwards, to-wit; on the ..*21*.. day of ....*Oct*.... 186*1*,
brought before me by ..... *warrant* ..... to answer to said accusa
such proceedings were thereupon had as that the said Defendant ...... *was h.*
in Bonds to keep the Peac
fined the Costs of sui
which were paid

weather this shade is not used (this I have noticed since as at the time I was at the camp I saw none of these shades)   This being the 3rd & as they said the last day of their grand meeting they were going to have a great dance &c

Out about 200 yards from camp they had built a large fire and I supposed as I saw it as I came up to the camp that they were only amusing themselves at the fire there as the wood was all burned in the immediate vicinity of the camp   but as I was leaving the camp I saw that something else was going on so I went by the fire and I found that they were painting and feathering three of their number for their grand Dance   (I did not nor do I yet know what the dance was for

The Diggers and Their Customs &c &c

only that it was one of their amusements had a[t] such meetings)   I will try to describe the way they were painting and feathering (however I will not to night as it is now about 10 of the clock of the night of the 1st day of *Nov* but without remark I will continue the description at convenient times &c)   The fire was built against a large oak log & by the fire was a number of Indians   3 of the number were being painted black & feathred   the paint made of charcoal and water & they were entirely naked except the breche clout   after being painted they were dressed by the others in a coat of feathers as follows   on the head from the forhead to the back of the neck lay a red & white strap of quills   the feather end of the quill (which were the quill of the hawk & owl) sticking out horizontally each way fastened in this position by a band of small feathers round the head just above the ears   then below this band of feathers hung the hair which they all wear long (some of them have hair nearly two feet long but the squaws always cut their hair so it never hangs below the shoulders)   then across their faces was placed several rows of down the soft white down of the Owl & Hawk   the rows were placed over the face so as to encircle the nose mouth & eyes & to hide the ears   then round their necks were many yards of beads decked with dangling pieces of the pearl Oyster shell which when they moved made a rattling noise   then up & down & round their bodies arms legs were places [placed] lines & spots of the white down stuck on by a thin mixture of pitch & grease which was

The Indian Dance

put on the places where the feathers were to be & the feathers then carefully placed on it   when they were thus dressed they began to move towards the camp headed by the Master of Ceremonies   as they left the fire they began singing & the Feathred Gents Danced to

the Music which was kept up with the voice   & each one of the
singers which were 8 or 10 in number had a stick some 18 inches long
split about ⅔ of the way so it would snap togather when they shook
in the right manner   with these sticks they beat time to the Music
while any quantity of outsiders danced to the music also with frequent
stops & turnings   they got to the camp & entered the round house so
I could not see them any more   they had during the day got the ½
of a hollow log about 8 feet long & put it in the round house for the
feathered hombres to dance on   this made a hollow noise when the
bare feet of the Dancers came in contact with it with any force   they
sung different songs   I could notice the change of words but could
not understand anything said   I walked up on the round house and
looked in through the hole in the centre but could see nothing but the
crowd round the different captains who were all collected near the
centre of the house   several Americans that came out said it was
verry much crowded & verry hot in there so I didnt venture in   I came
home at dark and after supper went back   Angier and his wife went
up after dark & were in the round house for sometime   I stood on the

The Indians and Their Customs

top & looked down at them for some time but I could not see the
dancers as they were to one side of the house though I could hear the
singing which was rather amusing then otherwise   they keep good
time with their sticks & some of their tunes are good   they sing
however as they talk in a kind of Gutteral tone as if within their
throats & their are shortend with a catch generally like for instance
Hatch-a—for man & Chumuck for to eat spoken in a short chopping
style   not more than a hundred of those in camp could get into the
round house so those outside kept time by hooping yelling singing &
dancing as the whim directed keeping up a perfect and most *beautiful*
confusion   I left and went home about 10-o clock but til after 3 I
could hear the old hollow log sounding & I suppose they kept up the
dance all night while a great many of them were drunk & some fighting
I saw two young fellows about 18 take a scratch which was nothing
but a scratching of each others faces & a pulling of hair though [it]
brought blood from each others faces pretty freely   I saw while I was
in camp during the day a squaw cutting her hair   their hair is straight
coarse & black   she to[ok] a small stick & would roll round it a small
lock of hair then with a knife cut against the stick thus severing the
hair where it lay against the stick   in this way she cut all over her
head making it look quite comical as it was cut so in little spots

Tuesday Feb 17th 1852

Worked as usual in our claim   the bed rock or Ledge today is of the rotton Granite & verry rough   we have descended as low as 8 feet from the surface & then rose again in the next foot to with[in] a foot of the surface   the crevices thus are deep & narrow   while in the deepest place we got a piece of Gold weighing 8 Dollars   then as we were working a crevice nearer the serface we got a pice of 5½ ounces   this piece was thrown into the tom and I got it on my shovel & was about throwing it out when I looked again & discovered it was gold   I picked it off the shovel (I was washing the dirt & the boys were digging) & stuck it in my pocket thinking to plague the boys after a while   but I was so tickled I could not keep it long so I showed it to them & then if ever there was 3 hearty cheers given we gave them over that lump just before finding this lump I had picked out a yellow stone about the same size of the Lump & was a little vexed when I found it was not gold   but finding the lump so soon after & of so near a size & coler to the stone I picked it up again & kept it to memorize the event   just above us had been working a company & thy had dug a deep hole in the Gulch   while digging they had a hose in to carry the water past the hole to keep it from interfering with their work & one of the company came down to see us when he heard of the lump and I suppose he felt a little vexed because we had found the lump   so to prevent us from work awhile he took out the hose and laid it on one side so the water was stopped by the hole until it was full therefore we could not work any more this evening   his excuse was that it was leaking round the hose & he thought it would as well be out not thinking that it would bother us   but he being an envious penurious & much disliked man we believed he done it to prevent us from work any more to day   his name was Tickett & was a Dentist by profession   we felt sure he done it to spite us for finding the lump   This day has been a beautiful clear & pleasant day with a white frost in the morning which was rather uncomfortable to our fingers when we first went to work

Feb. 18   We worked along the centre of the Gulch to day   the Ledge seems to be sinking a little & the bed of the Gulch rising so the digging is deepening as we advance up the Ravine   we got today something near 20 Dollars but we only guess at it as we have no scales to weigh   when we found the big lump we went to Angiers & weighed it   we all went to the Rich Gulch Store after supper   this Store is kept by one Dan Curry & is situate on the Rich Gulch about one mile below our camp etc.

Feb. 19   Came home this morning at daylight after playing poker all night & lost in the game 1.50   Tom & Bill come home about 12 of the clock last night so they felt more like work to day than I did though we worked only ½ the day & made about 3.00

Tom & Bill had came home about 12 of the clock last night though I got up as soon as they did which was about 9-oclock   we went to work but all felt drowsy or at least I felt so & thy were stupid as thy had imbibed pretty freely so they brought a bottle of Brandy down to the claim the first that we had at work & I hope the last   by night we felt better as the Brandy made us more lively   we did not make much so we knocked off tolerable early & at night Tom & Bill went to Angier to take a spree & I went to bed or to my bunk (our bunks were made of cow skin stretched over a frame of poles & two placed side by side on logs in the back of the tent & over which was mine placed over the other two on steaks driven in the ground   on these we slept all winter with 1 pair & a half of blankets or 3 blankets   my blankets were heavy and kept me tolerable comfortable but the boys complained of cold as theirs were light)   about midnight thy came home and were pretty tight   it was Toms cook week so he made up a loaf of bread & put it in the oven on the fire & laid down & went to sleep toward morning he waked up & was some surprised to find it all a crust well burned   so he then gave us a lecture on intemperance & said he would quit drink   (But subsequent circumstance have proven he did not keep his word)   however I had got up first & he called to me to see if it was baking well & had forgotten in his sleep that the night had slid away to him without his being aware of it   Tom is &

Friday February 20th 1852

had been for a day or two drinking in company [with] Steward   The Portugee & he is here asleep this morning & was with them last night etc.

An Irishman who has been to work here for some time in company with our Jo Wallace sold a claim to two different companies taking pay from both   they made a to do about [it] and called on the Miners to settle it   so they had a meeting   evidence was had in which it was discovered that they had taken out a few days ago a lump weighing 20 ounces   the lump was produced in the trial   thy had partners on the River & was concealing the lump from them & the Irishman was preparing to leave when he sold the claim but got caught so thy dismissed him by his paying back the money he had got & dividing the

lump with his partners & making every thing straight   this was
considered verry lenient as many were for flogging him but they gave
him a chance to leave in two days or take the consequences   so he
prefered the former & left the diggings. Wrote several letters this
evening one to Martin Igo at Indianapolis & one to D Brown Bloom-
field Iowa in answer to letters lately received

The day has been clear & pleasant etc   I wrote on a wine box
placed by my side on the bunk in our tent   this manner of writing
goes verry awkward as I have written no other way than on a table
since I left Mexico   but I find a man can suit himself to circumstances in most any form they may come   at least so far every change
with me has not particularly bothered me

Saturday Feb 21st 1852

We worked as usual   we had the Ledge sinking all day   we got
about 8 feet deep & had some verry large rocks to move some of which
we broke up with the sledge & by this means we got them out of our
way   we dont find much gold in such deep places   we got to day
only about 5.00   which is verry poor pay   we went to Angiers to
night to pay us a/cs & divide   we first paid Jo Wallace for his tent
which we have had borrowed til today   he agreed to take 10.00 for it
so we paid him that & now have a house of our own   we then paid
Angier 26.29 which was the amount of our bill including the $10.00
for the tent   Angier received the money for the tent as Wallace owed
him   we then divided what we had left & had each 39.20   this we
thought was making money pretty fast being about $6.00 per day   I
then paid my private Bill which was for the week 3.13

We sold the big lump to Angier for 18 Dollars pr ounce which made
our work for the week larger as Gold is only worth 17 Dollars pr ounce
The Indians I thought had quit their dance last wednesday but this
evening they are thicker than ever around & the Variety of dress with
the increase of number is larger if possible than I have before noticed
a great many wear bands around their heads decked with shells &
beads to keep the hair out of their faces though a Majority wear
nothing while a few wear hats   The passion for Gambling is very
prevalent among them   the principle game is "Monte" which is a
Spanish Game   they frequently Gamble away every thing thy have
even to the last piece of clothing if they happen to be fortunate enough
to possess any   I have frequently noticed them gathering up the old
clothes thrown away by the Miners & as fast as thy get apiece they

immediately put it on   in this way I have seen them twice as large
as common with clothing   I have seen as high as five pair of pants
on one Indian   on Saturday evenings is their best time for getting
their clothing as this is generally the time miners change and as they
scarcely ever wash   they buy new and throw away the old or if an
Indian is by give it to him   report says there is now about fifteen
hundred at this camp & that they have been coming in all week and
that they are still dancing though I have not heard the old log sounding any since the night I was there

Feb. 22   Some dog visited our tent last night while we were away
& stole some 2 Dollars worth of meat from us   we keep our arms
allways ready so we can kill them if they come

This morning is clear calm & beautiful   our tent is so situated on
the hill side that we have a clear view of the Valley & Bay between
Francisco & Sacramento that is when the Mists are all cleared away
so this morning we see several clouds of smoke from the Steamers
passing though the distance is so great we cannot see the Vessels   the
opening through which we see is made by the Moquolumne River
through the hills or lower Mountains

Sunday February 22n 1852

Early this morning several miserable ragged black & bare feet &
legged Indian squaws with their Pappooses on their backs & any number of dogs at their heels—came round our tent begging any thing to
eat or drink or wear   we had some bread baked & some old clothes of
which we gave them apart   they left & not long after more [came] &
we in like manner gave to them   but thy had not left but a few
minutes til more came & we soon had nothing to give   but during the
whole day thy kept calling for something   we afterwards learned that
whenever any of them got any thing give to them they told the others
& they in like manner would try to get more and in many cases hundreds have visited one hut or camp begging   in fact I find they never
fail to beg at all times when they [think] there is any chance to get
anything given to them   we soon learned their game and now this
evening we refused all that come and tell them to leave which they
generally do without this 2nd telling   There was again a large number
of the Miners Drinking and carousing at Angiers during the Most of
the night   I was over in the evening but soon got tired & left   they
said they were Celebrating Washingtons Birth Day so thy had a Drink
round of Champaigne Wine in which the toast was—Washington may

his memory be as lasting as the rocks of ages   In this I joined   it
was the first Champaigne I ever tasted   it is beautiful clear & sparkling but I did not like the taste of it as it is rather sharp & biting
especially to sore or chopped lips or tongue

Bill & Tom got quite merry in the spree but Bill came home with me
early in the evening & he went to sleep while I wrote two or three
letters home   Bill & me both tried to get Tom off but he was determined to stay as they wanted him to play the Violin for them during
the night but he could not do it as he was hardly able to get along
when we left   The day has been verry windy though clear & pleasant

Feb. 23   This is the 5th Anniversary of the Battle of Buena Vista
in Mexico between Taylor of the United States & Santa Ana of Mexico
& their respective Armies in which Santa Ana with 20,000 men was
beaten by Taylor & with 5000 men   there being several of us here
who participated in that Engagement we had a quiet drink of Porter
to the Memory of the dangers we there passed safely through   I could
not help but look at the changing scenes & places a man will pass
through in a few years   This day 5 years ago I was at the Battle of
Buena Vista loading and firing dodging & laughing at & to the Mexican
balls with a determination to kill as often as possible & to day in a tent
again some thousands of miles from there but instead of the Musket a
pick & shovl & instead of men to kill rocks & Earth to move with the
determination to get as much Gold as possible   We worked our claim
again to day and made only $12,00   the Ledge runs verry deep & we
are about the end of it & dont think what is left will pay   This morning was clear & beautiful   evening cloudy & looks like rain

Tuesday February 24th 1852

We worked til about 4 o clock and made only about $2,00   we
thought this wouldnt near pay so we quit this place as the Ledge was
still sinking & our claim nearly out   so we went down the falls about
200 yards where there is flat place of some 50 yards just at the foot of
a rock over which the branch comes some 60 feet high   we had some
notion to go to work here but there was so many verry heavy rocks to
move we thought it would not pay so we went back & concluded to try
the place we first worked in when we came here again   we had a visit
from Charly Andersan the one who was one of our partners when we
first came here   he brought one or two of his friends with him   we
happn to have a piece of beef boiling so was able to give them some
beefs broth togather with a small piece of the flesh   this broth we

dignified with the name of soup & we happen to have enough for all   I rather think if some of the good folks at home had seen us there feeding our friends they could have hardly suppressed their mirth or if they had to feed their Lady visitors on such fare they would think it rather hard times but in California this fare does very well   we also gave some of the soup to a Man who had stopped for the night with a load of cabbages & potatoes   so while he [was] helping himself to the soup Charley & Bill helped themselves to some of his cabbages which they carried back on the hill & hid til a more convenient time to cook them

The day was Hazy & pleasant

Wednesday February 25 1852

We worked to day hard all day in the place we had first worked when we came here though it took us about two hours in the morning to carry up our tools   we only made about 5.00   This discouraged us & we thought of going prospecting   the Gold we got to day seems of a lighter quality than what we have been getting   that it is (in) thiner more scaly & porous than any I have seen before & it has some Quartz mingled with it   The weather looks like rain   Cloudy & Misty

Feb. 26   Got up early & eat Breakfast & then went down the falls again & removed a few stones & rolled them over the edge of the next fall below   but the rocks being so large and the ground to us not looking favorable we gave it up & came back & worked where our tools were til night but did not make but about one dollar   we are much discouraged and think we will go to the River tomorrow and see if we cant find something there and see if our notices are up yet   While we were at work an Indian came to a hole of water where we were working to wash his clothes   he had on a calico shirt a good cloth Vest & casimere pants   he first took off his pants and washed them & hung them on the bushes and then his vest & then his shirt   he used the soap plant which washes nearly as well as soap   after he had got all washed he then put them on & got up on the hill side & set in the sun until they were dry or nearly so   we are working in a deep & good looking crevice which looks like it ought to have gold in it but we have not found much yet

Thursday February 26

The crevice or sink in the [ledge] runs square across the Gulch & is about 4 feet deep solid Granite on both side & is triangular   we have never yet found much Gold where the rock is so hard on the upper

surface of the Ledge though we hope there is something in this place
After supper we went over to Angiers & conversed with several Miners
who all had a good opinion of our River claim & hinted that some
persons were going to jump it if we gave them a chance   so we
thought we had better go down tomorrow & see if all was right   Several Indians were drunk at Angiers & he tried to make them leave but
they would not so he took a strap & *walloped em like blazes* .. until
they left   some of them run for the whipping but some stood & took
without winceing   they say if they whip them & make them mind
they like them the better just like a dog that licks the hand that
beats him

Feb. 27 Got off to the River pretty early & descended the hill
quicker than we did before as we went straight down only where we
turned on one side occasionally to avoid a rock or a cliff   the other
time we followed the trail which winds about & around the points so
as to admit horses etc to go up & down   so by going straight we saved
at least ½ the distance   the ground was soft so we could stick our
heels in and prevent our reaching the bottom sooner than we wished
to come up the same way we went down would be next to impossible

Friday February 27th 1852

We took with us some tools and dinner in a small camp kettle   Bill
carried the dinner & Tom & me the Tools   we all started up the River
Bank on the East or south side   this side the channel runs most of
the way to the forks where we wanted to go   we soon came to a high
rocky point that came to the water which was rather hard to get over
and at this Bill backed out & went no farther   he being rather childish
in doing any thing requiring strength & exertion   so Tom and I went
ahead up & down over cliffs and Boulders where sometimes without the aid of the brush growing in the crevices of the rock we wold
have rolled into the River which just below us was boiling Roaring &
Tumbling over rocks & falls on its onward course towards its junction
with the Sacramento   in about 2 hours we reached the forks which
are about a mile from where we come to the river   here as I before
stated is a high square pile of stone or a high pile of square stone which
appears as if built by hands & just below the junction a Ledge Island
which is some 10 feet above the water & is nothing but solid blue slate
stone   it is about 50 yards long   as we crossed the River here I
walked down to the end of the Island   the rock is filled [with] smoth
circular hole[s] perpendicularly down from 1 inch to 5 feet deep sup-

posed to be made by the current keeping small stone in motion in the same place until they are worn down in this manner   I got in to one which was about 18 inches in diameter   the depth was to my armpits I prospected several but found no gold at all

These holes are found all along the River & are what is called pockets and are often found verry rich   there is generally Gold in them when they are found below the bed of the River that is when the Ledge is covered with loose material

We crossed the River here on some logs that had been placed from the head of the Island to each bank for the purpose of damming the water so as to turn it on each side of the Island alternately   last summer as they were working the bed of the stream (that) they first turned the water on one side while they worked the other then cut away the first damn & turned it on the other side while they worked the [other] one   this claim I understand did not pay verry well   after we had crossed we prospected the bar on that side but couldnt get more than a speck or two to the pan   We then went down to our claim & found the notices all right   We prospected along the bank in several places but couldnt find it good enough to pay to work as what we found was generally at about high water mark which where the River was not verry wide was about 40 feet above the water at present   We got back to the log across where we first came to the River about 12 M we here found Bill   he had come back & stayed with some men at work here waiting for us to come back   The Men at work here are making from 3 to 5 Dollars a day   they are digging in the bank where the dirt is about 6 feet deep & some 20 feet above the water They bring the water to the Tom in a Hose about 200 yards long made of No 4 Cotton Duck   We left here some of our tools intending to come and work a while here & see how we can make out at it   A Young Man from Greene County Indiana came down with us   he has been here for 2 years & has worked the River below so he wished to come down the River some 2 miles to the mouth of Nigger Gulch which puts in to the River just above Angiers   so we came along with him we stopped awhile to rest at the mouth of Indian Gulch which is about ½ way   this Gulch at its mouth is nearly level with the River & (&) runs back level about 50 yards where it rises about 100 feet the water falling nearly perpendicular that distance   from the foot of the fall to the river is about 50 yards & it is about 30 feet wide   the rock rises on both sides nearly perpendicular & in one place nearly closes at the top so that in broad day it is hardly twilight in here   We went in to

the foot of the falls where there is a deep pool of clear water   in
coming out I slipped & fell with my side on a rock hurting it some
Just above this place the Ledge rises for about 50 feet on both sides
the river leaving a channel of only about 30 feet in width   through
this the water surges with tremendous velocity there being a considerable fall just above   while the projections of the rock keep it in a
continual froth   On the face of this gap some 15 feet above the water
on this side is a narrow shelf running through the gap   I undertook to
pass through this gap on the shelf while the others clambered up and
over the rocks some 200 yards farther up the Mountain   I got about
½ way through a projection of the rock on which there was no chance
to get a hold to swing myself round it & it lay so close the shelf I could
not pass it on my hands & knees so I had to return   I found it harder
to get back then it was to get in though   I got back after several
times nearly falling into the water   I then went up round the way
the boys had went just before   We came on down the balance of the
two Miles which I thought the longest two Miles I ever travelled and
I am sure I never [had] a more rocky and rough two Miles in my life
we came up the hill at the Mouth of the Nigger Gulch   The trail here
runs in a zigzag course up the hill but is not quite so long as the one
above that we went down   it took us about three hours to get up the
hill & as the day was clear and warm the exercise caused us to perspire
freely   we got home just before sundown & as tired as we could wish
thinking we would not again take the tramp for nothing

Feb. 28   We worked to day in the crevices & got 8.00   We are verry
sore from our ramble and scramble yesterday   my side is painful
though not verry severe   I feel besides hardly able to work yet   I
cant well loose time so I do what I can   The boys lets me work at the
Tom in this case which is easier than shovelling

Sunday February 29th 1852

We payed Angier last Night $16,00 which was all that we got during
the week   this did not pay our Bill by 4 or 5 Dollars   This morning
early we started down to Moquolumne Hill as we have never seen the
place we wish to see it once & I expect there is some letters there for us
From the Buckeye Store it is called two Miles   in this distance there
is several high hills & deep canons to cross   just after crossing a small
flat we gained the top of the hill & then opened to our view the Town
of Moquohumne Hill   it is built on a low hill surrounded by higher
hills & some lower ones   The one we crossed in going into the Town

was several hundred feet higher than the Town   All the Gulches
Ravines & hill sides around the Town are dry up   Thousands upon
Thousands of Gold has been got from this place   some holes have
been dug here and large quantities of Gold found to the depth of 180
feet   they have to dig & blast in the hills sides through a hard chalky
looking rock which is said to be Lava   this Lava varies & [in] depth
& thickness and generally under it is where the most Gold is found
The Town consists of several hundred houses & any quantity of tents
scattered round   some of the houses are on substantial frames. There
seemed to be a brisk business doing the Town being full of people.[12]
I got several letters one of them from Cap Reid who is yet in Stockton
trading at large being in no particular business of any kind   he says
he is doing well. The others were from Abner & were older than some
I already had got through another source than the post

We were in the Town several hours and took dinner at house kept
by an Islander from some of the Atlantic Isles   he had his wife with
him who was a verry genteel looking little woman. they charged me
(as I paid for the three) for the dinner 2.00   with a good drink of.
or a drink of good Whiskey punch hot it being the first I ever drank
it did not taste verry well to me. The prices of different articles were
not so high here as up at angiers   I bought 2 flannel undershirts for
which I paid for both $2,50   the price would have been or is $2,25
apiece. I also bought a couple of Buckskin purses for which I paid
25 cents apiece   they were about 6 inches long & would have been
worth in the States 5 cents apiece   we started home about 4 of the
clock & when we got to the Buckeye Store we stopped awhile & took
a drink of portin[?] which Tom made Bill pay for by forcibly takeing
the money from him   this caused a little dispute between them which
I left them to settle as they could   I came on home by the Rich Gulch
way & they each one came by themselves   they got home before dark
and we all had some words but soon settled the matter by putting all
the blame on Bill   The day has been verry cloudy and has been
showery all evening so that we all got wet comeing home & it being
verry cool we feel verry uncomfortable   but a good supper & warm
fire which I cooked and made soon put all to rights

Monday March The First 1852

Got verry cold during the night   snowed & hailed about morning
our tent during the night being wet got verry cold & my one pair of
blankets were insufficient to keep me from getting verry cold so I got

up & made a fire of a barrel we had for a chimney top which warmed
me up so I slept well til morning.   We made some calculations of
going to the flat down the falls & working a few days   so Bill started
about 8-o-clock down to the River after the tools we had left there   as
it had by that time quit raining & hailing & the clouds seemed breaking
away while Tom & me looked round   we went down to the claim
where our tools were but we felt so lazy we did not go to work so we
went back and got some wood made a good fire & then sit by it to keep
it company   I have all the wood to chop as neither of the Boys ever
chopped any or tried to chop any til they came here   The sun shown
awhile about 10-o-clock but about eleven it commenced raining with
heavy & cold gusts of winds from the East & North   Bill got back
with the tools about 1-o-clock   he had been on the way back during
all the rain so far & was verry wet and cold—as the rain was mixed
with snow & hail   I put in the day sitting over the fire & writing
letters home &c &c   the boys laid abed most of the evening   it
steadyly showers all evening & sometimes mixed with snow

Tuesday March The 2nd 1852

Last night after we were all abed a Drunk Frenchman who could
not speak a word of English came round the tent wanting to come in &
waked us up with his noise so that it scared us   we jumped up and
as we did so caught up our arms with a firm determination to defend
ourselves against all enemies of whatsoever kind thy might be   we
were verry still waiting for the attack when he began to curse in
French so we knew he was a human *Man*   so we opened the tent &
let him in   he was wct & cold and we punched up the fire so he could
warm & dry himself   Tom and Bill soon found he had a canteen of
Cognac so he and thy amused themselves verry much for some time
while I being sleepy amused myself with the Fairy sprites of dream-
land conjured up by their noise & laughter   The Frenchman took the
floor of the tent before the fire for his bunk at least he was there when
I waked up in the Morning wrapped up in his blankets which he had
with him   he could not talk English but he was good at sign talking
by which he made us understand he had got lost in the night as he
was aiming to reach rich Gulch   the day is wet being showery all day
& occasional gusts or squalls of snow   we worked about 2 hours
towards evening and made only about one dollar   We think we will
not work any more in this crevice which seems a long one as we have
got but little out of it

Wednesday March 3rd 1852

Rained all last night by showers that is   it rained nearly steady judging from the times I was awake to hear it   it rained all day steady but hardly ever 20 minutes with the same density at a time   even while it rains steady all day as it has to day it comes by showers & torrents   During the day a Deer was seen near by   Tom with several others put out to try to kill it but all they got was a good wetting   I spent the day writing to Friends whom I had promised to write to err I left home   Tom bought a dog which we have had tied to our tent for some time   he agreed to pay for him 8.00   we call him Stingo — *sharp name isnt it*

Mar. 4   This morning it did not rain for 2 or 3 hours so we put out as soon as we got up & went up by the Indian Gulch & looked at the Upper part of the Spring Gulch but we did not like the looks of it so we came back & after eating Breakfast we took our Tom & put it in the little Gulch called Jo Wallace Gulch which puts into the Spring Gulch just above the falls   we worked a little while but it commenced raining & rained the balance of the day so we quit work for the day

Mar. 5   Rained all day again as usual by showers   I have cut down a large Oak which was near camp so our wood is handy. Doc Ticket the Man that was so envious of our finding the lump came over to see us and after a look he seemed surprised to see us so well fixed up   we have a small table made by some pieces of wine boxes nailed on sticks driven in the ground on one side the fire place. Tom went out to kill Robins & got wet   he killed 4 or 5

Saturday March 6th 1852

I made a Mistake in writing day before yesterday   we had put our Tom in the Mouth of the little [gulch?] on the other side of spring Gulch which is just in front of Angiers but the 2nd one from the Store which is about ½ way between the Store & the hill where it starts down to the River   Tom & I went prospecting & dug a small hole in the flat above our Tom but the water prevented us from getting verry deep with it   We then went & turned the water at our Tom so if it quit raining we could go to work   we got wet while at work   it rained all day except about 2 hours in the Morning   Two Men came up off the River & reported the River up about 8 feet & still rising rapidly they had been camped on a bar on the opposite side of the River above the Mouth of Nigger Gulch & had to go down to Makelumne Hill to get across   the River haveing washed away all the logs across it up this way

They brought up with them what they called a Mountain or California Cat but I think it is really a Martin. It is about 15 inches long from the nose to the tail & its tail is about 18 inches long   it[s] feet ears and eyes were like the cats only its eyes were larger & rounder   its tail shaped like a cats but ringed with black like the raccoon   it[s] face & nose shaped nearly like the coons   its feet and body shaped like the cats only the legs were a little shorter & the body more slim   the color was gray something like the gray squirrel   it was very tame & gentle & was not verry wild when caught[13]   This evening as has been for several evenings back windy and disagreably cool & uncomfortable

Sunday March 7th 1852

Last night we were awakened sometime after midnight by a shock a shaking of the tent & a low short rumbling noise   we were all awake at the same time & each asked at the same time *what is that* but neither go an answer   we speculated awhile & concluded it was an Earthquake so went to sleep again   This morning we got up wet   it rained in torrents during the night & we found what had waked us during the night was the dirt wall (that had once been round the cabin that had been burned which was yet standing) within which our tent was pitched   a part had fallen in near our heads & had caught the tent at the bottom & had pressed it in against the ends of the bunks so the water had run in on the cowskins of which the bunks were made so we were verry wet   I felt verry unwell all night & dont feel much better yet   we built a good fire which after awhile remedied the disagreeableness of being wet   rained all day except about 2 hours this evening it cleared up a little in the west so the sun shown for a few minutes   The wind was high & just under the sun we saw the smoke of steamer on the Sacrementao   we cleared away the Earthquake of last night & fixed up the tent a little & got provisions from Angiers which was now a hard job as the Gulch (as indeed is all the Gulches now) is swollen to a roaring torrent some 8 feet wide & deep as reasonable   we managed to cross where some rocks were sticking up some distance above camp   I crossed with a hundred lbs of flour which strained me some   Tom fell in & lost some of his load & hurt his knee Bill would not undertake to cross at all at all

Monday March 8th 1852

This morning is clear & frosty a heavy white frost   we got to work early   About 7-o-clock we seen men running in every direction almost & all seemed [excited] most of them however were going towards the flat at the head of the Gulch on enquiry we found a rich lead had been struck at the lower edge of the flat by a Company of 3 who has been digging for some time & last night one of them got tight & told of it The news had spread verry rapidly and by noon at least 100 men were on the ground most of them sinking holes Tom & Bill were anxious to stake claims too but I did not feel like we could make anything so by my opposition to it we did not stake off only our Gulch Claim We washed out at noon & had just one bit or about 12½c In the afternoon most of the holes had been sunk to the Ledge but nothing found we sunk a hole in the upper end of our claim but got nothing we then moved our Tom up the Gulch a little farther but could not find the color

If we had not staked off our Gulch claim it would have been taken from us as men kept coming in all day wanting claims By night at least 10 acres had been staked & some of the holes up the Gulch had prospected well which increased the excitement but nobody seemed to be getting anything worth while except the first who had started the noise Capt Van Allen our partner in the River claim had found something his claim being next above the first diggers

Tuesday March 9th 1852

Blew up cloudy last evening & during the [night the] wind blew verry hard I got out & tightened the stays of our tent so that it weathered the storm the after part of the night it rained verry hard & wet our blankets but did not wet us much it continued raining till about 8 we then went over to work but the water was too high so we went prospecting to the Dutchmans Gulch & found 5 cents to the pan but we thought our claim was yet good so came back & went to work but got nothing in the 2 hours we worked A heavy Thunder storm of hail rain & snow came up in the evening with verry heavy thunder so we quit work the wind was verry high in the evening The excitement about the new diggings seems to have died away as nobody is about them but the 2 or 3 who had found Gold in their holes We all three feel unwell to day from getting damp during the night

Mar. 10 rained during the night & snowed this morning we all feel well this morning It ceased snowing pretty soon so we went to work working an hour or two & found nothing so we got discouraged with the place so we moved our tools to the Mouth of Jo Wallaces Gulch & worked a little while and got about $3.00 it commenced raining and wet us a little before we got home but the rain soon turned to snow which continued til dark

Mar. 11 This morning cool & frosty with a light snow on the ground We worked all day & made about an ounce of heavy coarse Gold   we think we have struck a good lead   The dirt is a hard sandy and Gravelly clay which is very hard to dig & harder to wash   the Ledge

Thursday March 11th 1852

is the gray granite & very hard   we find the gold generally mixed with the dirt to the top

This evening is clear & pleasant with the snow yet lieing on the hills around

Mar. 12 Morning frosty & clear the day rather cloudy   worked all day & made about 12.00   we had a shower of hail about noon   The water in Jos Gulch is running off verry fast   if it rains no more now it will soon be to low to work

Mar. 13 Rained some during the night   The day is cloudy sun shining at intervals & several showers during the day   we worked the most of the day & made only 6.00   We went over to Angiers & paid him all we had   except a couple of small specimens all we had was   38.43 leaving a balance Due Angier of   100.39 I then bought on a/c 100 letter stamps for   3.50

Mar. 14 Rained during the night & as it is Sunday I chopped wood while Tom prospected between showers of rain which continued all day   he found 50c in a place just opposite our tent in spring Gulch which we will work when we quit where we are now

Mar. 15 We worked as usual & made 7.00   Angiers Mule train arrived & by it I recieved several letters from home which was verry gratifying   I answered them to night   Rained several showers during the day & the sun shown at intervals.

Tuesday March 16th 1852

Rained during the night & — some this morning   a heavy fog came up the River & from that up the Gulches & so on til every thing was nearly as dark as night which continued til noon when it cleared away so we could go to work   We went to our claim but did not [work] any as a man was there who wished to buy it   after some chaffering we sold it to him for 2 ounces   we then washed off our Tom & took it up to Angiers to line as it was nearly worn through on the bottom

The Mule train did not leave to day so to night I wrote home again My letters are all deposited at Sacremento where Abner takes them out of the office and re-envelopes them & sends them to me through Angiers partner at Stockton   by this means I get them pretty regularly   When letters come through the pass to Mokelumne Hill they are frequently delayed for weeks   The last one I got from Abner by that means was 4 weeks on the Route   When I was at the Hill I sent by Express to Abner one letter & 3 ounces Dust including the three lumps we had found that I kept   I also wrote him to send me some picks which I expected by this train but they did not come

Mar. 17   Bill & Tom have not yet heard from home so they are anxious to get letters so Bill went down to the Hill to day while Tom & me Lined the Tom with sheet Iron   this took us most of the day & the balance I put in mending a Hose which we had just bought and paid for eleven yards   5.00

Wednesday March 17th 1852

Billy Spencer (one of the party that struck the new lead here) was on a spree to day & came to our tent in the evening & took a fight with Stingoe who was tied to the tent   the dog bit him severely   Bill returned at dark & brought me a letter from Reid who has not yet heard from me (I think he will when this train goes down)   Bill said he had been lost in the Mountains or he would have been home sooner to get lost is a verry easy thing when a prson is not acquainted with the country as all along the road roads are branching off in different directions   Tom went in the evening & got the money for our claim the [day] has been clear & pleasant but rather warm

This being St Patricks day the Irish have a spree at Angiers   they make considerable noise judging from the sounds I hear

Mar. 18   We dug a race round our claim by the tent this afternoon Bill & Tom being in the Irish spree last night could not work this evening so I washed awhile and got 2.00   Angier had an Extra Train of Mules up this evening by which I received from Abner 2 Dozen picks & one Dozen socks & a number of papers & a pr of Gold Scales   Sold Angier the two Dozen picks for   64.50
and paid him on Co a/c & private a/c   21.00
afterwards put all on Co a/c

Mar. 19   Tom being unable to work Bill and I went prospecting but found nothing   we worked awhile in the evening & made about 50c apiece   The day has been clear with flying clouds & pleasant

Saturday March 20th 1852

Tom & Bill went over into the Nigger Gulch to prospect   We have contemplated going there ever since we came up from the River that way & hearing last night that somebody else was going there to prospect we wanted to be first so thy went over to dig & picked a place but did not prospect any   I worked by myself during the forenoon & made $2.50 & in about 2 hours work   in the afternoon I made 13.00 the boys returned verry tired   we did not work [in] the evening   we paid Angier the balance of our bills which was   9.34 we then divided the rest & had each   5.35

Bill remained til late at Angiers   I felt vexed at him for it   he now owes some 30 dollars & has no money yet he stays round there til late frequently drinking & getting deeper in debt

The New Diggings are paying two or three companies verry well that is those that are working in the Gulch   several are digging in the hill sides but are not making much   The day has been clear & pleasant

Mar. 21   As it is Sunday we did not rise til late   I went & picked a panful of California lettuce which is a verry succulent pleasant tasted Vegetable & grows in abundance along the Gulches & on the flats   it tastes verry much like the lettuce at home only is not so pungent

Angier returned from Stockton & brought me some letters   Day clear & pleasant etc

Mar. 22   We worked in our claim to day & made 13.75   The day clear & beautiful I went down the Gulch for the first time since it was so full of water   the water has run off til there is not verry much in the Gulch now   everything along the Gulch was changed by the strong current that had run down during the rains

Tuesday March 23rd 1852

After Breakfast we went down the Nigger Gulch & dug a hole in the place where the boys had picked   we had verry hard digging as the roots were verry thick but after several hours labor & a considerable sweating & swearing we got a hole 3 by 8 down to the Ledge & found nothing   we then started home   The place we dug the hole was about a quarter [mile] from the River   we came up the Gulch which is a fall all the way to Sweenies tent which is on a flat where the road crosses   the sides & sometimes the bottom of the Gulch is thickly set with low bushes so we had a hard climb to get up to the road   the distance being about ½ a mile   we got home about 3-o-clock & worked an hour or two & made $2.00   After supper the Boys went up to the Indian Ranch to see the dance as they were again dancing   thy came home long after I was asleep & were tolerable tight etc   Day clear & warm

Mar. 26   Worked to day in the claim by the tent & made only $8.90 This evening Tom is taking a spree with Jack Nelson & Sandy the 2

partners of Billy Spencer which 3 with another company of two first struck the Lead on the Little Gulch in front of Angiers   Tom is getting to drink a great deal so I think we will soon part company The flesh flies are getting verry bad   we string or hang our meat up in the tree by a line thrown over a limb so we can let it down when we want   morning clear & evening cloudy looks like we would have some rain again

Thursday March 25th 1852

We worked til awhile after dinner & made 4.59   When Bill & Tom knocked off &went with Sandy & Jack Nelson on a spree which is to go to the Grocery & drink as much Liquor as they can   they were at the claim to day & had a bottle of Brandy with them which gave Bill & Tom a start so thy go this evening to finish it out   I worked by myself an hour or so & made 75c   I then went up to the tent & fixed for supper then came back in ½ an hour I made $6.50 one piece weighing $3.50 this was all mine as the boys when they quit gave me the liberty of making all I could this evening   Bill & Tom took supper at Angiers so I eat alone for the first time since we have been togather

The day has been clear with a high wind blowing all day

Mar. 26   We went to work as usual   Tom being not quite over his yesterdays spree got a bottle of Brandy this morning & by the time we went to dinner he was tolerable drunk   so him & Bill had a quarrel over some Onions cooking for dinner   I then proposed buying Tom out & offered him $35.00 for his share in the Company property   he refused to take it & went off   came back when we that is Bill & I were at work & said he would take it so we went up to Angiers & paid of[f] the Co^s bill which was $10.73   Bill & I then divided what was left making $7.24c apiece that is the 3 but as I had brought one share I got $7.24 more and what Bill & I got during the evening was 4.37 apiece. Tom goes in Company with Jack and Sandy in the lead in the little Gulch in front of Angiers   I think he has made a bad exchange as the company he is now in drink most all the time & drink up all they make   however Tom is not far behind them   Tom moved over to their tent with Bills assistance all his personal property   the tent is on a low hill the other side of the store about a quarter [mile] from here I was over to Angiers during the night & Stewart said he thought Tom had got into bad company which was just what I thought

The Day is clear & windy

Mar. 27   Bill & I worked most of the day & made 2.35 apiece   we are now working on a soft blue slate Ledge which is full of small cracks and crevices but we dont seem to be finding much   we are working

out to one side [of] the bed of the Gulch under the bank which is about
8 feet high   we have coyoted or caved under about 4 feet & still find
the ledge flat

The Day has been Hazy cloudy & cool & it rained & snowed some
during last night & a little at day light this morning

Mar. 28 Snowed & rained & cleared up & frosted & froze a light ice
(as thick as paper perhaps) over the ground during the night   This
morning is clear with a cool bracing breeze from the Nor East   The
snow looks to be several inches deep on the hills   I sit up til midnight
reading & it was raining when I went to bed   I feel like home would
be better than tenting thus in the open country   Tom came by on his
way to the Hill & asked if we wished anything brought from there
him & Bill are on as good terms as ever   rained hailed & snowed by
showers during the Day & the sun shown at intervals

Monday March 29th

Angier & wife left for Stockton yesterday and turned off all their
Boarders so there is 3 or 4 new tents going & gone up along the Gulch
also there has several companies of Miners came in here attracted by
the reports of the Lumps found here so we have now some 20 tents
along the Gulch and on the hills around

Worked hard all day & made (both of us)   7.46
This morning cool & frosty   ice ¼ inch thick
Day clear & pleasant evening cool

Mar. 30 Worked as usual & made for both   7.53
Morning & evening cool   Day clear & pleasant   Was over to
Angiers   a good many Indians about all gambling   Monte is the
only game I see them playing   they bet away to each other every
thing the[y] possess or can get hold on even to 1 old shoe at a time
that has been thrown away by some miner who has worn it out or
nearly so

Mar. 31 Worked til noon & then quit   made for both   5.75
I being the Treasurer paid on the Co bill   76.00 [?16.00]
I felt verry bad all day so got a bottle of Brandy to drive away dull
care etc but did not drink to drunkeness as I did not think it would pay
Forenoon of the Day clear & pleasant   cloudy in the afternoon &
begins to rain at night

April 1st Rained most of the night & most of the Day   as it was
raining we rose rose late bought 72 yds of *No 4* Cotton Duck to make
a Hose which I worked at during the day or evening

Apr. 2   Rained til noon & all night   cleared off at dinner   I got the Hose finished but had a sore hand by it never haveing used the palm & sail needle before   We worked about 2 hours moving a Stone & one hour cleaning out a crevices & got $9.50   thought that would do for an hours work anyhow

Saturday April 3d 1852

Worked to day til nearly night and finished the claim below the tent we got only $1.62

We then went up the Gulch to prospect but found nothing   then went to Angiers and paid him our Co Bill which was

Balance			5.49
Then Divided what we had left & had each			6.31

I here give a part of	Mar 26	8 lb Beef (fore quarter)	1.60
some Bills which I have	" "	1 " Candles (Stearine)	.75
yet showing the prices	" 28	21 " Potatoes	2.62
of things at this time	" "	12 " Beef (Hind quarter)	3.00
As I expect not to copy	" 31	5 " Salt (Table)	1.00
any more bills I have	" "	10 " Sugar (Manilla White)	2.50
picked out of several	" "	2 " Beefs liver	.50
these articles	Apr 1	1 Beefs head (whole)	1.50
	" 2	1 " Tongue	1.50
	" 3	4 lb coffee (green)	1.00
	" "	¼ lb Green Tea	.25
	" 4	1 Beefs shank	1.00
	" 8	4 lb Pork (salt)	1.00
	" "	3 " Salt Salmon	.60
	" "	5 " Cheese (Dutch Heart shaped)	1.50
	" 30	½ " Tobacco	.50
	" "	1 pick	4.00
	May 3	1 bottle Brandy (1½ pints)	1.00
	" "	1 Box Matches	.13
	" "	2 Bottles pickles (½ pints)	1.00

Went down to Dan Curries or the Rich Gulch Store and sold him 2 Dozen picks which I immediately sent for to Abner. Then came home & went to Toms tent & there I played my first game of Rounce which is a verry amusing game with cards   I left Bill here & came home & he came home after midnight drunk

April 4   Bill did not get up til the afternoon & then was not well enough to move round   I borrowed ½ Dozen picks from Angier for Dan Curry til his came up   Day clear & pleasant

Monday April 5th 1852

Out of a claim   feel as if lost   walked round the new diggings & down the Gulch but all is worked   talked of going off to some other part of the Mines   after dinner walked round while then set down to read awhile   then commenced digging a hole in a bar below the tent (a bar is a narrow flat or bottom on one or the other sides of the Gulch)   did not get down to the Ledge

Day clear & pleasant

Apr. 6   Went to work & by night had cleaned out the hole we commenced yesterday & had made   5.15

The Excitement again broke out about the new diggings   a company had took out several ounces further up the Gulch and in the hill side so another lot of ground was staked off and many holes sunk but as before none but the first found anything worth while   Bill went to get a claim but found all claimed that seemed workable   Day clear & pleasant

Apr. 7   This morning a large crowd are at the new diggings some to finish holes commenced yesterday & most to look round   I went over with Bill to sink a hole on anothers claim who had given him the liberty to do so but we found nothing   I was not verry well so I staid at home while Bill stayed round the new diggings   While sitting in the tent a Man who was passing came in reach of the Dogs rope & he bit him slightly on the arm   he was verry angry   his tent being close by he soon returned with a pistol & before I was aware of it shot the dog in his barrel which was at the tent door

Wednesday April 7th 1852

I sprang up & went to him with my pistol in my hand but found I was too late to save the Dog as he was already killed   I said but little to the Man but went over to Angiers intending to call togather some Miners and let them say what should be done   by the time I got there I thought better of it & went to The Mans tent (his name was McKinney from Maine) & asked him for damage but he wanted Damage for the bite which was a blue mark on one of [his] arms made by one of the Dogs tusks   the scratch was only about one inch long & not deep enough to bleed so I proposed to him to leave it to two men which he agreed to   we then went to Angiers & he chose Harris & I chose Rainy both Miners & after hearing the case from us they decided that I should have $40.00 Damage which he immediately paid   I then treated away to the crowd 5.15 & paid Tom the 8 Dollars for the Dog and then Divided the balance between Bill & me each intending to give the Man a part of his money back   Angier returned bringing me some letters from home & from San Francisco   Day clear & pleasant

Apr. 8   Rained during the night   A man staid with us so I slept on the floor of the tent & this morning my right leg is sore with the Rheumatic pains   Bill went to dig a hole while I looked round   he found nothing & I done nothing but write some letters

This evening my right knee is verry sore & stiff   The Day was cloudy but the sun set clear

Friday Apr 9th 1852

Bill staid out all night drinking came home at daylight   after Breakfast he went to sink a hole in a flat back of Angiers store called Snake humbug flat which Gold has been lately found in   he could not get verry deep for the water   I sunk a small round hole on the flat by the Indian camp but found nothing   afternoon we begun another hole on the bar below the tent

Tom has outdrinked the company he went to so they have turned him out   My knee is verry stiff so I can hardly work   I slept badly last night on account of it   The Day clear & pleasant

Apr. 10   Tom has bought a horse   he left this morning to go to the Double Springs for letters that being the place he directed his letters sent   he returned late this evening   he got some letters. We worked out the hole we commenced yesterday & got 5.80   We throw off about 2½ feet of dirt or loose soil & roots then come to a blue loose clay & gravel in which the Gold is found   we wash about 2 feet of this which lays on a hard Granite Ledge   Angier again left for Stockton

After supper I went down to Dan Curries

Apr. 11   Played Poker all night at Dans & lost 2.00   Bill & Tom rambled all day after Toms horse but did not find him   Black Jack who is mining here & is a sailor told me to day of a new place up on the Cosumnes River which he was going to start tomorrow to prospect & look at   he gave me a [model?] or map of the route (which I would defy the world to make sense of) to the Indian Diggings which are on the route to the place he is going   I think of going too tomorrow Day clear & pleasant

JACKSON VIGILANTES

Monday April 12th 1852

Went over to the flat & looked at the hole Bill had commenced but it was full of water   came back to the tent took what money I had & my blankets & started for the place Black Jack had told me of & left Bill to do what he could while I was gone   My knee was yet sore which bothered me some in walking. I overtook at Spring Branch Sweeney, Lang, David Ferguson & Mad Jack (called so from his mad ravings when drunk   his name is John Nelson) and at Mokelumne Hill Black Jack Bill & Bob Atchison   This was the company that was going on the trip   I stopped at the Hill & left at the Express office to be forwarded 4½ ounces of dust for Abner   we left the Hill a little after dinner   8 Men 1 horse 1 Mule & 1 Donkey   on these our tools & blankets were packed. We crossed the River at the Big Bar Ferry which [is] a rope ferry the boat being propelled by the current   They have dug a road up each hill from the River making it easier going up & down   we passed through Butte City which is on a small flat about a mile from the ferry & consists of some 50 canvas tents & clapboard houses   from this place we went up by the Butte Mountain [Jackson Butte] which is a peak some 800 feet higher than the surrounding Hills & is about 5 Miles from Mokelumne Hill   at its foot on the East side is a small camp of some 50 tents where there has been some Rich diggings[14]   here we got a dinner of crackers & cheese which cost $4.50

75

I know because I paid for it   We then moved on in a Nor East direction about 2 miles over high hills etc when we struck the south Branch of Jacksons creek at a camp of a few tents mostly Chleans called Secreta   we then went up that to another & larger camp called Clinton   this camp has about 100 clapboard & canvas houses in it & a Majority of Chileans & Mexicans   they have Rich Deep diggings here   Deep diggings are so called when the Auriferous dirt lays far below the surface   we took a trail here due North crossed the Middle & North forks of Jackson creek   in leaving the North fork we lost the Trail but kept the course til we struck the Sacremento Road then followed that through Grass Valley or flat to Valcano   Grass Valley is a beautiful flat some 1½ miles long & 2 or 300 yards wide   it is all fenced in for a Ranch & the owners have a house which is store tavern & etc   we arrived at Valcano about dark & stopped at Jim Dolons Gambling Saloon where we slept on the floor & got our meals at a Hotel for which we paid one dollar a meal   Valcano consists of about 300 houses built of clapboards & pine poles which make very comfortable houses in this country   it is situate in a verry pretty Vally surrounded by high pine capped hills those on the North presenting to the View from the Vally a rugged rocky appearance as the sides are of a whittish kind of rock thrown up in rough piles & high cliffs both piles & cliffs reach nearly to the top of the Hills

Tuesday April 13th 1852

Packed up early & struck out in a Northern direction on the New Emigrant Road which joins the old one at Leeks Springs   we followed this Road along the Ridge between Sutter & Dry creeks some 8 miles when we turned off to the westward & passed round the head of Dry Creek down a verry Rocky & high & steep hill into the south branch of the Mocosme or Cosumnes River   The hills on each side of this Branch are verry steep & high   the space between the hills about 100 yards & the stream some 50 feet wide   it is a beautiful clear stream running as all the Mountain streams do over a bed of rock & gravel   the water is verry cold at least I thought so when I waded across it   the crossing was verry easy   the banks being low   When we got up the hill on the west side we came to a beautiful small flat on which there was an Indian Ranch. All the flats are now beautiful & green and some are covered with a brilliant sward of many different kinds & colors of flowers   While the Vegetation on the hills has not yet sprung up   however for the last few miles as we have been coming Northward the Vegetation appears younger by a week or so than it does on the Moquolumne where we started from   At this Ranch we could find no Trail but an Indian boy pointed the direction to Indian Diggings so we took the course without a Trail   When we got on the hill out by the flat westwardly we found ourselves on the top of another fork of the Mocosmes hills & to look down looked like we could scarcely get along for the brush which on the west sides of the hills & along the streams grows verry thick   Though we could see from here the sugar Loaf Peak which is about 4 Miles to the South & Westward of the Diggings so guessing our course we started down the hill   Black Jack being the only one who had ever been over here in the crowd he was our guide so he took the lead   when we got down about ¼ of a mile we were on a point between two Gulches which came togather a few hundred yards ahead   looking in that direction I saw 4 Deer crossing the Gulch below the point & sung out to look who was ahead & had a rifle to shot at them   he raised up & fired when the Gun was about the angle of 45 & then turned to me and asked *where are they* which question I could not answer for Laughing at his motions   meanwhile the Deer had got out of sight over the next ridge   we got down to the stream with great difficulty as the brush were verry thick & when we got to the stream we were some time finding a place to cross as the banks were high & rocky   Mad Jack picked some Gold out of a crevice in the rock with his knife but we didnt stop to prospect as we wanted to get to the Diggings before night   After crossing we found an old trail leading up the mountain so we followed it to the top   About ½ way up while stopping to rest I noticed large quantitys of a kind of gray porous stone somewhat resembling pumice   I did not keep any of [it] nor have I since seen any like it although I have been over a great [d]eal of the country

Tuesday April 13th 1852

Near the top of the hill was some springs covering about an acre of ground   on the upper side was an old deserted Indian Ranch   from this Ranch two trails branched off   after consulting awhile & each one giving a different opinion our guide struck off taking the trail bearing North   after following this trail some distance we had got on a high hill which was flat about ½ a mile wide and we kept on it for several miles   looked like an old meadow as there was scarcely any timber on it   from this open place we could see the Sugar loaf hill & some thought we were close to the place while others thought we were not far enough North   This consultation was held where the trail we was following started down the hill

We continued North following the ridge & the guide   The ridge was running down to a point with a Gulch to the right so struck more North crossing another Trail which I wanted to take but could not get the consent of the others   keeping this direction we crossed several dry Gulches & one verry deep one that had considerable water in   the water tasted salty   getting up on the hills after crossing this Gulch we found ourselves on a sharp high ridge & no appearance of living thing around except an Indian dog we saw in chase of a hare   some of [us] judged from the shape of the country and the position of the sugar Loaf peak when we last saw it that we were passed the place so here a consultation was held & Black Jack unpacked his horse and

Out Prospecting April 13th 1852

started west down the ridge in hunt of a Trail or the Indian Diggings The rest of us unpacked the Animals rolled togather some fine logs & heaped on them a pile of pine burs which were plenty & set them afire it was now about the Middle of the afternoon & we had no provision with us so we were all verry hungry   some of us searched sometime for some pine seed but they were all gone at this season as the birds the Indians the squirrel & the Goofers all live on them partly   so after they fall they are soon destroyed   We gathered some acorns & roasted them but they were too bitter to eat so some of the boys laid down & slept while others walked round til nearly Sundown   when Black Jack returned with the intelligence that he had found the place   so we immediately packed up and started back a little to the right of the direction we had come & after going about 3 miles & down a long hill we came to The Indian Diggings just as the sun was sinking behind the western hills verry tired & hungry   by the industry of a cook at a Hotel our hunger was soon appeased & a little Hay on some clapboards on the joists of the house furnished us a place to rest   To day we passed 2 indian store houses at one of which there was a large collection of Indians but no camp   The store houses are built in a circular form & set on a stump 2 or 3 feet from the ground   They are built of brush lined with fine leaves some 10 feet high & are filled in the fall with acorns which are eaten out as necessity demands to be done

Out Prospecting April 14th 1852

Indian Diggings are so called from the Indians first discovering the Richest place which is a creek or large Gulch about two miles long from the Mocosme River or the south fork of the Mocosme or Cosumnes River to its head or where it branches into several small Gulches here is a large spring & here is situate the principle camp   it is built

along the Gulch from the spring down & consists of about 50 log cabins
& two clapboard houses   These two are Hotels Gambling houses &
stores each containing a bar   The Gulch is so narrow they have to
dig into the hill side to build   so the town or camp is in a string along
the bank   The waggon Road comes in from the North & stops at the
Hotels at the spring   the place being so narrow to permit waggons to
go through or by the place   The Gulch or creek is said to be verry
Rich all the way to its Mouth   We paid here one dollar a Meal & 14c
pr lb for Barley for the Mules

This place lies about 12 miles North East of Valcano on or by the
straightest route known

We bought provision here for 6 days & packed up & started early for
Chickemasee or Grizzly Flat which is said to be near the head of the
Northernmost fork of the Consumnes   We had for guides 2 Men who
had came from there yesterday & accompanied by a Man from The
Hotel   we went up the hill from the camp in an Easterly direction
after we had got on the hill we found we had been within a quarter of a
mile of the camp the evening before when we stopped to talk of where
we were & if we had taken the last trail we crossed in ½ an hour we
would have been there for that trail is the one we are now going on
We crossed the salty Gulch several Miles above where we crossed it
yesterday & bearing East of North we crossed the North fork of the
Mocosme ½ Mile above its 2nd fork   The hill between the forks is
verry low   in crossing the Main fork our Donkey came near being
washed away as the water was swift & belly deep to the horse   We
crossed on a drift a few yards below the ford   In going up the hill on
the North side we stopped about ½ way up at a pretty little [spring]
that makes out of the hill in a kind of basin that looks like it had once
been a slide or Avalanche   after getting up this hill we had before
us a beautiful rolling country before us but no Vegetation except tall
pine timber was visible   we begin to see signs of work & several tents
soon came in view & in a few miles we crossed the North fork of the
North fork of the Cosumnes & up that several miles we came to
Grizzly flat where we stopped about 3 of the clock just as the rain
which had been threatening all day began to fall   We built a shelter
of pine & Cedar boughs & a fire of logs & lay down & rested   rained all
evening   My knee bothered me all day & is verry sore

I noticed to day along the hill sides numbers of Grizzly tracks some
as much as 16 inches long & 6 inches wide but saw nothing else like
a Bear

Our shelter by spreading a couple of blankets over the boughs keeps
the rain off very well

Thursday April 15th 1852

During the night the clouds had blown away & after eating some
grub this morning we divided into two companies & Bob Bill Black
Jack & myself went west & the other 4 East taking with us our tools
to see if we could find any of the Ore or a place to dig for it that suited
us   We went west about two Miles & then started down a large Gulch
we here again divided and Black Jack & Bob going North while Bill
& myself continued west   we went down the Gulch or creek which
was thickly set along the sides with brush about two miles   we found
several companies at work but none seemed to be making much   we
prospected several places but found nothing   we then took up a
Gulch to the south & followed it some 3 miles to its head along it were
several companies at work but none seemed making much   we prospected as before but could get nothing but the coler in verry fine specks
we then struck for camp where we arrived about 2-o clock & found all
the boys had come in & all had found nothing that we were looking for
& all tired of the place   Grizzly Flat is about one mile long & ¼ wide
the grass is just beginning to grow on it   several holes have been
sunk in the flat in all of which Gold is found but at this time it is not
workable for the water which nearly covers the flat   a Company is
now digging a hole but they quit this evening as the water was in their
way so they could not work to advantage

Grizzly Flat or Chickamasee[15]

The people think when the Dry season comes this will be a good
place to work as gold has been found in all the holes now sunk in the
flat & several of the Gulches around which are now worked out have
paid well & one or two farther down the River are said to be paying
well now   There is two bars stores & boarding houses here now & one
or two more building   at one of them there is a woman which is a rare
thing in these Mountains   The Miners just at this time are scarce but
all that are here think it will be a place during the summer   This is
the farthest North I have yet been   the snow is yet on the ground
5 miles above and it has been off here but about a week therefore Vegetation is far behind to what it is down on the Mokelume where I have
been

We looked round the place during the evening & were satisfied it
would not suit us   Just before dark the Mules & horses on the flat

took a stampede   The Men that came with us thought it was a Grizzly that had scared them as they had been verry plenty here lately They went out to see if they could find them but could not so suppose an Indian or Wolf scared the Annimals

After some hard running they were caught & fastened up by the Larryats or long ropes always carried in the Mountains to picket the animals   to picket is to drive a pin in the ground and fasten the end of the rope to it so the Animal can feed round the peg the length of his rope   The Day is clear and pleasant   evening cool but a good log fire made all comfortable

Friday April 16th 1852

We packed up & started back after eating some & hanging an empty bottle on the top of a high pine which stood near our Camp   one of the sailors (sweeney) in [our] company performed this feat & said it would mark the place   we went back by Indian Diggings prospecting along the way but found nothing & went down the Indian creek & crossed the River & camped for the night opposite the Mouth of the Indian creek   where this empties into the River is a small flat which is fenced in for a farm   My knee has been verry stiff & much swollen all day so that it is with difficulty & pain I can keep up with the company

Day clear & pleasant

April 17   During the after part of the night a number of Indians which we had noticed as we passed the Diggings came by our camp & waked us up with their shouting & yelling as some of them were drunk Being near the water our blankets were wet with the dew which does not fall on the hills   We went up the River in order to find the place we had before crossed as we though we might find Oro there   We got to the place about noon & prospected it well but found but little Gold & what we did find was verry fine   we then went 2 or 3 miles further up to where several large Gulches came in here   we unpacked & my knee being yet verry sore I watched the Animals & the things while the others went up the Gulches but thy all returned & had found nothing worth working for

Saturday April 17th 1852

We then packed up & went up the stream some two miles farther above the Mouth of a large Gulch or small creek & prospected along but could find nothing   The creek came in on the south side   The brush was so thick along the creek we could not take the Animals along so had to send them up the hill some distance to get along   We then started up the hill on the south side   we had to cut a road for the Animals for some distance up the hill side as with out it it was impossible for them to get [up]   after considerable labor we got up the hill & went down the ridge ½ a mile or so & finding a place where the Animals could get food we camped for the night some 200 yards up the hill from the Gulch or creek   the water of this creek was some salty   tasted like weak brine

Day clear & pleasant   During this day we have seen no sign of Man only where one small hole had been sunk on the River

April 18   This morning the boys went down the creek to prospect leaving me to watch the camp as I was yet lame   they dug 2 or 3 holes which took them til about non but found nothing   We then packed up again & took our course for Volcano   struck the Trail at the top of the hill on the North side of the south fork near the Indian Ranch   passed through Volcano & camped for the night at the west end of Grass flat   we all took supper at the Ranch for which we paid .75

Day clear & beautiful   my knee is some better this evening

Monday April 19th

As I before said Grass Valley or Flat was covered with a beautiful coat of Verdure consisting of Various colered flowers and Grass   the grass about 6 or 8 inches high & coming as we just have down from the Mountains where the Vegetation had scarely started Makes this flat look more beautiful than it looked as we went up   Here also a heavy dew fell as the flat has considerable water in it at this time   we packed up pretty soon this Morning & went the Route we had come & arrived at Mokelumne Hill about noon   our ferry expenses were for each crossing 25c a Man & 50c a horse or Mule or Donkey   We stopped at The Hill some time   I took dinner at a French Restaurant which cost me $1.00   I got a steak fried potatoes Bread & Coffee served up in the Bar room on a small table a row of which lined the room   The other Boys got to Drinking so I left them and came on home where I arrived just before sundown   I went over to Angiers & found a letter from Ab & a box of picks which he had sent according to order also 17 other picks of his own that he sent for me to sell   the 2 Dozen belonged to his company   He also sent me some of their cards which were well gotten up under the Style of Nelson & Doble Blacksmiths etc   I cast up my Expenses for this trip & found I had Expended   27.00
of [which] I paid for clothing at the Hill   8.00

Day clear & warm   Roads getting dusty

Tuesday April 20th 1852

I find Bill has done nothing since I have been gone but loaf & spree he & Tom is talking of going to work togather in Jo Wallace Gulch in the banks as they prospect well   I certainly think I shall leave him pretty soon   he does not suit me for a partner at all   as soon as I can make it so we will seperate   I done nothing in the way of Mining to day though I took the picks to Dan Curry & sold him the 17 for 30.00

My knee is nearly well again so I can now move with ease

The Day is cloudy though not gloomy

Apr. 21   I worked to day throwing off top dirt on the bar below the tent intending to work it out   Bill worked with Tom   Forenoon cloudy afternoon clear & pleasant   night cool & windy   wind from the North

Apr. 22   This Morning was raining & snowing   snowed rained & hailed most of the day   ceased in the evening awhile as I worked an hour or two got a verry little Gold & wet feet etc

Apr. 23   This day was like yesterday only rained verry hard with a cold wind & snowed in the evening   worked some as yesterday   Got some letters from home by the Train which came up to day

Apr. 24   Forenoon cloudy   Worked part of the day & got but little Gold   have made this week 5.50   afternoon part clear rained awhile at evening   Bill & Tom is doing verry well   My back has been verry painful from stooping so much for a day or two

Sunday April 25th 1852

Played Poker at Curries all night lost 40.00   Think now if I dont I ought to quit this gambling alltogather   I have a love for that game but have no desire to gain money by it as I know Money thus gained is of no Value to the winner or at least I have never known it to do any good   I think now I shall risk no more money at it but will make no promises least I might break them   Tom is building himself a canvas house on the Rich Gulch flat for the purpose of Gardening there this summer   he is now living with us til he gets his house finished as Angier has again turned off his boarders as his wife is sick

Apr. 26   Got up early & went to work on the bar   at eleven quit & made only 1.50   feel verry much discouraged with the diggings think of going somewhere else   walked round til awhile after dinner with my pick & shovel on my shoulder as if prospecting but not finding a place that suited my fancy I went to work on the bar again & made during the evening 5.00   this put me in better spirits   A Miner by name Tappan came over to the tent this evening & we agreed to work togather on the bar tomorrow

Forenoon cloudy   afternoon clear & pleasant

Apr. 27 Worked with Tappan & we made 7.50   Forenoon Hazy afternoon cloudy and pleasantly cool   Tappan does not think the bar will pay to work

Wednesday April 28th 1852

Rained most of the night & til noon to day   looked round during the evening   at night clear   Bill & Tom made 30.00 this evening which they have been throwing off top dirt for two days to get at

April 29 Rained most of the night & til late this morning   Tappan came over and we went to work   we worked about an hour when one of his partners came after him to go to Sonora   he left in his place his other partner by name Jackson   we worked the after part of the day & made in all 6.00

Tom & Bill is doing well

Evening clear & pleasant

Apr. 30 Worked til noon & made only 1.25   when we concluded the claim had run out so we quit   I went down on the Dutchmans Gulch to see if any sight was to be had there but it is all worked over like the Rich Gulch

Stewart got badly hurt by a bank caving in on him this evening he was working on the lead in the new diggings   they think his hip is unjointed   he cant move for the pain when he attempts to   Forenoon clear afternoon cloudy & some rain at night

May 1st Scratched round a little in the Gulch & got .75   Then walked down Rich Gulch but thy are all leaving there   came back paid Angier our bill my part 9.80   Bill & Tom made but little

Forenoon cloudy afternoon clear & cool feels like frost

Sunday May 2nd 1852

Stayed about camp most of the day   was thinking of going to Independence this evening with Judge Hill & Tom Morris but did not get off   Tom & Bill went to the Hill & returned by dark   was over to see Stewart who is yet on his back   he is lieing on some blankets on the ground at Angiers as there is no beds of any kind there & is yet verry bad

May 3 Both The Boys I was going with took a spree to day & got verry drunk so we did not start   I was somewhat vexed at it as I did not know the way   I was down to Toms new house which is a verry neat canvas house about 8 by 12   he has it built under some oak trees on a little rise at the head of the flat & is a verry pretty place as the hill sides flat and all is now covered with beautiful flowers & every thing looks so fresh & green   it makes me feel as if I could always stay here   Bill & Tom took a spree for a house warming & got pretty gentlemanly Merry over it etc   Day clear & warm   evening some heavy clouds with Thunder over the hills East

May 4   Went up to Independence with Judge & Tom & 3 Miles above to where they are camped   Independence is on the same ridge Angiers is & about 8 miles above   in going to the camp we crossed one of the Branches of the Caliverus   got to the camp by night & found 3 other boys there who were partners of Judge & Tom

Wednesday May 5th 1852

Judge & Tom had brought some Brandy up with them & the company all but Judge got most gloriously tight & kept up the fuss til after midnight   they wanted me to join them in drinking but I did not think it would suit me   I went with them to the place they were working but could not find a prospect to suit me so I returned home by way of Independence   Up above this place there has been a large quantity of ground worked over but none of it has paid verry largely

One thing I have not before mentioned from the tops of almost all the high hills here we are in sight of the snow ridge which looks like a white cloud in the distance though there is snow now on most of the highest hills all round us   Day clear with high winds

May 6   Looked round in the forenoon & went to Curries and tried to buy a Mare of him but could not hit on the price   Came home to dinner & found Bill pretty tight & not able to cook or would not do it so I proposed a Division of the camp property which he excepted so we divided   I kept the tent & he moved into the house with Tom as they are better friends than ever   I am not sorry we are seperated as we never could have suited each other for Messmates although we never quarreled

Friday May 7th 1852

Went down to the River on the trail we went before   found there at work 5 men with a long hose & Tom   they were only making about 3 dollars a day & not that all the time   I cant work to advantage here for want of a Hose which it would not pay to buy   I came up & went down the Rich Gulch but there they were all idle or not making anything   I felt verry much discouraged with the place & think of leaving soon as I dont believe I can make anything here anymore

May 8   I fixed this morning to go south with Tappan & Jo Wallace prospecting but the Mule run away & they did not find him in time to start to day so another day is lost

Weather clear & beautiful

May 9   I fixed up my carpet sack & put every thing I had in it & hung it up at Angiers so the Indians might not steal it while I was gone & started for McKinneys on the Caliveras   We were 2 Mules & five men   The Mules Loaded with provisions & tools   on one we had a Tom packed which gave us a deal of trouble   we went down the Caliveras Hill to a Little Town or camp of 10 or 12 canvas houses & tents called Esperanza[16]   this is the North fork of the Caliveras   we went up the River from here some distance & took up McKinneys branch & after crossing the first ridge ½ a mile we came to McKinneys store on a Large Gulch [Wet Gulch?] running into the Jesus Maria a branch of the Caliveras   here we stopped for the night

Monday May 10th 1852

We went down the Gulch some ½ mile with a Man we fell in with here by name of Lawson   The Gulch is verry wide with considerable bottom or bar on both sides   We built a damn & dug a ditch & turned the water so we could prospect & then went up to dinner   in the afternoon I stayed at the Store as I felt verry unwell   the others washed some dirt but got but little gold   Day clear & pleasant

May 11   This forenoon we washed til about 12 & found but little Gold   I was not pleased with the place so I sold my share of what we had for 50c & came home where I arrived about dark

May 12   Went down to the Hill for nothing but to see what I could see   got home by noon & finished the day reading Dumas Works

Evening cloudy & cool

May 13   Day cloudy & cool with a steady light rain so I laid in the tent all day   it was not verry tiresome as I had books to read etc

May 14   I am now going down to the River as I think I can make board there until the River falls so we can go to work in it   Bill came up & helped me to take down & roll up my tent   I had engaged one of Angiers Buccaros (who was a Mexican & went by the name of Valentine) to take my things down on a mule so we packed up & went down[17]   I took possession of a tent that had been left standing here & threw mine over a log that lay against the foot of the hill   I put my cooking apparatus under the tent as there is plenty in the tent I went into   I bought a lot of provisions to bring down with me which I calculated would do me a Month   here is the bill

I looked out a place took my pan pick & shovel & went to work panning out but soon found I could not make board in that way   I became verry much discouraged so went & cooked some dinner & after eating felt a little better   tried it again but it was no go   then went and looked at the other company awhile but they were not doing well at all   by this time it was night

5 lbs sugar		1.00
3 " coffee		.75
1 " candles		.75
½ " tea		.50
¼ " pepper (box)		.25
10 " pork		2.50
11 " beef		2.75
50 " flour		5.50
1 " saleratus		.75
1 box caps		.50
2 box Matches		.25
½ quire paper		.25

Then for the mules to carry down the things 4.00
and one shovel 4.00

Day cloudy & cool   the air feels damp

May 15 Picked round among the rocks to day and got nothing The River is verry high so the bars are most all covered with water
Day clear & warm

May 16 Went up to Angiers with one of the men at work here & sharpened my pick & a piece of a crowbar that I picked up on the bar near my tent I sharpened for the purpose of breaking up the ledge which is all slate mostly solid but some times shelly & in the crevices where it is shelly gold is generally deposited   so not finding much on top I think to try the crevices   The Day is hot & verry hard getting up & down the hill

Monday May 17th 1852

Scratched round some   broke up some Ledge but could find nothing but a few fine specs

Got worse discourage than I have been since I have been in the country   in part I got the blues but had no notion of leaving the Mines yet as I wanted to try the River when it get low enough   I still kept at work all day & at night had only about 25c   I think I will try some other place

Forenoon foggy afternoon cloudy

May 18 Rained during the night   after breakfast I went up to Angiers thinking to prospect round there awhile & see if I cant find something   I stop with Cap Van Allen for board as he is one of my partners in the River claim   Looked round during the Day but could find nothing

Day cloudy but pleasant

May 19   I started this Morning down the River with my blankets on my shoulder not knowing where I would go to   when I got to the Hill I thought I would go over to Greaserville[18]   When I got there I heard that a man over on Jacksons creek wanted to hire hands so I went over to see him As it was only two miles   I found him carting dirt   he offered me 75 Dollars pr month which I did not like to take I then thought of my things that I had left on the River so I came back home   got back by dark verry tired and hungry although I had eaten dinner with a Man at the Hill who said he had been acquainted with Abner at Humbolt Bay 2 years ago   Day clear & warm etc

Thursday May 20th 1852

Old Ebby Hollis Cap Van Allens partner got tight last night & got mad at me because I did not like Mackcal and he made some fuss about me boarding with them so this morning I came to Dan Curries to board as Angier turned off his boarders so often I did not like to go there til he would get some cooks

I partly sunk a hole in the Rich Gulch this evening with Jo Wallace but we found nothing as yet   Day fair   Morning & evening cloudy

May 21   Finished the hole we commenced yesterday & got only about 12½c   I then went to the River & got my carpet sack and let the company at work there have what provsion I had there   came up and paid Angier some on my bill there *(Amt* **11.50)**

The Mule train has not arrived as was expected so I will wait another day as I intend to go for a couple of weeks ovr the other side the River   Day clear & warm

May 22   Laid round the store all day & read Dumas works   Train came up but brought no letters for me   Day clear & warm

May 23   After Breakfas I started for Jackson creek   arrived there about noon   Saml Watson the Man that offered me the 75 hired me at that rate for as long as I pleased so I engage to Work awhile for that   I was in the Town in the afternoon & at night   Watson & me went over to the town which is some ¾ of mile from his cabin   he went to attend the Vigilance committee & I went to look around

Sunday May 23 1852

The Town of Jackson which was formerly the County seat of Caliveras is situate about 5 Miles North of Mokelumne Hill & on the point at the junction of the North & south Forks of Jacksons creek between the two Branches   It consists of some 200 houses some of canvas some of clapboards & some that are verry good frames covered with sawed lumber   it has 10 or 15 stores 8 or 10 gambling houses of different kinds 4 American Hotels & 6 or 8 French & spanish Restaurants & Cafes and two spanish or chilean Dance Houses[19]   The country around here is not so hilly as on the other side the Mokelumne and the Gold is more generally distributed in the ground at least such is the name the Miners I have talked with give it

May 23   I got sleepy & left Watson in town last night   he came home after midnight and said they had a fire in town   one of the Dance Houses had caught & burned up   It was canvas so did not make much fire

I went to work this morning

May 30   I have been steady at work all week carting & washing Dirt   we haul & wash from 17 to 18 loads a day from which we have got on an average $1.00 to the load

The Dirt is a red gravelly clay not verry hard to wash & lays about 2 feet thick on the Ledge   we are hauling from the hill side about 400 yards from where we wash it   The Ledge is a soft yellow slate   The Gold is verry fine & is generally mixed with the dirt from the top to the bottom   The Gold is about like fine corn meal

Sunday May 30th 1852

The Earth in every direction is covered with a Many colered Mantle Vegetation is growing rapidly & the Grass is knee high on the flats Wild clover the first I have seen grows in abundance along this creek & is in bloom now   it is just the same as the red clover at home

Wild Rye & oats also is scattered about in every direction   Watson & me was speaking of the extensive Variety of flowers when he told me to walk in a straight line for the distance of 100 yards & see how many different kinds of flowers I could find   I did so & picked all the different kinds I noticed & on counting I had got nineteen flowers all of different colers sizes & shapes & there seems to be no partiality among them for the situation they grow in as they [are found] on flat & hill Mountain & Valley   I am no Botanist or I should like to classify them

Caraway also grows everywhere here & Tansy Mint & sage is abundant all growing spontaneously   There has been considerable excitement up about Clinton during the week   The Chileans have come togather there and ordered the Americans out of the place   The Americans then sent out to the different camps & gathered a large body of Americans & drove out & subdued the Chileans to peace again & all without any bloodshed & now all is again quiet in that quarter at least so says report

The people are considerably excited about several Murders that have lately been committed wtih a scope of 4 miles of this place   The Vigilance Committee is on the alert but no clue as yet is had to the Murderers   The Weather has been clear & warm without variation during the week   Watson paid me to day 15.00 for my weeks work he liking my work so well that he gave me the 3 Dollars pr day instead of the rates of 75 pr Month   I spent the day in walking round the Town & country   In Town the Gamblers & women were busily engaged at their different avocations which lead to misery & wretchedness & in the Country all Nature seems to smile & bid poor miserable restless Man *Be Happy*

June 2   The last two Days have been clear cool & windy   This morning a heavy fog obscured the sun for several hours & During the day heavy clouds were visible over the hills and towards the Mountains & Distant Thunder was heard from them occasionally but now [never] came near enough to give us any rain on the contrary the sun shown clear & brilliant all day after the fog went away

This Morning a Circus came into Town which performs two nights here   Circuses in this country perform altogather in the night as no inducements of that kind will draw the Miners from their work during the day   During the afternoon a courier or runner came round among the (the) Miners belonging to the Vigilance Committee warning them to meet at their Room in Town at night as a man had been shooting somebody or somebody else

Wednesday June 2nd 1852

Watson being one of the Committee he & I went down to Town just before night he to attend the call & I to look round & see what I should see   by talking with different persons I found the case stood about thus   Thompson a Gambler from Mokelumne Hill was in an Italian gameing Room & was Bucking at Monte against the Italian who had the Bank   after playing awhile they had a dispute about the ownership of a certain six dollars that Thompson had bet   after disputing awhile Thompson left the house & the money saying no more about it In passing up the Street he met Moore another Gambler of I know not where & Moore taking sides with the Italian renewed the quarrel and made some hostile demonstrations whereupon Thompson showed him he had no arms to defend himself   this stopped Moore a short time but he soon again drew his revolver swearing he would shoot Thompson anyhow & immediately fired   the ball passed through

Thompsons shirt just above the belt & some distance beyond went into a boys shirt sleeve where it lodged   The boy has the ball yet which is a slug or long ball

They were then in front of the Union Hotel & next door is a Bakery Immediately after the pistol was fired Thompson run into the Bakery & seized on old Musket that was in the hands of an Indian & returned to the door to look out for More

Meanwhile Moore had run into the Union Hotel & had returned to the porch & taken refuge behind a large dry goods box that lay beside the door next to the Bakery with his pistol cocked & resting on the box   Thompson being aware of what direction Moore was in was stooping forward with the Musket in his hand trying to get a sight of him when Moore again fired at his head & then ran up the stairs in the Hotel   Thompson drew back & remained where he was   A few doors below the Bakery was another Hotel with a porch in front   on this porch stood a Dutch Drummer belonging to the Circus

The ball from Moores pistol passed through the corner of the crown of Thompsons hat & [went] on & struck the Dutchman in the side of the waist & passed through & lodged in his clothes on the opposite side

The Dutchman fell & was carried into the Hotel & his wound Examined by a Surgeon & pronounced Mortal though he supposed it possible he might recover   One of The Officers of the place passing & hearing the firing but not seeing Moore & hearing of the wounded Dutchman etc took Thompson prisoner and put him in jail but afterwards coming to the truth Thompson was liberated & Moore put in his stead & now at 8-o clock Thompson is round telling how he tried to do & blowing considerable & The Committee is in its room holding consultation & Moore is in the jail & here they may stay til I take a walk round the circus tent & the jail which is close by

Wednesday Night June 2nd 1852

On hearing some Miners speak of the jail & its occupant I asked where it was and was directed to the circus tent as it was near by   It is a clear light night   The Moon is high in the heaven & seems to look down on Turbulent & restless Man within a pitying & Mournful light I took the direction of the circus tent guided by the Musick which sounded loud & clear on the still night air & passed out of the Main street by the first opening I came to which was a narrow pass between a store and a Mule Correl   this led me by the jail which stood about 50 yards from the street the back end ½ buried in the ground as it

was against & in the hill & just back of the jail on the hill which was
low stood the tent which was a small one for a circus & from which
issued at short intervals loud bursts of Laughter showing that those
within were enjoying the scenes therein passing   I walked round the
jail   it is built of fine logs hewed on two sides duvtailed together til
the flat sides touch leaving the rough & unhewn sides out & in (I
suppose in as I cant see)   a division as shown by the ends of the logs
cuts off about 10 feet in front leaving the back end about 20 feet square
in this backroom are two Iron grated windows on each side about a
foot square   It is covered with logs hewn square (as shows by the
ends) & laid close and over that a roof of clapboards   The door seems
to be a common batten door & is fastened with a common pad lock
hasp & staple of light structure

I walked round the circus tent but saw nothing but 2 or 3 horses
& some performers dressing in a waggon standing outside the tent as
thy had no dressing room attached & a crowd of Indians & loafers
about the door a Majority of which were Indians & a few of them were
buying tickets & going in   I reckon to see what it was the Americanos
or palefaces had that they should stick up so many big squares of
paper covered with curious figures for I soon returned to the street in
front of the Committee Room   just as I got there the door opened
& The Committee about 80 in number issued therefrom in double file
& took the course for the jail   on seeing this I went ahead & took a
station in front of the jail in the correl behind a pile of boards against
the fence   from here I had a good view of the front of the jail   A few
Moment & The Committee in double file issued from the back of one
of the houses on the street & at the command of the leader they formed
2 lines one from each corner of the jail in a square to the correl fence
Then the command *every Man draw his Revolver cock it hold the
Muzzle upward* was obeyed with alacrity   Then 8 Men from the lines
advanced one with a lanthorn to the door & after a few words of consultation held in a low tone one of them with a stick about 3 feet long
struck the lock a light blow & the door was open   just then I heard
several terrified yells issue from the interior   I suppose the prisoner
was some scared for to offenders in California Vigilance Committee
have a terrible name

The Committee or Sub Committee were now in the first or Ante
room & before them another door fastened much as the first

This was soon opened with a pick brought for the purpose   The
staple was pulled out & the door thrown open   when before them

stood Terrified & trembling with a revolver in one hand & a Bowie knife in the other a Young Man of 20 years or thereabouts rather tall & good looking well built & strong to appearance   he made no resistance but at command gave up his arms & was led to the Committee Room followed by the committee as they had come   The Room door was closed by the doorkeeper behind the last of the committee & with a deal of impatience the descision of the Committee was looked for   as most all expected by morning to see dangling from the limb of an oak tree growing in front of the *Coms* room the body of the aforesaid young man but this was not to be   fate had decreed otherwise as time will show   I loitered round the street til after midnight & no news from the *centre* of all *attention* so I went to a store borrowed a blanket of the storekeeper & seated myself on a sack of potatoes leaned back against a pile of boxes & fell asleep & dreamed of God knows what as the potatoes which were not level or smooth & the boxes whose corners were not very soft or downy kept me in a verry uncomfortable

Thursday June 3rd 1852

½ asleep condition til morning & every thing so confused that my dreams were almost forgotten   next morning when I was awakened by the oths and loud words of Watson & others who were displeased with the descision   Upon straightening up & rubbing my eyes Watson said to me come John lets go home   The Town Prisoner committee & all may go to—(I shant name the place but people say it is very hot) for me   On our way home he informed me that just before day they had got through the evidence & speeches when a Vote was taken whether it should be   Return him to the Civil Authorities or Hang him when a Majorty were in favor of returning him so they took him back to the jail & put him in shutting the doors but the fastenings being all broken the doors were only closed   when the sheriff was informed that the prisoner was returned he refused to take charge of him & while thy were consulting what should be done he (the prisoner) walked out & got upon a horse his Friends prepared for him and rode off unmolested   Watson was verry much angered at the way the committee had done as he was decidedly in favor of hanging for all such offences but was over ruled by the Majority

Friday June 4th   To day the report was circulated that the Dutchman was dead & several Miners here were with Watson in favor of stopping the Murderers career but fate or circumstance had ordered other wise so they chewed the cud of disappointment with many bitter words to soothe their wounded feelings etc

Saturday June 5th 1852

This evening the courier again came round informing the committee that Moore had been captured at Drytown & was again in the custody of the Officers & wanted the committee to meet & try it again but this time Watson would not attend however he went to town at night & staid awhile   When the committee met they found their Room occupied by the justices court so they contented themselves with watching the proceedings   About 9-o-clock the Prisoner made an excuse to retire from the Room & was attended by a constable & as soon as he got clear of the crowd he & the constable had a footrace in which the *Const* gave tongue freely but could not overtake the now free prisoner nor could any of those who came at the cry of the Constable   therefore he escaped

The Dutchman is not dead as was reported but is in a fair way of recovery   This lessened the excitement some

June 6   This Morning Watson paid me 16.50 as I lost ½ a day thursday by sleeping the forenoon   The last two days have been verry warm & sultry & so is to day   I left Watsons & came over to Dan Curries & find everything verry dull more so than when I left   I went up to Angiers & found some letters there for me — paid Angier   12.75 all I owed him & Dan Curry   3.00 all I owe in the Mines   I am now in a stew & dont know which way to turn

Monday June 7th 1852

Old Ebby Hollis is now living with Tom & Bill   When Bill first left me and went with Tom they laid off the flat for a farm or Ranch & dug up & planted a small space in potatoes Beans peas & Vines etc & when I left here this garden had begun to look as if it would make something but while I was gone they had another quarrel & one wouldnt & the other wouldnt tend to the garden so the Animals pushed the fence down & destroyed it or nearly so   so that now it is all gone to rack They are living in the same house but each buys & cooks his own grub

I was about going over to Valcano to day but Tom offered me a share of a claim he had bought on Poison Gulch which is a Branch of the Dutch Gulch & lies between that & the Rich Gulch   I was to help him & Ebby sink a hole & if I thought it would pay me pay him for ⅓ 20.00   & if I didnt like to do that take ⅓ of what we got out of the hole & quit so I am going to help them sink the hole

June 10   Yesterday & to day heavy clouds with thunder & lightning are visible over the hills to the East & North but none of them reach

here   The weather is clear & warm   We have been at work at the
hole in poison Gulch   we have started about 6 by 12 feet square &
ought to have it down now but Tom & Ebby drinks nearly all the time
so they dont work only about ¼ the time   I think when this hole is
done I will quit let it pay ever so well

Saturday June 12th 1852

This evening we finished the hole that we ought to have done in
two days   we got 14.00 apiece which is good pay for the time we have
worked but not for the time spent   If anybody had the claim that
would work steady I would take a share but with the present owners
it would never pay so I think I will go somewhere else to work as the
River is yet too high

June 13   Paid Dan Curry for my weeks board 9.00 & took my
carpet sack & blankets & came over to Volcano by way of the Hill the
same route we came as we were going prospecting   I stopped at the
Volcano House   I dont think the chance verry good for work here
although wages are good being six dollars pr day without board but I
havent yet found anybody that wants to hire though I have only been
here a few hours   I have here met with John Reaves & A F Smith two
boys that were at Angiers when I first came there   I have agreed to
work tomorrow for Gemmill the Tavern keeper I am stopping with

June 14   Worked to day for Gemmill [G. W. Gemmil] at shoveling
dirt into a cart   The clay dirt here is a blue tough clay and works like
putty when taken out of the ground   we have been stripping that is
taking off the top dirt all day so I dont know how it pays though
report says it pays well

Gemmill payed me & my board in   4.00

Tuesday June 15th 1852

I can find none who want hands so I shall leave   They have made
a law here that none that hire shall pay less than 6.00 pr Day   I find
many that would hire me for less but they dont like to pay that &
they dont want to break the law so I cant hire   I left Volcano & went
by grass flat across & down the big hill to the forks of the River to our
claim which I find all covered with water   I come down the trail a
fluming company that is going to flume the River below our claim have
made   it is a high steep point of the Mountain & has no breaks or
benches from the top to bottom & is about ¼ of a mile long   it is so
steep that timber started at the top goes to the bottom without any
other assistance   they are sawing out the lumber with a whip saw at

the top of the hill & bringing it down this trail   I took dinner with this company and then came up the hill another and longer way but not so steep & crossed the ridge to Jacksons creek & came down by Secreta to Watsons where I will stop for the night and probably longer

June 16   This Morning I went to work in Watsons claim scraping the Ledge where the dirt had been hauled off   I believe that there is considerable gold in the top of the Ledge that is soft so to day I scraped up two Loads & washed it this evening and got only $1.37   this Watson gave to me as it was so little & I had worked pretty hard to get it   Watson is from south Carolina & is a good man to work for

Thursday June 17th 1852

Came over to Angiers & stopped with him as he has got a couple of Chinese cooks & Dan Curry has quit boarding

They had here yesterday a shower of rain from heavy clouds that I saw to the East of Watsons   Angier has got a new store & dining Room built of fine poles & clapboards & this is all the improvement I see going on   They struck another lead in the new diggings & took out about 70 ounces in the last two weeks but it has created no excitement & the lead has run out

June 18   Had a shower to day with heavy Thunder & lightning & to night a heavy storm   prospected some & found *nix*

June 19   Weather warm & sultry several showers to day   sunk a hole found nothing etc

June 20   I started this morning to go to Volcano by way of the Forks   went down the trail at the mouth of Nigger Gulch & up the River to the Canon below the forks where I heard there was a log across

The water is so high I had a hard walk or climb along the cliffs and I think I will never try it again   I had to go along the hill side over rocks & cliffs as I could not go close to the water   the rocks were too steep   I went about two Miles in this way   the weather is verry hot & here under the hills no breeze so I suffered greatly from the heat When I got to the log I could not cross so I came back by our claim below the forks

Monday June 21st 1852

Rained verry heavy during the night and this morning a heavy fog came up the River and spread over the Mountains   it was so dark we could not see 50 yards for about 2 hours when it cleared away & the sky was clear & the sun shown most brilliant   I went up to day on the South fork to Musquito Gulch & crossed over the ridge to Colburgs

Humbug which is about 4 miles from Angiers   went up that Gulch to its head & down another Gulch to the Independence Road & down that home again   did not see nor hear of any good diggings   The Indians bring in considerable Gold but none can discover where they get it They are such slow Miners & bring in so much dust it is the general opinion that they have found some rich places & many are trying to discover its whereabouts but have not yet succeeded

They lost a child at this camp about a week ago which was buried at their burying ground in front of Angiers and ever since they have kept up a continual howling & Mournful singing at the camp   how long they Mourn for the departed I dont know but they make a deal of noise while they are at it   I see the squaws going about Marked & daubed all over with a white paint which is made of a kind of pipe clay which I suppose is their mourning color

They have left the camp up on the flat & burned it up round house & all and have built shades of brush opposite Angier across the Gulch near where my tent stood   I am informed that they move their camps every spring & fall because the two seasons Winter & summer require diffcrent kinds of abodes & the Vermin such as fleas & lice get so bad during six months they cant stay any longer so they burn their camps to destroy them

Day clear & Warm

June 22   This Morning cool clear & a light frost   Doc Ticket Abe McKinney (Brother to the onc that shot the Dog) & myself packed a horse with tools blankets & provision for 3 days for a prospecting trip up among the forks of the Mokelumne   we started after breakfast & went up by Musquito Gulch & Browns Ranch and crossed the South fork at lower crossing and then steered North to The Quartz Mills on the Middle fork   we here took up the Ridge to the upper crossing of the Middle fork where we arrived about noon and stopped to Lunch & prospect etc   After eating we [went] down the River about a Mile & prospected some bars found but little   came up & went up the River & prospected some bars & a Gulch but found nothing that would pay   so we packed up & left for the North fork about 2 hours by sun There is two companies at work here who are making about 5.00 a day but they have expended considerable in preparing for it   We went down the ridge 2 miles & then struck across for the North fork   we went down the hill without a trail & got to the River by dark & cooked some supper with drift wood   laid down among the rocks & went to sleep

Wednesday June 23rd 1852

The place we had come down the hill had been a large landslide & there was a bar in the middle of the River & the bottom or bank was so narrow & rocky we could not scarcely find a place to lie down   we had to leave the horse several yards above us & in a place where there was no grass nor anything else he could eat although vegetation was plenty   so this morning Doctor Ticket took his horse & went up the hill to hunt grass for him   While McKinney & I went down the River as close as we could to the water which was so high all the bars are covered   we went down some two miles & finding no bars out of water we turned up the hill   on the top on a flat where there was plenty of Grass we found the Doc herding his horse   we then let Doc go up by the upper crossing of the Middle fork (as he could not get a horse across at the mills) & he was to meet us at the Woodhouse Quartz Mill on the Middle fork while we went down to the lower crossing of the North fork to see if the bar there was out of water   when we got down to it we found it like the rest covered with water   we went down the River a mile or so but all was alike so we returned to the Mills where we found the Doc waiting for us   The Quartz Mills here are two each running 10 stamps by an overshot wheel of 30 feet [diameter]   there is so much fall along here that the troughs that carry the water to the wheels are only about 30 yards long   the bed of the stream is solid Granite over which the water runs with a loud noise heard to the top of the hill   each side the hills are so steep & rocky a horse cannot get up or down them   The Quartz is dug up several hundred yards back from the top of the hill & hauled to the top where it is hammered up into small bits & then run to the Mill in a plank shute   After eating some dinner we came home by the same route we had started   we arrived about 5 of the clock well tired of climbing the hills & Mountains

June 24   Collected some flowerseeds for the purpose of sending home & packed up a small box of curiosities such as stones chrystals seeds etc to send to the City to Abner & Loofed the balance of the Day

Day clear & pleasant

June 25   Went down to the River this morning & brought up some of my tools and left them at Toms tent   sold Tom & Ebby my Hose for 4 dollars which cost 6 dollars & a days work to make   I could not sell any of the balance of the tools at any price

Day clear & warm

June 26   Paid Angier for my weeks board 10.00 & started for Volcano   went down to the River at the Mouth of Spring Gulch expecting to get across in a canoe close to the Mouth of the Gulch but when I got there the water is so high I could [not] induce the man to try to cross so I went down the River along the hill side passing several canoes but none of them would attempt to cross as the water was so high   til I came to Whites Bar which is two Miles above the Hill   here they have a rope ferry so I got a cross

There are a number of miners along the River all doing nothing but about making their board   The walk or scramble along the River has tired me much & I almost loathe to undertake to get up the hill but it has to be done so here goes — two hour — & I am up the hill across the ridge — on to Jackson Creek — up that to Clinton past Clinton across the ridge to the Middle fork of Jackson — up that to its head & over the ridge to Grass Valley & here I stop to rest awhile   they are mowing their grass & Barley on the flat & offer me 3 Dollars a day to mow but I wont take that for I am going to Volcano where wages are 6 dollars   so on I came & arrived at Volcano about 3 & stopped at the Volcano house   here again I met Reeves & Smith   Smith has just finished a house at the spring and he offers me a place to Lodge which I except as lodging is two dollars a week   The house is new the floor clean new plank & clear of Vermin so I prefer lieing on this floor with my blankets to lieing on the Mats at the Tavern which are infested by innumerable Vermin   That a Man must be verry sleepy to sleep among them

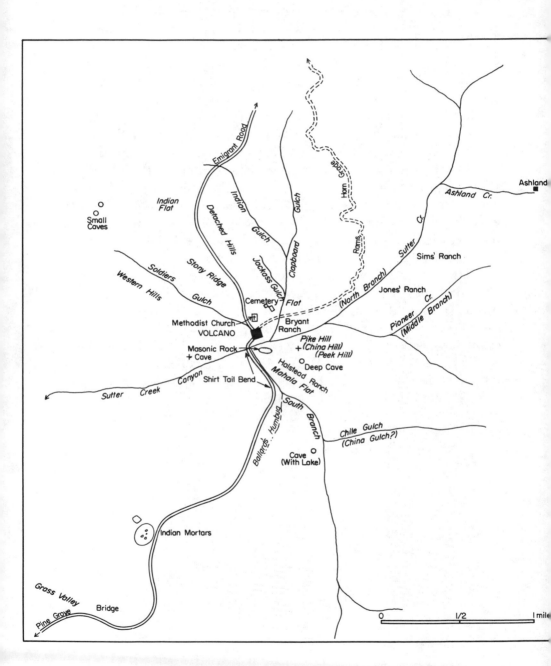

Ashland

Ashland Cr.

Emigrant Road

Indian Flat

Small Caves

Detached Hills

Indian Gulch

Clapboard Gulch

Ham Grade

Rams Grade

Sutter Cr.

Sims' Ranch

Stony Ridge

Jackass Gulch

Cemetery Flat

Jones' Ranch

Pioneer Cr. (Middle Branch)

(North Branch)

Western Hills

Soldiers Gulch

Methodist Church
VOLCANO

Bryant Ranch

Masonic Rock
+ Cave

Pike Hill
+ (China Hill)
(Peek Hill)

Deep Cave

Halstead Ranch

Sutter Creek

Canyon

Shirt Tail Bend

Mahala Flat

Ballard's Humbug

South Branch

Chile Gulch
(China Gulch?)

Cave
(With Lake)

Indian Mortars

Grass Valley

Pine Grove

Bridge

0   1/2   1 mile

VOLCANO

Volcano & Valley & Hills Around

Volcano is situate on both sides and at the Fork of Sutter Creek & takes its name from the supposed Volcanic appearance that exist in & about it   The Valley is bounded on the west by a range of hill running North & south   On the North by a range of hills or piles of Limestone Granite & Marble that run North East & South west & the East & North East by irregular hills & points of hills & on the south by the range or point of hills running down parallel with the North Branch & ending in the Forks   The south Branch comes in from the South East & joins the North Branch about 50 yards from the base of the west line of hills   When the two togather pass in a westerly direction through the hills forming a deep canon (canon is a spanish name for deep steepsided narrow bottomed Ravines or hollows & is pronounced Can-yon) & passes on down through hills & flats til it joins Dry creek about 18 Miles below here

Just in the Fork is a high detached Rock or pile of Rocks about 60 feet high and about 100 yards long nearly perpendicular on the North side with a few stunted bushes on the rocks & in the crevices and on the south side runs off with a gradual descent & is covered with Earth

101

and grass and is seperated from the hill between the forks by a flat space of about 100 yards & is seen from all parts of the North & South Valley   from under the Centre of this Rock on the North side Gushes a beautiful large spring affording something near 8 solid inches of running water the year round (at least I am informed it is never affected by wet nor dry weather)[20]   On the East side of this spring & close to it stands Smiths house at which I am stopping   one side resting on & against the rock the other supported by stone pillars about 4 feet high   Commencing at this rock & running south along each side of the south branch is a Vally or flat about 300 yards wide at the beginning & irregularly tapering til it comes to a steep & deep canon at about a miles distance   The Town Extends from the Bridge across the Main stream below the point of rock up this Vally along the foot of West hill in a single row of houses about 200 yards & this part of the Town is called shirt tail bend for want of a better name[21]   Up the North Branch about ½ a mile comes in from the south another Branch called the Middle Branch forming another small branch Vally The Vally then tapers up the North Branch about one mile where it ends in a canon   From the North East comes in what is called Clapboard & Jackass Gulches   Clapboard is a flat Gulch & verry wide & has been verry Rich in the precious metal   Jackass is a small Gulch coming down over the or through the ridge of rocks   on the west side of Clapboard is a low range of detached hills seperated from the rocky hills by a wide hollow called an Aroyo   these hills are about ½ a mile long & end at what is called Indian flat through which runs the Indian Gulch

Volcano & Valley

On the southern extremity of these detached hills stands the Methodist Church which is built of pine poles & clapboards & is about 20 by 30 feet square & finished on the inside with plank seats & pulpit of the Methodist style   From the North & running along the western hills comes in the Soldiers Gulch   The one from which Most of the Riches of Volcano have been taken   this Gulch joins the Main branch at the Mouth of the canon and along this Gulch on both sides of a single street & reaching from the base of the rocky hills to the bridge is the Main part of the town which is about 400 yards long   The North part of the Vally is occupied by Jones Ranch from the Middle branch North taking in about 160 acres   then up in the point is a small field fenced in called Sims Ranch   From Jones Ranch to the rock or spring & between the creek & the south hills is Bryants Ranch containing about 20 acres   then up the south Branch another small

field name unknown   The rest of the Vally between Jones & the
Town is occupied by the Miners for drying Ground   The North &
South Branches for ¼ mile down the Main Branch and up both
branches ½ a Mile are occupied by Long Toms & damns for turning
the water into them   some of these Toms have a furnace on which is
placed a wooden box with a sheet Iron bottom for the purpose of boiling dirt

Soldiers Gulch

This Gulch takes its rise some ½ mile back of the stone ridge on the
North of the Valley & runs down dividing the western hills from the
stone hills & then along the west side of the Vally at the foot of the hills
til it joins the creek at the Mouth of the canon

The Soldiers in 48 first found Gold in large quantities in the top-
dirt along the bed of this Gulch   then in 49 all its top dirt was washed
down several feet to a tough sticky clay something about the con-
sistency & tenacity of putty   the Gold was generally verry fine &
they used quicksilver Machines to collect it but those were found to
lose the Gold so they changed them for long Toms   After all the top
dirt was taken off that had Gold in it the blue clay was found to
contain Gold but it could not be washed just as it was dug up and
upon Experimenting it was found to dissolve rapidly in hot water
hence the boiling apparatus   also it was found that when it was dry
it rapidly dissolved in water hence the drying ground   holes were
then sunk all along the Gulch the width of the Vally & gold was found
as deep as they could go for water   also it was found to run into the
Hill as far as any had sunk holes & thus they kept working at it until
now they have it dug on an average 150 feet wide & 30 feet deep   the
bank in some places is 60 feet high   They have never yet got through
this blue clay & after the Main part of the Gulch was worked out Gold
was then only found in streaks

At this time There is only about ½ the Gulch that pays more than
wages   It has become verry difficult to keep the water out of the
way as they are now nearly on a level with the creek   All manners &
shapes of pumps are in use here now   This clay is generally of a deep
blue color nearly like stone coal though there is streaks & spots of red
yellow Brown & black clay intermixed with it   Also there is frequently met with large smoth irregular shaped stone that appear to
have once been subject to long & continual action of water & the small
stone & gravel are all round as those in the beds of the streams   however there is one spot of considerable extent that is a cellular porous
buff & white Quartz this found frequently chrystalized   it is in irregu-

larly square shaped cells sometimes of the size of a foot & from that down the partitions between these cells are sometimes verry thin & clear as Isinglass   The interior of these cells are all covered with a black scaly coating that looks like soot dried though it neither tastes nor smells only like dirt   through & among these rock the clay has considerable Gold in it which is extracted by hauling the dirt out & spreading on the Vally til dry or boiled & then washed   These burnt looking rocks & the rough hills around are the supposed Volcanic appearances from which the place takes it name of Volcano[22]

Sunday June 27

Laid & looked round Volcano all day to day & made the foregoing observations   There is one Spanish Dance house in this town & last night a fracas came off in which one man was slightly wounded by a pistol ball

Day clear & warm

June 28   Went up on Indian Gulch to see if I could find diggings but could not   we took the Road that runs North East from town & is the Emigrant Road up between the stoney ridge & the detached hills   Back of & over the Stoney ridge rises another ridge that is capped with pine like all the Mountains in this vicinity   we (another Miner was with me) came to Indian flat in about ½ a mile where the detached hills end to give place to another flat running up the Clapboard Gulch for ½ a Mile further   Indian Gulch rises to the North of the flat & runs down over the stoney hills & across the flat & into board Gulch   A company of Miners have dug a deep ditch from board Gulch up to the edge of the flat   from the Gulch up to the flat is about 200 yards   all this distance they have worked through   1st the top dirt a loose brown loam & gravel which pays from ½ to 1c to the pan & is on an average 18 inches thick   2nd a solid hard to dig strata of Quartz gravel & red clay which pays from 4 to 10c to the pan & is about 3 feet thick   3rd a strata of red soft stone easy to dig up without sand or gravel in it pays nothing & is about 2 feet thick

Indian Gulch & Flat

4th a strata of blue sandy clay verry soft about 4 inches thick & pays verry irregular though sometimes verry well   this lies on a hard blue slate ledge which is the Ledge all along board Gulch   They have now come to the white Marble or limestone of the ridge which is all over the flat & have lost sight of the slate ledge altogether   These rock seem to have been thrown togather promiscuously and the spaces

between them filled with a hard sticky gravelly clay in which there is
but verry little Gold   They are blasting through these stone & lifting
them out with what is here called a Derick which is a crane with ropes
& pulleys   We went on up the flat to its end   here the stoney ridge
turns to the North & sinks a little & forms a kind of cove down which a
Gulch runs   up this Gulch with a deal of Labor they have taken the
Emigrant road   to the west of the road in the cove comes out from
under a large rock another clear cool & large spring issues   we stopped
awhile here to admire the beauty of the scenery as facing the East
before us was a high range of pine capped Oak skirted Mountains   to
our right & left & behind us rose the rocky ridge where pile upon pile
& ledge upon ledge stood the time worn rocks rearing heavinward their
time worn points & sides   we next went across this ridge to the Indian
Gulch above where it goes over the rocky ridge   Just above the first
face they have struck a rich lead which commences just above the
falls & runs to the left of the Gulch at an angle of 20 degrees into the
hill   they have traced it for about 200 yards and are sinking holes &
tunnelling from the Gulch & taking out the dirt & piling [it] along the
Gulch to wash when the rain comes again as the water has all run off
here   the pay dirt here is a red clay & gravel with considerable Quartz
intermixed and not verry hard to wash   the Gold is generally fine
but some coarse lumps have been found   The first claim at the Gulch
where the lead starts has about 2 feet of top dirt on it & the hill
gradually rises til the last hole on the lead is 30 feet deep   The dirt
pays from 5c to one ounce to the pan
    We then went up the Gulch about 300 yards farther where it appar-
ently ends at a low ridge but on crossing the ridges we again find the
same Gulch   it here runs under the hill where a high pile of loose
stone are lieing against the hill   we looked at the entrance but did not
venture in as we had no lights although we have heard there was a cave
here   we then returned by the Gulch   came down over the falls
which are about 300 yards long   The dirt all the way up has been
picked out from among the rocks & washed   We got home after
dinner verry tired as the scrambling over the rocks is tiresome

Tuesday June 29th 1852

    Went over to Angiers by way of Whites bar to day & tried to sell
my tent & things I had left on the River but could not do it   The
River is yet verry high & it is thought it will be late before it falls so
it can be worked so I have concluded to go somewhere else to find
summer Diggings

June 30   Left Angiers this morning & came down spring Gulch & crossed the River in a canoe   it then took me about 3 hours to get up the hill as it is steeper here than any other place I ever came up it I arrived at Volcano after dinner awhile   I left my tools all except a pick & shovel that I brought with [me] telling Cap Van Allen to take them & keep them & if I never come back they were his   I started then for Shasta but intended to stop wherever I could or thought I could find Diggings

July 1   Watson came up yesterday evening & is going to work here I think now I will get work   I worked this evening in the creek below the spring in the water crotch deep   I worked for a Man by the name of Bill whose partner stays in the house with Smith & me   his name is Stewart   Watson will not give but 3 dollars a day so I wont work for him   The dirt here is old tailings run through the long Tom & quicksilver Machines   the branch is filled up about 5 feet with these tailings which pay well to wash as an ounce a day is nothing uncommon in the tailings

Friday July 2nd 1852

Worked part of the Day to day for Stewart as he was gone prospecting   I would have worked all day but Bill would not go in the water & he could not get a hand so I lost part of the day

July 3   This forenoon done nothing   after dinner I went up the South Branch to see a cave there   I found an Irishman up there who went in with me   The Entrance is in a large pile of rocks on the hill side about 30 feet above the branch & is near the head of the flat   It is a small irregular hole   goes down nearly perpendicular about 20 feet & then goes off downward in a slaunt 8 or 10 feet farther when it opens into the cave   we clambered down letting ourselves down by the projections of the rock holding in one hand a candle   I then clambered all through it in many place I had to crawl on my hands & knees it consists of 3 rooms of irregular & rough shape   sharp points of rock which are hanging with stalactites stick out on every side & on the roof the whole inside above the floor is full or was of stalactites like icicles the most of which are now broken off   I got a few & brought [them] home with me   The passage between two of the rooms is a double one that is one above the other & are just large enough for a man to crawl through conveniently   The floor or bottom is damp & covered with a dark vegetable & sand mixture such as is deposited on creek bottoms by high waters   The whole length is about 200 feet and width about 30 feet average & hight about 10 feet average

Sunday July 4th 1852

The past week the weather has been clear & pleasant   Started early this Morning with Stewart to see the Indian Gulch Cave   we took a torch & a couple of candles but the torch we could not use as the passage was too small   we went in about 100 feet   it was an irregular shaped passage & seemed to be only the opening between large Marble boulders thrown togather promiscuously   The Marble was verry smooth and had a tolerable fine grain   the passage ended to us in numerous small crevices between the rocks through which we could not go   so we returned home

After dinner we went up to the south branch Cave & this time took some pitch pins but that filled the cave with smoke so we soon had to leave it

I engaged to work tomorrow for Smith & Slator who are partners in the house at the spring which has a bar in it & does a good business

The Day passed off verry quietly there being nothing going on more than common as Most of the people had gone to a Celebration at Ione Valley

July 5   Worked for Smith & Slator to day in the Gulch by the town they have jumped a claim & are only working enough in it to hold it The law is a Man shall work at least one day out of every 5 or the claim is jumpable so this claim had not been worked for five days and they jumped it   *Sunday July 11th 1852*

Have been doing no work & would have left but I had lent Smith some money which I could not get   The week has been clear & warm I have engaged to work next week for Stewart who is going over on the Mokelume prospecting   The Methodist church have been holding a camp Meeting here for several days & to day I went to their camp which is up the south branch close to a steam saw mill which is about ½ mile above town   They have only a shade of brush supported by timber sawed out for a Ten pin Alley   The preacher was an elderly Man & preached a good sermon against Gambling Drinking fighting etc

They held evening Meeting at the New house but I had promised to put up Smiths sign so I could not go   The sign was *Spring Saloon* painted on Canvas which I fastened on a frame and set up on the comb of the house

July 12   Heard this morning of the Nominations of Pierce & King for the Presidential Election or Candidates   Also Gonzales & Old

Blaze the keepers of the Dance house here were arrested by officers from Sacremento for a Grand Larceny Committed some time ago which breaks up the Dance house   The people are verry well pleased that it is broken up for most every night they had a fuss of some kind there

The business Men are beginning to talk of the expected Emigration by this Route   *Sunday July 18th 1852*

The Circus that was at Jackson performed here Monday & Tuesday nights nothing else of Interest has transpired   The Miners those that have claims & work them seem to be doing well   The weather has been clear & warm though it has been cold for me most of the time as I have been working in the water for Stewart   I have worked 5½ days & rec for it   33.00
& have paid for board out of that   18.00
for the time I have been here   Started by sun up this Morning for Drytown with Stewart who has worked there before   we went from here North to the head of Rancherie then down that two miles then crossed the ridge & went down Dry creek til within 1 mile of Dry town where some of Stewarts Friends live   we here stopped & got some dinner   as we came down the creek we passed many Chinese at work they seem verry quiet & none that I have seen can speak English   The way we came was a verry rough one & has tired us verry much as there was no trail a good part of the way   after eating some dinner we went to Dry town   This consists of about 200 houses & is on the South side of the creek   we then went down the creek two Miles to New York flat [now New York Gulch] which is the head or upper end of Ione Valley   Sutter [sic] and Amadore & Rancherie Creeks come into Dry creek between Dry town & the flat   Stewart had worked here before and wanted me to take a claim which was jumpable but I did not want to do it as there might have been some hard feeling about it & I dont believe in jumping claims nohow   we returned to Dry town & by the place we took dinner & then struck across the ridge to Rancherie & came up that to its head   home again the way we came up was rougher than the way we went down   there is two or 3 Ranches on Rancherie & one large Indian Ranch   we arrived at home by dark verry tired and sore

July 19   Feel verry sore & tired for my walk yesterday   Board has risen two dollars on this week so I paid up mine   paid 8.00 for the last week & quit

July 20 Done no work to day but engaged to commence tomorrow for Whitfield the man that bought Smith & Slators claim a short time ago

July 21 Commenced work for Whitfield at four dollars & my Board pr Day he has his wife with him & boards his hands

Some Emigrants have arrived which created some excitement also several claims in Soldiers Gulch have been jumped and a Miners meeting called which decided in favor of the previous holders

July 22 More Emigrants their stock looks well as if grass had been plenty

July 23 More Emigrants They come in small companies on Mules no waggons have arrived yet

July 23 Worked for Whitfield since Wednesday have been hauling out to dry & havent washed any dirt yet but it prospects well with the pan *Sunday July 25th 1852*

The week has been verry warm during the day & the nights cool so a person could sleep comfortably under a couple of blankets passed the Day at the spring as it is the coolest most comfortable place in town as there is there no dust while up in Town the dust is continually blowing about by the winds which are verry regular during the day at this season

July 26 The Day is Hazy & smoky the woods have been on fire for some time which makes the smoke

July 27 As yesterday smoky etc One ox team came in today off the plains bringing one woman the first that has come in this way Also about 20 packers arrived to day They report the Emigration healthy and advancing rapidly & that grass was plenty on the way

July 28 The Day is cloudy more Emigrants on pack mules

July 29 As yesterday cloudy Two ox teams arrived to day Cattle look well

July 30 As yesterday cloudy the fires are visible from the Vally on some of the hills around

July 31 Clouds have disappeared the Atmosphere verry smokey 3 Ox Teams arrived & two women & some children

Some of the Rich claims in Soldiers Gulch were jumped & to day the rights of property was tried by a jury of Miners & decided in favor of previous holders *Sunday August The First 1852*

Have worked for Whitfield all week The weather has been verry warm in passing across the Valley we frequently feel hot flashes of the breeze which are verry unpleasant but of short duration   we have been washing dirt most of the week   Whitfield is a John Bull from the Borders of Scotland on the English side & has a head of his own and is honest to a cent   He dont pay any attention to the advice of the Miners and being Green at Mining himself we have not washed as much dirt as we might have done & the consequence is he is loosing Money so to day he turned off two hands & one cart   I being one of the hands   he paid me for my weeks work   24.00

Smith told me this morning that he had bought Slator out & wanted me to go into partnership with him as he owed 150 Dollars yet which he wanted to pay   so I bought ½ the house & bar for which I paid & am to pay   [300] 3000.00

He seems to be an honest well meaning Man & I think will be an honest partner   he has many friends here as I have learned from enquiry   I felt after leaving Whitfield verry much discouraged as by this time the Emigrants that have arrived have filled all the places where Men were wanted to work & at much lower wages than I like to work for   but the trade with Smith has set me all right again as I am to go to work for him tomorrow or with him for the work will be for both as it is the improvement of the place that we are going to work at

Monday August 2nd 1852

Went to work at leveling a place between the house & rock for a kitchen   Day fair & beautiful the winds having cleared away the smoke

Aug. 3   Commenced a wall of stone under the high side of the house which is built on pillars   the creek washes the base of the pillars so it is necessary to have a wall to keep it from washing down in the rainy season

Day cloudy though warm

Aug. 8   Finished the wall in two days & then put up the kitchen with clapboards & pine poles   The spring is to the west of the house about 20 feet   it has a large square box of timber to hold the water To the south of the house & about 10 feet from the west corner is a hole under the rock which is about 10 feet high & 8 feet across & of irregular shape this has about two feet of water in it which is so clear a(n) Man going in for the first time can't see it   this we call the cave it is a cool pleasant place   the kitchen is against the East side of this between the house & rock & is about 12 feet square   this makes things more comfortable   A number of Emigrants Teams & women have come in this week some of which are stopping here though a Majority go on to the plains   We have heard of the nomination of Scott & Graham & the whigs have formed a scott club   The Democrats are quiet & dont say much

Smith is candidate for county Assessor & the whigs here have appointed Delgates to a county convention to be held at the Hill & instructed the mto go for Smith for Assessor   They are greatly rejoicing over the Nomination of Scott & Graham   Several of the claims in Soldiers Gulch paid largely this week & this excited the cupidity of some who jumped some of the claims but a Miners meeting after considerable fuss decided in favor of the former holders

The weather has been clear & warm & the nights rather cool   Smith does not please me well   he wont work and I find he is rascally in playing cards which I dont like   however he appears honest in other Matters

Aug. 11   Smith went to the Hill to the convention Monday & returned this Morning   he was not nominated   he says he gave way for a friend of his that was a cripple though I cant more than ½ believe it   Another Smith came to me to day & wanted me to go with him to prospect a Gulch running into the South Branch ½ a mile above town & is the Gulch the Sacremento Road goes up   the hill in the Gulch is called Ballards humbug as a man by that name struck a good lead there & raised an excitement & some 30 or 40 holes were sunk & no more Gold was found[23]   The Democrat Electors & Congressional candidates speak to night here   they seem able men

Sunday August 15th 1852

The weather has been the past week during the day clear & warm & the nights are cool so 3 blankets are not uncomfortable   The Emigration is coming in rapidly at the rates of 10 to 20 waggons a day & every two or 3 waggons a family sometimes two or three

Many of them are stopping here & going to Mining so our town is now quite lively   I worked with Smith (2) in the claims in Ballards Humbug   Ballard had struck the lead we are working on and dug a large hole so he could run in with the cart   he had worked to a place where the lead had stopped & thought he had worked it out & quit it & when Smith prospected he sunk a hole above the big one in the Gulch & struck it again   we have made in the last 3 days apiece 32.00

The lead lies about 8 feet below the bed of the Gulch & is of irregular form about 2 foot square & is a red gravelly clay surrounded by what is here called ledge but is only clay   it is one side blue & the other yellow — the blue has sand & gravel but no Gold in it   the yellow has

neither sand gravel nor gold in it   we wash with a cradle in the big
hole that Ballard dug   there is no running water here now but some
seeps through the ground from a running spring above which sinks
before it reaches here   we use the same water all the time so it gets
verry thick with mud & carries some of the Gold with it as the gold is
tolerable fine   *Wednesday Aug 18th 1852*

The last 2 days we have made 27.00 apiece   the streak seems to
rise   we are following it by a small tunnel   I think from the manner
it rises that it will soon run out   The weather is fair & warm with cool
nights   a few more emigrants have come in   I have prospected some
of the loose black sand & gravel in the bed of the Gulch and find it will
pay well with plenty of water & a Tom   with a cradle we can make
about two dollars a day in it   I have bought 1 pr of boots at   4.00
& one pair of shoes at   2.00
& both have ripped in a few days   they were pegged   I just now
boug a pair of sewed shoes for which I paid   2.00
& I hope they will last awhile   I have also paid A F Smith on the
house since I bought it   125.00

Aug. 19   To day we sunk another hole higher up the Gulch & find
it is just on the end of the lead   the top dirt has prospected better
than below   we have here came to a slate Ledge   Bill Ryal my old
partner came over here last night   he says times are verry dull on
the other side the Mokelumne   scarcely any Mining going on

Aug. 20   Smith (2) went to Clinton prospecting to day & I worked
with Bill but the lead has run out   we only made $3.00 apiece   how-
ever I again found the lead had turned to our side & am going to see
where it goes to tomorrow

Saturday August 21st 1852

Bill Ryal left to day for Sonora   Smith & me followed the turn of
the lead & got $14.50   my half in dust was 7.25   was up town this
evening and a fight or ground scuffle between two Miners in which
neither whipped but both were some scratched & each had got his hair
well pulled   Emigrants coming more rapidly

Aug. 22   Played Poker last night & lost   6.00
& subscribed to help a sick man   1.00
Played this evening & lost   6.00
more   think I have bad luck & ought to quit

Aug. 24   Played Poker again last night & lost   6.50

Emigrants arriving hourly & mostly going on towards the Valley Bill Stewart & myself intend prospecting the big hole ballard dug as I want to see if I cant find the lead Smith & me was on   I hired an Irishman at 3.00 a day to work in my place with Stewart & Bill hired another Irish so they commenced cleaning out the hole this evening while I hunted for the lead Smith & me had lost as Smith has left the Diggings and gone to hunt better

Aug. 25   Stewart Bill & me worked in the big hole to day as the Irishman quit this morning   we hauled & washed all day & made only $2.00 & paid for the use of the Tom $2 & for the mule 2.00 & for hired help I paid $1.50 so I came out some looser as I made nothing while hunting the lead   *Saturday August 28th 1852*

Have been prospecting in different places but have not found anything   Stewart & me went up board Gulch to look at it to day but did not find a place we liked well enough to go to work in   we came back down the Road   Emigrants are coming in more rapidly than ever   the whole flat is now taken up with them   One family of 7 girls are now camped here   they are going on to the Valley of the Sacremento   The sun burn dust etc in crossing the plains makes them all look verry black & dirty about like a person would look after working in charcoal all day in June or July

Read some letters from home etc   Weather warm & clear

Aug. 29   Stayed about the spring all day & played poker some but neither made or lost anything

The Indians have been up in the Mountains attending their general gatherings & are now returning in squads of from 10 to 50   some are nearly naked while others are well dressed   a number of them have nothing but a shirt on   I see one big Indian who had on a shirt of fine Muslin & over that a satin Vest & British Military officers coat decked off with shells & beads & had his pants tied round his waist under his coat for a belt   he went through town this [way] which caused many to laugh   *Monday August 30th 1852*

Emigrants still coming and passing on towards the Valley   I commenced to day to build a Bathhouse on the opposite side of the spring from the house   went up on the ridge between the south & Middle branch of Sutter to cut poles for it   have already got the boards etc

Sept. 3   Still at work at the Bath house   I have begun to dislike Smith as he wont do any work at all

114   JOHN DOBLE'S JOURNAL

An Indian was shot for stealing by some Emigrants up the road 9 or 10 miles yesterday which has created a little stir among the Indians but not of any consequence   An Emigrant was taken up to day for trying to sell a horse he had picked up near here which belonged to a man in this town   he was let off with a fine

The Day has been cloudy & oppressively warm & sultry

Sept. 5   In removing stone bushes etc to make a place for the bath house I pulled up some of the poison oak & it being a hot day & I sweat verry much I got severly poisoned on my hand arms & feet & legs   the poison breaks out in large putrid sores and are verry painful

Played poked & lost   3.00

Emigration is on the increase

Sept. 6   Played poker & lost   1.50

Weather is clear & warm   Emigrants still coming

Tuesday Sept 7th 1852

Got up verry early this morning   felt verry well went to work & in an hour I took a pain in my back so severe I could not straighten it I had to lay idle all day on account of it   Smith went up the Emigrant road to day   when he returned he said he had got a woman engaged to come to live with him   she was an Emigrant & had parted from her husband after they crossed the plains   I immediately tried to sell to him as I dont want no woman in a house where I stay unless she be right but Smith could not buy me out so thus the Matter stands

Sept. 8   My back is yet verry painful so I cant yet straighten it Smiths woman did not come which I am glad of

A man by the name of Daily was killed on Chile Gulch this evening by a bank caving in   Chile Gulch puts into the south Branch about ¾ of a Mile from town   He was dead when taken from under the dirt which only caught his head which was entirely crushed

Sept. 12   The last two days felt verry well so I could work   last night after we went to bed we were aroused by what we thought was the scream of a woman but it as only a panther   after this I couldnt sleep so I put on my clothes & went up town & played poker all night lost   10.75

& to day I played again & won   1.50

the first I have won in California & I think the last for if I can resist the temptation I surely will from now henceforth & forever

Sept. 14   Still at work at the Bath house & will get it ready for use to day   I have discovered Smith has swindled me as there is a

Mortgage on the house although he says he can & will pay it off this week as he knows where he can get the money to do it with

Sept. 16 Weather still pleasant though the nights are some cooler A wedding was reported to have come off last night at the Ureka House which is a boarding house tavern etc so about dark a crowd had collected with tin pans dinner bells fiddles 2 or 3 key Bugles & some bars of steel & they cheveried the whole town they after some two hours were let into the house & drinked all the liquors & smoked all the cigars that the Man had The House is kept by a man by the name of Myers & he it was who was to be married to an orphan girl who had come across the plains this season with a widow woman they were both cooking at the house I was up to look at them awhile but did not stay long before I went to bed I heard the girl had backed out and that the wedding had not come off

Thursday Sept 16th 1852

There has been a couple of Emigrants sick at the house of Dr Morgan which stands just below the spring at the point of rock & in the forks of the creek one of them died last night he had the scurvy the other is nearly well The one that died was taken to the Graveyard by the New church & there buried This evening a woman just off the plains lodged a complaint before the squire here against a Negro for kicks licks & abuse on the plains and against her husband for permitting him to do so & encouraging him to do it The squire did not take hold of it but the Miners did They met heard both sides gave the Negro 50 lashes & divided the property between the husband and wife and ordered the husband to leave the wife which he did immediately taking his share of the property with him

Sept. 17 This evening the husband returned & has again joined his wife & they seem to be in quite good humor with each other again The Miners say the Negro may do as he pleases now for as much as they care Emigration still coming in rapidly A number of women have stopped here which makes the town look quite civilized Smith started to Hang Town to day as he said to buy a Ranch I am trying to sell him my part of the business as he is not the kind of Man I took him to be I am staying in the saloon til he returns Weather clear & pleasant

Sunday Sept 19th 1852

Smith returned this evening but said he had not bought the Ranch he went up on the flat to see some Emigrants so I did not say anything to him about the trade   I am determined to sell him my share of the business as I believe he spends all the Money he gets

Sept. 20   I pinned him close to the trade I offered & he gave me for my share   140.00
credited the balance on my note that he held & the balance in cash which was   5.00
The balance of my note being   135.00
so now I am clear of the business but I am afraid I will loose the house or the money I have paid on it besides the work I have done to improve the property & build the Bath house   unless he gets the Money to pay the Mortgage I am sure to lose it

Sept. 21   I feel easy about loosing the property as Smith has assured he he can get the money by going after it over to San Andreas

A large lot of stock passed through to day on their way to the Valley Emigrants still coming in rapidly

Sept. 22   I have been unwell for the last day or two   I would go to Mining if I was able but now I am not   I showed an Emigrant how to wash dirt & put him to work in Ballards Humbug to day   he found some gold

Sept. 23   Got a letter from F Hoop the first I ever got from him he is my brotherinlaw & I have frequently written to him   I feel verry bad yet   took some medicine last night

Saturday Sept 25th 1852

Hicks cattle passed through yesterday   they were 4000 in number & generally looked well   I feel some better to day but the poison on my hands & legs is no better   The weather has been warm during the Day & the nights getting cooler

Got a letter from Cap Reid in which he says he is going to the States to start the first of next Month   he says he is going to bring sheep across the plains next summer

I am again afraid I am going to loose my house as Smith has not got the Money yet to redeem it

Sept. 27   I am talking of trading my house or my share for a Ranch over on the head of Rancherie   so to day Slator & me went over there to look at it but I did not like the situation so I wont trade

I feel verry unwell yet   my feet and hands are verry sore from the poison   I am told it takes a long time to heal

Sept. 28   Smith Started to day over to San Andres to get that money   I agreed to stay here for him til he returned

Sept. 30   The Mountains are again on fire & the Atmosphere verry smoky & it is windy & cool   A lot of Emigrants passed through to day in which were 5 women   one Man & woman looked to be about 60 years old & looked as hardy as any of the young ones & they all seemed to be of one family   There was also a lot of sheep passed through to day   they looked well in fact better than any other stock I have seen that crossed the plains

Friday Oct The First

Since Smith has been gone the Bath house has not been patronized much as the weather is getting too cold

The Atmosphere is yet verry smoky   The Indians set fire to the grass at this season & follow up the fire and collect the grass hoppers bugs etc that are killed & roasted by the fire   I have seen them setting out the fire but I never saw them collecting the game killed by it   One thing I have not before mentioned they frequently wear small short pices of bone in a hole pierced through the division in the nose also in their ears but I have never seen one wear any rings of any kind yet I made a bargain with Doc Carpenter to day to go in partnership with him & put up a house in town   he is from Indiana near Greensborough in Henry County [He was a dentist.]

Oct. 2   Clouded up to day & rained this evening for the first this season   I am afraid Smith wont return   I find he owes considerable about town   more than he is worth considerable

Oct. 3   This morning verry cool the coldest weather I have seen in California   Smith returned to day but brought no money with him I am almost sure now that I will loose my ½ of the house   I find everything is Mortgaged even to his book & accounts   he talks verry fair yet so a person cant say anything harsh to him

Monday Oct 4th 1852

This Morning I agreed to give up my deed & let Smith make Slater a deed for the whole of the property   I know if I hold on to my deed the property wont sell for enough to pay the Mortgage & costs but by my giving up my deed and taking Smiths note for the 300 I have paid him I may have some chance to get at least a part for Slator promises that he will give me all he sells the property for over the 250 dollars & interest   that is the amount of the Mortgage   I took Smiths note for   290.00
& his cooking utensils for   10.00
making the 300   Doc Carpenter and I went up on the divide between

the Middle & South Branches to cut poles to build with   we cut all the poles only the sills & sleepers which we expect to get in town   we got back awhile after dinner   Smith has made Slator the Deed so now all the show I have for my money is in the sale of the house   The poison on my hands & arms & feet & legs is better   I am using sweet oil on the sores which seems to heal them verry fast   I have been unwell so long I have laid out all my money so now I have to go on tick if I get anything to eat   however I believe my credit is good Doc says he will do the most of the work on the house if I will furnish certain articles which I agreed to do   Weather cloudy with a little rain this evening & verry cool

Wednesday Oct 6th 1852

Went with Doc on the Mountain and cut the sills & sleepers for our house as we could not get the timber in town

Smith left to day   I dont know whether he will ever come back or not   he left his Books with me as Slator would not have them   they have a few not over good a/cs on them & maybe I will get some of my money back by them   I find he owes money to every Man in town who has a book & he has borrowed money from a good many

Oct. 8   We have been badly disappointed in getting our hauling done   as the Man we hired was already paid he was verry slow in doing the work so I have hired another Man & I went up today with the waggon & got a load of poles   set up the Most of last night in company with Doc Carpenter with a sick Man most of last night who is lieing at Myers Ureka house   This evening he had verry hard spasms & some think he wont recover

The weather is again most beautiful & not verry warm   The Emigration has ceased coming in   some come in yesterday morning report snow on the Mountains belly deep to a horse & more falling

Oct. 9   Got the Balance of our house timber down this evening Two drunk men took a knock down & one cut the other a little with a knife   weather pleasant

Sunday Oct 10th 1852

The Girl at Myers after having time to think over it concluded to take him for better or worse   so they were married and had a ball over it & danced all one night & now they are moving on the even tenor of their way again

I went up to the Office this evening & found a letter from Abe which contained verry sad news of the Death of my father   I will leave to those similarly situated to imagine my feelings as any words I can make use of will not describe my feelings   He died on the 12th of August so the letter informed me after nine days sickness

Oct. 12   Recd my trunk yesterday from the City with some presents from my Brother which are verry acceptable & I feel verry thankful to him for his kind consideration of my welfare

To day I mined some & made   .12

This I think is rather a slim chance

Oct. 13   Worked to day with Ben Owen near the head of the Ditch Which the Men quit after they had got into the Marble rock about 30 feet   they dug out a basin here some 20 feet in diameter but found nothing scarcely   a spring bulges up from the bottom of the basin that affords water enough the year round for a small town which runs down the Ditch   there are several men at work here who are making about 5 dollars pr day   We went into an old hole and commenced taking out the dirt when a Man at work above us came and told us we were on his claim and showed us his Stakes which he had stuck up Monday morning   I thought I had the best right as I had left my tools here on Friday last but I put up no stakes so we left [it] to some of the Miners who decided in favor of the other man   I was satisfied as the dirt did not pay verry well   we had taken out about 2 Cart loads which he said we might have   we couldnt get a Tom to wash it so we left it lieing there til we could get a Tom

Oct. 14   An Emigrant Train came in to day with 7 women with it they report the snow 5 feet deep on the Mountains   The last train that came in was said to be the last but it seems it was not   I went to work at the house to get it up before the rain comes   it is cloudy to day & looks like it was snowing on the Mountains   we have got the frame up & are putting on the weatherboarding   we buy the bolts in the woods and haul & rive them ourselves

Oct. 17   Have been at work steady at the house   Doc & I shaved to day   the first time for me since I have been in California   feel much better for it   The weather has been pleasant & the nights verry cool   so we were cold under 3 blankets   this is the coldest weather I have experienced in California although the days are pleasant

Sunday Oct 17th 1852

I have been sitting up with the sick man at Myers every other night but one   his name is Chas B Killmer   An elderly Lady has been his constant attendant during the day time ever since he has been sick

she has lately come to this country   Her name is Stowell   She has a
son here who is a reckless character who has killed one or two persons
& is now up in the Mountains collecting stock   we heard to day he
was killed by some Emigrants while trying to steal their stock   I
hope for his Mothers sake it is not true   she seems a woman of verry
tender feelings   her son has been here for two years & she came this
summer to see him   his name is Roderick Stowell   I heard to day
that Smith was at work on James Bar on the Moquolumne   I
intended to go down to the forks to day but did not get off

Oct. 20   I am still verry unwell but keep at work at the house & sit
up with Charly every other night as watchers are hard to get here &
I may be sick & want attention too   so I do all I can for him

Mining is verry dull here just now & a great many of the Miners are
leaving for other parts   The weather is yet fair & nights cool

Oct. 22   The days are getting cool   to day is so that an overcoat
is comfortable   last [night] there was a circle round the Moon which
is seldom seen in this country   cloudy this morning but cleared up
during the day

Saturday Night Oct 23 1852

Recd this evening news from home that grealty afflicts me as before
My Grandmother died the 2nd day of Sept   I can not write how
I feel

My Brother urges on me to go home but I fear I cant go

Oct. 24   Doc heat up the Bath to day and spent the day washing
clothes   I went up on Indian Gulch to wash the dirt we had taken
out there but could get no water   Charly Stewart came up to see
about some of his things he had left here   he gave me his Tom to use
til he called for it etc

Last night they had a ball at the house below the spring & this
morning a wedding & then went to Drytown for a wedding tour[27]

Oct. 25   To day the wedding party returned & to night they cheveried them as they did Myers   An Indian stole some Dust up the
south Branch and thy followed him down here caught him got the
Money from him & then gave him a chance to run for it & he made
good use of the chance   He was about the centre of town when he
started & the crowd followed hooping & yelling & scared him so he
could not run fast but nobody tried to overtake him so he got off

Oct. 27   Commenced our chimney to day   we are putting up a
stone fireplace to be topped out with mud & sticks

Cloudy & cool all day to day

Thursday October 28th 1852

Rained all day to day so we could not work at the chimney   so we
put in the floor & commenced the doors   Rod Stowel came into
Town to day contradicting by his appearance the report of his death
he is a small heavy set Man & looks to be verry good humored   this is
the first time I ever saw him although I have heard a deal of him

Oct. 29   Worked at the chimney & got it up to the arch   I went up
& put notices on the humbug Gulch as I intend to work there as soon
as there is water enough   Charley Kilmer has got much worse   he
[has] broken out all over the surface with large putride sores   I fear
he will not recover

Oct. 30   Set up with Charly last night   he seems some better   had
a Miners trial [in] the saloon to night in which neither party got what
they claimed but both seemed satisfied   The Days are warm & the
nights cool   after the rain there was a thick white frost

Oct. 31   Started early this morning and went down to the forks of
the Mokelumne   all the River companies had quit work as the water
had risen so they could do no more   in the River some Chinamen
were at work on the Bars   The Mokelumne Hill Water Company
that is taking the south fork in a flume to the Hill have got their
flume built below the forks   I came back by 3 o clock & found the
Doc complaining of being sick

Weather clear & pleasant

Monday November The First 1852

Got the chimney nearly completed   Doc is not able to work   some
preparation is making for the Election which comes off tomorrow

Nov. 2   Charly Killmer Died last night & had a funeral preached
today and was buried at the church on the hill   a collection was made
for to pay the expenses of the burial   The Election came off without
much ado only some loud Hurras for Scott & Graham   I went up &
Voted for Pierce & King & said nothing about it   The Whigs have had
a flag up here for the last Month & doing all thy could for their
candidates

Nov. 3   A young man died last night at Gemmills & was buried
to day

Got some letters from Ab urging me to go home but I cant go til my
debts are paid which are now about   100.00

Heard to night that Rod Stowel had shot a Man last night at Fort
Ana [Ann] on Dry creek about 4 miles from here

Nov. 4   Got the Front door up to day and to night moved in   Doc is yet unable to work though he still moves round a little   This evening the Town has been full of people called in for the purpose of taking into consideration the case of Rod Stowell   Rod came in last night badly wounded him self & is now lieing at the National Hotel (which is opposite our house)   His Mother whom I pity is attending him   There are none of the Miners who seem to have any sympathy for Rod but all pity his poor Mother   The Miners collected at the National called a Mr Whitmore to the chair & proceeded to examine the evidence in the case   there was but one witiness besides one of the parties interested who was a Brother to the wounded man   from their evidence Rod was much to blame   Rod has been up in the Mountains buying stock & keeping a store on the Emigrant Road having purchased several cattle   he brought them down to a Ranch 3 miles from here kept by a Mr Flint[24]   The fray came about in this Manner   one of Rods Steers escaped from the Ranch & was taken up by one of the Brothers (their names was Cairn & the one that had the steer is not wounded) and kept some 16 days   In the Mean time Flint made search but did not find the steer until last Monday   he wanted Cairn to give up the steer without any compensation for his trouble as he could get no more than the Ranch fees   this Cairn refused to do & demanded pay for his trouble   Flint then left him making some threats   Then yesterday Rod & Flint went over to Dry creek & (The steer was tied out on some grass near the camp of the Cairns) cut the steer loose & Flint immediately drove him off towards the Ranch informing the Brothers who were then coming up that there pointing to Rod was the owner of the Steer   Flint then left with the steer while Rod remained to talk with the Cairns but a few words passed when Rod drew his Bowie knife & made a pass a one of the

Rod Stowells Trial
Thursday Nov 4th 1852

brothers   the knife struck just between the 4th & 5th rib & passed through cutting the lights in its course & came out just below the 5th rib near the backbone   Rod was then drawing to strike again when the other Brother caught his arm & took the knife from him cutting his (Cairns) hand severly in doing so   Rod immediately drew his Revolver when the Brother that had the knife sprang behind a tree & Rod fired at the wounded who had fell   the ball striking him in the side below the knife wound & passed through in nearly the same direction

Rod then supposing he had done enough left while The Brother & the other witness carried the wounded Man home & came after a Doctor There was none who had seen any other arms than those Rod had nor none heard any other shooting but the one shot that Rod fired so it is generally believed that he shot himself to justify the deed he had done   I have here given the nature of the wounds with the evidence   but I have written it as I recollect from the Doctors statement before the Meeting or to the Meeting   There is two Doctors tending on Rod who both stated to the meeting that his wound was such that if they attempted to move him it would be almost certain death but this at first made but little impression on the meeting They continued to call for justice regardless of his wounds and a majority seemed in favor of hanging him immediately   The Esquire came in & read a passage of the Law which took him some time as thir cries of *justice Give* us *Miners law* ....*Dam* the *Civil* law &c &c men frequently repeated during the reading   at length he finished & after commanding them in the name of the people and State of California to disperse he left the room   They continued to talk and speeches were made on both sides & at length a guard of 12 was appointed from among the Miners & the meeting adjourned until Rod should be able to come before a court or meeting   just as they were breaking up a report came in that Cairn was dead (The Doctor had pronounced the case hopeless)   It was the Misery in which Rods Mother was that worked on their feeling enough to give him a little time to recover

During last night some Men came up from Sacremento & reported the City in ashes   also one man came in town and brought all the Flour up & immediately put it up to 40c pr lb   it had been selling at 18 & 19c previous   provision raised verry high on the recd of the news

Nov. 5 Doc is getting worse   he has gone to bed & to taking Medicine   Carpenter tools are verry scarce & I have a deal of trouble to get tools to make the other door & tables &c &c   however after considerable search I have found some planes & will now finish the house out & out if Doc dont get too sick

Friday Nov 5th 1852

The report of Cairns death was false although he had fainted so they thought him dead   some of his friends have been all the forenoon warning the Miners to meet here again to night so about noon they again began to collect & by 3 there was a large crowd collected   about

4 they collected (at the call of a bell ringer) in front of the National Organized appointed a President & proceeded to appoint a jury of Miners to try the case   Thereupon a Man got up & warned them that the sheriff was by & would take the name & arrest hereafter all who took part in the unlawful proceeding   but this had no affect   they began to appoint jurors & out of 25 who were called on by the Meeting but four would consent to serve   some were foreigners who had become Naturalized Citizens & had taken the oath of alligience & could not serve on a jury that was got up against law   some were lawyers & had taken the oath to support the constitution & could not serve against that oath (and some) & some felt that as nobody was yet dead & that the prisoner (who was now in the custody of the sheriff) being unable to move himself much less come before a court to be tried they could not serve on the jury   It began to grow dark when the sheriff in a speech said he would guard the prisoner & he should have a trial Sunday if they would disperse   they thereupon with a deal of grumbling adjourned the Meeting *sine die* & the sheriff summoned a guard of 24 men & placed 12 on duty to be relieved every 12 hours until the trial

Nov. 6   I made a table to day & then quit as Doc cant stand the noise   he is growing worse

The Town is quiet to day   the guard keeping watch over Rod are loitering about doing nothing hardly even staying about the prisoner

Nov. 7   When Slator got a deed for the spring Saloon he permitted me to stay there until I finished our house   so to day he came up from the City where he is stopped and I delivered the house into his charge

The Miners again collected in large numbers & were called to a Meeting by the Bell ringer   when as before they could not get a jury speeches were made but all on Rods side   They at length again adjourned *sine die* & concluded to leave it to the Civil Authorities to conduct through

The Civil Authorities commenced an examination of the evidence

Ben Owen & me went up & washed out what dirt we had taken out on Indian flat and got only $4.00   they are still at work there throwing up the dirt in piles to wash when water comes

Nov. 8   Doc is still worse   he seems to have scarcely any fever I think it is the Mountain fever working on him as he had a spell of it crossing the plains   The Mountain fever is a low kind of fever making a person sick all over & weak without much apparent fever

Monday Nov 8th 1852

The Authorities finished the examination of the Murder Case & bound Rod over to appear at the next court of Sessions at Mokelumne Hill   he is to be removed as soon as he is able to leave the jail as no bail is taken

Ben Owen & me worked part of the day in Ballards Humbug Gulch & made   2.25
I could not work all the time as I had to attend on Doc   he has called on another physician who is prescribing for him & I give him the Medicine

Nov. 9   The weather has been clear & pleasant until now   This Morning is cloudy but not any cooler   I hauled a couple of cart loads of wood & just as I quit it commenced raining & rained all day

Doc seems some better to day

Nov. 10   Cleared off after sun up & the [day] was clear & beautiful Ben Owen is gone   I suppose to the City   I worked by myself to day in the Humbug & made   3.75
I intened to work here until I work it out or the Gold runs out   Doc is better so I could leave him most of the day.

Nov. 11   I went to work & made only in ½ the day   .75
The Morning cloudy   commenced raining about noon & rained the balance of the day   Doc seemed better all day but this evening he is verry sick at the Stomache & is in considerable pain all over   his mouth is verry dry & the skin is cracked & so sore he can scarcely talk I suppose he has a deal of inward fever

Friday Nov 12th 1852

This Morning a heavy fog is settled on the flat   it is so thick we cant see across the street   Worked to day & made   3.25
got my feet wet & were cold all day so to night the Rheumatic pains trouble me a little   Doc is no better   he seems in great misery but cant tell if the pains are in any one locality   The disease seems generally scattered through the system   The Doctor thinks it is from inaction of the liver so he has commenced giving him colomel & oil

For the last two nights he has slept scarcely any & has eat nothing for several days

Nov. 13   Went up & threw off some dirt this Morning but did not wash any as I had to stay with Doc   he seems some worse to day   I am still giving him Medicine

The Day is cloudy

Nov. 14 Rained last night & to day steady til about 3 when it ceased with a high wind for an hour or so   evening cloudy

Doc was some better this morning but is as bad as before this evening

His Medicine does not seem to operate verry well

Nov. 15 Gave Doc a heavy dose of Colomel last night which has done some good as he seems a little better

Rained all day very hard so I had to stay in the house   I put in the time writing up this journal   I felt very unwell all day   I am up late giving Doc Medicine & it is still raining very hard   I think the rainy season or spell has set in   if it has is earlier than common

Tuesday November 16th 1852

This Morning a heavy fog was settled on the flat which went off with a shower of rain about 8-o clock   I went up the south Branch & chopped some wood & got a team & hauled it this evening   I got a little wet and lifted pretty hard to get the wood into the waggon so I feel verry tired & have strained my back which is painful   cloudy all day however the sun shown awhile this evening   Doc has taken another dose of colomel & seems better this evening   The weather is a little cooler

The price of lumber has gone up to 30 & 40c pr foot on account of the burning of the City   every waggon goes down now loaded with lumber & furniture   some men here who have plank houses are tearings them down & hauling them to the City & all the Miners that could leave have gone to the City   Mining in Soldiers Gulch is done for the season   the banks are caving in & the holes are full of water They have tried every kind of pump here that they could make or get but none have been sufficient to keep out the water

Thy have a Steam pump going for the last month which kept the water out awhile but it has been stopped for some time as it would not answer the purpose   They had two horse pumps in operation with an endless chain water lifter but they like the others soon gave out

Tuesday Night 10-o-clock Nov 16th 1852

Doc seems some better to night though I am still giving him medicine which now seems to take good effect

I have now written this journal from my notebook & Memory up to this time & just now got up   from now on while I can keep this with me I will write each day as it passes

A few remarks & I am done for to night   Rod Stowel is yet lying at the Hotel in a critical state so the Doctors say   While Cairns is some better but in a verry critical situation yet

The Roads are now verry muddy which is uncomfortable & what is not seen in the California Mountains more than once a year & sometimes not that

My Brother has written twice to me wanting me to go home   I would go if I was out of debt but as it is I cant go now although he offers me all the Money I may want

I feel like one of us ought to go as no others could see to some of Fathers business as well as one of us   I have urged him to go but he says he would make too great a sacrifice to go now so he cant go   I will mine a week or two and if I can pay up & come out even I will go that is if Doc gets so I can leave him to go to my work

If I leave the house there are none here to Minister to his wants so as long as he is not able to help himself I shall stay by him

Wednesday Nov 17th 1852

Doc seems some better this Morning   his Medicine seems to have a good effect   This morning a heavy fog was on the flat & a heavy white frost both of which were soon scattered by the sun which rose clear & the Day is clear but not verry warm though pleasant   I went to the office this evening & got a letter from A enclosing one from Liz She says M Wright of Shellyville has administered on the Estate   if so I dont think it necessary for either of us to go home   Abe thinks that Wright will do what is right so do I   I worked to day & made this afternoon   2.25
I threw off top dirt & waited on Doc in the forenoon who is about the same This evening   A number of Miners have prospected around the Gulch I am at work in & some have gone to work to day but the water has rundown so but one Tom can do anything there now

Wind raised at sundown & blew up cloudy   It is now Ten or Eleven o-clock   I have been in bed but not asleep   I have not been well to day   My bones are in misery with Rheumatic pains caused from being in the water all day as I have been to day & my boots get damped through & keep my feet cold all day   The wind has been high so far to night & several light showers of rain & now it is beginning to rain steady

Thursday Nov 18th 1852

About Midnight the wind rose to a gale   blew the top of our chimney off   was awake til the wind settled   rained all the time while I was awake

This Morning Doc is some better   Rained all day   I stayed in the house as I am not verry well   took some Medicine last night which has rather weakened me   this evening Doc is about the same his fever increases while the general debility lessens

I am holding 3 claims in The Humbug Gulch one for Ben Owen one for Doc & one for myself   Ben Owen being gone & the Miners wanting claims I am afraid I cant hold them much longer so I told a Friend by name H Bledsoe to join me & take Bens claim which he agreed to do as soon as the rain ceased

Nov. 19   This Morning cloudy with a heavy fog which cleared away about 5 of the clock   It has been a Moderately cool day with scattering clouds & Ditto Sun shine   I found my hole full of water this Morning & got my feet wet so I have had all day & have now the rheumatic pains slightly   I have not washed as much dirt to day as I have other days but it is richer   I made   4.50 to day which is better than before   Bledsoe came & looked at the claim but did not go to work for what reason I dont know   The Doc is much better   he has eat a ½ pint of milk & bread more than for any one time for two weeks

Saturday Nov 20th 1852

Worked to day a little more and harder than usual but only made 3.25

H Bledsoe did not go to work   another Man by name of Taylor took the claim & he is to go to work on Tuesday or Wednesday next as he is going to hangtown tomorrow

Doc seems better   has eat 3 times to day which is more than since he got sick   This Morning was clear & a heavy white frost which made it rather uncomfortable handling the tools as I commenced early

The Day was clear but not verry warm though comfortable & the evening is cloudy or clouding up   I wrote a letter to Liz last night urging her to come to California & one to Ab telling him I cant go home this year no how

Having oiled my boots last night my feet have been dry to day so I am not in so much pain as I have before been

Nov. 11   Went early & borrowed a gun to kill Doc some quails & got up on the hill west of town & among a flock of them & could not get the gun to go off so I returned it & went to work   [even] if it was sunday & made   1.60 & quit at noon   This Morning was cloudy begun to rain at noon and continued raining hard til night when the wind raised cold & raw & the rain almost ceased but is yet at 8 falling a little   the evening is the coldest I have seen in California   Doc is getting better

Monday November 22nd 1852

Chopped some wood this Morning and got a little wet   There was a heavy fog in the forenoon with continual light rain & it rained most of last night   I went to work after dinner in my claim but it was still raining lightly so I worked at a table which I nearly completed   The sun shown awhile in the evening but only for a few minutes   It is cloudy & threatening to night & I expect will rain during the night Doc is much better   he sit up some time to day & eat some hare with the broth   I think he will now get along well   this is the first he has eaten of any consequence or sit up for some time

The Acorn crop this year is verry short in this part of the country so the Indians have been up in the Mountains where they are plenties storeing them up   they have been passing either way in large companies now for some time   they have been stealing considerable lately one place or another & several have been wounded while thieving & some have been killed which has rather irritated the tribes in this vicinity though no serious trouble is apprehended from them

Nov. 23 Verry cloudy this Morning   commenced raining about 8-o clock & continued til 12 when it ceased for a while & rained by showers during the evening & I worked in the rain throwing off top dirt   evening cool & the sun set clear & high cool clouds

Wednesday Nov 24th 1852

Cleared away early last night & was verry cold   This morning a heavy frost is on the Earth   ice in many places ¼ inch thick & the ground froze over the top ½ an inch   worked all day made   3.15 A man went to work with me this Morning but concluded it wouldnt pay so he quit   Doc is much better   A bell ringer went through Town to night announcing a popular preacher to preach at the Meeting house to night   I did not go   I hear this evening of Websters death also Cairns is slowly Mending and the Doctor thinks now he will recover   Rod is mending slowly

Nov. 25 This Morning clear & frosty   the ground is froze over the top

Worked harder than usual to day made   3.25 only if I could find other and better diggings I would leave the Humbug Gulch sure   Doc is Mending slowly   Day clear & pleasant

The water is now verry cold so that my hands are benumbed every time I wash a pan of dirt & the cold weather has dried up the skin so they are verry much chopped & cracked open & are verry painful whenever they are dry

Nov. 26   Morning cool & frosty but not so cold as the two last Made to day   2.12

threw off top dirt part of the day   Doc is slowly Mending   The Day is verry pleasant & evening begin to look muddy & cloudy

Saturday Nov 27th 1852

This morning a light white frost   The Atmosphere is Hazy & thick & pleasantly cool   stripped off top dirt in the forenoon & washed dirt all the afternoon & made only   1.12

The Day is Hazy & the air feels damp   evening cloudy   The Dirt in my claim has slightly changed   the Gravel is now finer & looser & the Gold scarcer   I am much discouraged with it & will leave it if I can find any place that will prospect better

Nov. 28   Rained during last night & most of the day to day   so I was in the house reading most of the Day   Doc is still on the Mend

Nov. 29   Rained During the night & this Morning it is raining verry hard with heavy gusts of wind & the Atmosphere is some cooler Rained all day & harder than it has rained before   I went up to the claim after dinner & got wet   I cut a small ditch to drain the big hole that Ballard dug   I feel rather gloomy as I am out of Money in debt & not working any to get out of debt though I have good hopes that I will make enough out of My claim to pay all I owe   god send I may

Nov. 30   Rained Most of the night verry hard   ceased this morning for awhile   after Breakfast I got a load of wood hauled & then worked Most of the day in the claim & only made 1.37   Showery During the day & to night is raining hard again   I got wet while at work

Wednesday Dec the First 1852

Rained but little during the night   this morning raining lightly I went with Herman (an Emigrant of this season) up the Jackass Gulch & prospected & then took up a Tom & washed some in the afternoon   we only made apiece   .50

Rained lightly most of the day   I got verry wet & have a slight rehumatism   This evening is verry cool   some snow fell during the evening

Dec. 2   Rained but little during the night   I went up to Jackass Gulch and found the water had run off so that there was not enough to work with   so I took my tools & went to my claim in the Humbug with Herman   we worked all day and only made for each   1.75

Rained in showers all day so we got verry wet which now feels uncomfortable   The winds are high this evening & the rain has ceased & the Atmosphere is cooler   Doc is able to be up most of the time

Dec. 3   Cloudy all day & tolerable cool

Worked alone in my claim & made but little gold but did not weigh it   The Ledge I am working on now is sinking so that I have now 4 feet of wash dirt but the gold gets scarce as it sinks   It appears to be on the rise again   I am skinning off some to day which will bring me near the lead I worked last summer where I expect to make good wages &c

Saturday Dec 4th 1852

Rained during the after part of the night in Torrents & continued until noon to day though not so hard   it then ceased & the sun shone out   I went to work but it soon commenced raining again & I quit I made $1.12 & yesterday $1.62 making 2.75   continued raining steady til night

Many of the houses in town are built on the ground & the continual hauling of dirt out of Soldiers Gulch has raised the Streets so the water has flooded several of the houses   The creek is verry high covering the Road for some distance   Mining is generally verry dull

Dec. 5   Rained During the night and ceased at daylight   I went with a Yankee up the Jackass Gulch & worked about 3 hours & made for each   2.37

We quit at noon   The day is partially cloudy & cool   Evening clear   The creek has went down til the road is again clear of water but the Mud is verry deep   several cattle carts & a waggon mired down during the day to day

The Evening appears as if we would have a heavy frost to night

Dec. 10   The Weather has been verry variable this week   Cool warm clear & cloudy & this evening it commenced raining just at night I have been at work steady & have made since Sunday   26.25 & lost the Most of to day   Yesterday a companion across the plains of the Doctors came into town & has went to living with us   his name is James A Troutman[25] & he is from Cap country Ind   he bought plank yesterday & I made a Tom last night and to day   I own ½ the Tom for making it   Docs Mind has been verry unsettled & to day he eat verry heartily and to night he got verry crazy after supper & continued raving til a late hour   We gave him an Emetic but it seems to do him but little good   Got him to bed after Midnight   J A Troutman & I were summoned to attend as juryman tomorrow nine o clock at the Volcano House   At Midnight the rain ceased & seems to be clearing away

Dec. 11   Doc seems some better this morning though he seems somewhat deranged yet   This Morning a heavy fog was settled on the flat which cleared away about nine & the day is beautiful   Jim remained with Doc & I attended at the Volcano House as a juryman & excused Jim to the Court which was held by a Deputy Constable The case was a rights of property trial & kept us all day listening to the lawyers witnesses &c

A jurymans pay which I got was 1.00 & I divided with Jim as he had staid with the Doc   The House which was one of the Bars & gambling houses in town & the dispute was between one of 3 Mortga-gees & a purchaser who had a bill of sale   decided in favor of Mortgagee

Sunday Dec 12th 1852

Sunday being the day in California for all sales Meetings & any thing to call togather the Miners   to day the Bakery & all in it was sold at public Auction   the owners are preparing to go home   the sale was but slimly attended & property went low   The house oven stables & lot went at $562.50   being about one fourth of the cost Doc is better

Day clear & pleasant

Dec. 14   Yesterday I made 6.12 & to day about 50c   This Morning clouded up   there is a heavy white frost on the Earth & cold winds astir   commenced snowing about 11-o clock & snowed hard all the balance of the day with high cold winds   we staid in the house   Jim split his riffle box so I mad a new one to day   The snow melted off nearly as fast as it fell   Doc is mending slowly

Dec. 15   Was clear during the night & froze hard so as to bear a Man   the morning cold & frosty   clouded up at sunup & commenced snowing again about 11 & continued snowing all day but slowly   so there is to night about 3 inches of snow on the ground   the weather has moderated some & is not so cold to night as this morning   I worked awhile during the day & made   2.50

The water is verry cold & my hands are verry sore so that it is a disagreeable business working in the water

Thursday Dec 16th 1852

Appears to have snowed all night   the snow is about 8 inches deep & is damp and sloppy under it on the ground, commenced raining just after daylight & continued raining a light drizzly rain all day and the snow is gradually decreasing   the atmosphere is verry cool   some hunters report the snow 3 feet deep on the hills around here   Jim & I went up and dug a ditch around our claims so as to keep the flood from washing the dirt into our holes

The Oldest inhabitants here say such a winter as this is but seldom seen here

Dec. 17   Rained all Night verry hard   this morning the snow is reduced to about 2 inches deep and the streets are flooded   the creek covers the road for a hundred yards more or less   the rain continued heavy all day without any intermission & verry hard   the bridge across the creek is about going   the snow is all gone off the flat but is yet thick apparently on the hills   the creek is still rising & the rain falling hard   Flour has risen to 37½c pr lb to other provision in proportion   Doc is still mending

Dec. 18   Rained all night verry hard & is still raining hard   I went out after breakfast & looked at the creek which is now about 100 yards wide   that part of the bridge (which is built across both forks at their junction) across the North fork is gone & the rest is shaken some   several of the large toms are also washed away causing considerable loss to the owners   Rained without intermission all day & some hard winds blew in the forenoon

Sunday Dec 19th 1852

Appears to have rained verry hard all night   ceased at daylight & looked like clearing off   but continued all day with light showers high winds and occasional spells of sunshine   The Water is running off verry fast   the creek fell during the day some 2 feet   Jim & I went up Jackass Gulch in the forenoon and after dinner crossed the creek & went to our claims & found the water had been so high it moved our Tom & washed our holes full of dirt and buried Jims pick & shovel so we could not find them

Times look gloomy   provision verry high & a prospect of an increase in price and so much water we cant make much   The Bridges are all washed away so goods can not be got from the City   The snow is yet laying in spots on the hills around   snowed a heavy shower just before night & again covered the hills & at dark commenced raining hard with occasional showers of hail & cold winds   Ceased raining & hailing about 9 PM

Dec. 20   Got up this morning about 2 hours before day   it is perfectly clear at least there is no cloud visible   light cold & sharp breezes are blowing & the Morning is cool   Jim & I or we went up to Jackass & worked til 10 o clock & the owner of the Tom came and took it so we quit   we made each   .93
After dinner we went up fixed for working in Humbug   my claim I cant work for the water so I will work with Jim   Day clear & pleasant

Tuesday Dec 21st 1852

Clouded up during the night and commenced snowing at daylight snowed til noon then turned to rain & rained til night   we worked til noon & got wet & made for each 1.25 & then quit for the day   the creek has fell within its banks again but has left marks of its violence all along the flat   A cabin up the Middle Branch was robbed by the Indians this evening but the robbers were not found

Dec. 22   Snowed all during the night & the snow is about an inch deep this morning   snowed til about 1 PM when it ceased & partially cleared off   but clouded & began snowing again at night   we made for each 3.18 by working most of the day   The snow melts faster than it falls so there is none on the flat though the hills are covered   some hail to night   the creek is again low

Dec. 23   Snowed during the night and is snowing this morning snowed til about 3 PM then turned to rain & rained til night   we worked most of the day & made for each 1.62 & got wet   The snow & rain is occasionally hail but not much at a time   The Atmosphere is verry cool and the wind is rising to night   Flour has risen to 45c Butter 75   Pork 40c   Lard 40c   Candles 75   Meal none in market   hard bread 40c   Soda crackers 50c   Clothing Blankets etc etc has risen in proportion   hard times

Friday Dec 24th 1852

Snowed til 12 & ceased awhile then snowed & hailed by spells all evening & melted off as fast as it fell   about sundown commenced snowing verry hard & by dark 2 inches of snow lay on the mud & is still snowing to night   we worked all day and made for each .25½

Meal has risen to 30c pr lb   no flour in Market scarcely   the Bakery has stopped for want of Flour   where we are now working the(y) pay dirt is about 5 feet deep & the gold verry fine   we are working in the claim below & adjoining mine in the Humbug Gulch so the Ledge is the same I have before described

Dec. 25   Snowed during the night & is about 4 inches deep this morning & heavy and damp and a light drizzling rain falling   We went up & worked about an hour and made for each   .56

The rain continued all day with an occasional shower of snow & is raining to night verry hard by spells   Flour has took an additional rise to 50c pr lb

Dec. 26   Seems to have snowed all night & the snow is about 8 inches deep & is still snowing hard   continued til noon & then ceased & began clearing off & the sun set clear   Jim & I went up & brought our Tom home in order to go to work up in a side Gulch of Soldiers Gulch   in the afternoon we went up & looked out a place to work & I hired to a man to work the evening for 2.00

Sunday Dec 26th 1852

We concluded to go to work to morrow in the side Gulch   The Man I worked for made about $8.00   Last Sunday a man in Liquor attempted to cross the creek & fell in & was carried down by the current & was drowned & his body is not yet found   The banks along Soldiers Gulch are falling to a great extent   the Graveyard which was about 200 feet square has most all fallen in also   in front of Town a bout 200 feet of the hill has slid in also   several other places of from 100 to 150 feet have slid in   Provision is getting verry scarce in town Lard is now 50c pr lb   Pork the same & Ham is 65c pr lb   several roofs have fell in in town by the weight of the snow because they were not well tied togather

Dec. 27   Morning clear & cold & frosty   a hard crust on the snow & the ground froze so as to bear a Man   The day is foggy or Hazy but seems clear of clouds   We took our Tom up & prospected the side Gulch in two places but did not find much   we moved to the Creek by the saloon after dinner & worked awhile but did not get much gold we went up & looked at the grave yard   3 or 4 coffins are sticking out of the bank & one I saw was lieing on the ground that had fallen in entirely uncovered that is lieing bottom upwards on the ground that has slid in   I havent heard any thing said about fixing it up

Tuesday Dec 28th 1852

Rained during the night & all day by spells   we worked awhile and made yesterday & to day for each   3.68
The snow is slowly melting & the creek is rising rapidly   we worked to day on the creek by the saloon & got verry wet   Flour has risen to 80c pr lb & other provision in proportion

Dec. 29   Rained during the night & all day by hard showers & close togather   the snow is about all off & the creek is again high & it is yet raining hard to night   Jim & me chopped a load of wood & got verry wet   the rain is verry cold & uncomfortable

Dec. 30   Arose early (the rain had ceased during the night) & by daylight struck out to find something to pay for grub as we are out of money & had nothing for breakfast but boiled potatoes with seasoning   we went to the creek and found the water so high we could do nothing   we then started to the Humbug Gulch and a slight fear in crossing the footlog turned us back & we went up Jackass Gulch but found no Tom there that we could get as we expected to do   so we came back & borrowed a Tom (ours being so heavy we did not want to pack it) & went up the side Gulch in which we prospected the other day & worked all the balance of the day & made 31 [3] oz being for each 15.82½   commenced raining again to night just before dark

Friday Dec the Last Day

Rained verry hard during the night & in hard showers til noon when it ceased for the day   We worked in the side Gulch as yesterday & done well but did not weigh our Gold   The place where we are now at work is different from any place I have ever worked   it is near the head of the Gulch   the dirt will average 2 feet on the ledge   the top is a loose light loam & as it nears the ledge it grows more solid but solidest part is verry loose compared with any pay dirt I have ever seen   The ledge is a rough blue slate   In the dirt there is no gravel or stone except the slate & is the first place I have seen where there is no Quartz gravel   The Gold is coarse & verry smooth solid & heavy & looks most beautiful when in the water   The Creek is again falling but slowly   last night a man living one mile out on the Sacremento Road by name Sal Elsie a scotchman being drunk started to cross the creek & has not been seen or heard from since & is supposed to be drowned[26]   another man fell in yesterday & was rescued by the exertions of an Irishman by name of Owen   Provisions are still rising Potatoes have risen to 20c & many other things in proportion   This evening is verry cloudy but it not raining any and I hope it will stop a while

Saturday January The First 1853

Cloudy all day   Sun set clear & red   The clouds were light & wavy though thick enough to hide the sun   We done about as well as usual weighed & sold a part of our dust keeping out the largest pieces we had each 21.40 of what we sold   The water is running down verry fast   this evening there was hardly enough to run our Tom

As a general thing when I have before worked the gold is settled in the Ledge but here it seems to be generally distributed through the dirt the loose top dirt pays nearly as well as that near the ledge & the ledge is verry much crumbled on the top & verry rough

Jan. 2 Went to work as usual & worked about 3 hours & made for each 3.87
Then went up & looked at our claims on Ballards Humbug then came back by the Spring Saloon & I got the scales I used to have there so we weighed our coarse gold that we had kept out & we had each 8.20

Jim then wishing to write I went up to our claim in the side Gulch & worked about two hours & made 7.25

Some men are cutting a ditch to drain the creek from the mouth of the Canon up to the Saloon I am trying to hold a claim in it but I am afraid I cant The water in the side Gulch is now too low to run a Tom so we will have to work somewhere else til it rains again The day is clear & verry warm & the sky looks a little Hazy

Monday Jan 3 1853

Carried our Tom to the creek but could not go to work as other claimants had taken up all the ground We then went up the side Gulch and went to work worked the day & made for each 4.00

The water is verry low there being not much more than will run a cradl

The day is clear & warm Flour yesterday had fell to 60c & a still farther decrease was expected This evening late Flour is offered at 55 but has no demand Doc commenced Mining to day for the first time since we have been togather

Jan. 4 Worked in the side Gulch & made 7.05 apiece & Doc made $1.80 Day clear & warm Flour is now offering at 45c and in no demand Potatoes 18c dry bread 50c This evening some clouds in the west and look & feels like rain

Jan. 5 Commenced raining just before day & rained about 2 hours we bought 50 lbs of Flour at 45c pr lb the first we have had for some time having lived on potatoes etcetera in the Mean time we put out in the rain & borrowed a tent & carried it up & put it up to work under & by the time we got it up it ceased raining so we could not work for want of water after dinner we went up to our old claims & worked an hour or two we made but little cloudy & cool all day They are removing the dead from grave yard hill to the graveyard on church Hill all the graves on the hill has caved in & some of the coffins are covered up so they cant be found and some of them are split one was so broken they had to make a new one

Thursday Jan 6th 1853

Rained during the night & by spells all day   we got to work early
& had more water than when we quit work yesterday but scarcely
enough to do good work   we put up the tent which kept the rain off
so we worked all day & with the little of yesterday made 15.93 apiece
Doc is sick to day with diarrhea caused from overeating   The clouds
appear to be breaking away to night   There is no others working on
the Gulch with us for want of water except 2 men who are at work
near us

Jan. 7 Morning Cloudy—worked as usual   Commenced raining
about noon & rained til night   we made in the day for each   13.95

To Night the wind is verry high & cool & rain still falling   Doc
worked while it wasnt raining & made $1.80

Jan. 8 Rained all night & all day   we worked all day   the tent
kept the rain off us   we made all day for each of us   4.31
Showing the dirt is not so rich as before   The water is flush there
being now about enough in the Gulch to run 3 Toms   Flour has risen
again to 50c   The Creek is again rising rapidly &c &c

Jan. 9 Heavy fogs in the forenoon and cloudy all day   I made
about .75 by working ½ an hour   this evening it looks like clearing
off   Flour is now selling at 50c & corn Meal at 45c and potatoes 18c
Soda crackers 65c   Butter 1.00

Jan. 10 Clear during the night & cloudy all day with some rain
Made to day for each 21.25   we worked out a hole in the ledge about
18 inches deep which had the gold in

Tuesday Jan 11th 1853

Cleared off last night   a heavy fog on the flat   this morning day
clear and pleasant   worked all day & made 4.10   we think our claim
is about run out   evening begins to look cloudy like rain again   Doc
is out late   he went to chop wood this Morning & has no came back
we are uneasy about him   8-o-clock he is just come in

Jan. 12 Rained heavy during the night but ceased before day
Forenoon cloudy with high loose white fringed floating clouds   afternoon clear & pleasant   We worked in the side Gulch the forenoon
the water there failed so much we could not make enough to pay us
to work there any longer as we have worked out the rich lead we were
on   we went in the afternoon & worked in the Humbug & made 13.81
apiece all day which seems rather small after doing so well

Jan. 13 Day clear & pleasant   forenoon not a speck of a cloud was visible   afternoon few switchy clouds over the sky   we worked in the Humbug & made for each   5.10

Jan. 14 Day clear & beautiful   to night looks like rain   the Atmosphere is heavy & appears smokey   workcd & made 4.00 apiece Doc has commenced cutting timber up the Emigrant Road to make rails   My teeth ache a little   the first tooth ache I ever had

Jan. 15 Rained hard during the night and ceased off by sun up we work all day made .75 apiece   not a cloud was visible all day nor none to night

Sunday Jan 16th 1853

Day clear & pleasant   not a cloud visible during the whole day but the night is clouding up from the west   We hired a team and hauled two loads of wood & chopped it up & piled it in the house to keep our neighbors from helping us use it   The Moon was visible from 10-o-clock this morning all day

The last few days we have been sluiceing with a ground sluice that is to dig the dirt down in the Gulch & wash it [in] the ground then shovel up out of that on to the sand & gravel & wash it in the tom   in this way the gold generally settles to the bottom   so we expect to make more this week than we did last as we will turn off the water & wash up the bottom of the sluice which is the tunnel me & Smith dug out last summer

Our Town is again filling with people   More men in Town to day than I have seen in one day for a long time & several are drunk and were wallowing in the mud in the streets & are now making night hidious with their drunken ravings

Jan. 17 Was cloudy as we went to bed but is clear this morning with a heavy frost & remained without a cloud all day   We turned off the water & commenced washing up the bottom of the sluice & made all day 6.90   My left leg is slightly affected with the Rheumatism which gives me some uneasiness in clearing up the sluice   this morning I had to stoop for some time & hurt my back so I could not straighten it all day   The pain is verry severe

Tuesday January 18th 1853

This morning my back is verry sore though I can now straighten it Day entirely clear and pleasant   morning frosty   Worked as usual $7.25 is what we made apiece

Jan. 19 Worked as usual and made for each 14.00   Day clear & beautiful without a cloud

My back has quit hurting me & the Rheumatic pains have ceased though the frosty nights make my hands crack verry much so they are verry painful

Jan. 20   Day clear without a cloud & as usual the morning frosty The Atmosphere is cool & raw during the day so it only thaws in the sun & so it has been ever since it quit raining but is pleasant to work we worked the forenoon & made each .87 & prospected the afternoon but found nothing   Doc has been Missing since yesterday Morning & came in this evening   he will not answer any questions that are asked in a correct manner but I suppose he has been looking for a Ranch as he has been talking of taking up or jumping one   I have got to dislike him verry much as he shows a disposition to gain by others losses or to advance his own interests to the injury of others provided he can do so without being liable to the law   he appears to want to take all advantages he possibly can in all matters where money or property are concerned & as soon as I can I intend to seperate from him as I do not like to have a partner in whom I can not put full confidence

Friday Jan 21st 1853

Morning frosty   Day beautiful & clear   Doc sold his part of the house to Jim this morning for $125.00   Doc says he is now going to Ranching   some light white light clouds visible for an hour or two about noon   We done nothing but settle up in the forenoon & the afternoon Jim & I went up the South Branch about 3 miles to look about & came back & worked about an hour but did not wash out Town is still filling with miners

Jan. 22   Day fair & usual & night frosty   we worked most of the day & made for each   2.87 Doc went to Mokelumne Hill to get his land claims Recorded & has not returned   I sent by Express this evening to my Brother in Francisco 7 oz Dust being all I had except some 4 or 5 Dollars   I am now out of debt entirely except 30 Dollars I have yet to pay as security for Smith

Jan. 23   Morning clear   we went up on Clapboard Gulch & followed it up to the head where we think we will prospect after awhile We then crossed over to Russels diggings & then came home by way of Indian Gulch   There has been a great quantity of work done on Indian Gulch this winter   it now looks as if it might be all dug up that was good for any thing   after dinner we went to the Volcano house to hear a Mormon preach   he spoke well   One of the drowned men was found about a Mile below town   a jury was held over him Verdict Accidental drowning

Sunday January 23r 1853

Commenced clouding up at about noon & was verry cloudy at night feels verry much like rain   Doc made to day about 33 Dollars at Dentistry   A few pack mule loads of flour came in to day & sold for 35c pr lb which brought the Merchants down some

Jan. 24 No frost this morning   the Air is much warmer than it has been for some time

We worked hard all day & made for each   1.43

We think of prospecting for a better place

A child of 8 years of age fell in the creek to day & was drowned   he was found lodged against a rock about ½ a mile below town   he belonged to the family of the owner of the Miners house whose name is John Rule   Doc is again at work at his rail timber   Cleared off about noon & the evening is clear & warm

Jan. 25 Went up Clapboard & took our little Tom with us & worked all day near the head of the Gulch to prospect   we found it good   we Made for each   8.70

Day entirely clear & pleasantly warm   A Man on Yankee Hill lost some 10 or 12.00 to day   it was stolen from his cabin

Jan. 26 Day beautiful rather Hazy   made to day 6.95 apiece Sun set behind clouds

Jan. 27 Day cloudy & pleasant   Made for each 3.95   some slight sprinkles of rain during the day

Jan. 28 Rained during the night & lightly during the forenoon then ceased   cloudy all day   We went up after dinner & worked about two hours   I felt so bad we quit   We made each 2.06   I have felt verry unwell since yesterday noon   My liver & spleen seems affected so my side is verry painful at short intervals

Saturday Jan 29th 1853

Day clear & beautiful   Made each   3.92

Sun set behind clouds   The ground we have been working is a loose reddish brown-looking dirt with a large quantity of broken slate rock among it   it colors the water a deep yellowish red which shows that Iron is abundant   The dirt is quite loose & the Gold partly coarse and part fine   the largest lump we have found weighed $3.12½   it is generally roundish & heavy Gold with considerable rust in the rough places on it   The ledge lies generally 18 inches deep & the gold is on the top & is not as is generally the case pressed down in the crevices it is a loose soft slaty or slate Ledge which is easily broken up & picked into

Jan. 30   Many Men in town to day showing an increase in population   also an unusual number of Indians were about town   Day clear & pleasant   Clouds in the west at Sunset

Jan. 31   Clouded up & rained some during the night   We went up to work at daylight but the rain soon drove us home   Ceased raining about 9 & after dinner we went to work & worked the evening   we made but little which we did not weigh   Cleared off to night & is cooler   Doc is gone to work on his Ranch to day

Feb. 1   Day clear & beautiful   Made yesterday & to day each 5.50 I went over to Russels Diggings but could not find any thing better than where we were so we concluded to keep working where we are

Wednesday Feb 2n 1853

Worked most of the day & made each   2.40

I went over to Russels diggings to see but could not see a place that suited my fancy   so now we are out of digins   Day clear & pleasant morning frosty

Feb. 3   Did not work in the forenoon as we had agreed to go with Doc to help him put up a house   but he did not get ready so we were fooled out of the days work   we worked a little up the Gulch & then carried our Tom home   a considerable excitement was gotten up to day at the Mouth of Clapboard & some 3 acres of ground was staked off though nothing great was made or struck

Day clear & pleasant   Morning frosty

Feb. 4   Went with John Reeves (a Miner from Iown [Ione] Valley) who worked here last summer down the creek about 2 miles prospecting but found nothing   we returned by dinner & then I went & helped Jim finish a hole in the new *diggings* in Clapboard about 4 feet down we could get 2c to the pan but at the depth of 6 feet we could get nothing & the water came in & bothered us so we quit with the intention of working at it again when the water went down   all the depth is a solid or hard gravelly & sandy & rocky dirt just like the beds of creeks generally are

Feb. 5   Went prospecting up the S Branch but found nothing   in the afternoon I took a spree & got *tight verry bad sure*   Day clear & beautiful

Sunday Feb 6th 1853

A slight headache this morning as is usual after drinking much

Morning frosty   Day beautiful and warm   Doc has taken in [a] partner in the Ranching business   Flour has fell to 23c & other things proportionally   The Roads are drying up verry fast so teams are now coming in daily   Jim & me feels rather discouraged as we are out of diggins etc

Feb. 7   We got off by day light & went up on Johnsons Humbug & worked & made 4.00 each for the day   we will try it again tomorrow
Day clear & pleasant   morning frosty

Miners are still working on Clapboard flat but none have found much   I have got me a pair of Gum boots which I paid 12.00 for & I have now no Rheumatic pains for they keep my feet dry

The body of Saml Elsie was found on a sand bar nearby covered up with mud & sand to day & buried this evening[26]

Feb. 8   Morning Windy & frosty   wind high during the night
Day clear & pleasant with a few light thin clouds   we made 4.50 apiece   The Dirt we are washing is a light blue or Mixed blue & white & brown gravelly clay & verry hard to wash   The gold is smoth scaly & heavy   verry much like River Gold   The Gulch we are working in is a branch of the South Branch & where we find the Gold is near the head of the Gulch   there is none in the lower end

Wednesday Feb 9th 1853

Day clear & beautiful   Morning frosty   we worked most of the day & made each 4.60 & came home to see to our claim on "board Gulch flat   found it all right   we intend as soon as the water goes down to work it   some claims there are paying well   that is those where the ledge lies high so the water does not come in

Feb. 10   Day clear & beautiful   Made each   1.56

Feb. 11   Day Hazy & pleasant   Made each 3.30   Threw up the Gulch as we think we ought to make more   so we will now go prospecting again & see if we cant find something

Feb. 12   Day clear & pleasant   night cool & frosty   We prospected on the Clapboard flat but made nothing   then loitered round the afterpart of the day   There are some 80 or 90 men at work on the flat but none making much   The Miners called a Meeting to night to revise the laws of the camp   they Met & after some debating adjourned to meet on the flat at 1 tomorrow   The purpose of the Meeting is to alter the law of claims   the claims are now restricted to 20 feet square which is thought to be too small so they wish to enlarge them

Feb. 13   Day clear & beautiful   Night frosty   however the day was somewhat hazy & a cool air astir   The Miners had their meeting on the flat & changed some of the existing laws making a claim 50 feet square which is much better than the old law of 20 feet square for claims

Monday Feb 14th 1853

Having found no diggings otherwheres we took our little Tom & went up and worked on Johnsons Humbug & made 8.70 each   Day pleasant   forenoon cloudy   afternoon clear   at night I went to the Consolation Hall at an exhibition of Spiritual Manifestation but did not learn any thing nor see anything but what I though was verry Natural   The Exhibiters are tolerable smart Men but are Humbugs

Feb. 15   Day clear & warm   Made each 3.78   Ball at consolation Hall to night   The Atmosphere looks a little murky like rain this evening

Feb. 16   Day cloudy & warm   Made each 7.00   Some Men on the flat are making large strikes but they are few and only just enough to keep up the excitement   the Most that has been struck is ten dollars to the cart load

The continued fair weather has brought provisions down verry much   flour has fallen to 15c   Meal to 14c   pork to 25c   Ham to 40c   Butter 75c and all else in proportion   so Miners can now live verry well

Feb. 17   Cleared up during the night & a heavy fog on the flat this morning   Day clear & warm   made each   3.10

Rained a little during the night *but little*

Feb. 18   Worked all day & made only for each 3.12   so we quit the Gulch again & I think for good this time   Day clear & warm with a heavy frost this Morning

Saturday Feb 19th 1853

Looked round a little & done nothing

Clear during the Middle of the day but cloudy morning & evening & a little rain falling this evening   Charley Stewart came up this evening & leaves tomorrow   he is going home soon &c

A Necromancer exhibited in town to night at a dollar a head Showed some slight of hand & some magic lanthorn tricks &c &c

Feb. 20   Cleared up during the night   Day clear & pleasant with high wind during the afternoon   Charley went back to day   Jim & I went with him to the Grass flat Quartz lead where we got some specimens of some kind of Metal which is mixed with the Quartz supposed to be Iron pyrites

Feb. 23   Monday was clear & cool   yesterday & to day was cloudy & to day it rained all the forenoon   We have made nothing but have been prospecting all the time   This evening I bought (or I should say we as Jim is in with me) of Taylor (the Taylor that was going to work with me in the Humbug) his share of the creek claims below the Saloon which was one seventh of all that part of the creek below the foot log & above the Mouth of the ditch for which we have paid him 20.30 apiece   Making $4000 [40.00] for the claim price   Men worked to day at it & made in all $60.00   so we think we will make something out of it

Thursday Feb 24th 1853

Day cloudy & cool   We went to work in the creek   I worked as owner of the claim & Jim hired at 4 Dollars pr day   one of the partners did not work nor furnish a hand so six of us made about 7 ounces one of the Company takes the Gold and keeps it til Saturday night those who shovel the dirt into the Tom have to work in the water crotch deep which is verry uncomfortable   Commenced raining about sun down & is raining hard now   Flour which was down to 12c is now on the rise & is selling at 15 now   this rain is supposed to be the commencement of the spring rains & is expected to continue for about two weeks

Feb. 25 Ceased raining during the night   Day cloudy & cool Jim Worked in another claim higher up the branch to day on the shares or at 5 Dollars   he haveing the chance of the $5 or 1 half Our company made about 90 Dollars though I did not see it weighed

Feb. 26 Rained verry heavy during the night & snowed so the hills are all white   hailed verry heavy from 9 til 12 & melted off the flat as fast nearly as it fell   We made a division of our work to day & Jim & me received $23.75 making for each 16.37 leaving what Jim made yesterday in the hands of his company   Rained all day

Sunday Feb 27th 1853

Day cloudy though sun show at intervals   A meeting at the Volcano House of the Miners   Made some laws in regard to unchartered companies

The Company I am Working with consist of 7 Members Who are known as fellows   Herman Chris Dan Pete Aron Wilson & Myself or John [Doble]   We are now working where the Road crosses the creek & will have to build a bridge so we can work the ground

Feb. 28 This Morning we fixed up our damns which the rain had washed down some & went to work   The company appointed me Captain or Boss secretary &c   After working awhile after dinner we knocked off & went at the bridge which we finished about sundown   I have to clean & keep the Dust so I can now tell how much we have we made to day at $16 pr ounce just $42.54 & only washed about 3 hours   Sunday Night a wedding came off at Taylors between a Mr Lewis and a Mrs Kark this being her 4th husband living   the boys had a big spree over the wedding last night

Mar. 1 Worked to day as usual and Made $164.20 & quit about two hours before night   the boys got some wine on the strength of the good strike & in consequence quit work sooner then usual

Tuesday March the First

The Butchers this evening brought up some More Spanish beef and two of the steers broke away and the Buccaros had a hard chase after them   after catching one of them they chopped his hornes off close to his head so he could not hurt them and well it was they did so for he run his head against one of the horses several times with considerable violence   they could not get him in to the corral but got him throwed at the gate & tied all of his legs togather in a bunch & let him lay til he got cool

Day clear & warm

Mar. 2 Day clear & warm with some wind   We Made $95.10 which we think is doing verry well   I recd to day from My Brother Paynes Age of reason which I will read &c   We have made several ineffectual attempts to drain the water off the ground we are working but as yet have not succeeded so we still have to work in the water about 3 feet deep & the water is verry cold so we dont work only about ⅔ of the day   Several of the claims on the flat are paying well and some of them are yielding as much as 50 Dollars to the Man a day   a load of flour was sold to day in Town for 8½c & cabbage sold for 15c potatoes are yet 15   Beef 35c & verry poor pork 37c & Ham & salt beef 25 & a further decline expected

Thursday Mar 3d 1853

Day clear & warm   Worked as usual & made $119.50   Jim Worked in the other claim as usual & he got a division so we had for each 8.00 & some dust left to divide hereafter

Mar. 4 Worked as usual   Day Warm & clear   We made $149.22

Mar. 5 Worked til 2-o clock & knocked off & divided our Dust all but 161 Dollars that had quicksilver on it   We had each 70 28 Making 35.14 each for Jim & me   Then Jim & I divided What he made in the upper claim & we had each 27.50

The Quicksilver being mixed with dirt lead & other impurities does not leave the gold on being heated but colors it a heavy lead color which injures the sale some   we sold the gold we could not get the silver off of for $16 pr ounce which we are to get 2 weeks from to day We are still working in the Water   there being so much in the ground that we can not keep it out so we have to work in it   it is verry cold and disagreeable but the pay is good so Men are plenty who will go in it   I have not yet went in the water as I am afraid of the Rheumatism but I have to furnish liquor to the others for taking my place in the water   while I wash the dirt they shovel out   The day is clear & pleasantly warm

Sunday March 6th 1853

Day clear & Warm   Town showed more lively than it has yet been this Spring

Mar. 7   In the forenoon one of the company being dissatisfied with my keeping the proceeds of the company we took it to Herman he living on the same side of branch that the rest of *Com* does & the reason they or he said was he wanted it on the same side of the branch where he lived nor I could find that he had no other reasons   the rest of the company were satisfied to have me keep it but I did not wish to in opposition to the wishes of any one of the company

Day clear & warm   evening some cooler & clouding a little with a heavy cool Atmosphere

Mar. 8   Forenoon is cloudy   commenced raining just before dinner & rained steady & light til night & is yet raining lightly   we quit work about 3   we made $52.20 to day & $112.00 yesterday

Mar. 9   Rained all night & all day hard

The creek is rising rapidly   work is stopped everywhere   the appearances indicate heavy rains   we bought some flour at 11c to day

Mar. 10   Day cloudy cool & windy or I should say cold with several light showers of snow & occasional spells of sun shine   The creek is so high we can not work so I done nothing but prospect some

Friday Mar 11th /53

Worked with Herman to day on the Bank near the upper end of our claim

Day cool with high loose black clouds & a light sprinkle of snow about 2 of the clock P.M.   There was a Ball at the Eureka House last night at which there was a large crowd   about 15 Ladies in all

Sat. 12   Clear in the forenoon   about 2-o clock a heavy black cloud came over the Mountains and gave us a heavy shower and cleared off so the sun set clear   We divided our Dust and after collecting all we had made we had 303.08 apiece all we made this week

Jim has now bought a claim in the upper claims which is the one he has been working & me [he] paid $10.00 which was all that was asked

Sun. Mar. 13 Day clear windy & cool   A shooting Match came off in Shirt tail Bend (South Volcano or across the creek) for chickens to day   I was not there though I hear the chickens were set up & the first Ball struck the chicken took it   I sold Jim ½ the cooking utensils for 5.00 so we are partners in everything now except our tools & blankets   A Man wanted to buy the house to day   we asked $350. for it   Our population is still increasing & think it will continue to do so til the Emigration comes in

Monday March 14th 1853

Our Damns being all washed away we spent the Day in rebuilding them

Jim worked this afternoon and made something   Day clear til just before sundown when it clouded up & looks like rain & verry windy & cool   we have got every thing ready to go to work tomorrow Morning

Last night was verry cold with a heavy frost & ice ¼ in[ch] thick & every night since   the rain has been equally frosty but to night it feels quite warm

The Indians that live on the Dry Sutter Amadore & Rancherie creeks are between here & the Lower settlements which comprises a District of some 8 miles square in which there are no Mines & consequently no whites settled in are said to be getting verry troublesome to travellers   they are supposed to be incited to rob and steal by the band of outlawed Mexicans & Chileans known as Joaquins [Murrieta] band   There has been lately several Murders committed near Jackson Amadore Drytown Campo Seco & Moquolumne Hill & two or three of the band have been taken up & he is said to wear a shirt of mail so that all who have yet shot at him have not affected him any in this neighborhood all has been quiet their range not being near here nor in this direction

Tuesday March 15th 1853

Commenced raining just after dark & rained all night & all day til 2-o clock then ceased   The tops of the Hills were covered with snow this morning & are yet in the same fix   The Day has been cool and verry disgreeable   we have done nothing only chop some wood this evening by which we saved $3.00 apiece

Wedns. 16 We went to work at our damns but could not get the water stopped as the snow Melted off the hills & raised the creek

although the day was rather cool   The snow is all gone this evening
The Day has been partially cloudy with some hard winds   The water
is verry cold

Thurs. 17 Worked & made but little   forenoon nearly clear
afternoon cloudy & rainy   commenced raining after several light
showers about 4 of the clock & rained til night   I played a Game of
Rounce this evening for Liquors & Cigars & lost $1.50 & I now think
I shall never play again for Money or property of any kind & unless I
forget this I now swear never to play again for any thing of any
intrinsice Value   I have not gambled any since last summer (or fall)
only to play for Liquors & I have frequently thought of renouncing
all togather but have always been afraid to say positively or swear to
it for fear circumstances would make me break my word (which I
have lately tried to keep in all cases) but now I am determined to quit
the evil practice of Gambling

Friday March 18th 1853

Morning cloudy & heavy fogs with an early shower of rain   clouds
light loose & scattering during the day and at evening heavy clouds
eastward which showed a rain bow the first this winter seen here   a
light shower of rain fell at dark & then cleared off & is now clear & light

Sat. 19 Day clear & warm   We divided our gold this evening   I
made $15.50 this week & Jim made $15.50 which gives us 75.50   also
a bit that Jim had of for each .85   also we got the 161 Dollars from
Hanford which upon Dividing first with my company 23 Dollars to
each then between ourselves we had each 11.50

Sun. 20 Day clear & Warm   Town full of people   Indians in
abundance

Mon. 21 Day clear & warm   Jim was summoned on a jury this
evening on a case between two Miners in regard to ½ or 1 share in
the claim I am working in   The former (or present) owner had taken
up the claim with the company & worked it by a hired Man While
he worked at other businesses & on last Thursday the other Man
jumped the claim   The question to decide was whether a man can
hold a claim by hired work or not   decided that he can provided he
has no other claim that he works or hires worked   This descision was
made on & by the Miners law entirely

Wednesday March 23d 1853

This Morning began to cloud up   in the afternoon a cold breeze
from the west set in & just before dark commenced raining & hailing &

is yet 8 o clock P.M. continuing hard   we finished working off the top of our claim & commenced working again at the lower end to day we worked at the top in order to wait til the water fell so we could get to the bottom but it is not yet down enough

Thurs. 24   Cleared off just after dark last night & a heavy frost was on the ground this morning   The Day however was pleasantly cool & quite clear   not a speck of a cloud visible above the Horizon

Frid. 25   Some Clouds all day   Air cool and rather disagreeable at noon I quit work & went into a Store for a Mr L M Duke who keeps in Town here to attend to the business for him until he came back from the City where he is gone to buy goods

Sat. 26   Day clear & pleasantly cool   My company took in a Man to work in my place to day & gave him what he made which I think was rascally but I cant help myself now as it would cost more than it would come to to try to get it   I have made besides what Duke will pay me this week $46.50 and Jim has made $16.46   Making each ones share for the week $31.32

Friday April The First 1853

Sunday Morning was dark and cloudy & commenced raining at noon & continued raining with occasional gusts of hail until Tuesday night and Wesday Morning   it was clear & remained so til now   The weather has been cool & rather uncomfortable & since the rain frost at nights   Duke came home this evening so I will go to work in my claim again tomorrow

The Creek rose so as to wash away all the damns so we will have to rebuild again before we can do anything   The Miners are now Organizing to drain the flat   they have got a ditch dug up & down through it several feet deep & and are now making arrangements to Drain Soldiers Gulch & to cut down the Canon low enough to carry of the water   I have not attended any of their meetings so I do not know how they are organzed   if indeed they have any organization at all

Sat. 2   Day clear & warm with a pleasant breeze   We built a part of our Damns to day & will finish the Weathe[r] permitting Tomorrow I have recd my money from Duke & have made altogather since the last calculation and entry on this Book $30.00 & Jim has made $8.33 Making for each   19.16⅔

Jim chopped Wood one day which we have not recd anything for yet   we get $2.00 a cord for chopping wood

Monday April 4th 1853

Went down to go to work on the claims & sold out Jims & Mine altogather for 33 Dollars with one pick throwd in with the claim   the Money we are to get some time this week   Jim then went to work on the flat carting dirt & I will go to work at carting in the same place tomorrow we are hired at 4 Dollars pr Day   I chopped some wood this evening   The Weather is yet clear & to day was disagreeably warm

Sun. 10   Jim Worked all week on the flat & I worked 4 days   The weather has been generally clear & warm   Jim recd for his work 23 Dollars   I worked [for] a Mr Martin who I think is slow pay   The Man we sold our creek claim to came this morning and payed us 30 Dollars on it & said he would not pay us any more unless the claim paid better than it was now doing   we divided what we have & had 26.50 apiece   I have counted up all the cash I have now which is

in Dust 119. "   (Making in
in Coin 37.62   { all $156.62

This evening it clouded up some & turned cooler   looks much like rain   The Town was unusually full of people to day   Rod Stowells trial was to have come off at the Hill last week but nobody appeared against him so he was set at liberty for want of evidence

Monday April 11th 1853

Rained during the night but not verry hard   Morning cool & chilly   I *recd* on my last weeks work $10. which was 5.00 apiece Rained steady til about two o clock & in the evening when it ceased awhile & rained again hard during the evening with cold winds

Tues. 12   Morning windy & cool with high cold looking clouds floating in the air   We went prospecting but found nothing & in the afternoon took guns and went up in the Mountains to Doc Carpenters & Maries Ranches   they are situate on the heads of the south and Middle Branches of the Sutter creek & are verry pretty flats containing considerable Meadow land surrounded by a rich alluvial & behind that the Barren & rugged hills   they are from ¾ to a Mile in length & from 100 yards to ¼ of a mile wide   we saw 3 deer which were yet in what is called the Blue   the hair being blue & white   we did not get close enough to get a shot   Doc has some Barley sowed and has a cabin under way & I think will do well on his farm   we arrived home at dark verry tired &c   the weather continued about the same all day

Wed. 13　Day cloudy & cool　　commenced raining about ½ past 4 & continued raining til dark　　there is to be a Ball at the consolation Hall to Night but it is supposed the rain will prevent its going off with eclat &c

Thursday April 14th /53

I went to the Ball last night & stayed all night　　came home at daylight & then slept away the most of the forenoon　　I put on a white shirt Eceterus the first since I had left San Juan Del Sul　　The Company consisted of 14 women & 37 men and time passed verry agreeable & everything went off much the same as such things generally do The supper was excellent consisting in part of Oyster soup Candies & Pound cake Etc Etc　　The night was cloudy & cool but the Day is clear & warm　　I feel verry stupid to day

Sun. 17　We have not worked any this week only to chop wood one day　　The weather has been clear and pleasant til last night when it clouded up & rained heavy during the night　　We have been trying to buy a Mule & cart which we succeeded in doing last night　　We paid for the Mule & cart $125.00 & for a 30 foot claim on Clapboard flat 74.00 which we intend to go to work in as soon as possible　　My ½ of the whole is 99.50　　besides we will be & have been at some more outlay for tools Tom &c　　the Tom we have not yet got nor do we know where we will get one　　we bought a set of Harness for $13.00　　the Harness we got with the cart being all out of order　　My part laid out in all taking 6.50 for the Harness is $106.00

Sunday April 17th 1853

Continued Raining until near night　　the forenoon the rain was hard and steady　　the afternoon the clouds were broken & showers in rapid succession & verry hard with some heavy thunder but no lightning that I saw

To night we bought a lot of Books comprising Shakespeares entire work　　A General view of the world　　Frosts *Am* speaker　　The Mexican War and 8 Novels 2 letter writers & advice to Bachelors a small work　　all of which we got for the sum of $10.00 my part 5.00

The clouds seem to be breaking away to night　　the air is cool

Tues. 19　Yesterday was clear　　to day is cloudy　　commenced raining at ten & rained the balance of the day　　We commence work on our claim yesterday & worked til noon to day　　We sold the undivided one third of our claim to a Man by the name of Wᵐ Reeves (My ½ 25.00) for the sum of $50.00　　he was glad to get it for that & surprised us verry much by paying us the Money immediately　　we agree to furnish the Mule & cart to work out the claim   The rain is verry cool & disagreeable   seems to be clearing off to night with a western breeze

Wedn. 20   Day cool with high dark floating clouds   thickened up & commenced raining just at night   We finished stripping the one half of our claim & will go to washing tomorrow if the weather will permit   Reeves worked with us to day

Wednesday Apr 20th 1853

We bought a Tom this evening (that is the 3 of us) for which we payed 10.00 apiece making $30.00   The Tom is in a good place   is 20 feet long by 3 wide   has a riddle weighing 85 lbs & is made of 1½ inch plank & is worth according to cost of Material & labor to Make &c the full sum of $50.00   it is now (8-o-clock) raining verry hard The Mule strayed off last night so that we were hunting him til after nine this morning so we did not work much in the forenoon   we found him 2½ miles from here at Russels Diggings

Thurs. 21   Does not seem to have rained much during the night but rained heavy During the forepart of the day   ceased about noon a cool western wind blew all the afternoon with high cold looking clouds   we hauled wood during the afternoon as the ground is to wet to work in our claim   There is a company formed (under what rules or law I dont know but they [are] at work) for the purpose of Draining Soldiers Gulch   they are now Digging a ditch from the Ditch formerly dug to turn Sutter creek into clapboard Gulch into Soldier Gulch for the purpose of sluicing out all the tailings that are now in the holes in the Gulch   The underground ditch which they had through it last summer being filled up   the wholes & low places are all filled with tailings in some places to the depth of 30 feet

Friday Apr 22n 1853

This Morning a heavy white frost was on the Earth & a cool sharp breeze blowing and a light fog on the flat   The sky was cloudless throughout the day   we washed dirt all day & Made only $15.15 we were washing dirt off the top of the pay dirt   we think it will pay better when we get deeper

Sat. 23   Day clear & pleasant   Worked at washing dirt to day & Made $25.00 & then we divided & had (being 3 of us) for each 13.42

Sun. 24   Day clear & pleasant   Duke was verry sick last night so I staid with him or in the store for him til 12 today when he was able to again take the charge of the store   he paid me $2.50 which divided

makes 1.25 for Jim & me each   Another of those disgraceful brawls &
fisticuffs took place to day in town in which two men of this place
got their faces badly bruised & several others were slightly disfigured

The ground we are now working is on the flat which I have before
mentioned & our claim is adjoining the ditch company claim   we
have about 4 feet of wash dirt under about two feet of loose soil which
we have to haul off in order to get at the pay dirt   we have taken
some more ground by the claim we bought so we will have work to
keep us most of the first half of the summer   the bottom of the gravel
which we now wash rests on a tough hard to wash blue clay which is
said to pay about three cents to the pan but can not be washed without drying

Monday 25th April 1853

Worked most of the day ditching our claim to take the water off
which bothers us verry much   washed 6 loads this evening & made
$6.62   Day clear & pleasant   a cool breeze most of the day

Tues. 26   Day clear & pleasant   Made to day and washed 23 loads
$17.05

Wed. 27   Day clear & pleasant   Made $41.17 & washed only 17
loads   the dirt seems to be the richest on the clay   This evening
clouding up in the west & seems some cooler

Thurs. 28   Day cloudy & cool forepart of the afternoon   showery
afterpart   steady rain which commenced with a hail storm which
was verry hard for the space of 15 minutes   We washed 16 loads of
dirt to day & made $63.87c which rather surprised us as we did not
expect to make so much   The rain increased towards night

Frid. 29   Commenced snowing before sunup and snowed hard til
12 & then rained til near night & then cleared off   The Day was
windy & cold   I went up to the Claim & found it flooded with water
which will cause us some work to bail out &c

Sat. 30   Morning clear & cool   snow on the hills   Day cloudy &
pleasant   clouded up in the forenoon   This morning a heavy fog on
the flat   On weighing our gold we had $129.25 which was for each
$43.08 out of which we have paid for grub feed repairs &c &c $7.59
apiece including 172 lbs Barley which will last sometime ahead   I
found it verry difficult to get coin as it is verry scarce in town at this
time   we have besides the above that was left out .35c apiece which
was not counted with the rest

Saturday April 30th 1853

We fixed a shed to Dukes house for which we got 1.00 apiece   we
then went & washed out the load of dirt we had left in the tom and

got 2.75 apiece (that is for the 3 of us)   some light sprinkles of rain during the afternoon   We hauled some wood which we have to go ½ a mile for   the wood near town being all cut   The creek is again all taken up with Tom claims as good diggings are now found at the foot of Jackass Gulch   The Gold that is found in Jackass is all verry fine and in fact all the Gold we find about this camp at this time is verry fine

Sun. May 1st   Day clear & cool but not unpleasantly so   passed the day in reading writing & loitering round &c

Mon. 2   Spent the forenoon in hunting the Mule bailing the hole &c and in the afternoon we washed eight loads & got $23.95   Day cloudy windy & cool   this evening it begun to rain & at dark is raining hard our hole is about 3 feet below the drain & it fills with water during the night so it takes nearly ½ the day for two to bail it out

Tues. 3   Day pleasant   Morning cloudy & foggy   afternoon clear We washed 18 loads & got 60 Dollars to day   we had to hire a hand as the water came in so fast one could not pick & bail &c   the clay is rising so I think we will not make so much in a day or two

There is to be a Meeting in town something about the Ditch Companies   another organ grinder in town

Wednesday May 4th 1853

Day clear & warm   we bailed out this morning which took us til ten o-clock   we then washed 15 loads & got $38.00   The water bothers us so we will strip for awhile & see if the water wont go down some

Thurs. 5   Day clear & warm   We went to Stripping to day   I hurt my back in lifting at the cart bed to dump it so I did not work in the afternoon but paid $2 to the boys for my time

Frid. 6   Day clear & warmer   my back is better   I went to work to day although my back is painful yet   after dinner I sold my ⅓ of the 30 ft that we bought of[f] of Scott to John Reeves for 75 Dollars 50 of it down & 25 when he takes it out of the claim   I then Staked off 3 full claims including the part sold for to work when they finish the 30 foot claim which will be I suppose in about a Month   I loafed the Balance of the day

The above was the bargain but to night he paid us only 15 Dollars the Balance to be paid shortly   Jim & me had 7.50 apiece of the 15 we divided what we made this week & after paying $12.75 of Expense for the week we had each 36.00

The claim was paying so well I would not have sold it only I promised to stay in the store for Duke while he is gone to the City   he proposes to go down Sunday & intends to stay 2 weeks   so I will get good wages for that time at least

Sunday May 8th 1853

Weather clear & beautiful   The boys washed dirt ½ the day yesterday and made 14 Dollars   I am going according to agreement to stay in the store for Duke while he goes to the City if nothing prevents

Mon. 9   I commenced for Duke yesterday & he left at noon for the City yesterday   We bought The Spring Saloon of Slater this morning for which we paid him one hundred Dollars down (which is 50.00 apiece) & one hundred & fifty more as soon as we can make it out of the property or sooner if convenient to us   this I think is as good a bargain as any man could ask   as we have our own time to pay the balance

There is now in this Town Eleven stores 1 Restaurant 3 Bakeries 6 Hotels 3 private Boarding Houses & 3 Bars & Gambling Houses one of the Bars is in an Apothecaries shop which leaves only two Gambling Houses

The large amount of goods makes competition high & the competition makes goods verry low so they sell here cheaper than any where else I have been in California   I have never eaten any eggs in *Cal* until I come into this store   Duke left some here which I now am using which are excellent having been so long without them   nor have I used but verry little milk   I find a person may be easily weaned from any luxury he may be used to as I never have any longing for milk which used to be my favorite drink

Volcano May 9th 1853

As I am now so situated as to have time to write I will try to give some idea of Matters & things in general   The Ditching Company first Organized have got their ditch nearly low enough to drain clapboard flat   about ½ way they have struck a ledge running across the ditch which is about 50 feet wide through which they will have to blast through to the depth of about 4 feet   after this is done the balance of the work will be comparatively easy   as I have before said we are bothered considerable by the water which will be taken off when this ditch is complete   our claim lies at the head of the ditch & will be the first one drained as through ours the rest will have to drain theirs They have run a ditch through Jones yard which brings Sutter creek into the ditch at the head of our claim   a portion lies in Jones yard & now all his yard & stable lot is taken up for mining purposes which is a great inconvenience to him as it will oblige him to Move his residence or fense out of the ditches & holes from his house   as he has a large family & it will be verry dangerous for the children who are all small for the ditches to remain open

Volcano May 9th [10th] 1853

The next company formed was the Soldiers Gulch company   They have a ditch coming out of Sutter creek some ½ a mile higher up the creek which comes down across clapboard and falls into Soldiers Gulch near the upper end of Town   this ditch is calculated to sluice out all the washings & (&) top dirt along the Gulch so as to get at the clay near the bottom with less labor   they are progressing finely with the work   I do not (not) anticipate that they will get it complete this summer as they have a deep ditch to cut through the canon before they will get it low enough to drain the water off of the best pay dirt in the Gulch

I suppose the flat company will get their ditch finished in the cource of 2 weeks as they are busily engaged at it now   we are anxiously waiting for the completion of it as we cant work to advantage until it is completed

The feeling is general that the blue clay in the flat will pay well as it prospects tolerable good on the top & most miners think it will pay excellently well nearer the bottom   but none have yet went through it as the water has been so much in the way they could not

Wednesday May 11th 1853

Yesterday was cloudy & cool with high sharp winds during the day it commenced raining after dark last night & seems to have rained steady all night   but not verry hard   Continued showery through the day   Wind raised towards night & the weather cool & chilly Clouds thick & heavy

Thurs. 12   Rained heavy during the night   ceased shortly after daylight this morning   still cool & chilly   Clouds become more scattering during the forenoon   Rained verry heavy but not steady during the afternoon & at night   is nearly clear & the air is quite pleasant having Moderated considerably

Frid. 13   This Morning is a gloomy dark and cool Morning   The hill tops are hidden by the Mists   Jas Bell was last night married to Mary Read both are living at the Volcano House

The Mist or fog fell in a light drizzle and by 10 cleared off leaving some floating clouds   about noon clouds thickened up again & again cleared away in the afternoon   then at night thickens up again & looks as if it would rain again & the air is colder

Sun. 15   Day clear & beautiful   Dukes Team came up to day bringing some goods &c

A man by the name of [John] James and Hannah Else is being Married to night   about 100 persons are collected with promiscuous music & are now making night hidious with their infernel clatter

Tuesday May 17th 1853

The weather is now supposed to be settled for the summer   To day is warm   in the afternoon the clouds are heavy to the North & East   The Day has been nearly clear until those clouds settled over the Mountains about 4 PM   they began to move westward with heavy thunder &c   between 4 & 5 a light shower fell from them as they passed over   Thin clouds all evening that nearly obscured the sun & looks like it would not stop raining yet though the air is not cold like it generally is when it rains here   Business is tolerable lively for the last 3 days   A considerable noise is made about the gold found in Jackass Gulch   though I do not hear of any large strikes being made there   there has been some disputes about claims some of which have ending in a fight & afterwards a Miners meeting which generally settles matters equitably & justly & to the satisfaction of all parties   The claim that I sold on the flat has not been worked since I left it on account of the water which comes in so fast since the Ditch has brought their water across the claim   but we are told that they will have the water out of the ditch in a few days so we can work it to advantage

I hope they may be as good as their word

Thursday May 19th 1853

Yesterday clear & warm most of the day

Some heavy clouds with some thunder over the Mountains but no rain reached here

To day is warm   forenoon nearly clear   afternoon cloudy with some thunder & a light sprinkle of rain near night

Frid. 20   Seems to have rained lightly all night   This morning looks gloomy the clouds are thick & heavy & the rain still falling lightly   I heard this Morning 2 Men were killed near fort John by a couple of Indians   one of the Men was said to have been too free with the Indian women which give rise to the Enmity   Continued

Raining steady through the day   lightly this evening   the ground is disagreeably muddy   This is the latest rain that has ever been known here

Sat. 21   This Morning cool & cloudy   heavy fog hanging round the hill tops   cleared off by 8 & the Day is clear & pleasant

Sun. 22   Day Warm   forenoon clear   afternoon heavy clouds with thunder over the Mountains   evening cloudy   Cleared off at dark   night beautiful & clear

Tues. 24   Yesterday was warm   forenoon clear   afternoon cloudy To day is cloudy and cool   forenoon the Mists & clouds are settling down on the hill tops concealing the trees from sight   afternoon the clouds are higher & more broken upon the whole a cloudy day

Thursday May 26th 1853

Yesterday & to day cloudy & warm with occasional flashes of sunshine   this afternoon heavy clouds with Loud Thunder over the Mountains Eastward   I have not heard from Duke for a week   I dont know what to make of his silence

Frid. 27   Day warm & clear overhead but there were heavy Dark clouds hanging over the Mountains all day from which issued at intervals throughout the day loud thunder   the air is cooler this evening   A man at Myers had an Epileptic fit to day   I heard his groans for ½ an hour before I went to see what it was   the reason I did not go sooner was I thought it was a sick animal that was about when I went to him he was by himself & had threw himself off the bed & was lieing on the floor   The folks of the house were in the back part of the house so they could not hear him   he is better now

Sat. 28   A heavy fog & cool raw & damp air this Morning   There was a dance at a house ½ a mile up the Middle fork last night   Doc & Jim was there   I had to stay in the Store so did not go

Cleared off by noon & was clear the balance of the day   Duke got home this evening so I am out of the Store

Jim has made since I went in the Store $81.50 & 11c on the claim which we divided & had each 46.25   I commenced collecting money for the Broken leged man this evening

Sunday May 29th 1853

Day cloudy & cool   towards night a verry light sprinkle of rain

Mon. 30   Morning cool & foggy   I collected yesterday $46.87c which I paid to the Man that nurses Dutch Fred who got his leg broke some time ago by the kick of a Mule   Day cloudy & cool & rained by

showers all day   Duke started again to the city this morning with
his Team & I am staying for him til he comes back

Commenced raining harder about 5 of the clock & rained verry hard
til night   during this time a bright rainbow was visible for some time
but the sun did not show itself

Tues. 31   This morning heavy fog round the Mountain tops
Cleared off by 10   Day clear & cool   cold western wind all day
except a short time during the afternoon when it was quite pleasant

Thurs. 2 June   Yesterday clear & warm   to day cooler & cloudy
in the forenoon & in the afternoon warmer & the clouds settled over
the Mountains & hung there in dark Masses til night   just before
sunset a heavy cloud came up from the west & scattered as it passed
the Zenith   from this fell a few drops of rain

Sun. 5   Duke returned to day at noon   we settled   he paid me
$6.10 and owes me yet 60c   this is the Balance after taking out our
Bills   Jim has made the last week $39.80 & we recd on the claim $35.00

Sunday June 5th 1853

we then divided after paying some other small Bills & had each 40.60
Day clear & warm

Mon. 6   Day clear & sultry   I went to work at repairing the
Saloon which I will finish in the course of 2 or 3 days

Thurs. 9   The weather is still clear & warm   I got the Saloon fixed
Tuesday   yesterday at noon Reeves (John) Struck the Mule over the
head with his fist & knocked his little finger out of joint so he is not
able to work   I worked for him ½ the day yesterday   to day I fixed
up things & this evening we moved in to the Saloon where we are all
in a Mix as everything is out of order

Frid. 10   John Reeves & me fixed up our things while Jim & Ed (the
other partner in the claim worked)   this morning was almost cool
enough for frost & rather cool all day with some clouds & this evening
the clouds are thicker & just at night a high wind blew & a light shower
of rain fell but not quite enough to lay the dust

I Recd the 6 Dollars that Martin owed us & we divided it which
was for each 3.00   Jim sold some Dust which was for each 2.12

Sat. 11   Morning clear & cool   Recd from Duke some Money as
the Bal Due me after taking out our a/c   we divided & had 17.80
apiece & some other *rects* making for each 1.12   Mrs. [Lewis] Holstead [James L. Halstead] that was married last fall here at the house
by the spring Died to day near Eleven o clock after an illness of some
3 Months[27]

Saturday June 11th 1853

She gave Birth to a child about 2 weeks ago (on the 24th May) which is supposed to have hastened her decease   The child died 3 days ago   I am going to sit up to night at the wake

We recd on the claim 20.00 & Mule hire 1.50 & Jim Made $49.00 which is for each 35.25

The claim paid better to day than it has all week

Sun. 12   I feel verry stupid to day from having sit up all night I sold the bath house day before yesterday for 40 Dollars which I got on order for on Lafayette Mace the which he excepted this morning though he has not yet paid the Money   Mrs Holstead was buried at 4-o-clock

Mon. 13   The weather is clear & pleasant

Jim is sick to day so I worked in the forenoon in his place   in the afternoon I sold the Saloon for $325.00 $200.00 in cash the balance in three Months   we paid on the Saloon to Mouckton for Slater $75.00 then Divided the rest which was 62.50 apiece   We have traded what wood we had left for Boards which we used on the Saloon & for living in the other house

We moved back to the other house this evening   We give possession of the Saloon tomorrow morning

Thus. 16   Weather clear & warm   Thermometer in the shade at noon stands at from 87 to 95 & in the sun from 110 to 125   The Boys are now about finishing the part of the claim I sold so I will get to work again next week

Thursday June 16th 1853

My private Expense for the Month of May was

I went in the store for	May 1st	1 Knife	1.00	
Duk on the 8th so my	" "	1 pr shoes	2.00	
Bill while there is as	" 2	3 plugs Tobacco	1.00	
here set Down without	" 3	Postage	.13	
any Items as I have lost	" 5	1 Segar	.12	
the Bill	" "	Hired Man ½ Day	2.00	
	" 6	Washing	.25	
	" 7	6 Segars	.50	
	Dukes Bill		7.25	
	Washing for same time			
	the Bill run		2.50	
	June 1st Amt Total		$16.75	$16.75

This I put down as an average expense for Myself aside from My
Board

My Board has been as follows commencing Oct 8th 1852
& running to Nov 4th   Cost for this time   18.41½

Carpenter was taken sick here & I payed My own Board
up to Dec 1st 1852 Which Amted to   20.16

Then from Dec 1st to the 9th was   7.41

Jas Troutman then come Jan 21st 1853 Amt to this time   56.30⅔

Carpenter here left to go on his Ranch   Jim & me continuing togather from this time to Feb 20   The Amt was   28.04

Mar 2 Amt to this time   12.26

"   20th Amt to this time   14.50

Apr 10th Amt to this time   7.94½

May 1st   "   "   "   "   19.46

Making My Board from Oct 8th 1852 to May 1st/53 $184.49⅔
The sum of $184.49⅔

Friday June 17th 1853

I went yesterday with a Mr Worley & took the level of the ground
from the head of Indian Gulch to the head of Jackass for the purpose
of getting water into Jackass   we found the ground good for cutting
a Ditch & will probably go to work on it soon

I went to work to day with the boys   I commenced bailing water
& in two hours I hurt my back so I am not able now to work   The air
is verry warm   Thermometer in the shade 98°   in the sun 120°

Sat. 18   My back is verry sore to day though not so painful as
yesterday

The Dutchman that I collected money for some time ago has been
without any attendance for several days   he broke his leg over again
stripped all his clothes off   tore off all bandages & let the flies in so
the wound was filled with Maggots   To day we concluded to remove
him to the City so I have been most of the day preparing to take him
to the Hospital at Sac City   we propose starting early this evening
and travelling through the night   He has been ½ crazy ever since
he got the wound

Thurs. 23   Returned from Sac City last night about 10-o clock
We had the waggon fixed with a spring bottom and then a thick bed
of Hay on it as that we had but little Trouble with him on the way
we travelled all night & got to Sac City next Day about an hour before
sundown   we left him in the Hospital which is an old hull lying at

the wharf near the lower end of Town   The weather has been verry
hot   my face sunburned til it is sore   Jim has made since last settlement $31.50 besides 6 or 8 Dollars that he has not yet Divided & he
got the balance on the claim & Mule hire which was $19.50 & I made
(which I got) in going the trip $20.00 which we have divided   Making
for each of us $35.50   John Reeves has quit the claim as he has got
his part worked out & Ed has quit because he thinks it wont pay   Jim
& Me calculates to work it awhile yet   I expect to go to work on the
Ditch perhaps tomorrow   I have had a severe headache all day   The
weather is verry warm   My face sunburned in the Valley which was
verry sore but is now about well

June 24   I feel worse this morning   my head still hurts & My
bones ache & my flesh seems sore all over   the reason I cant tell unless
it is sleeping in the waggon which has given me cold

John Reeves left us this evening & is Boarding at Gemmills   I feel
some better this evening   Jim stripped enough ground to day for us
to work on a couple of days   Those working on the flat are generally
as far as I can learn doing well   but none are doing anything more
than making good wages

Saturday June 25th 1853

I went up with Worley & we leveled a part of the Ditch & will go to
work Monday at digging it   Jim worked in the claim with a hired
hand

They made after paying the hand $18.25 which is for each of us 9.12

A Man they call Sam was badly injured to day by a bank caving in
on China Gulch   I went to a Temperance meeting to night   the
society consists of 40 members and is doing well though they dont
seem to be any verry thorough going men among them

Sun. 26   Day some cloudy & Morning rather cool   Jim Divided
what he & Ed Made last week and his share was $6.25 which was for
each of us   3.12

The day throughout was cloudy & cool so that an overcoat was
quite comfortable & just after noon a verry slight sprinkle of rain fell
which is uncommon for this country   To night is clear & chilly so
much that I am now shivering with cold

Mon. 27   This Morning the Thermometer was at 42° which is cool
for June   Ed come back to the claim & went to work with Jim this
morning while I worked on the Ditch

Tues 28   Worked yesterday & to day on the Ditch   Jim and me took up a claim on the Soldiers Gulch which lay across the back end of our house & to day some men went to work on it   I am now trying to get them off   they seem verry stubborn about it   I will try them again in the morning & see what I can do with them   weather is verry warm

Wednesday June 29th 1853

Jim worked on the flat   I went round among the Miners this fore-noon & got a good number togather at 1-o clock to say whether the jumpers of our claim should have it or not   but the Miners refused to decide the Matter so it stands as it was   we give Ed an Equal share with us in all our ground so he is now a partner with us   we have nearly concluded to go to work on the claim in the Morning

Thurs. 30   We concluded this morning that if we drove the fellows out of the claim they would sue us & it would cost more than it was worth & if we sued them they would have nothing out of which to make the cost so we would let them alone & save our money rather than spend it for what is uncertain return   by doing so we run the risk of gaining the ill will of some of our Friends   as some of them wished us to drive the fellows out of the claim which we felt verry much like doing for awhile

Frid. July 1st 1853   I am still working on the Ditch & Jim & Ed is working on the flat & Making money   The weather is verry warm There is one case of the small pox in Town but the friends of the diseased have moved him to a house seperated from the rest so we think there is no danger of the disease sprading   The Miners Gener-ally are doing well   There is no hands to be hired here as all are Mining for themselves with but few exceptions which shows the Mines are good at this time

Saturday July 2nd 1853

Jim & Ed Made this week altogather $124.27   Jims share $62.12 Then I got for Mule hire &c $9.37 Making for each   37.25 Out of this we have kept in a purse altogather $25.12 in fine Gold which we intend to divide at some future time   we got the ditch so near completed that we will finish it in two days more if nothing prevents   That case of small pox is now at its worst   The cabin he is in is on the South Branch Trail & daily men are passing near it also many of the Indians are looking in when passing   so it is feared the disease will spread among all the people

Sund. 3   I have Made one way & another the last week aside from our work   5.12 Several loads of snow have passed through here going down to the

Mines below to cool the drinks of the thirsty where they are not blessed with cool Mountain Spring water like we are here   Several companies of Traders have crossed the Mountains to meet the Emigration & one or two companies are forming to cross the plains home

Our Board has cost us the last week apiece   5.62
The Temperance Men are making preperation to celebrate the 4th A Man deceived two other Men here by saying he had a large amount of Money & wished them to go with him & buy stock in the Mountains they believed his report of the Money & sold their claims and otherwise made preperation to go with him   but when they urged him to get his money ready to start he could not find any   They then got each a whip & whipped & Beat the fellow verry severely   The people collected to the number of 150 this evening & went to the house of the two men with the purpose of whipping them in return   but after talking awhile they concluded to leave it to the civil authorities   The Man is a Drunken Vagabond of a Welshman and the only wonder is that they could be so deceived as to put their property out of their hands until they were sure he had been telling the truth   What vexes them Most is they have sold their claims & now have no place to go to work in   The two^s names are Wm Lee & — Griffin   Lee is a yankee Griffin is a welshman as is also the other man who is the deceiver   his being a Welshman and a countryman of Griffin is partly what caused his word to be believed with more readiness   The Men were summoned before a justice to night but I have not heard what is doing with them

Mon. 4   Temperence Men had a speech or two at the Meeting house Duke left for the City this forenoon so I am in the store again so I did not see or hear the speaking   Those two Men that were taken up for whipping the other man whose name is Robert Roberts compromised the Matter with Roberts to day & got off by paying the cost The Boys & some Men have amused themselves with firecrackers & Liquor   The firecrackers have kept up a continual cracking nearly throughout the day   *Monday July 4th 1853*

The Town is fuller of people to day than I have seen it since I have been here   a(re) number are drunk but there has been but one fight which is better than common as whenever a crowd gets togather here a fight is apt to come off

July 5   Some of the remnants of the 4th are visible to day in the form of several drunken men   two of which took a fisticuff just after dinner but neither was hurt to do any good   Our Town has been since

I have been here clear of Dance houses but we are doomed I suppose from what report says to have one or two of these pests among us Tis said two of the houses in Town are preparing to receive the women which are said to be all spaniards   how true it is cant say

Wedns. 6   Last night a Man by the Name of Geo Addison Died he has been sick but a few days   The disease was supposed to be Lung fever   he leaves a young Wife   he settled here last fall   came across the plains last season   is an Englishman by birth   his wife is an English Woman   Will be buried this evening   There are several cases of the Billious Fever now about town & in the town   it is feared by many that it will be sickly here this fall   There is More sickness now than has been here since I have been in the place   though all that are sick are those that came in last fall

Thurs. 7   Yesterday Morning when I got up my legs to my hips and my hands to the rists were covered with purple splotches showing a stagnation of the blood of some kind which I do not understand   This

Thursday July 7th 1853

Morning it is about ½ gone   I feel no bad effects of it but the sight is disagreeable   My blood was in the same way once before but I paid no attention to it then   I eat a verry heavy supper the night before so I attributed it to an overloaded stomach but how that could affect the extremities I am at a loss to say or I dont know   The spots have entirely disappeared from my hands but are still on my legs up to the hips   Pack Trains are still passing through here on their way to meet the Emigration   I conversed with a Physician in regard to the purple spots or splotches on my Limbs but he could give me no information as he knew nothing of it

Frid. 8   Jim Did not work to day   he has made with the Mule hire $20.38 which is for each   10.18

We have now $580.00 Loaned out which we think is as good as the Money itself &c

We agreed this evening to let a Man go to work with us in the flat he is a stranger just came up from Ione Valley   his name is Thorpe & has been in the country nearly 4 years   We paid eight Dollars of the above Money for hired hand which is 4 Dollars each out of the 10$ There is now a general complaint of Colds & ill feelings supposed to be caused from the changes now going on in the weather   the Thermometer ranges now from 60 to 97 & has been greater   these changes are verry regular being at the highest from 9 A M to 4 P M & at the lowest from 10 P M to 5 A M

Sunday July 10th 1853

Thermometer at ½ an hour after sunrise stood at 55° During the Middle of the day stood at 88° Another of those disgraceful fist fights occured in town to day Many Indians are drunk though this has not been an unusual thing Several Teams & about 40 Men arrived to day from Salt Lake being the first of the Season coming across the plains they all look well &c

Tues. 12 This Morning sunrise Thermometer 52° We agreed to rent the house this Morning to Worley & Davis for 25 Dollars a Month they agree to take it 6 Months & we fix it up a little such as putting a counter & shelves in one side for a bar & a narrow porch in front

Thermometer at noon 82 at 4 P M 86

Two Men of the Soldier Gulch Ditch Company had a difficulty to day their names were Farrel & Easly Easly struck Farrall in the back with a Bowie Knife & cut him severely but not dangerously Esly broke & run jumped the Ditch which is about 12 feet wide & 10 feet deep & took over the hills Eastward One Man pursued him to the Ditch but could not cross so easily as Easly did so he let him slide

An Indian Came into the Store this evening drunk his face all bloody and washed in streaks by the tears from his eyes his shirt being bloody the other Indians pulled his shirt bosom aside & revealed a gash just over the heart about 1½ inches long like the gash of a Bowie or some other knife

Tuesday July 12th 1853

The Indians said or we understood them to say that another Indian had done it but others say a spaniard Mexican did it The Doctors say the wound near the heart is a verry severe one after the blood was washed off several small gashes appeared on his face & one severe large one on his forehead it appears that one of the Indians did the Mischief Duke returned this evening Two Dutchman took a fisticuff in the upper end of Town to day

Wed. 13 Went to the Mill & got some lumber to fix up the house Settled with Duke & he paid me $27.00 for the time he has been away also $3.00 interest on four hundred Dollars we loaned him some time ago we Divided & had after Deducting some Expenses paid for provision we had each   12.97

Jim Made $6.75 & Mule hire 2$ Which we divided Making for each 4.37 & for Mule hire besides the above 2.75 apiece

Thur. 14 Made a counter & shelves in the house to day & Moved across the street into a house for which there is no owner it is the house formerly used here for a dance house & the Man that used to keep it is in the Penetentiary so there is no owner for it here   we intend to live in it until somebody says they want it   we were going to buy the house but found we could not get a good title to it so we would not buy it   the Man that wanted to sell it to us is an irresponsible Man so we could get nothing of him

Sunday July 17th 1853

I have felt verry unwell for the last few days   To day is clouded up about noon & commenced raining slightly   a lot of cattle & horses & 2 waggons passed through Town to day from off the plains   Jim & Me commenced Boarding out yesterday &c   The Rain continued steady & light til night & it now looks like clearing off   This is something News to all here as rain in july so far as I can hear was never seen in July before in this country   although it has been falling all evening steady it has been so light that the dust is not laid nor is the top of the ground wet

Mon. 18   We recd this Morning the Balance of the first Months Rent on the house but this I will set down at another time   We bought this Morning a claim on China Gulch for which we pay $145.00   we get the 6th part of a Ditch running the water into the Gulch and 2 Carts & harness & one Mule one house Toms water privilege and Mining Tools   if the claim continues to pay as it has done we will make something of it   there is supposed to be dirt enough to keep us all summer   Day clear & warm   Morning Cloudy

Tues. 19   To day another strike was Made near the Lower end of Town & some dozen holes are going down between the Middle of Town & the flat Ditch   they got five dollars to the pan about 42 feet from the surface & in the water   in fact the water Bothered so they had to cease working & some of the other holes are to the water & got good prospects

Wednesday July 20th 1853

Sold our small Tom to day for 2.50 which is 1.25 apiece   I commenced work on the Ditch to day but my back is not strong enough yet to stand it so I had to quit   I got a letter from Ab to day asking me to come down & take charge of his Ranch but I am so situated that I cant go now   I would like to go verry well if I could   Another case of the small pox in Town or it is said to be the Variolord   The people up the south Branch burned the house that the other case was in for fear this case would be taken there   The present case refuses to be removed   it is not known what will be done with it

Thurs. 21 Clouded up & rained a light shower during the night the clouds are settling away to the south & west this morning Day clear & hot cleared off entirely by 8-o-clock

Fri. 22 Morning cool day hot an overcoat felt verry comfortable this Morning Watermelons the size of a Mans head have been selling the last few days from one dollar to one & a half and Muskmelons accordingly cucumbers have been selling from 50c to $1.00 pr Dozen all spring & Onions 37 to 50c a Dozen for small sized ones & 25 to 50c a pound for large ones the Market is now supplied plentifully so the price is down to about ½ the above

Sat. 23 Jim worked the forepart of the week & I worked the latter part To day we only worked ½ the day the dirt only pays 50c to the load so we have nearly concluded to let it lie til the rain comes & then it will pay to sluice we may try it once more but I think we wont

Saturday July 23d 1853

The Mule we got with the claim is a large Black Mule & to day he backed the cart into the hole which was about 5½ feet deep the Harness held him up until he floundered out of the shafts so that he did not get verry badly hurt though his legs were considerably skined We have only made the last 3 days about 2 Dollars a day we recd for our share of the weeks work $8.50 & for Mule hire $8.25 for ½ days work that Jim done extra Making for each 8.37

We quit work at Noon and concluded as it would not pay to cart we would leave it til the rains this winter and then sluice it off as it pays 50c to the load it will pay verry well to sluice when we get plenty of water in the Ditch

Sun. 24 Day verry hot we can as yet find no other claim so we are now in a *fix* & dont know where to go to find claims to work a situation in which I find Miners are frequently placed We might spend several days prospecting but all the prospecting I have ever done yet has been verry unprofitable so I am always against doing much at it unless nothing else can be found to do & again all the Mines here so far as I have tried them are so spotted that it is two chances to one that a person will not find the Gold when they only prospect with the pan I prefer prospecting with a Tom & washing a day or two before taking the pan as a Tom is a better test than the pan

Monday July 25th 1853

Last night some person or persons unknown Entered the Store of Klebitz & Beckman and dangerously wounded Beckman who was

sleeping in the Store   8-o-clock A.M. I have just returned from
seeing Beckman & saw the Doctors dressing the wound   he was found
this Morning lieing in his bunk   head & one arm hanging over the
side of the bunk   one deep (to the bone) wound or cut across the
right side of the right eyebrow & a slight bruise across the nose showing
that a wide edged instrument had been used   another wound just
over the corner of the forehead right side showing a hard blow with a
blunt instrument in this place the skull was broken in   The surgeons
made an incision one inch wide & three inches long commencing at the
edge of the hair over the right corner of the forehead & running back
parellel with the centre of the head   found a large clot of coagulated
blood showing that it had been done early in the night   one piece of
the skull nearly square & an inch across was taken out   another
section running down towards the eyebrow was considerably depressed
which the Doctors tried to raise but did not suceed   They then closed
up the wound & applied cold wet clothes & I left   suspicion fixed on
no particular person nor does any here know how much money was on
the premises   there was near 40 Dollars found in his pants pockets &
some more in his desk amounting in all to near a hundred dollars
some say he had 7 or 8 hundred in Dust which he kept under his head
which can not be found this morning   there is no goods missing so
far as any know

Monday July 25th 1853

There was a dull heavy poled axe found lieing near him which was
supposed to be the instrument used as there was some hair sticking to
one edge of the poll of the axe   the door was found standing open
(the Back door) & the window up & his dog was in the house   it is
supposed some one intimately acquainted with him did it as the Dog
is verry surly to all persons only those belonging to the house

We have hired our mule to go after Klebitz who is Beckmans Partner who is now at the City having left here only yesterday morning or
Saturday   I am not informed certain which day   it was 9-o-clock
suspicion rests now on a sailor by name Harry [Fox] who has been
staying with Beckman[28]   they on the hunt of him now   The Doctor
tells me that a large portion of the right lobe of the brain has oozed out
& that they got the bone raised so there was no portion of it resting
on he brain   the supposition is he will not live the day through   it is
said he was seen to weigh out 15 hundred in dust after dark last night
none of which can be found this morning   Companies have gone out
in every direction   12-o-clock Beckman is supposed to be dieing
some 3 or 4 Men are Missing from Town some of whom are suspicioned

½ past two   Beckman Died a little after one   several of the parties
have returned and found nothing of two of the Missing Men who are
most suspicioned   they are sailors & are known by but few persons
around This place   new parties arc starting on the hunt for them

Tuesday July 26th 1853

Klebitz arrived about 4 PM   no further information in regard to
the amt of Money stolen as yet   Two Men were seen this morning
early near the New York Ranch who are supposed to be the Murderers
Several companies have been out & are out on the hunt but none have
had any sucess as yet

Wed. 27   Our Mule returned from the City to day   he is none the
worse for the trip   no further news of the Murderers   Beckmans
Partner is going to put his business belonging to the firm into the
administrators hands so we will not get the Mule hire for some time
yet   Two Emigrants from the States arrived here today being the
first that come through this way

Thurs. 28   We bought a claim on Chinese Gulch of Aron Rice for
which we pay him 60.00 apiece   we get a Tom & Tools & Mule & Cart
with the claim   Two Men were Murdered by the Mexicans near Jackson a few days ago   the Murderers are not known

Sat. 30   Jim has worked yesterday & to day in the new claim   they
have been stripping most of the time   they washed some today &
made $4.50 apiece & paid for Barley two dollars apiece & I made to day
$3.50 which when we divided we had each 3.00   I have done no
work this week only to day I hired out

Sun. 31   The day as usual verry hot   we spent the day looking
round   Emigrants are coming in slowly & Traders going out regularly
One or Two families have passed through here in the last week

Wednesday August 3d 1853

We commenced building a house 12 by 16 feet square this week in
company with Dr Carpenter to live in this winter

Jim is still working on the Chinese Gulch claim   they have not
washed much dirt yet as they have been hauling off top dirt most of
the time

We sold our Mule & cart this evening for $125.00   which is for each
of us 62.50   we have to credit a part of it for awhile but the Man we
think is good

Sat. 6   I have Made in cash 3$ which is for each   1.50
& Jim hasMade $16.87 which is for each   8.37

The Weather is still verry hot   the Thermometer ranging from 50 to 105   This Morning was the coolest we have had this summer   the Thermometer was at 49 before day this morning

Flour has risen 4 & 5c on the pound so Board has also raised one dollar on the week

Sun. 7   We went up on the Emigrant Road to see a lot of Emigrants that were reported to have stopped there but found it hoax

We moved our place of Boarding to day as the house we have been Boarding at has raised the price to $8 & as he dont set as good a Table as they do on this side the creek   we think we had better take the best when it costs no more

Sat. 13   We have worked (Doc & me) the most of the week on the house & have got finished nearly & will move in as soon as possible The Emigration has been coming in some during the week

Tuesday a Waggon came in & a woman that was with it reported having seen two Men on the Eastern summit of the Sierra Nevada over which the road passed & from the discription are supposed to be the Murderers of Beckman   so Wednesday Morning 3 Men started in pursuit   we have heard nothing of them so far   Jim Made this week $30.62   after paying the feed expense we had each   13.87

The Company in which we bought a share in China Gulch some time ago have commenced work again & we have had a hand hired the last 3 days for which we paid 12.00   as soon as we move into the new house I will go to work myself   The ground that Jim is working now is the most spotted ground in these diggings   to day they made 40 Dollars   this being more than they have made any day since they have been at work at it   the spot they have now struck bids fair to hold out for some time   the dirt is of different colors & mixed with clay or there [are] spots of clay which has no gold in it   there has been a hole sunk 40 feet in the claim & the same kind of dirt at the bottom that there is near the top   they are now working under the edge of a bank 30 feet high and the dirt has paid in spots all the way from the surface   it is a reasonable supposition to me that there has been a large slide in which the clay & gold dirt being in regular strata have in the slide crushed each other & mingled togather there thus making the paying dirt so spotted

Thursday Aug 14th 1853

We got a division of what was made in the claim on China that we first bought which was $3.37 to the man   Making for us 1.68 apiece for Jim & me   they only washed yesterday having been engaged making a damn & road &c the other two day   this amt was what we had after deducting expense for Mule shoeing Barley &c

The whig candidate for Senate in this county speaks at the Volcano House to night   One of the Men who went out the Emigrant Road after the Murderers returned this evening & reports that they overtook one of the Men described by the woman & that he was crazy & raving about a Murder &c but that he was not one of the Men suspicioned   he had a partner who has been gone on towards the States the other two Men went on in pursuit of him while this one returned The probability is that the one gone on has taken all the Money (if they are the Murderers) and gone on to the states   The crazy Mans name is Murrill & is not much known here ther fore he is not suspicioned   Though suspicion is beginning to gain ground as he raves about a Murdered woman & being hanged &c   He had not money or Scott (the Man that has returned) would have brought him back   I have not heard whether the one that has gone on is known to be one of the suspicioned ones or not but suppose from what I have heard he is not from this place   One of the suspicioned has a verry notable Mark which is the absence of nails on his fingers & toes   they have been frozen off

Monday Aug 15th 1853

We hired a hand to work in my place   while Doc & me finished the house & moved into it   we made a shed over the front door & intend to put another back & a chimley also   I have kept an account of the cost & find it as follows

Lumber for floors & doors &c	21.50
Nails (23 lbs & some others all at 15c)	4.37
Lock Latch Butts & screws	3.75
Tacks & canvass for Light hole (back)	.50
Clapboards	25.00
Team for hauling	4.00
Sash & Glass 7 x 9 one window 12 light	5.00
Use of Grindstone	.50
Pencil	.25
14 Days work to build @ 4$	56.00
	120.87
½ Days work overlooked	2.00
Making a Total Cost of	$122.87

We cut all the poles & hewed them on the Mountain before we hauled them down

Tues. 16   I went to work this Morning & Jim and his company quit work & have concluded their claim will not pay as they only made ½ an ounce yesterday & this morning   they prospected could not find the color   I am working in the Mouth of the Gulch or where it comes into the flat   the pay dirt is about 8 feet deep with some seven feet of loose loam and sand which we have to strip off   The pay dirt is bedded on a yellowish reddish & blue clay or rotten stone & is a reddish Brown sand & gravel dirt & has spots in it of yellow sand and gravel & clayey gravel all of which pays about a dollar & a half pr load

Wednesday Aug 17th 1853

Democratic county candidate spoke to the people at the National House last night by the light of burning Tar Barrels &c   Jim and his company commenced prospecting their old claim again yesterday evening   they are finding some dirt that pays a little and are in hopes that it will not be as they expected that is "run out"   This evening they have got down about 10 feet & find dirt that pays $2.12 to the load so they are in a good humor   My claim is not paying so well we have the dirt to haul about 200 yards so we can haul & wash but 12 to 15 loads a day which yields us from 17 to 25 dolars a day & some times less

Aug. 20   Recd second Months Rent on our House which was $25 Making for each   12.50

There were Many Emigrants passing about all week   some went through & some have stopped to Make this their home   among them two young Ladies have stopped here   We have been at work steady but have not done over well   I made after all expense of work is paid $22.50 & Jim made $16.95   Making for each   19.72 5/9 Out of this we have paid $4.00 for hired help while I finished the house The ground I am working is not so good as we anticipated   we expected it to pay at least two Dollars to the load   but it only pays about 87c   we will continue to work awhile longer & if it dont do better we will have to find other diggings which I do not wish to do as prospecting is verry expensive

Sunday Aug 21st 1853

The two Men who pursued the supposed Murderers beyond the Mountains returned to day & repot that they are convinced that they were pursuing the real Murderers but that they had got into a company of Indians & white Men near the sink of the Humboldt so they were afraid to pursue them farther   There is some talk of a company going out again after them but I think there is not interest enough here in the Matter to raise & support that company   The Editor of the Chronicle printed at Mokelumne Hill is addressing the people in front of the National tonight

Mon. 22   While at work this evening we heard a Man had been shot four times in town & on inquiry after coming down I find Collins a Miner & occasionaly a Gambler had been shot during the evening by John Stephens who is a worthless fellow & followed Gambling mostly Collins was drunk & Stephens was lame with the Rheumatism though sober   before dinner Collins had whipped Stephens in a Gaming quarrel & after dinner Collins wanted to fight again & when he went at Stephens he (Stephens) drew his Revolver & shot Collins   the ball struck the left side of the Breast bone a little above the heart & glanced a little to the right and passed between the ribs through cutting the left lung a little & came out near the left shoulder blade   the doctors say he can not live   some Men are in pursuit of Stephens who left immediately after the deed was done

Monday Aug 22d 1853

The foregoing is the first report I got after coming into town   since I have asked & seen & heard several eye witnesses report what they saw & heard so the following is as near the facts as I can learn   Stephens being crippled did or could not resist Collins when he beat him in the afternoon and after beating him he told Stephens to go & get his pistol while he did the same   Collins got his pistol & some one took it away from him   he then went back to the Gambling house and layed down on a table & became quiet   after awhile Stephens returned after procuring a revolver & came into the house & fired at Collins twice   both balls striking the (the) table   this aroused Collins & Stephens ran to the door   at the door he turned & fired again twice   one ball struck a post in the rear of the houes & the other took affect as before described only the ball came out under & to the left of the left shoulder blade   There was no one in the house but the bar keeper & he was so scared he can tell nothing of the matter   though several that were in the house adjoining heard all that passed   Stephens had picked up the pistol in a bar room in town   he returned the pistol & then left while Collins was taken to the *Dr*   Collins is what is called a kind good hearted Man but Gambles when he has money & mines when he has not   Stephens Mined some time but for the last year has done but little besides Gamble & he is generally considered a worthless fellow

Wednesday Aug 24th 1853

I attended the Ball at the Eureka House last night & had quite a
pleasant time   There was 18 Ladies & 29 Gentlemen Dancers & 4 or 5
more Dodging round   Danced til Daylight this *Morn*   I feel rather
stupid after loosing sleep &c

Frid. 26   I attended a Ball at the Volcano House last night at which
there was 56 Men & 20 Women   also a Political speaking came of[f]
while the Ball was in Motion   There was quite a crowd at the speaking as both Democrats & whigs spoke

I paid for My Ball Ticket   6.00
Tuesday Evening the weather thickened up & has been cloudy ever
since   This Morning it looks like rain   The Ball broke up at daylight this Morning And I feel verry sleepy from having staid all night
The Man that was shot is not expected to live   he is swelling in the
chest verry much

Emigration still coming in bringing with it a large number of Cattle

Remained cloudy all day except about two hours at noon when the
sun shows clear

Sat. 27   Jim has been prospecting & working all the week on China
Gulch & has Made clear of expense $3.25   While I have worked all but
one day on our other claim in the Gulch and I made $15.86 clear of
expense which is for each   9.55

Jim & his company have quit their claim as they cant make anything
of it any more & I am afraid the other claim is not going to pay verry
well   two weeks now have not paid any thing & I dont think it will
pay well at all til water comes

Sunday Aug 28th 1853

Last night about 12 Collins the Man that was shot Died & will be
buried to day

The Doctors tried to find how the Ball had passed through but he
was Mortified & they could not trace it   he leaves a wife & children in
the States

A drove [of] some 6000 sheep—passed through town from [New]
Mexico   the drivers were mostly Mexicans[29]

My back is verry sore to day from having stooped so much during
the day yesterday but I think it will soon pass off

Mon. 29   All of our company except Myself and one other were not
on the Diggings as we only washed 3 loads & got $3.75 which was for
Jim & me   1.37

The Balance of the day I helped the boys build at a chimney to our house   The clouds have all passed away & given place to a clear serene sky with a fresh cool bracing breeze from the west

Sept. 2   The weather is still cool & to day is cloudy & looks like falling weather   we have been at work at the house and have got an addition of 12 feet square to the back end and a chinley & fireplace on the front part so we are now fixed to live comfortable this winter   I engaged to work with Carpenter for his partner at building a barn for their place   The reason we put the addition to our house is that Jim is talking of gitting a wife & if he does we will want more room than the 12 by 16 that we had built   The Emigration is still coming in rapidly & nearly all are from Missouri   some are stopping at this place   The Town is improving   several new buildings going up and a large store house in front of our house

Sunday Sept 4th 1853

I went up the Emigrant Road to day to try to trade for a team but did not succeed   The day has been pleasantly cool   The Town has been unusually full of people to day & business lively in proportion   There was several large trains of Emigrants passed through town to day   Several young Ladies have stopped here to remain the winter and in consequence the young Men are all on the quivive & looking out for Wives   12-o-clock at night   We attended a social singing party at the Eureka House at dark to night & left there a few minutes after 10   we went to bed & just as we were asleep we were aroused by the cry of fire   on looking out we perceived the Eureka House on fire we drew on our pants & ran out & assisted in tearing up buildings & carrying water &c   I worked a few minutes to try to save the house & finding that useless I commenced carrying out our property assisted by my two partners   we soon had the house stripped & had a man on the roof to whom we gave water in plenty & thereby saved our houses & have now all our thing back safe

The fire spread no farther than to Dukes Store which stood some 30 feet from the Eureka House   one small building was torn away which stopped the fire in that direction & a space between Dukes House & the next stopped it in that direction   Duke owned a store which he had in his house (he is at the City)   The man attending for him saved some few things but nothing of value   I suppose that $8 000 will cover all the loss   Myers the keeper of the Eureka lost everything his wife escaped in her night clothes only   most of the Boarders lost all their clothing & some apart of their Money[30]

Monday Sept 5th 1853

This Morning nothing is left of the two houses but a few smoking fragments   Several of the boarders had Gold Dust in the house which they are now washing up the coals & ashes to get   There was no wind astir while the fire raged so it was not so hard stopping its progress We have lost nothing of any consequence for which we are verry thankful   Myers with the true California spirit is going to work to rebuild Duke has not yet returned.

Tues. 6   Duke returned to day & is going to rebuilt & continue in the business   Myers had about 300 Dollars Made up for him besides what he borrowed & started to the City for furniture &c for to continue his business   My partner Jim was taken last night with a hard chill & to day he is verry sick of a fever both billious & intermittent we are giving him Medicine which I think will soon restore him again to health   I hurt my back to day & it is verry painful to night

I give Myers   10.00

Thurs. 8   Jim is worse to day   his disease has determined to the lung fever after he had taken Medicine to break the billious intermittent   I fear he will have a severe spell

Saturday 10   Jim is worse to day than he has been before   The Doctors say his lungs are inflamed & in consequence a high fever rages almost continually on him   I have made this week working by the day $13.00 which will pay board and no more   We have been sitting up the last two nights with Jim & giving him Medicine but it appears to take no verry material effect as yet

Sunday Sept 11th 1853

I traded for a Waggon & two Yoke of Oxen to day for which I gave $430.00 which is for each   215.00

Jim is no better to day   we are still giving him Medicine steadily

Mon. 12   We sit up with Jim last night as we have for the last 4 nights   though the two first nights we did not stay up all night   This Morning about 3 of the clock his mind began to wander by spells & he grew more quiet & apparently easier

The Doctor thinks he is a little better

This evening we think he is worse than ever but he is under the effects of the Medicine so we cant tell with any certainty

I have kept an account of my private expense for the last 26 days which is as follows

July 17	July 17	1 Box Brandreths Pills	$1.00
	" 18	1 Glass Sarsoparilla Beer	.25
	" 20	1 " Strong "	.25
	" "	1 Pr socks washed *35* Postage *10*	.35
	" "	Paid my Board for this week	7.00
	" 23	Washing *37* 1 Bottle Beer *50* Do ale *75*	1.62
	" 24	1 segar *13* 2 sticks candy *25* 1 watermelon *50*	.87
	" 27	1 Watermelon	.50
	" 28	Phrenological Examination	.50
	" "	Chart of head	.50
	" "	Fowler on Matrimony	1.00
	" 29	1 Watermelon *50* 1 Bot Sarsoparilla Beer *50*	1.00
	" "	This weeks Board	7.00
	" "	1 Box percussion caps	.25
	" "	1 Muskmelon	.12
	" 31	Washing 3 pieces	.75
	Aug 2	1 Muskmelon	.25
	" 4	1 " *12* 1 Watermelon *25*	.37

Carried Over

Volcano Cal a/c of Expense

1853

Aug 7	Washing two pieces	$ .50
" "	Board for this week & one day over	8.00
" 10	1 Watermelon	
" 14	Board for this week at another house	8.00
" "	4 Watermelons 1.00	1.00
" 16	1 "	.25
" 20	Cloth Dress Coat	17.00
" 21	1 pr suspenders *75* 1 pr shoes *2.00* melons *1.00*	3.75
" 23	Ball Ticket	5.00
" 25	" " Another Ball	6.00
" "	1 *Bot* Cologne *25* Melons *50* Wine *50*	1.25
" "	2 Glasses Port wine	.50
" 28	This weeks Board	8.00
" "	Honing razor 50 Hickory shirt 1.00 Melon 50	2.00
" 29	1 Melon	.12

Sept	3	Mending Coat	1.00
"	"	Washing 87 Wine 25 Board *8.00*	9.12
"	4	Melons	.75
"	5	Give a Man that got burnt out	10.00
"	7	Postage	.05
"	8	Wine	.25
"	10	Washing	.50
		& Paid for Board last week done our own cooking	7.50

Leaving out Ball & Dress expenses this a/c shows something near an average of My expense the year round as near as I can judge

Wedn. 14   Jim has been about one thing til about 4-o clock this evening when he seemed to decline rapidly & now (½ past 6) his pulse is verry low & his breathing labored   the Doctors have stopped giving Medicine and we do not expect him to live til mor. though he is Stout enough to move his head and limbs about without assistance

Thursday September 15

This Morning at 15 minutes past 2 James A Troutman Died   about 4-o clock yesterday evening he took a change for the worse and continued going down til Death stopped farther progress   This is written at daylight before I go out to make preparation for the funeral

6-o-clock P M   We have just returned from the funeral   We had a sermon & service by Mr Beady Episcopal Minister   Now am I again alone   the only heart I have found that beat in unison with mine suddenly torn from me   Almighty God Mysterious are thy ways Guide & direct me that I may never be found wrong & May I never complain at thy decrees as thou knowest the right & doest it

The day was cloudy & several showers of rain fell which prevented the Ladies from attending the funeral but there was a large number of Men more than I have seen at any burying except one (a Ladies) in this place

I have never met a Man in life as generally respected as was Jim he had no enemies & none who knew him but what speak verry well of him   he was entirely clear of all the Vices for which *Cal* is so noted he used strong drink in no form not even Tea & coffee   he made use of no profane Language at all nor did he ever grumble in any Manner to my knowledge   he was raised a strict Methodist (Episcopalian) & his actions remained the same until his death   although he has for the last six months been a firm believer in Deism which belief he

adopted as soon as he knew what it was & he further has told me he
always doubted some of the Doctrines taught by his Church though

Friday September 16th 1853

he never permitted his mind to run on the subject until he had seen
what Deism was & then the more he thought the more he believed the
Doctrine   This love of the truth was verry great   I never knew him
not in the least things to vary from it & falsehood he always denounced
whenever he saw or knew of it

Forenoon of the day cloudy & pleasantly cool   cleared off towards
night

Jas A Troutman was Born January 10th in the year 1829   Died
Sept 15th 1853[25]

Mon. 19   I sold my spy Glass for   3.00
The weather is again warm after being chilly for the 8 or 10 days past
I have felt verry unwell & have not been able to work   but to day I
feel better

Tues. 20   I send by Express a small box covered with black glazed
Muslin containing a blank pocket Memorandom   not blank but with
sundries writing in a note book the Psalmist and in specimens $57.18
to John Troutman James Father   also by mail a letter informing him
of his sons Death   Jim was engaged to be married to a Miss Jane
Cummins [?] who lives in town here   he wished to see her before he
became deranged so I went and saw her & she agreed to come but he
became deranged so he could understand nothing so she did not see
him at all after he became sick   she seemed to take his death hard

Friday 23   Our partner sold our Mule & Cart which we owned on
Chines Gulch for which we recd 52.00 apiece   counting our work at
4 Dollars a day we have lost on the claim $37.25 & have let the claim
go for good   *Tuesday October 4th 1853*

A few day since at a Meeting of the Citizens I was appointed to cir-
culate a subscription for the purpose of raising money to build a Bridge
across Sutter creek which is verry much needed   I stired round with
it for 3 days and got 699 Dollars subscribed which we thought would
build the Bridge   last night I was appointed one of 3 Commissioners
to see to the building the Bridge   to night we opened the proposals &
found that we had not money enough to meet the lowest proposal   we
have 522 Dollars Cash & the bid was 662 Dollars   so we expect to get
the balance tomorrow & then give the contract as we have over enough
subscribed we think there will be no difficulty in collecting enough to

make the amount   I have not mined any for some time but expect to
go at it as soon as I can get clear of this Bridge business

Miners generally are doing well here though are many Emigrants
here who are without money & many who are not able to get work at
any price   wages are rating from 50 to 75 Dollars pr Month   There
has been several Temperance Meetings here & several Meetings at the
Methodist Church I have attended in Company with a Lady for the
first time in California[31]

The Meetings of both kinds have been well attended & the Temperance order is increasing rapidly

Wednesday Oct 5 1853

We let the Bridge at 661 Dollars that being the lowest bid   we got
nearly all the Money collected to day   to night I attended a show
which was a panoramic view of crossing the plains price $1,00   quite
a crowd attended   I hired a hand to day & engaged to give him 50
Dollars a month & Board him

Thur. 6   This evening we received intelligence that [Harry] Fox &
[Chris] Stevens the supposed Murderers of Beckman were captured
that they had been captured On Board the Steamer Brother Jonathen
while on her downward trip from Francisco to San Juan & that they
had confessed the Murder[28]

The Excitement is intense   some talk of Meeting them on the Road
& bringing them to this place

Mon. 10   Yesterday evening a Meeting of the people here appointed
a committee to take out a warrant to go to the county seat & see if
they cant get Fox & bring him to this place as we have heard that
Harry escaped & are afraid the Fox will do the same   the committee
left last night & we have not yet heard what they are doing   we have
recd no certain news where Harry escaped as yet but that he is gone is
certain   The excitement here is still great if either of them ever gets
into this town he will certainly be hung   Last night it rained a heavy
Shower so the dust is well laid to day

Thursday Oct 13th 1853

Today Last night the committee returned from the Hill & reported
that Fox was committed for trial that the Grand Jury had found a
true Bill against him for Grand Larceny   his trial is to come off in
three months

The Emigration is supposed to be all in or nearly so as there has
none passed through here for the last three days   The weather is

quite warm now & the nights cool   we are looking for more rain soon
as the the atmosphere is murky & feels like rain

Oct. 15   Saturday night   I worked on the Ditch on Jackass to day
& intend now to go ahead until I finish it   The hand I have hired
worked the last seven days for another Man   he will go to work on
the Ditch on Monday

Tues. 17   To day I went up on the Emigrant Road to see a Ditch
& to see if I could get water to bring into mine & worleys Ditch   they
offered to let us have the water for ½ the profits of the Ditch for a
Months & then give them up to them all our interest in the ditch but
I could not take it so I came back and offered the Ditch for sale & will
know to night whether they will take it   we have been promised
water by the company I offered to sell to but they now talk of running
a Ditch along near ours & taking the water ahead of us so we think
we had better sell it to them

Tuesday Oct 17th 1853

I got back home by 3 o clock and traded the house I have had rented
for a claim in Soldier Gulch and give besides the house one hundred
Dollars as soon as I take it out of the claim which will make it cost me
325 Dollars   The Ditch company came in to see us & offered us 80
Dollars when we want 135 so they left without any final conclusion
We do not wish to dig the Ditch [at] all now as they are going to Dig one
into the same Gulches so that the two Ditches will bother each other
& for this reason we offer to sell to them

Our Town is now being visited with some sickness   there has been
in the last week two Deaths & one expected to night which is a child
about 18 months old sick with Dysentery   though there are a number
sick it is not considered sickly as there are many people here   the
Town is supposed to contain 3000 inhabitants at the present time
The weather is cloudy this evening & looks as if rain was near   I hope
it is as I have made nothing for some time for want of water   if it
would rain a week steady I could now go to work & make something
though I will probably make something of the claim I bought this
evening

Many of the Miners are now only waiting for rain to commence
operations and should it happen to be a dry winter the disappointment
will be severe

Wednesday Oct 18th 1853

To day I had my hired Man at work washing some dirt which was
on the yard & dried ready for washing   we got out of 8 loads $92.75

there being only 2 shares in the claim we had each   46.37
which was for me clear about $40.00   we will not have any more dirt
to wash for some time as we have 5 or 6 days stripping to do where the
bank has caved in except 5 loads on the yard not yet dry enough
to wash

Thurs. 20   We commenced stripping to day   I washed 2 Loads &
got 75c   was for each   .37
but this wont pay so we throw away the dirt & get to the bottom as
soon as possible

Sat. 22   We washed 4 Loads of dirt in the forenoon & got $26.50 &
washed 5 Loads in the afternoon & got $4.37 after paying all expenses
I had   7.81
a part of this expense was for hired help   the dirt we washed was
some we had on the yard drying   we will not get out any pay dirt for
at least a week yet

Sun. 23   The Ditch Company paid us 80 Dollars for our Ditch on
Jackass my part   40.00
which is just $4.50 less than cost on each share   we would not have
sold it so if we could have got the water into it without any trouble
but we found that we could not get water so we sold it   My prospects
for a good winters work are now better than I have had since I have
been in California   *Sunday Oct 23d 1853*

I bought an Indian Pony of Mr Cummins to day with a saddle &
Bridle for the sum of   30.00
which I think will pay Poco tiempo

Mon., 24   Worked on the claim in Soldier   Abe (the hired man)
is digging potatoes for Holsted   The boys began work on the Ditch
on China Gulch to day

Wed. 26   I sold my claims on China Gulch to a Mott for $250.00
one hundred in cash & one hundred & fifty as soon as he takes it out of
the claim   this I thought would be better than to try to work both
my claims as I think he is an honest Man   I recd a letter from my
Brother to day which informed me he would start home in Dec but I
am going to try & pursuade him not to go so soon as I think it better
to go in the spring when it is warmer weather in the western States

The claim in Soldier is about 35 feet deep now & none know the depth
of the pay dirt as some holes have been sunk 15 feet below the lowest
place worked & still find good dirt   I calculate that I will have a good
winters work & then a good summers work afterward   The Cave

which fell in the day before I bought it was about four feet thick & some 16 feet wide but we took down 4 or 5 feet more so as to keep it from caving again so that we will not more than get to the pay dirt again until Saturday about noon when we expect to take out some good dirt

Thursday Oct 27th 1853

We have made arrangements with a Mr George who has a Lady & no children to come & live in our house & we give him the rent of the house for cooking for us   I expect to be here steady the winter but Doc has bought the ½ of a ranch near here & sold his half of the other Ranch to his partner Mace so he will stay at the Ranch most of the time   Doc worked on the house to day preparing it for Mr George to move into   I went to the Mill & brought a load of slabs with which to floor the back Room & some lumber to make door bedstead &c   We will probably get all the top dirt that caved in off tomorrow so we can begin to get at the pay dirt

Oct. 29   To day I have written 2 Deeds one from Carpenter to Mace & one from Freet to Carpenter   he have sold his Ranch on head of the Branch & bought one lower down on the same Branch   We got our claim ready to go to taking out the pay dirt Monday after a little more shovelling & pumping   we are now five feet below water drain and dont know how much deeper we will have to go before finding the Ledge   I anticipate a good winters work but dont know anything certain as all the Mines are uncertain

The draining company are putting in a blind drain which will give us some two & a half feet more drainage which will give a great deal better chance to work

Sunday Oct 30th 1853

This evening Mr George and Lady came into my house and are calculating to stay the winter with me   The Miners had a Meeting to day to revise the Laws but did nothing but Make a law reserving the grave yard from all Mining purposes &c

Mon. 31   We expected to have begun taking out pay dirt to day but when we got to work we found we had more top dirt to take off so we have been all day clearing to get to pay dirt tomorrow   We are bothered some by our neighbors who are blasting rock but that will not last long as they are nearly through with it   the rock is a kind of grey Marble which appears to be of a fine quality & susceptible of a fine polish and could be got out in verry large slabs

Nov. 1   We got out 21 Loads of pay dirt to day which is about what

we will average all the time   we have some large Marble rocks to
encounter   all that are small enough we pound up & haul out   those
that are verry large we dig round   one rock is about 100 feet long
one way the other way it goes under the bank so we cant tell its size
we have traced [it] to the depths of 6 feet & dont know how much
deeper it goes   The companies drains go through near the Middle of
the rock which they are now blasting through

Sunday Mov [November] 6th 1853

For the last few days the weather has been cool & felt like it would
rain   to day was cloudy with no wind of any amount   I spent the
day in fixing up the house   Mr & Mrs George seem as well pleased as
could be expected and I am excellently well pleased with them as they
are just the kind of people that I think I can always agree with

Mrs George is an excellent housekeeper & cook   in fact I think she
is the best cook I have known in the country & I hope they may continue in the house as long as I stay in the place   We have been taking
out pay dirt all week & have got out about 70 loads   the water
bothers us a great deal but the Ditching Company will have a blind
clear water drain in which will give us a drainage of at least four feet
more than we have at present   so that we will probably have as much
dirt as we can haul out in two or three weeks & we will not probably
wash any for a week or two   Mr Worley my partner is gone north
prospecting and will probably go north if he can sell out when he
returns   his son is working in the claim in his place & is a verry poor
hand   I shall be verry glad when his father returns as I will then try
to have a better hand in his place   Doc seems to be well satisfied with
his trade & is going ahead fixing up the Ranch he lately purchased

Sunday Nov 13th 1853

The past week has been generally cool   forepart of the week cloudy
& wednesday a light shower of rain & since having frost of nights   We
have done but little work in the claim this week as my partner was
gone from home and his son being in charge did not do his duty so we
have been lieing idle for two or three days   we washed to day made
14.37 apiece   I hired a man in my place & hauled poles to bridge the
hole so we could get to the end of the claim   the ditching company
have got their drain nearly in so we will not be so much bothered next
week with water as we have been

A Wedding came off over the creek this evening   Mr Holsted
[James L. Halstead] who was married a year ago & whose wife died last

June was married to a Miss Brown who crossed the plains this season as usual the boys gave a Cheverie & were treated by the groom in Liquor to the amount of about thirty Dollars[27]   This evening the clouds have again thickened up and it now looks like rain again & the afterpart of the day has been cool   though to night it has again became warmer   I got a letter this week from my Brother which informs me that he will not go home the first of next month as his former letters stated   the reason he did not give

Tuesday Nov 15th 1853

Rained all day yesterday   to day was partially clear   we washed yesterday & got about 20 dollars which goes towards paying the debts to night Mr George bought Mr Worleys half of the claim for 250 Dollars to be paid when Made out of the claim   This is 75 Dollars less than I give for my half which I think makes the claim verry cheap we did not work to day as the ground was too *muddy* but we expect we can work tomorrow

Sun. 20   To day is clear & pleasant   since Tuesday it has been cloudy with several showers of rain   we have only worked ½ a day on the claim as the Road has been so muddy that we could not haul out more than ½ a load at a time but now the road is drying up so I think we will get to work tomorrow again   We helped Mr Freet dig potatoes one day this last week so we made by it   4.00 & yesterday we made sluice boxes all day so that if water enough comes we can go to sluicing

The Ditching company have got their sluice in so they are ready for the wet weather if it comes

The Miners generally are not making much now as most of them are waiting for water   some few are making money out of the deep Diggings but they do not number more than ¼ of the population here

Friday Nov 23th 1853

The weather has been clear up to yesterday afternoon when it clouded up   During the night last night the wind raised & blew verry hard & continued verry windy all day   at about day light this morning it commenced raining & rained hard by showers all day   Worley & me washed dirt yesterday & to day until about 3 in the afternoon when it go so wet we could not wash any more   for the present we made yesterday & to day for each   48.56 out of this we have the expenses to pay which is about $2.50 a day besides board   this evening it is getting quite muddy so we will not

be able to cart any more out of the claim until it dries off again   we
have got some sluice boxes made with which we intend sluicing off the
top with if we can get water to do it with   The Ditch *Com* are rather
contrary so that we may have some difficulty with them but I hope
not   they have already refused to give us drainage as much as we
want but that we can get along without if they do not throw any other
inpediments in our way   we want a sluice way which we think we
have the right to take anyhow & I dont know how we will yet fix it

Saturday Nov 26th 1853

Rained all last night verry heavy & thundered & lightened considerable & continued raining throughout the day in light showers & to
night it is again raining steady & hard   We washed the balance of the
dirt that Worley had an interest in & made for each   31.83
out of this Expenses are to be paid which is just $4.50 apiece   We
commenced putting in our sluices this Morning but stopped to wash
the dirt   the Ditch company object to our putting in the boxes but
they can give no good reason for the objection   the persons we
bought of had taken up the claims before the Ditch *co* took up their
claims so we believe we have the right to run our tailends where we
please   but I dont know how we will yet fix it   I believe their idea
is to drive us to sacrifice the claims to them but I dont believe they
will succeed in it

Sun. 27   Rained during the night & several light showers during the
day   We fixed up the stable during the forenoon & in the afternoon
we washed a Tom of dirt that had been partly washed & got 2.37 apiece
The Company that own the Ditch & claims on Chinese Gulch are
about selling their claims to an old Spaniard who has a lot of Peones
to work it   I got a hint that Mott (the one I sold to) was going to
take French leave of me & not pay me when he got the money so I
am going with them to Butte City tomorrow where they expect to get
the money   *Monday November 28th 1853*

I bought Day before yesterday of Hanford & Downs a revolver
Colts Patent for which I give   27.00
I went to day to Butte City with two of the boys but the old Spaniard
wouldnt buy so we had our trip for nothing   I am convinced that Ab
intended to give me the slip if he could have got the money in his
hands so I am satisfied that I watched him close even if I didnt make
anything by it though I feel verry sure that I shall get the money after
awhile   George Made to day for me   4.50

& for himself $8.50 that is taking his days wages out of what he made The day was clear except about 3 hours this evening which were cloudy

Tues. 29 We washed Tailends most of the day & Made for each 6.00 out of which we have to pay 1.00 apiece for Water rent The day is cloudy & cool We ascertained to day that the Ditch company were mistaken in the lines which will give us some 3 or 4 feet more of the good ground We believe the Captain was intending to cheat or lie us out of all he could &c The owners of a Claim adjoining us are talking of going in with us and putting in a long sluice & both sluice togather if we do join companies we will put in about 400 feet of sluice Since the rains have begun there has a considerable slide come into our claim some ten feet of the bank has slid in which would take us some two weeks to cart it all out but we think we can sluice most of it

Wednesday Nov 30th 1853

To day I bought Carpenters one third of the house for which I paid him 70.00

& Took Troutmans at the same 70.00

Doc wanted me to sell verry badly to a man he had found but I wished to live in the house til spring so I thought it best to buy his part which I did

We made to day for each 5.00

We are washing the dirt wet as the rain has soaked it so it washes with considerable rubbing if it remains clear & dry as it is now we will have to dry & pound as it is getting too dry to wash well now however we will wash tomorrow & if it does no better we will stop for the present

Dec. 1 I took a chew of Tobacco after breakfast this morning which is to be the last for a Month if I dont forget it on the (the) first of January next in the Morning after breakfast I will take a chew of tobacco & not before on any terms We washed ten Loads of dirt to day & got for each 10.37

we will now quit washing as the dirt has [been] too dry to wash wet and is too wet to wash dry that is it is now about ½ dry & is verry tough so that it balls up & will not wash clean The weather is now clear & we are afraid it will not rain any more so we will have to cart out the dirt that has caved into our claim though we may have water enough to sluice off the top though I think it doubtful

Saturday December 3d 1853

We have been stirring up the dirt on the yard & getting wood for the last two days   the weather has been verry pleasant & clear & we are now doubtful that we will not have water to sluice with until spring

Sun. 4   To day we had a verry light shower of rain & a rainbow in the evening

For the last 2 weeks the Merchants and traders have had a notice up that they would close their houses to day and this Morning all kept closed except one til about 9 when they discovered that the one was open   they all opened so the notice was of no effect   This evening we had Oyster soup for supper and some of our neighbors (a Lady & gentlemen) to help us eat it   The Ditch Company now seem to have given over opposing our sluicing for the reason I suppose that they know that they cant keep us from it as we have the right to sluice whether they are willing or not   The Methodists have a quarterly meeting here now which I undertsand is well attended & I hear they have several excellent speakers   I was going up this evening but have a headache & feel unwell otherwise so I have not went

The Sons of Temperance have been organized for the last 3 or 4 weeks & I hear are progressing finely though I know nothing about them

We find it will be difficult to get enough water to sluice with unless it rains more than it has yet done   we intend cutting a ditch from the upper end of our claims to clapboard Gulch & get the water from the Gulch & from the toms along the Ditch

Monday December 5th 1853

The day was Hazy & cool   we went on the Mountain & got a load of poles for to put up our sluices on   I spoke to Grady (the Captain of the Ditch company about sluicing & he now says we shall not sluice at all unless we make a sluice way of our own   while we think we have the right to sluice along the Gulch   Grady got verry angry this evening & made some ungentlemanly remarks to which I made no reply   I have spoken to most of the Lawyers in town & they all (that I have spoken to) say that we have the right to sluice & they cant prevent us only by brute force which it is supposed they will not resort to   We purpose commencing a ditch to bring water into our claims to sluice with

Wed. 7   The nights now are cool or cold with heavy white frosts

last night ice froze as thick as glass & to night is verry cool   To day
about noon was so warm that it was comfortable working in light
clothes & the sun was so hot that it felt uncomfortable through a
wool hat

We commenced digging the ditch to day and got 4 or 5 rods completed   we have to dig it about 4 feet deep

Thurs. 8   To day I hauled a load of slabs for which we paid 4 dollars
at the mill   Our Ditch crosses the Road so we have to bridge a considerable distance   Millers had three hands on to day while we only
had one & a half   Mr George was unwell so he did not work this
afternoon   he seems to have something like chills or fever on him &
is in considerable pain

Friday December 9th 1853

About an hour before day this morning the rain fell heavy   at daylight it ceased and only a couple of light showers fell during the day
we worked at the ditch which we will probably finish in two days more
so that we can put up the sluices   I have been conversing with many
persons on the subject of our sluicing & find most all are of the same
opinion of ourselves that we are entitled to sluice if we want to   we
have said nothing to the company since but will ere long try & settle
the business

Sat. 10   Rained heavy during the night and til near 3 in the afternoon when it cleared away so the sun shown beautifully & warm   our
ditch caved considerably so it will take us a day to clean it out again
remained clear til night & is cooler   Old Californians prophecy a dry
winter which will be hard on the miners if it is   The most of them in
this camp are depending on the rains for their winters work

Sun. 11   We washed dirt most of the day   we made 15.00 apiece
we worked because our dirt was soaked so it washes good & we were
afraid we would not get it done if we did not push the matter so we
worked to day   Heavy frost this morning   day clear & pleasant

Mon. 12   Day cloudy & cool   a light shower of rain this evening
at dark   This morning was the coldest we have had this winter   ice
froze ¼ inch thick   We made today 29.00 apiece   The Frost was so
heavy this morning it looked like a light snow

Tuesday December 13th 1853

Rained considerable during the night & a light shower or two during
the day

We washed 21 cartloads of dirt & made 31.70 apiece which is about
24 Dollars over expense

To night the Sons of Temperance had a torchlight procession   I
have heard nothing said about it previous to this and dont know why
they chose so muddy a time for it   there were about 40 men in the
procession wearing Regalias & they looked verry well   Their appearance so unexpected in the streets created some astonishment which
soon however subsided

Wed. 14   We washed ½ the day to day & made 10.62 apiece   this
is the last dirt we have to wash this winter as we dont expect to get
any more out of the claim until next spring   We will now finish the
ditch and try how soon we can get to sluicing

I understand the Sons of Temperance had a lecture as well as procession last night   A Ball in Town to night

Thurs. 15   We got a small stove to day which we paid $32.00 for
it is the smallest size premium patent with the furniture   that is the
cost here   This morning was the coldest this winter   looked like a
light snow   ice ¼ inch thick   we sent to the mill for a load of slabs
to day for our ditch but could not get them as they were none there
so we will have to make another trial   In the road across where our
ditch runs we found in the bottom of the ditch good pay dirt some of
which payed 2/– to the pan & some as low as 2c

Friday December 16th 1853

This morning was the coldest one this winter   frost was heavier &
ice thicker and more of it   The day was clear & cool   the ice did
not thaw in the shade during the day which is something unusual here

There is a company just forming to bring water into this camp from
the Moquolumne River or from one of its branches   they propose
bringing it through Robisons & Cos ditch which runs to Russel diggings
There is already a ditch from the same branch begun which is to bring
the water in by way of the south branch so that I dont think they can
get the water at all as that company will want all of it   People are
turning their attention more to ditching now than ever before as that
is now considered the surest way to get plenty of water & that (that)
is clear to mine with   Every branch & Gulch that furnishes any water
worth while is now ditched & turned away for mining purposes
There is a company at work now digging a ditch to drain the bed of a
part of the South Branch of Sutter and it is generally supposed they
will do well   also there is another company at work digging a ditch
through Grass Valley for the purpose of draining it so they can work to
the Ledge where they have found some verry good prospects in sinking

holes   The Mining on the flat here is now nearly all stopped for the winter except a few who are sluicing & preparing to sluice

Saturday December 17th 1853

Mace came down from the Ranch to day & tells me I had better take my cattle down on to a Ranch on the valley as the frost has nearly destroyed all the grass up on his Ranch   I think some of taking them down on the (the) San Joaquin

Last night was equally as cold as night before last   I went to the mill this morning & got a load of slabs for making a Sewer in our ditch as we think that the best way   We make a box of the slabs & lay them in the bottom of the ditch and then fill up the ditch again so by this we will not have to clean it out again as we would have to do if we had bridged it as we first calculated   we would box it in this way all through if we were able but as we are not we will have to have a part of it open where there is no road crosses   The Ditch is about 9 feet deep on an average

We have talked some more with the Ditch Company & they now say if we will wait until they can sluice away a part of the lower end of the Gulch that we may sluice into the place they sluice out   we intend to give them a little time & see if they are going to do anything & if they do not we will immediately commence sluicing into their hole

Sunday December 18th 1853

Last night was another cold night and it continued to freeze in the shade til ten o clock this morning   The day is clear & the sun shines warm   We made some sluice boxes to day which is the last we expect to have to make   we have now got 18 boxes which makes 216 feet which we think will be all we will want   The company who went out yesterday to prospect the ground for bringing a ditch into the North Branch returned this evening & report the snow deep on the hills & the ditch verry hard & long to dig   they think it cant be dug nohow at the present time as it is too cold & they say it will have to be at least 25 miles long to get the water into the North Branch of Sutter from the main Mokelumne so that the ditch will not be dug now at all

Mace says the company that is now digging the ditch into the South branch of Sutter will have their ditch complete in the course of a fortnight   This will be of considerable advantage to the Miners on the south branch

Mon. 19 Last night was not so cold as usual   the day was warm We worked on the ditch & did not quite finish it but we will finish it by noon tomorrow if nothing prevents   The day was clear but clouded up about sunset & looks like rain   I have had the rheumatism all day in my back hips & thighs down to my knees & this evening I can scarcely move

Tuesday Dec 20th 1853

We finished the ditch a little after noon   I feel verry sore to day my knees & back are so sore they give me considerable pain   The day was cloudy & a cool light & sharp breeze from the west   The Grady Company having agreed to sluice out a ditch below so we could sluice we are now waiting on them so we can go to work

Wed. 21   The forepart of the day frosty cool & cloudy   the afterpart clear & pleasant   We got wood today as we had nothing else to do to advantage

Thurs. 22   I went up to the Ranch to day to take my Cattle away I found them looking worse than they have looked before   I took them to Grass Valley where a man is gathering up Cattle to take on the lower valley to Ranch   I took 3 of maces Cattle with mine   I find I have worked the Cattle too much as they are poorer now instead of fatter while cattle that crossed the plains the same time they did & have not worked any since are looking well

Fri. 23   This morning was the coldest yet   ice was thicker than it has been this winter   the day was clear & pleasant   the evening cloudy & cool

A Ball comes off to night in the new Hotel that is built on the Ground that the one was burnt off of last spring[30]   all the burnt ground is now built over again & looks as if a fire had never been there   I cant go to the Ball as I dont think I am able

Sunday December 25th 1853

Rained most of the day yesterday, This morning frosty   the day clear & warm   We had a pan of Egg Nog this morning   we paid for Eggs $2.50 pr Dozen   A great many of the Miners are taking their christmas that means getting Drunk   The Miners generally are not making anything as they are waiting for water which does not seem to be coming soon   Most of the old Californians say there will be no rain this winter of any consequence   they say there is generally two open winters & one hard one every three years

This Camp is now more prosperous than it has yet been   that is there is more people in it just now & it is the opinion of some that it will begin to go down again ere long as there is supposed to be not enough of water to keep the men that are here at work the winter

We have some doubts of getting water enough to sluice with ourselves this winter as the Ditch company use most all the water that comes in to the flat from the north   though we will know this week what we will do   Mr George & Lady & myself took dinner at a Friends in town to day   we had chicken for dinner which is the first time I have eat chicken only at a ball since I came into this country   was as good a dinner as I have eat in the country

Sunday December 25th 1853

I have felt for some months past as contented as I ever have been in life   I believe that a person to be happy must take the world as it comes & make the most of it   There is no happiness in a continual strife with all that we meet for us

The easiest way is the best & the mottoe "Do as ye would that others should do unto you" is the best to follow as near as may be or as circumstances will permit us to do

I have now been so long from home that I do not feel so anxious to get back there as I did the first year I was away   I thought then of soon returning to my native place but I think now that this is as good a country as is in the world & that I can live here as well as anywhere else   The Climate suits me better than it did in the states & money is plenty enough so a man can always get plenty to live on comfortably & that that is all a man can make use of in this world & this is all that is necessary to happiness

A man who always endevers to do as near right as his conscience & circumstances will permit will seldom ever go estray & that a man who does so is an honest man

I believe that to do nothing to others that you would not like to have done to you is the true definition of the word Honor

Monday December 26th 1853

This morning was the coldest I have seen in California   a verry heavy frost   the road froze so as to bear a horse

We have not worked any on the claim since last Tuesday til to day we worked to keep them from jumping the claim

The Law here is now that a Man can hold two claims provided he works a day for each claim on either of them every week so we have worked to day to keep them from jumping ours

Wed. 28   We chopped wood yesterday & to day til noon   I went up on the hill and got some pitch pine for light wood   Clouded up during the night & some light sprinkles of rain fell during the day

The Miners are cheering up considerable with the hope of plenty of water now though I verry much fear we will not have enough to do any good   we cant do any work now in our claim until it either dries up or more water comes

Thurs. 29   We did nothing particular to day   We have concluded if we can buy water of Grady & Co to do so   The day was clear & pleasant it having cleared off during the night   I feel a little like the blues as I cant work the claim to advantage nor cant prospect to advantage because if I leave my claim somebody will jump it although the Law allows a Man two claims   I cant leave this one as I have more than one claim here

Saturday Dec 31st 1853

To day we commenced hauling out of the claim on to the Road but soon quit as we could not get dirt that we did not want to sluice During the week it was understood that all who would would gather on the road & fix it near the creek where it is verry muddy   so after I hauled a few loads out of the claim I went & worked with the rest & hauled tailends so we got the road in tolerable good order but it will want work again soon

A Trial came off to day in which both parties were considerable loosers   The dispute was for a claim which is not believed to be verry good   worth perhaps $50. & the cost to each party was not less than $150. so it is with most all the law suits that come off in this country therefore I will always try & keep clear of them   We think of trying to buy a sluice head of the Ditch company instead of bringing it in the ditch we have dug   if we buy the water it will put a stop to the dispute between us about sluicing in the Gulch   I feel some Dubious of (of) asking for the water as they may think they have us fast & refuse to let us have the water so we may be forced into a ruinous Law suit

Sunday January the first 1854

The Morning Cold & frosty as it has been for several morning

The day clear & pleasant   The evening Cloudy & cool   The Town was filled during the day with people Many who were strangers to me Many were drunk & many nearly so   Some passed the day shouting &c &c

We had an Oyster Dinner & had four Men & two Ladies and 4 children to help us eat it   This seems to me much more pleasant than ranting around town or passing the time in Lounging about town thus we keep up a Miniature society which to me is another Portion of

what the world is seeking which is pleasure or happiness   every
moment that we can pass by with pleasure is so much more of our
share of the good things of this world   We have now exchanged Civil-
ities with two or three families in Town which I think is a rare thing
for California

This morning my promise expired & I took a chew of Tobacco   it
tasted as well if not better than it ever tasted before though I will still
smoke in place of chewing until I take a notion either to go to chewing
again or quit the use of the weed entirely

I will now make a Statement of what I am worth

Statement Jan 1st 1854

I have

In Specimen Dust	16.00	
" House	225.00	
" Cattle & Waggon	430.00	
" Horse	50.00	
" Hogs	40.00	
" Mule & Carts	100.00	
" Mining Tools	50.00	
" Claim in Soldier	350.00	
" Note on Mott	250.00	
" " " Parsons	30.00	
" " " Reeves	8.00	
" House furniture	30.00	
" Revolver	28.00	
" Wearing apparel	50.00	
" a/cs that are good	45.60	
" " uncertain	80.00	/ 1782.60

I Owe

In note to Tyrrell	95.00	
" " " Davis	46.00	
" a/c To Troutman	236.67	
" " " Hanford & Downs	63.00	
" " " Duke	18.37	
" " " Carpenter	7.50	
" Small a/cs	20.44	486.98
		$1295.62

This is as near what I am worth as I can tell just now   I have put
every thing at what I think it would sell for provided it could be sold

at all at a fair price though I might possibly not get more than ⅔ of My calculation

If the claim is near as good as is generally supposed I will realize at least 2000 of it next summer

Monday January 2d 1854

The day warmer than has been for some time & clear with a light breeze

The New years Ball comes off at the Consolation Hall to night

This day two years ago I landed in San Francisco   This is the longest I have ever been away from my Relatives & I now find a person is easily weaned from home   I do not feel so uneasy now as I have formerly when I would be away from home for a short time

Tues. 3   This Morning clear & frosty   I spoke to Grady this morning again to buy a sluice head of water & he spoke favorable to it though he said he could not give us an answer until he had consulted the rest of the company   so I am waiting for his answer while George & Lady are sleeping to make up for the time they lost at the ball The day is warm & pleasant   The day has past & Grady has not answered me yet   I have not talked with George yet but I think we will not wait any longer but try & get water in & go to work

Wed. 4   To day we put up some of our sluice boxes & tried to make some arrangements about getting water as Grady has not answered my application yet

The day was clear & pleasant

Thursday Jan 5th 1854

We finished putting in our sluices to day   I talked with Grady & he refused to let us have water so we must now try to get it otherwheres

The flat Ditch Company have dug a ditch around the head of the Soldier Gulch companies ditch & have taken the water away from them so they havent water enough to work with now more than ½ the time   They are now gone to the hill to get out an injunction against the flat company to prevent them from taking the water   We are now going to try to get water from the Middle Branch   The day was the coldest throughout of the season although it did not freeze there was a cold North wind blowing all day & is blowing hard to night

Fri. 6   This Morning is the coldest I have seen since I have been in the country   I was up the Middle Branch this morning & found it froze over wherever there was water there was ice   I saw icicles 18 inches long which are the first I have seen in the state   It was a cool

day throughout although the sun shown clear & pleasant   I have been
up the South Branch to night & find it freezing again apparently as
hard as it did last night   We did nothing to day for want of water
which we cant get

Saturday January 7th 1854

This morning was about as cold as yesterday but the day is warmer
I was talking yesterday about hireing water from a ditch that comes
into the Middle Branch below Gradys Damn   The Grady company
have now got a damn built across the Middle & North Branches up out
of the valley for the purpose of catching the water over night to work
with during the day   The ditch that we are trying to get water from
comes out above the reservoir damn on the Middle Branch & has been
dug for some time so it has the oldest right to the water   by making
the ditch large enough to carry most of the water we can get a good
sluice head here   Grady is trying to buy the ditch but I think they
ask a price that wont be given   We have tried to get the water that
runs in the flat ditch but they have cut their ditch above Gradys &
think they can hold the water so they will not let us take it out until
the difficulty between them & Grady is settled

We are doing nothing and in consequence have the blues a little
but we think if we cant get water to sluice we will go to carting next
week & try to get out some pay dirt before the spring rains set in
From what I can understand the times are more dull now than they
have ever before been in California   nearly all are waiting for water
and in consequence money is scarce

Saturday January 7th 1854

The Merchants during the fall & summer kept all the teams running
that they could get so as to have a good stock on hands provided the
winter set in as it did last year   They have got their stores full & the
roads are dry   prices remain nominal   the demand is decreased so
that trades are dull and money scarce   Most of the retail trade is now
done on time here & from what I can hear it is generally so throughout
California   such however is the effect of a dry winter like the present

On last thursday week I paid 5c for a letter which was the last money
I had & I have had none since not because I could not make as much as
I thought I ought to by work so I would make nothing rather than
work for little and such is the way with the generality of Miners
They will prospect a place & if it is good they will wait for a chance to
work it & do nothing rather than hunt another place & run the chance
of loosing the good prospect they have got   The Law allows us to

hold two claims which we have got here so we cant leave to prospect otherwheres as if we got a good prospect we could neither sell nor work it because we have got all the Laws allows us here

Saturday January 7th 1854

This evening I understood that Ab Mott was going to leave so I went up & found he is gone

I find he has sold ½ his claim for $150.00 for which the man owes him $50.00 yet which I probably will get & the other ½ I may sell for something   He has promised to return tomorrow week but then I do not believe he will return at all nor do I believe he is honest   The Democrot & Whig candidate will speak in town to night

Mon. 9   I went this morning & saw the Men owning the upper ditch on Middle Branch & they promised to give us a head of water

I came back & found that Grady had promised to give us a head of water as soon as his companies difficulty was settled with the flat ditch or as it is called the Volcano Ditching Company   so I went back & told the Men we would wait on the Grady Company awhile longer The Men using the water in the creek are on a spree to day so we turned their water into our ditch but there is not enough of it to do us any good in sluicing   I do not understand the way Grady does alto-gather though I suppose time will show what he means by being so fair   I hope he means no harm   The weather is warmer & to day is cloudy & a light shower of snow & hail fell during the forenoon   This evening the clouds are heavier & looks more like rain

Hired the mule awhile & got   .50

Tuesday January 10th 1854

The election for a Member to the Assembly or State Legislature to fill a vacancy caused by death came off in this county to day   George worked with the mule & cart to day for another man while I did noth-ing   the day was clear & pleasant   this evening is some cloudy but does not look much like rain

Wed. 11   The day was cloudy & pleasant   We hauled wet dirt all day and washed 8 loads to try it & got only .50 apiece so that won't pay   guess we wont wash much more until we get a sluice head of water   I commenced chewing tobacco again to day   I do not feel that I cared to deny myself so much pleasure as it would be to quit chewing tobacco

Thurs. 12   This morning when I awoke it was raining & continued so all day without any intermission   we have water enough now to sluice & will go at it as soon as we can

Fri. 13 Seems to have rained verry hard all night & rained with but little intermission all day   Our ditch caved in in several places   so it will take us a days work to get it in order to work again & we are afraid that the boxes are filled so that the water will not pass through some of the bank caved in & knocked some of our sluice boxes down

Saturday Jan 14th 1854

Rained verry hard during the night & some showers during the day The wind blew up cold in the morning and the day has been cold & several light showers fell during the day   We worked on the ditch & got it nearly cleaned out though I fear we will have to continue throwing out as it looks as if it will cave more   The creek is now up considerable & plenty of water for all the Miners

Sun. 15 I went up on China Gulch to day & find the boys at work with plenty of water   To the surprise of all while I was there Ab Mott came up according as he said he would when he went away   This somewhat shakes my belief in his dishonesty though I cant entirely believe he intends to pay the debt he owes me   The day is cold & windy with some light showers of snow in the forenoon   Davis sold his house to a family yesterday and they moved in last evening   so we have some neighbors of the feminine gender besides some children they are new comers to the country   In the afternoon the snow fell steady & is yet snowing (at 8 PM) the ground is covered with it only where it is too wet to lay on   We staid round the house most of the day & did no work   only Mr George took the mule & cart & hauled a couple of loads of boards up to Jackass Gulch

Monday January 16th 1854

Seems to have snowed all night   the snow this morning is about 4 inches deep & still falling

We turned the water into the ditch & find the boxes are clogged but I think the water will work its way through in a day or so

The snow melted considerable during the day & was showery all day (snow showers)   I have taken cold & feel verry bad this evening suppose it will wear off soon so I wont take medicine yet   To night the snow falling is all rain & looks as if we would have considerable more rain

Tues. 17 Snowed considerable during the night & most of the forenoon today   cleared off in the afternoon but is again cloudy to night The air is not cold   it has been thawing or melting ever since the snow begin to fall   I have felt verry unwell all day   I was not 20 feet from the house all day   this is the first day I have been kept in the house all day by sickness since I have been in California

A boy badly burned on the face was brought here for Mrs George to take care of til he gets well   he was burned by water falling in a hot bed of coals & the fire & ashes flew up in his face   the skin is off most of his face & is considerably swelled so much so that his eyes are closed   he is about 5 years old

Wednesday January 18th 1854

This morning was clear & cold   the ground was froze so as to bear a person on the soft mud   the day was clear & cold   thawed but verry little this evening   clouded up & commenced snowing awhile before night & is snowing now (8-o-clock) verry fast   I am still verry unwell but going about   George has made a little yesterday & to day washing tailends

Thurs. 19   The snow quit falling about bedtime last night & cleared up during the night & froze considerable & the day was clear & cold & this evening it began to freeze about an hour before sundown & is verry cold to night   it thawed a verry little during the day   I did nothing to day but walk round   I feel nearly well again & would go to work if I could to advantage   Our ditch bothers us so that I have proposed to the ditch company to buy water of them to sluice with   they are to answer us tomorrow morning

Fri. 20   This Morning was the coldest within the Memory of the oldest inhabitant   The thermometer was down to 2° above Zero   My bed was covered with frost this morning & every thing we had in the house was froze   The potatoes in this valley are injured to a great extent   all the Merchants lost some & the farmers considerable   the day was clear & cold & to night it is again freezing the little it thawed during the day

Saturday January 21st 1854

The day was not so cold as has been and was a little cloudy   but to night it is clear again   thawed but verry little to day   A company has now got to work digging a ditch from the mouth of the Canon up the south Branch for the purpose of draining off the flat so they can work it   The other company above are progressing with their ditch the cold weather however has stopped mining for the present as most of the water is froze up

We went up on the ridge to day & drawed down a dry log of pitch pine   poor light wood   we found the ground not froze any under the snow & the snow is only about 8 inches deep on the low hills around this valley

Sun. 22 The day was cloudy & cool   commenced raining awhile before dark & is now raining steady   the ground has thawed some but not much   the snow is melting slowly

Mon. 23 The day was cloudy & cool still thawing but verry slowly seems to have rained all night lightly & part of he night it seems to have sleeted   rained none during the day except a light shower this evening   I went and seen the ditching company this morning and they could not give me any certain answer so we went to work to digging out the ditch so as to open the boxes where they filled up last rain

Monday January 23r 1854

we had been to work about an hour when Grady came & told us we could have water at $5, a day for a sluice head as long as we wanted it So we quit work on the ditch and went to work to cut a light ditch up the street to get water out of the companies Ditch   we got it nearly completed & will finish it by noon tomorrow   We wouldnt buy the water only we apprehend some difficulty about getting the water out of the creek above

Tues. 24 Rained hard all night & all day so we did not work only a verry little

Wed. 25 Rained some during the night and some showers this morning   it cleared off about noon and is clear to night   We finished our ditch & put up our sluices & are ready to go to work tomorrow

Thurs. 26 Day clear & pleasant   Morning frosty   we sluiced a part of the day and did not wash out

Fri. 27 Morning frosty   day clear & pleasant   after we got to work this morning a considerable part of the bank caved in & carried one of our boxes down into the hole which is now ful of water so we could not get it again   we were bothered some time before we got to work again   Mellus had two hands to work this evening as they could not work their other claim for want of water

Saturday January 28th 1854

Day clear & pleasant   no frost this morning   Weather considerable warmer than has been   we two sluiced to day   Melluses did not come   suppose they are at work on their claim up Soldier Gulch

Sun. 29 The day quite warm   the mud dried up considerable We cleaned out our sluices & had $11.50   paid water rent $9.00   had left each   1.25 We moved our sluice near under the bank so we can pull the dirt down into them for awhile without shovelling

Feb. 2   The weather is still fair & pleasant   Gradys Company had some fixing to do to their sluices so we stopped work & cleaned out our sluices & got $29.50 & paid $10.50 for water rent   Mellus worked ½ a day & his share was $2.50 so we had each   8.25 $1.50 of it I got after we had first cleaned out by picking it out of the rough places in the sluice   what we first washed out was just $28.00 We got the water in again this evening but did not sluice any   Mr & Mrs George has gone to a dance this evening at the Volcano House

Fri. 3   The day was cloudy with some rain in the forenoon   We sluiced all day though we got a little damped with the rain   I am not verry well though I work steady   I have the rheumatism some but it is not settled in any one place

Saturday Feb 4th 1854

The day was cloudy & pleasant   We washed out to night & had only $3.00 which did not pay for the water by $3.00   we will move the sluices tomorrow & I think it will pay better next week

I sold my share of the pigs for   30.00 by this I loose   5.95 but I had to sell them to pay a debt for which I could not get the money any other way I sold to Mr George

Sun. 5   Rained hard during the night & nearly steady all day   we fixed up our sluices & moved them in nearer the bank so we can now sluice the whole length of the claim without again moving them   It rains verry hard to night

Mon. 6   Rained hard during the night and was showry all day About 50 cartloads of dirt caved off the bank during the night & knocked down apart of our sluice   we have been all day fixing up & running off the cave dirt

Tues. 7   Morning foggy   Day clear and pleasant   We sluiced & washed out this evening & had $9.35   paid for water $6.00 which left for each   1.78 We have to pay $3 a day for water while two of us are sluicing & five dollars when five of us are at work   The dirt we are now working is a red clay & washes verry hard

Wednesday Feb 8th 1854

The day was clear & pleasant   Morning foggy   The Grady company were changing their boxes to day & had the water out so we could not work   so we chopped wood   Mace who is boarding with us came down from the Ranch to day verry sick with a fever   he is now taking Medicine   Cloudy to night

Thurs. 9 Mace is much better this morning   sit up all day   is well only weak

We sluiced ½ the day   was fixing up the sluice in the fore part of the day   we had washed two or 3 sluice fulls so we washed out & had $4.35 which was for each   3.18

The day was cloudy & to night it is raining a little now (8 PM) The dirt we have to wash now is what has been hauled out of the Gulch & is a red & blue clay & washes verry hard so we can not save what gold there is in it but we are satisfied to get enough to pay water rent

Fri. 10 Rained hard Most of the night   This Morning I turned the water out of the sluice & picked up $1.25 which was for each   .62 We then concluded we would not work all day so we cleaned out the sluice & had $5.58 which was for each   2.80

Ceased raining at noon   we worked the afternoon   Mellus told us he would go to work in the morning so we washed out this evening & had $3.75 which was for each   1.87

Pay for water rent   3.00

Commenced raining just before night & is now (8 P.M.) raining hard

Saturday Feb 11th 1854

Rained verry hard during the night & caved in a part of the bank and mashed one of our boxes & flooded the companies hole so they were sometime this morning repairing

We fixed up but could not get enough water to do much with so after trying awhile this evening we quit til we can get water

Cleared off early this morning and the day was clear & beautiful

A Report has lately reached us that the United States have bought a part of Northern Mexico [Gadsden Purchase] with Lower California which has created considerable excitement   Many are making their preperations to go there as it is supposed to be as good mining country as any part of California   I see by the New York Herald of the 5th January that the purchase is not made certain but that Negotiations are going on to that effect   Should Uncle Sam buy that part of Mexico as large an Emigration would flock there from California as came here in the year 1850

Mining has improved considerable since the rain set in but the Town does not present as lively an appearance as was generally anticipated last fall though thare are about as many people here this winter as were here during last summer

VOLCANO — LATER FIFTIES

John Doble's volume ends on the last line of its last page. He must have kept up his journal. If we know John Doble, nothing except dire calamity would have prevented him from keeping up his journal. In fact, he mentions his "journal" in a letter of July 30, 1861, from Volcano. The publication of this one may lead to the discovery of the others.

John Doble lived at Volcano from 1854 to January 1861 when he moved to Jackson and took a job as "Deputy Clerk" in the Amador Court House. He remained only until April 17, when, disliking "secesh" arguments with his associates, he returned to Volcano where he probably could not always avoid the tussles between the Volcano Blues and the Confederate "Knights of the Golden Circle." The cannon, "Old Abe," was imported from San Francisco by the Blues to overawe the opposition.

Preserved among the Doble papers is a receipt for $3.00 evidently expended by John Doble as advance payment for a book that has not been found and may not have been printed: George H. Campbell, "The Plains and California," 1855. Geo. H. Campbell on April 20, 1850, ran for County Judge of Calaveras County, according to the

Stockton *Times*. And he is listed as holding that office from May to November, 1852, having been defeated in 1850. (Coke Wood: "Calaveras," p. 148.)

We also welcome an item which seems to refer to the "Platt" of the Platt-Slater Guidebook. *Calaveras Chronicle,* vol. 2, no. 23, March 19, 1853: "Col. Platt has returned from the State of Illinois, and will practice law as heretofore in this county. Offices at Jackson and Sutter Creek."

John Doble, a member of the Independent Order of Odd Fellows (Grand Lodge of the State of California), became its District Deputy for Amador County on May 11, 1855. This document is among the family papers which also show that John Doble attended the Second Annual Ball of Amador Engine Co., No. 1, Oct. 30, 1856: tickets $5. [Fire prevention was a perpetual problem, and was never too successful.] Doble was also a subscriber to various ditch and canal companies bringing the necessary water at great expense, to run the sluice boxes at Volcano.

John Doble was appointed Deputy Sheriff of Amador County on January 2, 1857, and on September 19, 1857, he was elected to the office of Justice of the Peace in Township Number Three, Amador County, California. He was re-elected on September 1, 1858, and again on September 20, 1859.

Among the Doble papers are many receipts for sums of money transported to various points in Amador County by express agencies, particularly Wells Fargo and Co., through their Volcano agents, Hanford and Downs, in the early 1860's.

On October 7, 1861, John Doble was elected Associate Judge of the Court of Sessions at Jackson, County Seat of Amador County.

Early in 1863 he joined his brother Abner in the iron working business in San Francisco. They lived in a cabin at the back of the lot on which the shop was situated. There John stayed until his trip to Mexico in 1865.

The pages of the *Volcano Ledger,* as well as reminiscences in Doble's letters record some of the happenings during the period between the end of the journal (1854) and the beginning of Doble's letters in 1860. Entries in Alfred Doten's remarkable "Diary" cover the two years before the *Ledger* was started on October 27, 1855. Thus Doten says on September 19, 1854, traveling north, that he went, "down through James Bar and crossed just above. Passed through 'Greaser' and other small places. Stopped at Clinton a very pretty little town" and put up at the Clinton Hotel. He reached Volcano at sunset and went up the emigrant road to "the second trading post." On October 9, Doten was back at Volcano stopping at Chili John's National House. Chili's brother, Antonio, was then running the Empire House. He visited Fort Grizzly in "Pi-Pi Valley," seven miles from Indian Diggings, also Ft. John and Philbrook's Ranch.

Doten returned to Volcano on January 24, 1855, when he "went to a diorama now on exhibition at the 'Volcano Hotel.' It was pretty good—American views, Swiss scenery—Entrance fee $1.00, ladies free." On February 25 he passed Hartram's Ranch north of Volcano. March found him working his Indian Flat claims as well as those on Eddy Flat. On March 18 he met the "Morton boys," who used to keep the 'Empire House' in Volcano." On March 26: "Ft. John is a snug quiet little village of a dozen camps and a store." This town was exceptional. It was 90 per cent "Temperance."

On May 5, Doten "engaged the team of a Mr. Foster who is residing here at Russel's [Diggings] ... saw the 'rich tunnels' in the hill. These diggings are not very extensive, are situated at the head of the south fork of the 'Dry Creek' near the main emigrant road, and were discovered in '50 by a Mr. Russell."

On May 28, 1855, Doten saw Len and Marshall's circus at Volcano, and "Batchelders" Daguerreotype saloon on wheels charges $5.00 for a likeness.

On June 16, he mentions "Doc Ishmael's [Dr. J. B. Isbail, the dentist's] camp on Stud Horse Gulch." On June 18, he attends the grand opening of Vance and Curtis store in Volcano. On June 25, "Volcano Lodge No. 56" has a Masonic celebration. On July 8 he visits Masonic Cave. On July 29 he stops at "Greaser or Butte City." On August 25 he witnesses a performance of the "San Francisco Minstrels" at "New Hall—Volcano Hall." On August 27 he hears "Gov. Bigler, Col. Sabriskie and Jim Farley spout" at Volcano, the last kind of spouting that this particular Volcano ever did.

By the end of 1855, Volcano, in its insolated mountain vale, has settled down to its lyceum and debating societies, its theatricals and a spanking new newspaper. But there are still some rough edges. Contributors to the *Volcano Ledger*, all anonymous or pseudonymous, sign themselves: "More Anon," "Conridy," "Eye-Witness," "Flint Lock," "Zigaboo," "Gimlet, the Royal Dane" and the long-silent "Frat." It is feared that, "Frat has fallen victim to some female Vigilance Committee." On October 17, 1863, Mark Twain enters this arena of wit and beauty with a squib on: "How to cure a cold."

John Doble's card: "Notary Public, Volcano, Amador County, Cal."

runs through the first forty-four issues of the *Ledger,* from October 27, 1855 to September 6, 1856. On February 28, 1857, a letter on "Batchelors Hall" signed, "Theophilus Single" sounds a lot like J. Doble, Esq. The *Ledger* moved to Jackson on April 18, 1857. On October 3, 1957: "John Doble, Esq. will open his office in the room next door south of Hanford and Downes, Monday, Oct. 5th." And in the next issue we find the card of John Doble "Justice of the Peace." Doble's office stood beside Soldier's Gulch near the corner of Consolation Avenue and Main Street, and adjoining Hanford and Down's store, on the south.

Shortly thereafter, on November 10, 1857, the *Ledger* carries the notice: "Married: Mr. J. F. Johnson and Miss Caroline Yeager both of Drytown, by John Doble, Justice of the Peace in Volcano, Nov. 9, 1857." It may be noted that "Drytown" at that time was distinguished by its support of no less than twenty-six saloons.

We are pleased to see that John Doble, J.P., was "determined to maintain due decorum in his court. On the first of this week, a gentleman of Volcano, of extensive legal experience, was found by a decision of the court, to submit to a non suit, and in conversing with his lawyer at the door of the court room, used derogatory language to the court. He was at once arrested and fined ten dollars for contempt. If the explanation of the matter did not sufficiently purge C - - - - of the contempt we would advise him to take Brandreth's pills," *Ledger*, vol. 3, no. 10, November 24, 1857.

This completes what the *Ledger* has to say about Doble, but it continues to regale us with examples of local wit and journalism—letters from mines as far away as the Greenhorn Mountains in Kern County, letters and reports from Upper Rancheria, Fiddletown, Clinton, West Point, Poseyana ("Quite a village of this name, or some other, is located in Minister's Gulch"), Sutter Creek, Slug Gulch, Drytown, Ione, Ft. John, Amador, El Dorado, Lancha Plana, Poverty Bar, Sandy Gulch, Puckerville, Cooper Centre, Mogul, and Monitor, as well as a screed on Russell's Diggings by "Rodney Swivelshingle."

We may be sure that Doble was interested in two first-hand accounts of incidents in the Mexican War. One by "Eye Witness," a member of the 2d Regt. of Ohio Volunteers in support of Genl. Taylor at Buena Vista where Doble was engaged (vol. 1, no. 20). Another by Richard Everett on the Battle of Molino del Rey (vol. 2, no. 29). He would also have read a letter written from the battlefield of Gettysburg (vol. 8, no. 43, August 29, 1863). Communications from a Union soldier who signs himself "Foo Ching," were sent in from Ft. Whipple,

DEDICATION BALL.

The Company of Mr. .... and Lady is respectfully solicited at the

NEW ASSEMBLY ROOM, EMPIRE HOUSE, VOLCANO,

One Tuesday Evening, March 20th, 1855.

Committee of Arrangements.

A. J. HOUGHTALING,   P. P. MARTIN,
E. PEARSON,   E. GRIFFIN,
DR. G. MUNCKTON,   G. GATES.

NEW YEAR'S BALL.

AT THE EMPIRE HOUSE, VOLCANO.

THE COMPANY OF

Yu respectfully solicited at the

EMPIRE HOUSE, VOLCANO,

One the Evening of Monday, the 1st day of January 1855.

MANAGERS:

Volcano—
W. P. Coursen,
J. D. Mason,
E. G. Griffin,
P. R. Frey.

Jackson—
W. A. Phenix,
Charles Boynton.

Ione Valley—
A. R. Courtwright,
Cook's Bar, Cosumne—
Wm. Davenport.

Mokelumne Hill—
A. I. Houghtaling,
Mr. Medley,
Mr. Moses.

Drytown—
Dr. Charles Fox,
B. F. Richmoyer.

Sutter Creek—
D. Crandall,
Jas. Porterfield.

Willow Springs—
Grove Williams.

Floor Managers:

A. I. Hooghtaling,   Wm. P. Coursen,
W. A. Phenix,   H. R. Martin.

Arizona Territory (vol. 9, nos. 18, 21 and 27, March 1864), all very interesting.

John Doble would have been affected by the execution at Jackson on December 19, 1856, of Nathan Cottle who had stabbed one, Cole, to death at the Union Hotel, Volcano, on January the 8th, 1856 (vol. 2, no. 9). He should have been especially interested in "The cave above Pike Hill," as he had once roped himself down into that very dangerous cave (vol. 1, nos. 28 and 44). This cavern, now called the "Black Chasm" was boarded up after a boy had been left dangling on a rope in its depths all one night. The hill, now called Peek Hill, rises just east of Stony Point (Masonic Rock). The settlement around the Rock, including the old "Spring Saloon," was vulgarly known as Pike Town in 1855. About then, the cool recesses of Masonic Cave had been fitted up with a bar, H. M. Bowden in charge, where "ice cream and jelleys" were served along with the drinks.

There were 210 houses and 170 families in Volcano in October, 1855. John Mahoncy ran the Eagle Theatre, A. I. Houghtailing was Deputy Sheriff. Those who "ate out" were happy to hear that H. G. Smith and J. Ford's "Antelope Restaurant and Saloon" was featuring venison steaks on their menu. Grizzly bears were visiting the vicinity of town, and a "fight" with one is described (vol. 2, no. 15).

Those who wanted portraits to send home had the choice of visiting Fayette Mace's Daguerrean Rooms opposite the Empire Hotel (where the Post Office now stands), or Beal's Daguerrean Rooms on Consolation Avenue opposite the Union Hotel (near the brewery). This hotel has recently been restored through the personal efforts of Walter Blomquist. In 1856, the Empire Hotel was in charge of Miss Ann Hallett who took over the Volcano House in April, 1857.

The Lyceum topic in September, 1857: "*Resolved,* that the discovery of gold in California has been productive of more evil than good" (vol. 2, no. 47). It might be instructive to know how this came out. Doble's library was a solace for the reading public and the intellectuals, while the musical instruments he kept in his cabin were there for the sole use of his guests. He could not play them himself.

"Flint Lock" wrote most of the short stories printed in the *Ledger*. One of these: "Minnie Eastfield; or, Second Love," dealt with the Volcano region in 1853, the arrival of the emigrants—Minnie among them—and the antics of old "White Plug," an habitue who wore a pale beaver hat and in honor of whom Plug Street, where Doble lived, was named (vol. 3, no. 2). Flint Lock's reputation had been built on previous stories: "The girls of Sandy Bar, a story of '49" (vol. 2, no. 15), and "The Fatal Card" (vol. 2, no. 25). But "Clara Calico" ran him a close second with her: "Midnight Marriage" (vol. 2, no. 13).

The "Amador Democratic Club, No. 1," A. M. Ballard, President, W. I. Morgan, Secretary, J. K. Payne, and T. A. Springer, editor of the *Ledger* met during the year '56. All this plus the doings of the Slumgullion Boys, and the "Calico" parties tended to pump life into the old diggings while the placers diminished and the miner's drifted off toward richer dirt—Frazer River, and the Washoe. Dull times and the town "full of loafers." No jail in '56, before the present boiler-plated edifice was built. Fastidious ladies found it unpleasant, returning from church, to have to take to the center of the street to avoid the drunks lolling and yodeling on the sidewalk (vol. 1, no. 21).

Volcano survived the strains of Civil War days, but by 1873, ten years after John Doble had moved out, it became reduced to one hotel and a small population, mostly Italian, grubbing in the abandoned claims. The town was by that time "all torn up," the houses were going to pieces, but several new quartz mines had started—*Daily Alta California*, April 20, 1873.

John Doble's letters tell what was happening to him and what he was thinking about during those outlandish years at Volcano. He became a thorough-going bachelor and his correspondence with Lizzie Lucas failed to shake him out of it. Like so many of the old prospectors who survived the first flush of the gold rush and chose to remain in the sleepy mountain towns, he had developed a few unsocial traits. Foremost of these perhaps was his dislike (or fear) of women, except for the idealized figure of Lizzie, whom he had never met. Also, and perhaps associated with this, was carelessness in personal appearance, sloppiness in the running of his cabin, his primitive cooking, and washing, his tobacco chewing, and his unkempt beard. He lived about as he pleased and this didn't tend to please his relatives.

Good tempered and easy going, perhaps inclined to be garrulous, hospitable, friendly and ready to assist the unfortunate, Doble upheld his principles and standards, never drank or gambled to excess, bought and read the books in his private library and provided food and entertainment for his friends when they visited his quarters. This might be of slight interest or importance were it not true of so many old California miners, relicts of '49 and the '50's. The "boys in grey beards," sometimes the victims of "cabin fever," living in hope of the "rich strike," full of "tall tales," given to horse play and boisterous amusements, unwilling or afraid to enter the bustling world so far from their quiet hills, forests and valleys, and old-time cronies.

John Doble "batched" it in a small clapboard cabin on Plug Street near Consolation Avenue, in Volcano. In this cabin, shared frequently with friends, he kept his library and his curios. He liked Volcano and at one time planned to stay there for the remainder of his life.

Abner Doble's wife, Margaret, visited her brother-in-law, John, at Volcano. She gave him the name and address and a description of her cousin, Elizabeth E. Lucas of Pennsylvania, thinking that the old bachelor and the old maid who had never met might enjoy a romantic correspondence. The resulting letters, preserved by the families, are transcribed as a sample of the way things were done in those days.

John unburdened himself to Lizzie but she evidently wearied of this transcontinental courtship extended over the years. And when the faint-hearted John at last hinted that she might ask him to marry her during leap year, she flitted away with another man.

The final days of John Doble are largely forgotten. He joined his brother Abner in the San Francisco iron works, and went to Mazatlan, Mexico, on a cotton-buying venture during the closing weeks of the Civil War. The cotton market blew up. John returned to California desperately sick with malaria, dysentery and small pox, as he says in his last letter to the already-married Lizzie.

CORRESPONDENCE

[MARGARET DOBLE TO ELIZABETH LUCAS]

San Francisco, Cal.
June 3rd — / '56

My Dear Cousin

Your letter of April 14th did not reach me untill the 22nd of last month. The delay was caused by a fearful accident on the Panama rail road by which scores lost their lives, and many are cripled for life. . . . I believe I have not written to you since we left York: Oh me, when I look back and recall all — but that is impossible, I can't recall half — the accidents and incidents crowded into those two months, it is more like a dream than reality. I am twice as old — don't be frightened, I believe *I look younger* — as when I penned you my last. I have had a variety of experience, and sometimes wonder if I am *really myself*. Well we left York the 5th of Apr. on the Mail Steamer Illinois, with 1,100 passengers of all sorts, sizes, and conditions. Before we were outside of the Harbor I — and the lady I mentioned who was to occupy a bearth in our room — were in bed just as sea sick as mortals well can be, and with the exception of two or three days, when we managed to ballance our-selves sufficiently to get on deck — spent the greater part of the time untill we reached Aspinwall in bed — and none of the softest, either, I can assure you. Sea sickness is anything but agreeable, but you get no sympathy, and feel none for your companions in misery. Carrie (our room mate) had the lower berth, I the middle, and D[oble] the upper. I would take a vomiting spell — D would have to hold my head and the

215

wash bowl at the same time, as soon I would get through he would have to go through the same performance with Carrie. You can imagine what an interesting group we were sometimes.

D would laugh and make fun of us both, and we both took our turns at laughing at each other. He was not sick at all, and his seat at the table was vacant but once, and that time it was occasioned by his sleeping untill breakfast was over. We put into Havanna Cuba about noon the 9th (or 11th) and left at sunrise next day. The sight of green trees never did me as much good as on that memorable day — I never saw anything so beautiful. We did not go on shore, but the view from deck was perfectly enchanting. There were hundreds and hundreds of vessels of all nations and all discriptions lying at anchor in the harbor. You can't believe or imagine the emotion I felt at seeing our own stars and stripes floating from the mast head of a goodly number. It seemed just like meeting an old friend. I, for one, never knew before what it was to 'be *proud*' of *my country*. The morning of the 15th we landed at Aspinwall — a place that looks as though it had sprung up in a weeks time. At noon we took the cars for Panama, were three hours crossing the isthumus. I must confess I never enjoyed a ride more than on that occasion. So long pent up on Ship board — out of sight of land and here everything so green and luxuriant. The road is very crooked, winding round through the hills, and in sight of the river a great part of the way. The jungle — so thick that you can see but a few feet into it, rises on both sides of the road, with here and there a naked spot doted with the huts of the natives — said huts composed of poles placed upright in the ground very close together, and thached with cane. Sometimes we would be whirled past broad grassy plains, without a tree or shrub, and covered with cattle, sheep, horses, and such like grazing in a perfect state of contement, and seemed not the least disconcerted by the frightful screams of our locomotive. I suppose you have seen enough of the Panama riot in the papers, so I may be brief on that point. The Mail Steamer cannot — on account of the shallowness of the water — come nearer to the town than 3 or 5 miles, there is a small steam boat carries the passengers, etc. out to it where the other steamer is anchored — and *it* can get in and out only at high tide — so much for explanation — The passengers are obliged to have their tickets registered at the office in Panama before they can go on board the vessel. I was waiting in the depot — an open shed — untill Mr. D could get our tickets, when the riot commenced and was but a few feet from the first man shot. The whole of it grew out of a drunken American refusing to pay a native for fruit he had taken from his stand. — I stood my ground, getting in as sheltered a spot as possible, of course, untill D succeeded in getting out, which was an hour or more after the first shot was fired. Just as he got through the natives attacked the ticket office and when we left it the balls stones and all sorts of missles were flying round our heads like hail. I was not frightened — but I know not *why* I was not. We went into a private house thinking it would be all over in a little time, but not so. About dark there were several wounded persons carried into the house where we were — we began to feel our situation anything but safe. (There were two Ladies and a little girl with us) I proposed concealing ourselves in the woods or jungle, the house being in the outskirts of the same. No sooner said than done, we made good our escape, and a little while after the house was entirely demolished by the natives. Mr. [Abner] Doble was at one time surrounded by eight or ten armed men and would have been cut to pieces had it not happened that one of them recognised him and thus saved his life. They had no intention of harming the women or children—farther than robing them of nearly everything they had on or about them—but were determined to butcher every man they could lay hands on—and, they, being utterly unarmed, had no means of defense. We kept concealed untill midnight, when the tide had raised so that the boat could get out: the firing had also ceased and we made our way on board and before day light were in our State room on board the John L. Stephens. We put into Acapulco the night of the 22nd to lay in coal and water. Up to that time the weather had been very warm so much so, that I began to think another weak like it would put a finish to me, but from that time out clocks and shawls were in great demand. The fare on the steamers is of the very best—all that troubled me was that I could not eat a double portion when I was at the table to make up for the times when I was not able to fill my place. I grumbled a good deal while in the hot climate about the water—it was about as pleasant to drink as warm dish water. They had but a limited supply of ice on board—and were obliged to save it for the wounded—of whom there were twelve. The measles and scarlet fever broke out among the children also, which made it more unpleasant. On child died a few minutes after we landed at the wharf which was the only death on board—out of 1,333—the number we had on this side the Isthmus. - - - When the wether got cool I was taken with chills and feaver—they call it the Panama feaver, and is brought on by exposure to the night air on the Isthmus; it seemed to be a very mild form of the typhoid feaver. I was able to be up and about most of the time, but still it was a very disagreeable disease.

The 1st day of May we entered the Golden Gate, and from the deck of the Steamer, as we passed up the bay, I had my first view of the Nelson & Doble ranch. Beautiful indeed it seemed to me—a broad garden in the highest state of cultivation, streatching from the beach back over the top of the hills—a gradual slope of a mile or more, with a snug white cottage near the center—the veranda covered with honey suckle climbing roses, fucia etc. in full bloom. Took a carriage at the wharf and came direct out here—two miles—and I have not been in the city since.
...Ds brother John has been down from the mines to see us since our arrival—they look very much alike, only John is not quite as large as Abner....

Your affectionate Cousin—Margaret—

[MARGARET TO LIZZIE]

San Francisco, Cal. .
Wednesday evening—
Sept. 4th /56

Dear Cousin Lizzie—
...On what condition could *you* be persuaded to come to Cal.—Lib? Be sure and tell me next time you write—for I'M altogether in earnest about it. You would like the country, I know. Besides I have a gentleman acquaintance here who was just made for you, I am sure—and I have been puzzling my brains ever since my arrival—how I could bring matters about. His name is Ross—and he has one of the nicest houses in the city—and all that.—The ladies here dress rather extravigantly—(at least we would think it so at home) they do not consider themselves dressed at all unless they have silk on. There is a great quantity of silk brought

here from China, and it is cheaper than we can get it at home. All kinds of dry goods are cheap here as I ever saw them in Wheeling—bonnets are the most expensive articles of dress—ten dollars is considered a very cheap bonnet, and they are often twenty and twenty five. It is never too warm here for woolen dresses—they can be worn the whole year around one gets the good of their clothes here—provided they are thick ones. We still live with Nelsons—and I'm afraid will have to for some time yet unless our luck turns—the ranch was robed last week of 175 dollars—that together with some other losses has rather discouraged me. You see I have not been here long enough to get used to such things—the folks here think nothing of it comparitively. Fruit is abundant here. I never saw as fine peaches and pears before—and grapes without end. Dobles step mother was married five or six weeks since making the fourth out of that family since the 1st of February, four more will finish them off, and more than likely they will be married before the year is out. . . .

Yours truly

E. E. Lucas   Margaret
P.A.

[MARGARET TO HER COUSIN LIZZIE]

Short Creek, Va.
June 24th /63

Dear Cousin Liz

. . . I hear from [Abner] Doble evry week—as usual. He is in good health—but says he is tired of keeping batchelors Hall. Wm has gone to the Owens River mines, in the employ of the same man for whom he has been working for some months past in San Francisco. . . .

Father Abraham issued a proclimation the 15th inst calling out ten thousand militia from West Virginia to serve for six months—consequently all the men have been kept in Wheeling for more than a week past, dangling around. They have not been organized yet, and no body not even the officers—seem to know what they are there for, or what is to be done with them. Will Darling got hime for a day or so, but has to go back again—you can judge how well it suits the farmers at this season of the year to be taken away from their homes. There are many farms left without a man at all to do a turn—substitutes charge five hundred dollars—and there are not many who can afford to give that. Two or three men here hired other men over age to take their places. The truth of the matter is, about this—they want to frighten the men into inlisting, same as they did last year—but they cant do it. Not half a dosen out of the Liberty regiment would take the oath. . . .

Yours as Ever—

M. B. Doble

[JOHN DOBLE TO LIZZIE LUCAS]

Volcano   June 11th 1860

Miss Lizzie E Lucas

An entire stranger may at times address another (even if not apropos) without provoking that derisive smile which is the most common answer to self evident presumption and hoping that this may be one of those times I venture to address you. I assume it you are unmarried and if so that natural love of the romantic common to most all the human family may induce you to look with more favor on a strangers attempt to establish a friendly correspondence   And believing there *can* no harm arise even if no good is done from or by it I address you to ask that you will favor me so much as to answer and thereby commence a correspondence that may afford amusement for the time even should no advantage accrue to either. You are a resident of a part of the world where the arts and sciences are flourishing where the luxuries and polish of a society have a being and the scenes surrounding you when written would be a bit of new history to me. I am staying in a wild rugged uncultivated ungoverned part of the world where beings from every quarter of the globe meet almost on a common level where polished or even well regulated society does not exist only to a limited degree and where most likely the scenes surrounding me would be intersting to you even when written in my rough unfinished manner.

Your address I learned from Maggie McFarland that was who is your cousin. She has been stopping in this place for the past two weeks and has discribed to me many of her friends and relatives at home and you among the number   And from her verry favorable history of yourself I am induced to believe you will not pass unnoticed this communication   I have been a resident of this place and of California for the past 8 years and expect to remain her for life   And am so situated that I can find time to write and therefore ask you to favor me with the privelege of writing to you   I am a Bachelor — an Old Bachelor   And am inbued with a love of the romantic to which I must attribute my boldness in attempting a correspondence with a Lady whom I never saw — coupled of course with the glowing description given me by your cousin of yourself.

With my best wishes for your happiness and prosperity and hoping that you may condesend to favor me with an answer

I will remain
Expectantly
John Doble
Volcano
Amador Co
Cal —

P S   Volcano is located on the 58th parellel of north Lattitude on the western slope of the Sierra Nevada Mountains about 160 miles East of San Francisco Bay

Pleasant Ridge (Pa.)   July 19th 1860

Mr. J. Doble

Sir: I was somewhat surprised a few days since by the reception of a note penned by the hand of an entire stranger one who to my recolection I had not even heard of. But finding the writer to be a friend (and as I have supposed a relative from the name) of my Cousin Maggie in whom I have ever placed the utmost confidence and that it is (at least in part) through her influence that you have addressed me. Beside, as you have rightly supposed me, being like yourself "imbued with a mutual love of the romantic" I shall very cheerfully comply with your request in responding to your communications. And anything with respect to the scenes and transactions in such a part as you are staying shall be truly interesting to me as I am acquainted with but little of the world at large having seldom strayed many miles beyond the limits of my Fathers farm.

I should be pleased to know something more of Cousin Maggie she has not written to me for more than a year. Suppose she has been visiting at your place or perhaps was on her way to some other quarter.

You say you are an "Old Bachelor" there is sometimes a difference of opinion respecting the age at which a gent should arrive before receiving the appelation of Bachelor. However I don't suppose you are one who has borne the title very long. Presume Cousin M[argaret] has given you all particulars (and perhaps with some exagerations) relative to myself so that anything further on my part would be unnessary at present.

I am Respectfully

Lizzie E. Lucas

Volcano   August 27th 1860

Miss L E Lucas

I was verry agreeably surprised yesterday in receiving you letter of the 12th *ult* And most cheerfully avail myself of your permission to again write to you even at the risk of being thought as presuming too much on good nature

I will first answer yours and then put down any thoughts that may pass through my mind

I am a Brother of Maggies husband   For the last year or more Maggie has been verry unwell and I verry much fear that she is permanantly diseased with a lung complaint   The Climate of San Francisco is verry damp and cool during the summer months and this summer when the cool winds set in there she grew worse and at my solicitation she came up here to see if our Climate would not improve her health We have here I presume the finest climate in the known world throughout the summer we have a pleasant breeze with a clear atmosphere and although the thermometer frequently rises to 100 and sometimes to 115 we seldom hear of any injury from the heat   Maggie came here a few weeks before I wrote to you   when she came she was suffering from a pain in the left shoulder and breast and coughed verry much at the time   I wrote she was nearly well again and had begun to be anxious about getting home again   The trip I think improved her health verry much but I hear now that she is worse again and I verry much fear she will not entirely get clear of the disease through life   She is one of the most plesant amiable women it has ever been my fortune to become acquainted with and you think truly when you say it was her who recommended my writing to you   An her description of your character was highly flattering She promised me to write to you in a short time after she left here which I presume she has already done I love the Grand and Sublime in nature And here is as fine a place as is in the world to gratify that Love Volcano is about half way between the Summits and the foot hills of the Sierra Nevada Mountains and is in a deep small valley bounded on the North by a ridge of Marble about 2500 feet high and on all other sides by high steep mountains covered with a dense growth of the vergreen pine Maggie will undoubtedly give you a picture of our scenery here and which will no doubt be more interesting than I can give but which I will try at some future time should circumstances permit Yes I feel that [I] am an old Bachelor I will be 33 years old in February 1861 and think I am fully entitled to the appellation as usually given me by my Female acquaintances Yes as you say it is only [a] matter of opinion which every person must decide for themselves

Yes Maggie gave me a description of you but I am so forgetful of personal descriptions that I have really forgotten most all of what she said in regard to your appearances, and would be much pleased if I could see her again soon to have her repeat it in such a manner as I might remember it though I now verry distinctly remember that her picture of you was a verry pleasing one

An outline of my own history might not be out of place I was brought up in Indiana received a common school Education and served a time at the Blacksmith Trade—Quit that to learn the Mercantile business—became a book keeper, came to California in 1851 Mined the greater part of 4 years and done any kind and allkinds of work to make a living And since the first day of January 1857 have been holding a Petty public Office [Justice of the Peace] I am poor as the world calls it but I am rich in [being] tolerably contented I have been fortunate enough to have a home since I landed here although that home was at times only a canvass tent I never could enjoy myself at a Hotel or Boarding house but felt at home only when I had a place that I could call my own

I am five ft 9 in high weigh 147 lbs blue eyes one of which squints—dark hair and Sunburnt whiskers—Was rather a wild and reckless youth but have grown more steady in later years An now think that the value of life is measured by the good we do in the world and therefore am trying to increase the value of mine I have got together a small library of 200 volumes consisting of Law Medical Religious poetical and other books which are not only useful and entertaining to me but are useful to those around me I have I think been very fortunate in life in always having around me many warm true hearted friends but have been either careless or unfortunate I don't know which in never meeting with that one *friend* who is the only one to fill our cup of happiness in this world

Maggie was continually hectoring me while she was here because I had not got a wife And I finally told her my reasons which were that before I left the States I had never thought of Marrying And since I had came to this country though I had frequently thought of it I had never met with a being here with whom I could hold that relation—The population of Volcano is about 3000 and in all that number there are only 6 Girls that are old enough to Marry And those 6 grew up here and have been accustomed to the attentions and flattery of the rougher sex since they were 10 or 12 years old Consequently they possess peculiar characters which did not suit my taste There has at times been more Girls here but the general characteristics were the same because there has always been from 10 to 20 men—young men I mean to one Girl and I find invariably that excess of flattering attentions turns the head to use a common phrase or so largely increases self love that it is verry unpleasant to come in contact with   With these reasons Maggie was satisfied that it was out of the question for me to ever expect to Marry And like her I am half convinced that it is my lot to pass through this world alone—that word *alone* has for me a dismal doleful sound at times—I feel when I hear it as if I were seperated from all the world and the air even echoed back the sound—I meant at times when I hear it —at other times of course it passes unheeded   I told Maggie that I had not a single Female Correspondent and on that she spoke of you—   And I thought how pleasant it would be to have a chance to write my thoughts occasionally to one whom I believed from her description given would appreciate circumstances generally and excuse the informality of an absent introduction   And upon the strength of that belief I have in this letter followed my mind in its impulsive meanderings without regard to order Grammer or regularity in any manner   I am writing in my office and at the same time attending to the business of the day which frequently interrupts me   I have taken no pains but write as I would were I writing any other matter and do so because I wish to convey to you an idea of my real character When you once understand that then should I be able to write anything that would interest you   it would possess no false charm but would be appreciated for its intrinsic merits only and should I be so unfortunate as to excite only derision instead of respect then our correspondence would cease without running to an unnecessary length

When there is no congeniality there can be no sympathy And therefore the necessity of truth in all things

Feeling as I believe this necessity I have written as you see in a rambling manner And I hope that it may not displease you

Your part of the Country I have never visited and anything descriptive of it would undoubtedly be to me interesting

Hoping that you will make due allowance for any errors in me and this and fully excuse them   And hoping too that you will be sufficiently pleased to answer my rambling yet I hope truthful letter   I remain in expectation

Truly yours

Miss Lizzie E. Lucas   John Doble

Good Intent (Pa.)   Oct. 20th '60

Mr. J. Doble

Sir: Several weeks have elapsed since I received your letter dated Aug. 27th. A week later I receivd another in which you apologised for the manner in which the first was written. But I think I understood it in the manner in which it was intended and so was not offended as you had thought. But on the contrary found it very interesting and perhaps I should here offer something by way of apology in not answering you sooner. My first is I have been waiting thinking to receive a letter from Cousin Maggie but have as yet been disappointed. The next I shall offer is there has been a lady here—an acquaintance—sick of fever and I had taken upon myself to act the part of nurse principaly and the care and loss of rest consequent accompanied by other duties continually devolving upon me I was entirely void of that frame of mind necessary for me to write anything intelligibly even could I have found time sufficient for the task. But she is now recovering and I feel greatly relieved   Though I confess my natural want of intellect is not repaired in the least, of which quality you will undoubtedly learn from my letters I do not possess a very large supply. But here I am too far straying from what I intended and will return. The information you gave me concerning Maggie was more satisfactory than anything I had heard for a long time   I had heard of her ill health but did not know what she complained of. I feared her lungs were diseased. Still I would hope she may so far recover as to be able to visit her old home by next spring as I hear they talk of so doing. I should like to see her very much indeed.

Since you have favored me with a short history of your past life and a description of your person, I shall try to give you a faint idea of how I look as you say you have forgotten Maggies description of my personal aperance   I am 29 years of age rather small of stature   Measure 5 ft in height rather slender, hair very nearly the color of Maggies   a little wavy inclined. black eyes, wear false teeth, am plain in evry sense of the word. I like simplicity probably because I was brought up to appreciate it rather than anything else.

Like you I was rather wild and giddy in my younger days but think I have become quite sobered down of late   I have learned something of the deceitfulness and vanity of the human heart in general, but I think I have a heart that can appreciate what is right at least to some extent although I often err as well as others.

I have always resided as you are aware in the country 20 miles from any large town though there are quite a number of villages all around us the nearest of which is two miles distant.

Society is good though not refined to any very great extent. Most of the people here are members of some religious denomination. We have plenty of Churches and school houses all around. The nearest Presbyterian Church of which I am an unworthy member is five miles distant   the road is good and it is quite a pleasant drive when the weather is fine. There are other denominations nearer.

The Country is rough and hilly   productive of all kinds of fruit and grain though the soil is not very rich.

From your description of Volcano I imagine the scenery must be very beautiful and anything further descriptive of the Country there will be truly interesting to me. I cannot imagine why Maggie has not written to me as you say she intended doing it, a long long time since I have had a line from her but perhaps she is not able to write.

I have written this at different times partly by candle light and have been interrupted in different ways so you will please excuse some failings.

Hoping to be able to write something more interesting hereafter, I remain respectfully

Lizzie E Lucas

Mr J Doble

Volcano   Nov 29th 1860

Miss L. E. Lucas

Yours of the 20th ult is read and contents noted and I proceed at once to answer though slightly indesposed from the effects of a change in the weather. For the past week or so we have had cool hazy cloudy windy weather all moderate and last night a verry heavy frost to day as warm and pleasant as heart could wish Thermometer 68° in the shade. During the fall and spring here these changes usually effect the human system more or as much as they do in more cold and damp climates. I am much gratified to find that you seem to understand the spirit of my letter as I feared you might only see the uncultivated manner instead of the spirit and I will say here which is true too that I have not received a letter in the last three years that has given me as much real pleasure as yours has And I see in it either fancied or real a deep current of sound and valuable intelligence And only regret that I possess not the ability to answer or write as you have done however as we have begun the Correspondence for the purpose of affording each other amusement or gratification as the case may be I will go ahead and do the best I can or perhaps not the best I might do under other circumstances but the best I can for the time being. When Maggie was here she promised me to write you verry soon and once I thought she would write while here but for some reason unknown to me she did not do so. I have received one letter from her since she went home and she has failed to write since though my Brother frequently says she is going to write   I heard from her last night and she is still wavering between severe illness and comparative health. I am thoroughly convinced that her disease is of the lungs and that she will never entirely recover. She will undoubtedly be at home next spring unless prevented by Providence. I have never been much with her as I have lived here ever since she came to California but so far as I know her I have a high opinion of her qualities. She really is one of the most amiable women I have ever been acquainted with.

An apology was entirely unnecessary and if it had been the one you have given is most complete   our duties to our suffering fellow creatures are such that society itself depends on their close observance   And therefore you did right in letting other considerations go to attend to one who needed your assistance. Although you may have had an unpleasant tedious time yet when done conscience the source of our worst pains and sweetest pleasures approved and pleasure the result. I have had many friends in this state sick and have neglected some but never did so without suffering in mind for it. And it is most true that when we have a suffering friend near the mind cannot seperate itself from the immediate presence without that vigor that at other times it is wont to do. If as you say your intellect was not repaired , , since the convalescence of your friend then I shall anticipate extreme pleasure hereafter in reading your letters should you be so kind hereafter as to favor me with any   And on the other hand if I am to be so unfortunate as to fall under your displeasure as to provoke your silence I will deem one of my sweetest pleasures lost.

I am under renewed obligation to you for your description of yourself   from what I can remember of Maggies description yours corresponds with hers and is nearly the description of my beau ideal of what woman should be and your preference for the handmaid of nature as I deem "SIMPLICITY" to be is I take it a good evidence that you are a true woman. A person who has lived in our age cannot even of the lowest intilligence be so blind as not to see some of the working of the human heart and to see is to know of the uncertainty of outside appearances   I have sometimes felt that I could not depend on anything human but after wearing off the first pangs of disappointment and viewing all matters connected calmly and coolley I have invariably come to the conclusion the human heart of whose deceitfulness we are so apt and often complaining of is *our own* mind and heart. When Causes combine we wish certain objects attained our wishes blind us and we see not the certain indications of failure that to disinterested minds are apparent. I have so often failed in wished for objects and so often traced the real cause of severe disappointment to My self that I have actually once or twice failed and not felt it as I would have done had I not made those observations   That person who can divest himself or herself of the influence of interest when an object however remote presents itself for contemplation never fails but the moment that interest or the wish steps in then we view only the obverse side or if [we] look at the reverse at all it is only a passing glance and we see nothing. To use a common expression "I know the world is deceitful" and yet I know I am seldom deceived without in a great measure being to blame. To err is human and therefore we should forgive the error in others and the more severely blame the error in ourselves. In a country like this where the great objct of life in all is wealth and but few seem to regard anything but the means of obtaining it all who join in the struggle must expect to meet with reverses greater or less. I have several times failed in what I deemed a sure fortune and seldom failed unless by putting dependence in untried friends so that when you spoke of the deceitfulness of the human heart it struck a chord in mine that is verry sensitive from frequent disappointments and this I say as an apology for trying to philosophise on the deceitfulness of the human heart and I further say by way of explanation that I have been deceived in every thing else in the world nearly (that is I mean within my sphere) except Love and Women   I have seen many I liked well but none that I loved and I never put confidence in a woman yet that deceived me. I must acknowledge though that it was not my faculty for observation or my ability to see what might be done but that it was the force of Circumstances and the experience of others that has on two or more occasions prevented great loss to me by trusting to women and appearances. In this country we have many women who buy borrow sell and lend and live single because the scarcity of women here assure them of great respect from men and it is of some of these I spoke. Our country however is fast settling down to something near an equality. Emigration and growth is fast equalizing the sexes   in many parts of the country they are allready equal but here in the mountains the old inequality still exists. If I forget not I wrote you before of their relative numbers if I have not I will in the future do so should opportunity offer.

Should you here notice a change it is explained by the fact that I was interrupted by business and resume the writing after several hours.

I prefer the country far before the City and living in a country village I deem the same   I suppose those who are brought up in the Cities prefer to live there and vice versa   My Brother has offered me every inducement to go into business in the City but I am so pleased with this part of the country that it is now my intention as it has been since 1853 to end my days here   were I wealthy I might travel some but here would still be my home   The Pleasant climate the pleasant and ever varying scenery and the excitement of digging gold all conspire to confirm me in that resolve.

I am not a church member as I believe I told you before but never interfere with those who wish to be   I take for my religion the words of Christ, "As ye would that others should do unto you, etc." And I do try to live up to it but I sometimes fail in it which is nothing but human   When I was at home I mean in Indiana I frequently went five and six miles to the various churches and enjoyed it much Were I there now no doubt but that I should resume old habits and attend church regularly as formerly

I will finish answering your letter and then endeavor to answer your request for description of some parts of the country around here

Why Maggie does not write is as much a puzzle to me as it seems to be to you My Brother writes that she is doing her own work most of the time so she certainly can not omit writing on account of sickness   I will write and ask her what is wrong You ask me to excuse failings etc the excuse would be good had there been *many* failings but I have carefully read your letter all over for the 5th or 6th time and have not found a single wrong letter in or left out nor a word misplaced or the slightest unnecessary scratch in it   On the contrary it is neat plain and properly written in every particular and such being the fact I could not help but notice it

This Country being newly settled is as a matter [of fact] far behind older countries in improvements   buildings are much lighter in structure and of less durable material   In this town we have several fire proof buildings about 14 [I] believe built of stone and brick togather Stone and brick alone and Groat (Groat is a composition mortair that is put into the wall a layer at a time and allowed to dry before the next is put on) these materials are good but they are put up more hastily and carelessly than in older settled countries   Consequently the general character of improvements are much lighter and unsubstantial than through the states yet they are sufficient for the country   I have lived through the winter here in a canvas tent and lived as comfortable as I have since in a more substantial structure

The soil where there is any is good and verry productive but requires irrigation throughout the summer season except in verry few spots   Irrigation is usually so expensive that but few are able to cultivate in that way   Water sells for 25 cents the inch that is what will run through a hole an inch square for one day   It would take two inches to irrigate one acre and that would soon eat up the crop   those who are able to own running water do well but those who are not can not farm it or as we term it here Ranch it therefore almost all the ground cultivated here is the Isolated plots and bottoms that chance to have a springy soil   All the streams here run through deep narrow hollows what we call Canions and verry seldom have any dry level land on either side   now and then there is a spot of a few acres along their sides and when there is it is verry productive   The Main occupation of the people is Mining   There is gold every where in dirt and rock but frequently so fine and thinly distributed that it will not pay to work the dirt for it and many places that will pay well when water can be had without buying   There are many ditches leading the waters from the rivers on to the higher grounds but all sell the water   We have the Mokelumne River on the south which supplies by Ditch about 80 by 10 miles of Country with water through Ditches   Our Ditch starts out of the River about 40 miles east of here which this place in part this Ditch has cost about Six hundred thousand dollars and is now making a good interest on that amount We have the Cosmines [Cosumnes] River on the North which is a smaller stream and supplies a smaller extent of Territory also a part of the country around this place   And the remainder of the country is supplied by Sutter Creek the small stream which runs through this place   A great deal of heavy mining is done here there are now in operation 2 steam Engines and 6 overshot water wheels now in operation in the immediate vicinity of this place all engaged in pumping water and hoisting dirt out of the deep places up to a level where it can be washed

There are many Caves in the vacinity one about two hundred feet down from the surface to water and nearly perpendicular   it is nothing but a confused mass of irregular fissures in the rocks and when a person is on the water they can see but a few feet up or down by the light of a candle and I had no other light when there   It is a muddy disagreeable place to be in and I have been there but seldom Another one about a mile from the place has two open spaces of irregular form some 40 by 60 feet square that it is a pleasure to visit the whole roof is covered with glittering stalactites the jutting rocks around the sides are covered with chrystalized lime that has the appearance of Roman Sculpture   It is beyond my power to describe it to you I can only say that I have never visited it but what I have been filled with indescribable sensations of Awe and wonder

For fear that I will so tire you out reading my scribbling I will soon close If you can manage to read it intelligibly it is all I could expect   I will not ask you to excuse me because you will then have the letter and I could not remedy the defects   But if there should be defects as there is most likely consider the intent and not the act   Hoping that you will be so far pleased as to answer at your earliest convenience

I remain

Respecftully

Truly Yours

John Doble

Miss L. E. Lucas

[MARGARET DOBLE TO JOHN DOBLE]

"Home" (San Francisco)   Jan 14th '61

Dear Brother

I have undertaken to-day to set myself right in your eyes, on that 'letter' question. I do not know what nonsense AB' wrote you—neither does he remember, himself the precise words he used. But you must have mistaken his meaning; as Lizzie has said nothing about being in a 'scrape'. I am sorry that anything has been written to offend you—where no offence was intended. Before he commenced writing to you, we were speaking about Libs letter—and I remarked that I was afraid *I* had got into a 'scrape' as she had asked me some questions I was at a loss to know how to answer. He said "How are you going to get out of it" I answered—I dont know—"you will have to help me".—That is about the sum total of what was said on the subject. Lizzie speaks of her correspondence with you, to me—said when she received your first letter, she took for granted that I was at the bottom of it all, and having implicit confidence in *my judgment* (save the mark) and liking your off hand manner of writing—She thought onely of replying: But when month after month passed away without receiving a line from me—She began to ask herself if she had not acted precipitately: Had some misgivings that I was enjoying a practical joke at her expense—was feeling a little indignant about it. In short—belabored me severely—though nothing more than I deserve, I suppose.

But now there are two horns to the dilemma for by getting into a 'scrape' with her I have got into a 'scrape' with you. And I fear I shall come off onely second best, quarreling with *two* of my best friends, at once. I don't suppose that your correspondence will do either of you any harm,—even if it does not amount to any thing proffitable. I do not know what your motive, or intentions are in addressing myCoz —in all probability you have never asked yourself the question. If it is merely to while away an idle hour—I for one, think there are many worse ways of doing it;— and so long as you can entertain each other—why, what's the harm? I shall write to Lizzie this week and make all sorts of apoligies for neglecting her so long—and she will forgive me:—of course she will, the dear little soul. But I am afraid your honor will be loath to excercise the same Christian virtue towards our offending self. But if you will do so *this once*—I shall promise in consideration thereof, never to *brag* about any of my *cousins* in your presence again. What say you? Our friend Darbyshire has taken to himself a wife. He was married in Sac.—the week before Christmas to Miss Fanny E. Towle—whose acquaintance, with that of her family, he made on the Steamer as he was returning to Cal. last spring. They spent the first week of their honey-moon with us. The only objection I see to the match is the disparity in their ages—she being—twenty—while he is thirty six and looks all of forty five, 'with a wig on' at that.

The last of the Dobles—'Femanine'—is married before this, I suppose. Have done pretty well—six inside of five years: —Hurry up now and add *your own* to the list before the five years are fairly out. It will never do for you to be the 'lone' one of the family. We are having magnificent weather here for a week past— merry warm sunshine—it is now after four oclock, and I am writing with the doors all open, and without a fire. I wish you would come down now, so that our Frisco climate might have a chance to redeem its character—'in your eyes.'

I am feeling stronger and better than I have done for a couple of years. I still have palpitation occasionally—with pain in the region of my heart—but neither so often, or so severe as formerly. I think a trip home would cure me up, entirely; but we must wait, and let Nelson have his visit first. Hoping that we may understand each other hereafter—I remain

J. Doble

Yours truly
M. B. D.

[MARGARET DOBLE TO JOHN DOBLE]

"Home" (San Francisco)   Feb. 24th '61

Dear Brother

Your kind letter was duly received—and for which I am thankful. Since you take it so coolly, I may as well tell you what I wrote to Lizzie. I had told her all that I think it is necessary to tell her about you—before I received your letter. I did not flatter you—trust me for that. I gave her *exactly* my own opinion of you, and think they are very nearly correct. I gave you credit for being rather better looking than the common run of men—and could improve your looks still more (but I did not tell Lib. so) by more attention to the 'outward man'—pronounced you—intelligent well read—but did not think you had made a very good use of the talent nature has given you thus far. Believed you to be kind hearted and generous to a fault— in short gave you credit for many good qualities both of head and heart, but told her you had *four* serious faults—first—that you smoked—second chewed tobacco

—third drank whiskey sometimes—and last but greatest of all—was a sceptic in religion. This last would prove an unsurmountable barrier in the way of you ever being more to each other than friends if there was nothing else in the way: for Lizzie is a sincere and consistent Christian as well as professor of religion. I may have erred in some of my estimates of your character, but I was at least honest in all I have said. You wrong your friends in Volcano, in supposing that they had given me your history. They said but little about you, and nothing in a fault finding way. I know it grieved them, as well as myself to see some of the errors into which you had fallen—errors, the danger of which they could see— much better than yourself. But they all gave you credit for having the ability to be something very different from what you were. I say again, as I have said more than once before—you lack *ambition* and *perseverence*—nothing more. I think you can correspond for a long time, and no mischief come of it, if there is none untill *I* lay the foundation it will be long enough, at least. I have not had any news from home since I wrote you— I am so lazy about answering their letters, they have had sufficient cause long ago to disown me altogether. I should be delighted to accept of your kind invitation to make another trip to the mountains—and delighted to again meet those whom I am indebted for so much kindness—on my first trip: but I cannot tell yet how it will be. If we find that we can make our visit to the states—I shall not have time to spare to go around any—and would need to economise also—for a trip home will take a snug fortune, you know.

Mrs. Darbyshires family live in Butte county—She has been trying to coax me to accompany her up there as soon as the traveling is good; but I cannot, unless we find that we cannot go east—in that case I could go as well as not—It is true— I *do not* like to leave my homliena long—I know he is lonesome, and the house comfortless when I am away—and so long as he is obliged to stay at home and work, I feel it my duty, as well as pleasure, to share his toils,—or at least—lighten and brighten them as much as I can. But we will know before long—what we will do, and then perhaps I shall make you a visitation the coming summer—My kindest regards to the Ladies of Jackson and Volcano with whom I am acquainted—and my best wishes for your own prosperity—

J. Doble	Affectionately Yours
Jackson	M. B. D.

Mr J Doble   Good Intent (Pa.)   Feb. 20th 1861

I have received your letter of Nov 29th and found it quite interesting as well as instructive and as the present is the first opportunity afforded me (though late it may be) I take advantage thereby and will attempt to pen a few thoughts in reply. I own it is with a rather increasing delicacy in the thought that I am addressing a stranger that I write, but thinking again only a little romantic amusement as well as information to be gained thereby (particularly on my own part) is the object of our interchange of thought I dismiss all misgivings and proceed to perform my part without further delay....

Should nothing unlooked for occur ere another letter could arrive here we will have left for our new home. So you will address me at Lyndon Station, Ross County Ohio.

	Yours respectfully
Mr J. Doble	Lizzie E. Lucas

Jackson   March 26th 1861

Miss Lizzie E. Lucas

Yours of the 20th ult is recd and contents carefully noted   I had almost concluded that my last letter to you was so uninteresting that you did not think it
worthy of an answer but am indeed highly gratified to find it is not so   Your
scruples were proper and natural and your conclusions I think just   We were so
far separated that certainly no harm can arise from a correspondence that is merely
friendly and for the purpose only of amusement and purchance information And
we or either of us can cease writing just so soon as our letters no longer afford an
incentive to write or when we think it proper so to do   And I have no doubt we
will do so so soon as our letters become uninteresting or disagreeable which I
sincerely hope will not be the case so long as we both are able to write of what we
do think or see

When I first wrote you at Maggies suggestion I wrote to one whome I believed
from her description to be endowed with all the qualities requisite to the struggles
incident to human life in a moderate station and one who was described to me as
an exact model of my ideal female purfection   And so far as I am able yet to see
from your letters the picture was not overdrawn or in the least exaggerated and
therefore am the more anxious that naught should occur to stop the communications between us and as you say it will afford us a little Romantic Amusement if
nothing else and being myself somewhat inclined to the Romantic I would follow
it up even if I were satisfied no information or purmanent pleasure was to be therefrom obtained   I admire verry much the calm reflection you seem to have given to
the act before writing as it evinces a knowledge of the world that I have seldom met
with and I find Maggie was not mistaken when she gave you credit for sound
thought and strong reasoning faculties this much by way of answering to the
"increasing delicacy" of addressing an entire stranger and I will go on and answer
your letter as it occurs making at the same time such remarks as may occur to
my mind   I am sorry however that time and circumstances did not permit you
to write more at length   I hope when you get settled in your new home you will
have an abundance of time to write me your thoughts on the world in general as
you see it and the neighborhood in particular as you know it

I did not conceive that your remarks on the deceit of the human heart could in
the least apply to yourself but that they were induced by the universal cry of
deceit in all   Human appearances I know are deceitful   the human heart I believe
is always true to its purpose   We naturally believe everything we hear and always
incline to speak the truth and it is only our experience in the world that leads us
to disbelieve or speak falsly   speaking false is like taking medicine we never do it
without an object and when we do we feel the sting of a disapproving conscience
When we are led away so as to violate these rules of nature we feel in proportion to
disappointments the necessity of so regulating our conduct as to meet the approval
of that all pervading providence to which all are amenable.

I heard from Maggie lately and her health was improving some but I too fear
she is not long for this earth   they seem confident that they will go home this
summer or coming fall and I do hope they will get off because I know that Maggie
is extremely anxious to see her mother

I am somewhat differently situated as to family   I am one of 11 children all but
one living   I am the 5th child and the oldest boy and now the only one unmarried

instead of having brothers and sisters to keep me company they have all other and more dear companions to keep them company while I am alone in the world and in all probability destined to continue so through life I have lived at home most of the time in this country that is I always had a house of my own and done my own cooking and housekeeping though generally rough I always felt more at home than when around the boarding houses that we have here I was going to give you a description of a Bachelors den but will defer it for the present and until I have a better chance to know whether it would be of any interest to you to read a description which would apply to about one half the habitations throughout this part of the world I have moved since I last wrote you and am now residing in Jackson in the same County which is twelve miles south of Volcano in a more level though mountainous country this place is the County seat and I am here to help the County Officials to keep matters straight though no officer I am aiding the officers in their business at which I make a reasonably good living

Like you I do most all my letter writing at night when no person is likely to disturb me but the duties of my position here keep me most all the time in the office so that I have but little time at my room

I will look with no small degree of interest for your first letter from your new home as everything will be new to you you will of cours tell me what you think of it and what kind of a population surrounds you whether you like it as well as your old home or not, etc., etc.

I have been in this place now some two months and have been so constantly engaged that I have had no opportunities to make acquaintance and therefore can not tell you exactly what kind of people I am among

I commenced this letter last night and was prevented from completing it as I was somewhat unwell and to night I am but little better and therefore beg you to excuse the style and manner of my writing should you find anything not exactly correct or in good taste in it

We have just had an unusually heavy storm thousands of dollars worth of property have been destroyed by high waters most all the bridges throughout the Country are gone and we have had no mail here for two days And a prospect of being several more days before we have any

I will endeavor in my next should you think this worthy an answer to give you an idea of the kind of people we have here I did intend also to attempt a description of the population of Volcano but must defer it all until my health improves which has not been good for several days

Hoping that you may have a pleasant trip to your new home And find it all that heart could wish

I remain Most

Miss Lizzie E. Lucas

Respectfully yours

John Doble

Mr J. Doble   Lyndon Station (Ohio)   May 31st 1861

Once again and in my new situation I have taken my pen for the purpose of attempting a reply to you. Yours of March 26th reached me only a few days ago in the perusal of which I was considerably interested. And now before I proceed further will just say that I know of nothing to write in turn that would prove very interesting or amusing to you, at this time owing partly to the cause that since I have been here my correspondents have been somewhat numerous and I have not yet become sufficiently acquainted with the place and people to know much of them, and what I do see and know I have so often written that it has become somewhat stale to me, and thereby seems to me to have lost the ability to interest others. I shall however try to answer yours to the best of my ability at present as well as give you whatever else enters my mind that might be at all worthy of your notice or the least interesting to you.

Were I very easily flattered I might think from what you say of Maggies description of myself to you (also your own opinion of me formed from my letters) that I was all perfection, but there is no human being perfect, and perhaps Maggie forgot to mention my faults, to most of which I am not insencible of possessing my share as well as others. I heard from Maggie a short time before leaving our old home and since have heard that she has written home that owing to the difficulties now impending in the States that they think it unsafe for them to attempt the journey home which I suppose would be the case as matters now are, but I am sorry to think that they can not, and perhaps may never be able to come. . . .

I shall look for a description of a "Bachelors den" in your next. I assure you it would be quite interesting to me to know the particulars as well as general appearance of habitations where there are no women to attend to the *thousand and one* duties necsesarily belonging to house keeping cooking etc.

Also a description of the population where you reside or travel would be perused with much interest by me. I am sorry your health was impaired so as to prevent you from writing all you intended but hope ere this time you are again in the enjoyment of your usual health. We had a tolerably pleasant trip coming out here notwithstanding the pain of parting with old friends and associates, and our old home, around the spot there are many associations connected that shall ever hold it dear to my memory. But I must close for the present. I see I have made some blots and mistakes, but you will please excuse. I have written at different times.

                                        Yours Respectfully
Mr John Doble   Lizzie E. Lucas

                                        Volcano   July 30th 1861
Miss L. E. Lucas

Your interesting letter of the 31st May came to hand a few days ago by the first daily overland Stage   I have been so situated for 6 days past that I could not answer but am now at home again   My pardner who resides with his family about 4 miles up the Creek from this place met with an accident by which his arms were paralized for several days and therefore required constant attention but he is now in a fair way to entirely recover so I can leave him to the care of his family

When I last wrote you I was Deputy Clerk in Jackson   My employer is a Tennesian and a disunion sympathiser as also was the other Deputy in the office   I was and am an unconditional unionist and this gave rise to frequent disputes which engendered ill feeling and as soon as that was shown I left the office although against the expressed wishes of My employer   I was satisfied that in a few months the disputes would end in an open quarrel which I prefured avoiding as that would bring about a discharge from the place   by leaving when I did I avoided a discharge and had the merit of sacrificing place to principle   I left the office the 17th day of April and have since been working at the Carpenter trade here with the exception of about two weeks time   I am now in my home again better contented than when in the office where political discussion was all that was talked of outside of business

You say truly that when we write several times to friends of things that interest us we then feel that those things have lost their interest even to those who know nothing of them   That difficulty I have often felt in the writing I have done to my friends at home   Yet that which you have frequently written to others would be new to me although to you it would seem to have lost all interest   I had no design at all to flatter and nothing was further from my mind than to give you the impression that I thought you perfect   I firmly believe as you say that "no human being is perfect"   I wished only to convince you that I was convinced by your letters and the description I had that you was one of the *superiors* in *mind* and *heart* of your sex that you was a *true* woman and an ornament to the sex that faults you had undoubtedly but that the good qualities were so strong as to show themselves only and generally hide all the faults and that in whatever position you might be placed you possessed the grace and dignity to maintain and adorn that position   There was a time in my life that I would probably have contended that you had no faults because that when I saw none that none existed but I have had experience enough in the world to believe that faults exist even when I cannot see them or find any traces of them as in this case

Maggie I think gave me a verry impartial description she mentioned some faults which I consider recommendations   She said you possessed a firm steady will which might be at times called stubbornness this I consider one of the most valuable traits in the human mechanism because without it where would our self dependence be   this with several that grow out of it were the faults she named and I considered them all virtues when applied to the travelling gear of the journey of life though they might be faults when shown in play houses or stopping places along the road And now should I at any time write flatteringly I wish you to understand from it that I mean you are only human adorned with most of the leading virtues common to the family and that (that) at most times those virtues were so plainly seen that the faults if any existed were entirely hidden these are my thoughts drawn from the lights I have   I think Maggie will go home this fall as they are now calculating to go as soon as Nelson their Pardner returns from England where he is now gone The last letter I had from my Brother told me they thought of starting about the first of September or sooner if they could   I am anxious for Maggie to go as her health is so poor and her desire to go so strong that it makes her worse to be continually thinking over her disappointment in not getting away however her health is much better this summer than it has been for the last year

I too am deeply grieved to see our beloved country in such a deplorable condition as it is now but sincerely hope it may be settled ere long and that the channels of business may be again opened and resume their wonted course   We do not see and feel the calamity here so strongly or plainly as you can do there but we can sympathise and thousands here are ready to go at the call and fight for that beloved flag which has so long waved triumphantly over us　I trust in God the matter will be settled before a further call is made　It is horrible to think of Brother Father against son and even Mothers and daughters taking sides against their relatives but with all that I would go at once to maintain that Government which has brought us to that unexampled prosperity we had arrived at before this war began　We are so far away from the scene of trouble that there is but little hope of our having anything to do with the war but our hearts and best wishes are with our friends

Your general opinion of the world I think a just one　I have a theory of my own that I am frequently studying to see if it is correct　that is　Good and evil are equal in quantity in this world and we only see either when the perfect balance is broken　That we can appreciate nothing only by comparison by pleasure we know pain without trouble we cannot enjoy quiet and ease and that one is as necessary to us as the other in order that we may know both　Tis only a theory with me and I have not yet convinced myself that it is true but it at first looked reasonable when I thought of it and I will continue to think until I convinced myself or til I find I cannot do so reasonably

I can imagine that the surprise party was a real surprise to you　You a stranger not yet used to the peculiar ways of the neighborhood not yet acquainted with those peculiar little things that exist in every community and go to make up a whole and to have them all brought before you at once as they would be in a company of 16 and you expected as a matter of course to take part You wishing to please and afraid to move for fear you might go rong leaves you as it were alone among so many　This you will undoubtedly soon get over because when thrown among them they will soon become natural to you

I have a notion that society is not so far advanced there as in Pa that the country is newer and society only beginning to emerge from a wild state just beginning to throw off the wild natural ways of acting and beginning to be constrained and directed by the rules and usages of what is termed better society A person brought up where those rules are observed finds it at first hard to fall in with the ways of a Community where none of these rules are observed　Yet in a little time they find enjoyment there as well as they did before

I will expect you to tell me if these ideas are correct and how far correct　As you will undoubtedly know whether anything congenial exists in your immediate neighborhood

Bachelors Den—a place where men have their abiding place and from which women are excluded

I have for some time lived with a family but my cabin is close by where I lived many years with one and sometimes two men with me

I will try to describe it to you as it is now with 2 men and as it was when I lived there and one description will suit both

Cabin 12 x 14 feet square built of boards floored and lined with cloth. I have just been to look at it. Step in to the front door on the right in the next to you stands a cupboard

"A store house of Commical oddities　Things that had never been neighbors before" next to that about the middle a stove black greasy and rusty in spots behind the stove a bench with water bucket stove pots and pans and between the stove and cupboard books mining tools and trash on the left in the corner a table with Cupboard on it containing a few dishes knives and forks etc. under the table a bread pan with ½ an inch of dough dried all around the sides showing it had not been cleaned perhaps for weeks   on the table the dishes standing as last eat from various traps scattered round among them from this to the back of the house the wall over the beds covered with clothes varying from a good cloth coat to a dilapidated pair of socks   under the clothes against the wall two beds 3 x 7 feet square consisting of pine boards made into a shallow box on legs 16 inches high filled with straw mattrass 2 or more pairs of blue and red blankets tumbled about as they were when last used in the centre of the floor and about the house several chairs with back and rungs crippled and 1 3 legged stool the whole appearing black and grimy as if never washed or scraped   The floor covered with dust fragments of potatoe skins and chips etc. etc. Each man has his plate and eats off it without washing until he takes a notion to wash it which is sometimes several days   The house is never swept only on Sunday mornings and sometimes not then   this is a medium picture most of them are worse some are better   We sometimes but very seldom wash dishes every meal and never make up a bed so long as we can get under the cover anyways near straight   The stove is never washed or cleaned only when it can't be used without cleaning and then as little done as possible

This is the cabin as it is now and about what it was when I was there   I had my book case and writing desk etc. there and had to keep the things a little cleaner because of my business in fact I got so at one time I kept it tolerabel fair order so that my visitors would compliment me on my housekeeping

About one fourth of the whole population here live in such places   about one fourth have and live with family about one fourth have good comfortable houses and take a pride in keeping things in order and about one fourth sleep in their stores and shops and board out at Hotels and private houses

I have seen many cabins here belonging to men who had been brought up in comparative wealth who kept their cabins in much worse plight than I have described in fact they are generally more careless than those who have not been raised so well

Our population is mixed up of men and women from every state and every part of the Globe   There is only about one woman to every ten men and some contend that there is in the state only about one woman to every 15 men   from this you can readily see that our society is verry poor yet we have society have balls and parties verry often but there always 2 or more men to every woman that attends

I have no doubt you feel deeply the severing of old ties and associations that love for such things which is so generally possessed is a natural and beautiful sentiment and one that goes largely to make up the sum of our happiness and one that clings to us so long as we live   It makes no difference how long we live nor where we those old associations come up in our minds and make us feel happy for a time in their contemplation   I sincerely hope you may be as happy in your new home as you seem to have been in the old one

On the 12th of April last I wrote a hasty description of a cave I had visited for the purpose of copying my journal   I was going to give you an idea of it but as that is on a sheet of paper I enclose it in place writing

Did I at any time tell you of Maggies walk from the Ranch up in the Mountains down to this place when she was here if I did not I will when opportunity offers

For fear you will be tired out reading my scribbling I will stop now and await
an answer from you before writing more

Hoping that your life may be as smooth and pleasant as the ever purling stream

I remain

Miss L. E. Lucas   Respectfully Yours

John

[ENCLOSURE]

Written at Jackson   April 12th 1861

It was reported through Town on the 9th of April during the forenoon that
Joaquins (pronounced Whau-Keen) Cave had been discovered   by noon the report
was so well circulated that many were going to see it as it was only about 3½
miles below Town   I was somewhat excited by the report and concluded to go with
the rest of them   By one oclock all was ready   twenty two of us in company
and on foot we followed the road from here to Lancha Plana (a town in the lower
part of the County on the Mokelumm River) for about two miles then turned off
to wards Jackson Creek down a long Gulch after travelling about 3 miles our guide
stopped on a low ridge near Jackson Creek and about 400 feet above the bed of the
creek and says there is the Cave   we looked around but could see nothing but
brush hill and hollow then he pointed us to a dense thicket of Buckeye bushes
and said there it was   we went to it found a hole in the ground about 15 feet
in diameter at the top tapering down to 3 feet in diameter at the depth of about
7 feet and completely hid from view at a short distance by the Buckeye bushes   we
lighted our candles a number of which we had along and descended through the
bottom of the hole as it appeared from the top about 8 feet supporting ourselves
by the projecting rocks as we went down when we came to a sloping bank of loose
soil which sloped off at an angle of 30 degrees for about 50 feet   We had to descend
one at a time and many were exclamations of delight half mingled with fear in
some of the party when we had got clear from all influence of daylight   We found
ourselves in an irregular shaped opening about 100 feet by 50 square the bottom
sloping as before stated the top an irregular rough rock some places 16 or 18 feet
high and others only 3 or 4 feet   On making a thorough search all around we
found no evidence whatever of its ever having been inhabited only by wild animals
of which there were abundant evidences   We found some 5 or 6 squirrel and
rabbit sculls and other bones and one wolfs Jaw bone   I took a round starting from
the entrance and going as far as I could into every little opening of which there were
many but could find none that seemed to open into any other rooms though I
found 2 that I could not see the end of by the light of my candle after I had
crawled in as far as I could on my knees I found 2 or three places where stalactites
were forming but none of any length had yet formed though those that were
forming made a pretty glittering appearance in the light of my candle

When about two thirds of the way around day light was visible on a closer
examination here another opening was discovered coming in from the hill side
which was nearly entirely closed by rocks and dirt falling down in which opening
undoubtedly at one time was about on a level with the bottom of the Cave from
here to the first opening on my return I found nothing but rough rock and decaying

limestone   At one place a quantity of silicious limestone and Quartz rock found as was evidenced by numerous glittering Quartz Chrystals that made a brilliant appearance when two or three candles were held near them   After about an hour spent in searching around we all returned to the surface satisfied that it was not Joaquins Cave but well satisfied with our trip as it was an interesting cave whether it was ever inhabited or not   The entrance where we went in was nearly on a level and was and is the only cave I have ever seen where the rock around its mouth is entirely covered with Clay and Soil   The side opening is in a layer of rock 20 feet high and would be much the easiest way to enter if it was opened   Joaquin was a noted Spanish robber who infested this part of the country during the early years of the gold excitement and this neighborhood was where most of his depredations were committed   He was frequently pursued and the officers reported that he sometimes mysteriously disappeared in this neighborhood which gave rise to the report that he had a cave somewhere here that he made a stopping place hence the readiness with which the report was credited when it was said Joaquins Cave was discovered

My idea is that he had no such Cave but escaped from the officers because of the roughness of the country and always went to some other part of the state until the pursuit was over

In returning to town we came up Jackson Creek which is from there up verry rough the cliffs on each side sometimes rising to the height of 200 to 400 feet and sometimes nearly straight and is more barren and rugged than up Sutter Creek Though there are several bars or flats where the hills recede from the Creek where numerous Chinamen are at work mining   We had some fun coming up as one of the Company gave out and another came verry near falling into the water when climing a round a sharp point of rock   This was only fun to us as the one that gave out was all right when rested a little and the fall was not dangerous if he had fallen

[LIZZIE'S REPLY OF AUGUST 30 HAS NOT BEEN FOUND]

Volcano   October 24th 1861

Miss Lizzie E. Lucas

Your verry pleasant and interesting letter of the 30th Aug reached me on the 10th of October; which shows that the Mail does not travel so fast this way as it does the other

I am sorry to hear you were ill but am flattered with the hope that you have long ere this regained your usual health and are now filling the place you name; a place that all western Farmers daughters are eminently calculated to adorn. Our country here is verry healthy the number of deaths are 20 per cent less than in the Atlantic States and one third of the deaths throughout the Country are caused by accident. One Man was killed about half a Mile above Town yesterday by the falling of a stone in a Tunnel where he was mining. You will see I am answering your letter as it occurs; that is I have your letter before me and when an idea is exhausted go to the letter for a new one.

I agree with you perfectly in not quarrelling. I deem it a mans duty to avoid it on all occasions when it is possible. I have never had a serious quarrel since I have been in this state And if I can avoid it never will have one while my residence is here.

By passing by unnoticed frequently intended insults those who give them are ashamed of their actions and when they are real men will most always do the Amende honorable or in other words amply apologise at a convenient time and thus save as you say "an increase of ill feeling" we are but erring creatures at best and what little we can do to soften the aspiritin of life is so much done in the divine cause.

Self control which but few possess in any considerable degree is in my estimation one of the finest attributes of the human character. And the nearer we can come to that the nearer we come to the standard of perfection laid down by him who was sent to save the world.

I have nothing to "pardon"   the hint you gave me was nothing but the natural reply to what might have been flattering words to one who possessed the qualifications I deemed you did possess. I have mingled much in female society here and have found almost a total want of what is considered a proper style of general action in the countries I had lived. At first I felt lost not knowing scarcely how to act but by close observation and care I could adapt myself to the circumstances surrounding me to a certain degree but never fully because as I suppose it was impossible for me to use so much of what I would call *gross flattery*. Yet it may be possible that my words were more than were justifiable under the circumstances and I ought probably to apologise which I most cheerfully do but in so doing will not take back what I said in regard to my *impressions* of your character from representations made and from your letters because had I really been in error before your present letter would undoubtedly have caused me to say the same things I have before said I have not seen a better letter written in all my corespondence Male or Female I do not mean in Penmanship but I mean purity of diction and clearness of ideas showing that your mental capacity is superior to any I have had the pleasure of knowing or corresponding with   I hope you will not think *this* flattery even should you feel that it is flattering because we are only writing each other for information and amusement and would certainly confine ourselves to our *actual* impressions and feelings when speaking of them   As I first said to you I write along as the thoughts come to me and write as I *think* not as policy would dictate   I write rapidly but not *well* and should I fall into any errors in orthography Language or grammer I hope you will attribute it to the hand and head and not to the mind or heart. I think we that is you and I who are entire strangers when ever we are speaking to and of each other should always write truthfully and so thinking I will certainly not in the least prevaricate   Least I might tire your patience with this long answer to your reply to my former letter I will now follow your example and change the subject

My theory on good and evil—I hope you will give me your opinion of theory I have not thought of it since nor do I ever stop to think of it only in idle moments when no other things present themselves for my consideration in fact theorys do not interest me now so much as formerly   when a man has a business it is apt to drive all theory from his mind and I have luckily and for some time past a Lucrative business that has left me no time to think of other things

Your statement of the feelings facts and condition of persons who happen to possess a little more refinement than those whom they are thrown amongst are most appropriate and strike *me* forcibly   I grew up I think about 150 miles west of where you now live and belonged to the *Community* as I grew   strangers from the east came into the country and were frequently greeted as you have described and then I felt and acted with them (the community) but soon after I had got my *schooling* and went away I began to see the true condition of the matter and so seeing endeavored to inform myself thoroughly—how I have succeded you must know from what I write—It is an old adage that "when you are in Rome you must do as Rome does" and to get along smothly this adage must be in part followed. That is a person need not loose any of their self respect but may yield to the Notions of others without giving up their own that is let others acts as they may still *appear* to consider it alright not by words but by saying *nothing*   And whenever anything is passing in which a part can be taken then take part actively and zealously   Your description of the schools was in effect about as I would suppose My picture of a Bachelors home was I think correct so far as it went in the Main but there are many *worse* and better   Your answer to it is most appropriate and about what I would think provided a few of you could just step in and see us at any reasonable time (I wish to God you could)   But wouldnt you Dear Creatures be apt to say a little harsher things after leaving the premises such as—those are nasty creatures have no taste at all—ought to keep things more nicely—shame to spoil that fine chair in that manner etc. etc.   The cabin I then described to you was my own then occupied by two old Bachelors   Since then I have moved in one has left and 2 *old* Bachelors are still there   I have changed things a little for the better but cannot say that it is verry much improved but I have got the Bread pan cleaned and the books arranged the Dish Cloth washed and manage to wash the Dishes once every day and sweep the house at least once every week   My Office is down in Town so I am not at home only at Meals   Were you with some of your friends to step in now you would find the books arranged on the shelves the tables clean bed half made the 2 x 4 ft square piece of carpet in front of each bed verry dusty the floor Ditto the stove and kitchen furniture moved back into the Kitchen lately built and the house in a general better condition than before described but stop I have come to the story about the "fellow" but you did not tell it—well I wil look for it in your next if that should come.

"What kind of figure would Old Maids Hall be" I'll tell you my idea.

House large and roomy—carpets of Sombre Cast—furniture rather abundant and gay—2 Cats 1 Poodle and 1 Parrot to each inhabitant—everything kept in a scrupulously neat manner—even to the Poodle—Wardrobe large and well filled—Beds verry thick wide and soft Toilet Bureau Large Glass Pomaturn   Powders and Perfumery scattered all around   Kitchen well stocked with furniture but provisions to be seen only when visitors were about—but hold—maybe I am not describing what your notions would be of Old Maids Hall so I will wait until I hear from you again and then I shall expect what you think they would look like

What me think you "are trying to make sport of me" *never* you write too truthfully for that you describe the natural acts of every body to well therefore I say next time dont stop so short but write out all you think and if I don't like it I will tell you so—Gone Crazy did you say—Now I want to know if even a Crazy person was guilty of writing connectedly so long a letter—no I don't say so at all at all—Me "think you are writing for vanitys sake" not by any means so long as you continue to write such sensible philosophical letters as you have so far written—Yes I did feel proud and highly flattered by the compliments of my *Married* Female Vistors but not a bit elevated by the half concealed sneers of my single Lady guests   mark the difference the Married would *praise* while the unmarried would only *approve*—and although I might work all day the 13th of Feb to get up a good dinner and reception for the 14th still that general grimness would appear which the married would excuse but the unmarried would or could not look over but then bless their souls how could they help it they who were so perfect to come into a grim Bachelors Cabin (I dont mean a grim Bach but a Grim Cabin) merely because their Brothers and sisters or parents did and not because they had any inclination *themselves* to see how Bachelors lived

Maggie was in readiness to leave for the States but Nelson did not return at the time they expected so they had to post pone their visit till spring and I know it was a sore disappointment to Maggie   her health is not so good as it was last summer and I believe the disappointment now affects her health

I am sorry to hear that any of Maggies relations sympathise with Secession Because I think Secession has no solid foundations and Civil war is one of the greatest curses that ever could afflct a nation   War is also the principal topic here we now get the news by Telegraph every day and every night the dispatches are eagerly sought after to furnish food for the next days conversation and we all are eager to see how the war is progressing   One company has been formed here and is now gone to Oregon to supply the place of the regular soldiers who have been withdrawn to go East   No doubt you have escaped a great deal of trouble and anxiety by your removal and I sincerely trust that the calamities of war may never come as far North as where you live   Business here too is much affected by the war but I suppose not so much as where you are now

I have been in the Office of Justice of the Peace for 6 weeks now and have done more business than at any one time of the same length since i first began my official duties   I came back here as I wrote you and was elected by a verry flattering majority and this will be my excuse I hope for delaying to answer your letter

Maggies trip or walk down the Creek I will now speak of

Volcano is situated at the junction of 4 streams heading respectively 6 6½ 8½ & 12 Miles Eastwardly from Volcano   The elevation of the Mountains about the heads of the streams is at least 4000 feet above Volcano each of these streams come down through deep narrow canons (pronounced Kan Yon)   four miles above Volcano on one of these streams lives an old valued friend of mine with his family When Maggie was here I took her up there in a buggy   the waggon road runs up over the ridges and round over the hills and down to the Ranch or farm upon which they live which is about 5 acres of ground around a springy place on the side of the ridge about half way down from the top and only about 1 acre of it being anyways near level   the scenery from this Ranch is verry interesting   looking down Volcano can be partially seen and about 12 miles of the hill tops below are in full view   looking up a sucession of hills rise one above another for some distance When we got there Maggie thought she would like to stay awhile so I left her and came home   At the end of week I went after her on foot and found her willing to undertake the trip on foot   We started the good wishes of the family who had become much attached to her and her child Lizzie following we descended the hill to the Creek about I think 1500 feet (the distances I give are all guesses) then start down the stream which is here about 50 to 200 feet wide (the flat or bottom on each side of the creek is so wide the creek is itself only a rivulet that would run through a 10 inch cheese hoop) and the hills rising on each side verry steep that is at an angle of about 30 Degrees and covered with a heavy growth Pine oak and Cedar trees   The trees are of unusual height being from 2 & smaller to 8 feet in diameter at the ground and from 80 feet and shorter to 320 feet high (I have measured two poles that were 10 inches at the but and 120 feet long and I have measured one tree on this flat 332 feet and one a mile above here 341½ feet high) We came down the creek about one mile over about such country above where we entered the canon   here the trees all disappear except a few live oaks which grow here and there out of the crevices of the rocks which now began to take the place of the hills above and rise almost perpendicular from the sides of the stream   We came down over an uneven narrow trail for about ½ mile further when we arrive at the first upper fall where the stream pitches down over a solid rock about 40 feet   the last 100 yards of the trail has been over rocks and rivulets from the Mountain sides sometimes climbing over broken fragments of rock sometimes sliding a few feet down the smooth surface of rock   here at the falls we now come   I carrying Lizzie Maggie with her shawl and work basket   My friend with her bundle of clothing and his daughter (14 years old) with some other things in her hands   We all stop on a level place of rock not more than 4 feet wide and about 20 feet long and look down at the water pouring over the smooth face of the rock then look up   before us the rocky hill sides rising not more than 60 feet from us at an angle of 50 degrees up up up to the height of some hundreds of feet   Maggie is wondering   My friend is careless   the Girl is chattering and Lizzie is playing with my whiskers and talking with me while I am alternately talking to Lizzie explaining to Maggie and answering the girl and Admiring the Magnificently picturesque scenery around us   We are standing on a projecting precipice about 30 feet high to the first notch in the rock and about 10 feet from the bottom of the fall   yes 90 feet as the water passes through the notch below for as many feet below the first notch in the rock the width between the rocks on each side being only about 20 feet   After standing for some time being tired we all set down against the perpendicular rocks at our back and talk for some minutes of the grandeur of nature the friendly shade of the stunted live oak growing from a crevice in the rock protecting us from the heat of the sun behind us up for 500 feet nothing but a bare irregular rock is to be seen while above and below our immediate vicinity for some distance the hills are covered with a low short bushes   After resting sometime we started down descending over rocks and rough places that caused Maggie frequently to catch at the bushes or rocky projections to prevent herself from falling into the abyss below   for about 100 yards the stream now falls over three more precipices from 10 to 25 feet high we are now at the lower falls here the live oak trees grow thickly from the crevices of the rock on all sides   the bottom of the stream is only about 10 feet wide the water purling and dashing over the rocks beneath in a succession of falls for some 40 yards the falls being from 6 inches to 2 feet high   Again we rest   Maggie is in great wonder and much pleased   we are entirely shut in from sunshine by the almost perpendicular Cliffs and live oak trees growing from the Crevices in the rocks the hills or cliffs rising for some hundreds of feet almost perpendicular then sloping off to the top of the ridge   After resting for some time and Maggie becoming satisfied we start again   Now we meet a succession of rises and descents in our path down over the rocks up over the projecting precopice and now along a smooth rocky surface all the time the stream some 60 feet below us still rapidly descending and its musical plashings distinctly heard as we now and then descend towards it and lost when we start up the next declivity   in this way we descend some half mile further and we are through the canon   then the creak widens to a greater extent than above the canon and we come into the upper Volcano Valley a beautiful little flat on each side of the stream of about 100 acres and from thence we come into Town along a good Waggon road that has been in part cut into the hill sides Maggie was much pleased and well satisfied with her walk down the Creek and will probably tell you all about it when she sees you next spring

I wish I could only have been there to go blackberrying with you   I know you must have enjoyed yourself amazingly   We have a similar sport here which is plumming there is a small plum grows in abundance up in the mountains   but I will tell you about that when I hear about that *fellow* you mentioned

I have written so far in my usual hasty business style without any regard to uniformity or beauty of appearance and as you try to read this letter and figure out what certain words mean or what sentences means that lack words you will or can form a correct estimate of my usual way   I have written this rapidly almost as fast as a person talks and done it so you would see my poorest as well as best writing   I have not looked over a dozen lines of the whole and therefore expect you will find many errors in it which this intended to apologise for   And should you find anything unintelligible I will explain in future   I have taken your letter for a prompter and a good one it is too and have now I believe got to the end of it except that I have not returned my sincerest thanks for your kind wishes which I now most heartily return

And hoping that no shadow may ever cross your path in life   And that pleasure in proportion may always attend you

                                                  I remain Most

Miss L. E. L.   Truly & Respectfully Yours

                                                    J. D.

Mr J. Doble   Cedar Ranch (Lyndon Station, Ohio)   Jan 14th 1862

Several weeks have passed since your last letter has been received and as this is the first favorable opportunity presented me for answering Shall with pleasure improve it by writing you a response. . . .

Am glad to hear of the improvements made in your Cabin since the last Bachelor moved in. Presume the *dish cloth* and Bread Pan look something pleasanter of their washing. So you have carpet too but why dont you sweep evry morning. Then you would not have so much dust to raise and settle on your Books Clothes do, as when you sweep but once a week. I fancy you dont take time to *clean up*, except on Sundays, tell me if I am right in my guessing. But do you attend Church on that day? I think you told me in a former letter that you had preaching in your town, (or Churches rather), and if I remember aright preaching too. What kind of Sermons do you have? Here we seldom hear anything except *War Speeches* I think they might be called, for though the text is taken from the Bible the Sermon is principally from the *Daily Papers*. Ministers are excitable beings as well as other men, but I think they would accomplish more of their mission by preaching for the conversion of sinners than preaching war, the abolishing of slavery and so on. But to return to the Cabin.

How far is your cabin from town? Who does your cooking   do you each one do your own share or one cook for both when two are there. Your idea of OLD Maids Hall is amusing. As you ask my opinion of how they would appear, beg leave to differ with you in some respects. Of course I suppose, as you say all would be kept scroupulously neat and clean—House large enough to be convenient on all occasions, were I one of their number might dispense with some of the quadrupeds, think one or two of each or one Poodle and two Cats sufficient for one house or a large dog instead of the Poodle would be my fancy. Pomatums, Powders, or Perfumery might also be disposed of, as things I could find no use for particularly the two former articles. Furniture just what was necessary and convenient. Provisions, plenty at all times, though perhaps a little more particularly and expensively got up when company were on hand. One bed would serve two individuals, while Bachelors have one apiece. Wide ones of course I for one single Old Maid give you credit for your taste though I never seen a "grim cabin" provided the Bachelor didnt look grim, might excuse the Cabin. . . .

I think my letter quite long enough as I am tired of it and fear you will be trying to read it. But I havent told you of "that fellow." It wasn't my intention to write it. But since you insist Shall give it in the fewest words possible. Dont remember it verbatim but presume you would prefer it in my own words. It was your Bread Pan covered ½ inch with dough reminded me of it. A gent was paying his devoirs to two young ladies. Couldnt decide which to choose for a better half, at last hit upon a plan to test the matter. Went to one told her his horse was sick, wanted some scrapings of her Bread Tray for medicine, being informed she had none, went to the other with the same request. Was supplied with a large amount. The result was he chose the first, as best housekeeper, and *better half*.

Now for your plumming expedition. . . . I dident find anything unintelligible in your letter, and only a few slight errors, not so many as I've found in my own and have not looked over it all either.

But hoping you will excuse I bid you Good Night.

Wishing you pleasant dreams

Yours Respectfully

Lizzie E. Lucas

Miss L. E. Lucas   Volcano   Feb 22nd 1862

Your letter of the 14th ult was by me received yesterday and perused with much pleasure and deem it fully as acceptable as any which have preceded it—I have nothing to do to day it being Sunday and so have got my office in order a good fire in the Stove and the doors closed and at my desk to answer your letter—as usual I will reply to it as each subject occurs therein.

If parties are numerous around you I wonder that you can find time to write at all but then I suppose they only occur semi occassionally which would give you time to write at various times. I am verry thankful however that you have the time to write.

Many is the time I look back over my life at home and wish myself there again to go to singing to parties and to church each and all of which were deeply interesting to my then young mind. I can imagine with what interest and delight you all go off to singing or to play and only regret that such is not for me any more. In this country young folks are scarce. We have no hospitable farm houses filled with more hospitable families that general warm sympathising hospitable feeling exhibited throughout the Western States in the farming communities is almost entirely lost in the universal chase after wealth here. When a stranger appears instead of receiving an invitation to enter and partake of whatever is present he is looked at with a calculation of how much can be made out of him and he is left entirely to demand what he may need and to pay for it when got—I hear from some of my friends here who have settled in the valleys that such is not the case in the farming communities here but it is actually so in this part of the state. I have never been over the valleys but little since I came here but I hear it is about the same there as in the States.

I am truly gratified to know your health is so good for without health life cannot be enjoyed—I have been quite sick with billious fever for the past two weeks but thank kind Providence I am again able to attend to my usual business—speaking of health—I received word from Maggie yesterday her health is much improved and she will be among you there once more about next June or July should not unforseen circumstances prevent—The general health here is excellent not withstanding the extreme hard winter we have. Yes health is one of the greatest blessings Mortals know and yet if we were never sick how would we know the value of health. My ideas are that we know nothing in this world only by comparison by pain we know the value of pleasure by sickness we know the value of health and by Poverty we know the value of wealth Therfore I think it is necessary to our happiness to be sick at times. In this country sickness is so scarce comparatively that one half the population do not know how to appreciate health only as they have learned it before coming here.

You express the natural feeling af a person settling in a new neighbrhood everything around you is strange and frequently contrary to your notions of propriety and etiquette but in the course of time you continue to mix with those around you— exert yourself now and then thinking of mixing some of your own ideas or learning with theirs to make the batch more palatable and finally things become so natural and easy that you wonder at yourself for not thinking them so when you first became acquainted   and [in] time you will find among them some congeniel spirits that will make you forget that you had missed the ones you formerly knew— this is my idea of the natural course of the human mind—That something wanting which you speak of I Judge likely you will find ere long. In this country that something wanting is probably felt more strongly by all persons than in any other part of the globe   here we all are in a measure eagerly chasing the fickle Goddess Fortune and in our zeal forget partially that we are human and surrounded by beings of our kind and are only awakened to a full sense of this situation when we are down in the world or when fortune deceives us. I have chased the Taunting Goddess for 10 years now and several times had my hands upon her but always by some Magic that I could not understand she has managed to elude my eager grasp and I have thus found plenty of time to moralize over it.

Yes I must admit the washing dusting sweeping etc. makes the Cabin much plesanter to stay in And I commenced this morning and think I will take your advice and sweep every morning. I have since I have been in the cabin washed my dishes every meal and I find that much more comfortable than having them stand— in fact I begin to think I am a first rate house keeper for California.

One thing troubles us old Bachelors sorely and that is mending our clothes   we are compelled to do it from the fact that we can not always hire it done. I have to spend about 3 or 4 hours every week in mending—I mean in Sewing—Your guessing is correct   Sunday is the day to clean and straighten things up. Sunday is not observed here as it is at home indeed it was not observed at all until the last year except by the few.

We have 4 churches in Town and Preaching in one of them everry Sunday. I sometimes go. The Churches are so weak here that it will not pay good Preachers to come and those [who] do come usually do the cause of Religion more harm than good by their poor preaching and curious conduct   one or two years since I came here we had a good preacher and then the churches grew but the others done so poorly that the churches sunk in proportion. We have a Methodist Church North and Church South a Baptist Church and a Catholic Church to each of which I go sometimes and give my mite to each—believing as I do that it is my duty to encourage all moral institutions whether I am a member or not. Our Ministers are inclined to talk war too but the church members have forbidden it so we do not have war Sermons—I—likeyou—think that Ministers of the Gospel should at all times refrain from Preaching of Temporal things and confine themselves strictly to the spiritual. And I have made it apoint never to go a second time to hear a Preacher who forgot his calling and talked politics or about any other Temporal matter of a general nature—And this I believe is a general feeling in the State as one in Sacremento and two in San Francisco have been dismissed by their congregations because they would pursist in preaching politics and these three were the most eloquent men known in the State.

My Cabin is in Town on Plugg street about 100 feet from Consolation Street the finest street in town and is about 300 yards from the Business center of the Town— Sometimes one does the cooking sometimes another and one only cooks at a time and cooks for all who are in the Cabin. I am alone now most of the time as those who did live with me have gone off to other places, but then every day I have somebody with me as I am well acquainted over most of the country—whenever an acquaintance is in Town I take him home with me and give him such as I have and then I always do the cooking myself. In fact, I keep house in every way only in washing that I hire done and pay 25 cents a piece for all shirts and such like and 12½ cents for Towels socks etc. this is the heaviest expense we old Baches have here except Board which costs us when we Cook ourselvs about 4 to 4½ dollars a week. The regular price at the Hotels is 7 dollars a week   the 3 dollars we can save each week by Cooking for ourselves we deem worth the trouble and therefore cook for ourselves even where Boarding houses are plenty.

The old Bachelors of California are as Jolly a set of Men as a general thing as it is ever seen although we may be laboring under a fit of the blues or the escape of fortune or any other mishap that may effect us   Just let a pleasant face make its appearance and you will at once see us up and lively with a broad grin on the visage and an expectant compliant look—as much as to say At your service Maam anything required promptly attended to   take a seat (handing a stool or broken back chair)   excuse my old Bachelor ways etc. etc.   although the cabin is dingy and dirty in a verry short time everything may look bright and lively through the medium of the brisk conversation that thus insues and for that day at least the old Bachelor forgets his troubles and endeavors to enjoy the life he has   Sit down perhaps and sing some song that is well known say like "The Girl I left behind me" or "Maggie by my side" or "Do they Miss me at home" or any other popular or pleasant song to beguile the time until the hour that nature requires rest and then sink into the Land of Dreams happy as a Lord that Angel Woman has once smiled upon us without asking us to kneel and bequeath a blessing   When I was mining my general pastime was singing and seldom an evening ever passed without rehearsing some song or learning some new one   I got together some 8 Note Books 6 or 7 small song books a Fiddle and flute (cant play a tune on either) And with these and my partners we managed to pass the time pleasantly   Those things I have yet but since I have been in the law business I seldom ever look at or touch either of them

I yield the Palm to you as it regards Old Maids Hall though I was only guessing at what it might be   You being a Country girl of course would prefer the big Dog but if you should propose such a thing to the village or City Girl she would look at you in wonder and perhaps say you was crazy   I knew one old Maid here who was a school teacher whose house was described when I drew my picture of Old Maids Hall   an excellent Lady she was too but the Poodle was her constant attendant and she was always frightened at the sight of a big dog

Aint that enough about the Hall?

It is indeed Terrible to think about the present condition of our Country but then I hope it is the purifying ordeal that all nations heretofore have gone through to more firmly establish their Governments and that when we get through this our Government will never again be troubled by anything of the same kind   I was some in hopes that England would pick a quarrel with us   believing that war with England would more effectually stop the rebellion but in that I may be wrong Should England commence I for one will be in the Army but at present I do not wish to fight nor will not until I find a necessity for it then I will go   The troops collected in this State will have to keep the forts here and that kind of service I do not like   If I was at home in Indiana I would no doubt be in or would have been in the Army   Maggie was indeed very tired when she got home, but still well satisfied with her walk in coming down we met with no reptiles only Large butter snails and I believe one water Lizard a small red lizard found in streams here We have never been blessed with Saint Patrick here though there are plenty of his reptiles to be found among us   We have a few Bottle yellow striped red house and tree lizzards   Horned Toads and frogs with the Terrible Centipede and Taruntula to scare the nervous persons with and Scorpians to sting the unwarry   The Scorpion is the most abundant the centipede and tarantuala next and the *Rattle* snake rather scarce   The Tarantula is a species of spider whose body is about the size of a nutmeg with legs 2 to 3 inches long and is considered the most poisonous of all insects or reptiles we have here   There have been many persons bitten by the rattle snake within my knowledge but none have died   I have heard of but one death by the tarantula and none by scorpion or Centipede

That is all I know about the snakes at present   in future what I may learn I may communicate

You say one bed would serve two individuals (this I believe) Old Bachelors have one apiece wide ones of cours You are right again   Mine is 4½ feet wide and frequently serves 3 individuals   I have sometimes 2 friends to go home with me and having only one bed per necessity occupy it   And then too we live in the faint hope that some dear friend may yet come to stay with us for time

I expect from the number of men that have gone to the wars that you (I mean the Ladys) are largely in the Majority like we men are here if so I have no doubt you can sympathise with us in our loneliness and indeed I believe we sometimes need sympathy sorely when we fully comprehend our lonely condition   God send that kind fortune may so far favor me as to allow me to visit my old home and friends in the next few years   Now only those who have been far away and alone from their earlier associations can appreciate the earnest longings that come over us to again visit The scenes of our childhood the fields and the meadows where weve strayed

I sincerely wish you had been with Maggie in her walk. I know you would have enjoyed it verry much. We talked of you as we came down the Creek and Maggie then expressed a wish that you were there —

Now you may have been in tired in writing the letter but I assure you that you were mistaken when the idea entired your head that I would be tired with reading it. I could have read on to the end without ever loosing a particle of the interest had it been 20 times as long and indeed I was so much interested in it that I was sorry there was no more of it.

That Man deserved a good wife because he took such a cute way to find out the right one. The story is new to me and I must say it is verry applicable to the matter we were talking of. However he was not as bad off as we poor old Baches are here or he would have been happy to have got either. We would think ourselves supremly blessed if any single lady would lend an attentive ear even if she was inclined to be sloven (barring those that are here.)

The plumming expedition, Yes, well as I have written you before we live half way between the summit and foot hills of the western slope of the Siera Nevada Mountains. Here the Mountains are high and steep along up the ridges between the streams for some 20 miles above here the sides of the ridges near the top is covered with a stunted growth of plum bushes which bear a red sour plum about ¾ of an inch in diameter. These bushes never grow more than 4 feet high and frequently not more than 18 inches to 2 feet and some seasons they are loaded with plums down even to the ground which plums make excellent preserves—fruit being verry scarce they are eagerly sought for for preserving.

In the fall of 1859 we made up a company of 8 Ladies and gentlemen 2 Waggons Camp equipage tents etc and went up the mountains about 10 miles to where they were supposed to be most plenty and found a good Camping place and pitched our tents and prepared for two or three days plum gathering. The weather was warm and pleasant the earth dry no rain having fallen for several months so it was as pleasant camping out as if we had been in the house. We numbered 2 wives and their husbands 2 widows and their beaus and 4 girls ditto and 2 drivers for the Teams one of whom was a fiddler   we had encamped on a beautiful small grass flat down the center of which run a good clear stream of water. After the Ladies had done up their dishes we had a dance on the green for an hour or so and then turned in to seek gentle Morpheus' embrace when about to sink to sleep were aroused by a most hidious roaring sound. The Men spring to their arms (we each had a gun) and the women huddled together (so they said I did not see them) in their tent as if to seek protection from each other—we had left a large fire burning and it was a clear starlight night. The men soon left the tents in different directions through all kept their backs to the fire so they could see beyond—soon after we had passed from the fire the roar was repeated in so loud a tone that echo answered from every hill around—the Ladies screamed the men fell to their faces for the purpose of getting a good shot as we then knew it was a California Lyon that had come down for water. I was on the opposite side of the fire from him the men on that side crawled towards him until one of them saw his eyes shining and drew up and fired at them cutting a hole through one ear. The Lion then run across the flat towards the hill near the other man on that side who drew up and shot him through the heart. We hauled him up to the fire and assured the Ladies that all danger was passed but it took some time to pursuade them to come out and see what had so terrified them. They came however at last and seeing the animal dead became reassured. We then renewed our fire and for several hours run jokes on each other about being terrified. The Lyon was about the size of a Newfoundland dog and of grayish color—We slept little during the night as several other roars were heard—besides the howling of many wolves. We kept a good fire however and none came so close as this one did. The California Lion is not dangerous as he never attacks Man—We were up early and after breakfast started out each with a basket to gather plums. The flat upon which we had camped was some 500 feet below the tops of the ridges and hills around. We went up over the ridges and scattered ourselves along the sides of the hills found plums in abundance and in the course of a couple of hours had our baskets full—had some play among us running and throwing plums etc and about 10 of began to collect together to return to camp which was then ½ mile off when a few of us who were nearest the camp saw others coming down the ridge towards us in full run screaming a Bear a Bear. We soon saw Bruin coming along the ridge Leisurely about 300 yards behind them   our guns were at Camp so we all made good time to Camp and the men with the guns returned to look after the Bear but we could not find him as he had disappeared down some other Glens there abounding. Our only wish was to drive him away as were loth to attack him he was a large Grizzly and such are extremely hard to kill. We returned to Camp with two hares that we shot and thought them better than the Grizzly. We made a good dinner of the hares and other provisions we had—when the Ladies unitedly demanded a return home they being too much frightened to remain longer   The Men reluctantly consented and we came home that night with about two bushels of plums and a firm resolve not to take women on another such trip—I have been out on horseback several times since and gathered plums but not with no such adventures. For many months afterwards the words "a bear" was enough to make either of those Ladies nervous.

This I believe answers your letter all but the last line   This is the story as well as I can tell it hope it may pay the perusal

We have had a winter of rain snow and flood such as none now in California ever saw   The rain commenced falling on the 9th day of Nov last and it is still raining from that time to this we had 12 days one day at a time without rain and in this Month one week of clear weather

The floods higher at 3 several times than ever known before   Immense amounts of property of various kinds have been swept away by the floods in some places whole villages have been swept away by the resistless current and many lives have been lost   In our Town several houses were washed away and the earth was cut away to the decpth of 10 feet and about 200 feet wide the whole length of the flat The damage by Flood to the inhabitants of this place will amount in the aggregate to about 15000 dollars and we have suffered but little in comparison to the other places   The farmers and stock growers suffer worse still than others   All the valleys have been flooded and fully one half the fences in the Country have been swept away — The long continued and cold rains have killed over one half of all the live stock in the State. In this County One Man had 1500 cattle 900 are dead — one had 70 Cows 64 are dead, one had 60 cattle and 47 horses 55 cattle and 27 horses are dead, one had 2500 sheep 1100 are dead one had 180 hogs 154 are dead and so on — I might name hundreds who have lost from one fourth to nine tenths of all the stock they possessed and in proportion to these losses. It is prophocied by many believed by more and feared by Most that the suffering during the next summer will fill the proportion. We expect actreme hard times for the next 8 or 10 months

The rain is still falling and none can guess when it will cease —

Flour is now selling for 12 cents a pound Beef 20 Corn Meal 10 Bacon 25 Hams 20 Pork 25 Rice 22 Sugar 20 to 30 Candles 50 to 100 Potatoes 10 Rye 2 Wheat $3\frac{1}{2}$ Barley $5\frac{1}{2}$ Lard 50 and Beans 16 cents per pound — this will give you some idea of the costs of things here, that people must have to live and keep their animals on

About every 10th man here owns a cow a horse or a lot of stock and some who only owned one or two have lost them   they do not die from want of food as has been proven by fat stock dieing as fast as the poor   they seem to get chilled through by the continuous cold rain and when they lie down never get up again The ground is soaked so soft that one half of the whole surface of the mountains here will mire down any common animals and whenever one gets into these soft places they never get out unless the owner is near to assist

I have strung out my letter to a length that I fear will tire you sorely before you get through with it but I hope that you will consider that it is from a garrulous Old Bachelor and make due allowance herefore   And I hope too you will allow for the circumstances that is We are here alone (alone what a doleful sound that word sometimes has) and whenever we think we are speaking to one who may take an interest we are apt to say more than under other Circumstances

I would have said something about the mines etc. but think I will have tired you enough already so

Hoping that the foregoing may pay for the trouble of reading And that Peace plenty and prosperity may ever be your constant servants

I subcribe myself
Most Respectfully

Miss L. E. Lucas

Yours to Command
John Doble

Cedar Ranch (Lyndon, Ohio)   May 9th 1862

Mr Doble

It is characteristic I believe of *Old Maids* to be punctual   And presume particularly so in answering *gentlemens letters* . . .

I should think it must be unpleasant to live in such a community as the one in which you live, where there is so little (or as you write) no hospitality or sympathy of feeling on the part of the people exhibited and all the finer feelings which should occupy a place in the hearts of all human beings lost as you say in the "universal chase after wealth" for what enjoyment can there be in the possession of wealth without friends? As friendship begets friendship and love begets love I presume it follows that where there is none given there can be little or none received "or what shall it profit a man if he shall gain the whole world and loose his own soul" and is there not great danger of the latter when there is none but selfish motives followed or perishable wealth sought after?

But I suppose that all are not equally alike lost to all good to God and their fellow men. And from your letter I take you to be one of the few who have not lost all, and that you at least entertain what *I* would suppose to be the right kind of feeling for those around you of your fellow beings. And perhaps too there is some advantage to be gained by some persons by living in such a community as yours, as they will undoubtedly learn to depend more on their own resources in the way of pecuniary affairs which is better than trust to others as too many are apt to do in such places as I have always been. But enough on this. . . .

I am pleased to learn you are still improving in your housekeeping and shouldent wonder if you did feel a slight sensation of pleasure and pride when any of your friends enter and find everything neat and comfortable.

Sunday here is not observed so strictly as in Pa. . . . War is becoming an old story and we dont here so much of it in the pulpit as formerly. Enough on that also. So your cabin is in town I had taken from something said that it was a little distance out. I commend your liberality and kindness in taking your acquaintances home and treating them to what you have. Your expenses in board and washing we would think very high here though in the "land of gold" suppose it is considered less extravagant. I suppose it is the case the world over as a general thing where you can make money you are nesessitated to spend just in proportion so that after all one part is as easy to live in as another so far as wealth is concerned, so I sometimes think. Perhaps I ought not accept the palm you offer as regards Old Maids Hall as you described one you knew there. Mine was only an imaginary one, and had none in minds eye when I gave "my picture" though believe I gave my idea nearly of how I should do were I so situated. But how is it an "excellent Lady" is permitted to remain an *Old Maid* when there are so many *lonely disconsolate* Bachelors (if such you will allow me to call them) though you appear to enjoy yourselves well from your letters. If the aversion of the latter to the *Poodle* is the obstacle I'll venture she would dispense with it in the event of the possession of a more *worthy* and *noble* companion on which to bestow her affections. But it may be her choice so to live and perhaps well for her. And she may see some object of adoration with the Bachelor that is equally detestable to her as the Poodle to them, which if you will allow me will venture to guess might be a *Tobacco and sigar box* if nothing worse, some other things I might enumerate but lest I should be mistaken will forbear at present

The war comes next. It is truly heart rending to hear the accounts of the battles fought in this once peacfull and happy land. Some of our community have visited Pittsburgh Landing since the dreadfull battle at that place. Also the hospitals filled with wounded and sick, some of the sick and wounded have returned to their homes who were there they tell us no one can have the least estimation of the dreadfull scenes who have not been there, and dreadfull indeed it must have been. But I am happy to know that Secessiondom is growing small by degrees and beautifully less, and that there are now indications that peace shall shall shortly reign once more, and our brave soldiers shall be again welcomed to the hearts and homes of their anxious friends, but how many shall be missing is sad indeed to contemplate, how many hearts and homes are already made dessolate. But like you I hope our Government will be more firmly established than ever and that our Nation will proffit by this calamity which I believe to be sent for that purpose by him who has all things at his disposal. I mean for the good of the Nation.

I dont think I should like to come in contact with any of the Reptiles you were so kind as to give me an account of for I have a particular hatred to anything of the species. Although I never get so nervous as to *scream* and *run* should I find one in my path.

I was deeply interested in the account of your plumming excursion and do not blame the Ladies of your company much for not wishing to remain another night in Camp. Think you should not have left your guns behind when you scattered out in search of the plums. The story fully paid the perusal, and anything more of your experience in the like excursions traveling or mining would be perused with an equal amount of interest. I had read in the Papers accounts of the rains and floods in California though nothing half so satisfactory as yours, and I am sorry that hard times and still greater suffering is yet expected. The past winter here was one principally of rain and mud though not much injury was done by high water, excepting along large streams I believe there was considerable. At times the roads were almost impassible and I believe altogether for teams. We had but very little freezing through out the winter and then only a day or two at a time. Spring opened up pleasantly and we now have beautiful prospects of plenty for the coming season, particularly of fruit of every variety which will be abundant should no future accident befall it, and which luxury will be gladly hailed as there was none scarcely last season, excepting Black Berries. . . .

Please excuse blots and blunders as there are quite a number I am aware. Thanks for your kind wishes, and may the same good fortune attend you through the rough sea of life.

Yours respectfully
Lizzie L.

Volcano   July 19th 1862

Miss Lizzie

Your verry interesting letter of the 9th of May is received and has been perused with much pleasure

I do not know much of Old Maids but think I should like them verry much if they are all as I suppose you to be from your letters

Indeed apology is unnecessary as I am glad to get a letter early or late and feel that I am under obligation to you for condescending to correspond with an old Bach and feel myself much honored by it and in consequence shall exert my self to make what I write you interesting as possible

I did not mean to say that there was no sympathy but that in the general haste to get rich sympathy was seldom seen or rarely exhibited only to intimates   When persons become intimates & friends here that friendship is much stronger than is generally seen in the Mississippi Basin because of its scarcity   Yet when a person becomes accustomed to it things pass along smoothly   he falls into the general track and goes along as the balance and it is only by stopping to think that he can see the difference   I am naturally of sanguine temperment and My passions are Strong   I do feel strongly for those around me and have endeavored since I have been in this country to carry out the adage "Do unto others etc." Yes many have lost their all here by placing confidence in others and it does cause many to depend on themselves more   Your conclusions are exact and to the point

Maggie will no doubt be with you before you get this and she will tell you more than I can write the only fear I have is that she will give you such a bad account of me that you will not care to correspond any more with me but I do hope that she will be charitable to me as I know it is her nature to be charitable to all   I am truly charmed at your ingenious way of arguing the question and the truth in your conclusions are so strong too   The reason they are not married is because they can not get a man to marry them   I gave you an idea of the character before and that always disgusts a man when he comes in contact with it   I mean the rough thoughtless self concieted action that is so common here in fact old and young are flattered petted and praised until they think all men should Kneel to them and Mens nature will not stand it therefore in place of being wives as they should be they are now old Maids

I have often cried over the details of the battles in our country   I know the terrible effects of a well fought battle   I was in Mexico and at the battle of Buenavista and saw all the horrors of a battle field and can appreciate what is now going on in the states   God send that it may soon cease

I hope it may be settled soon but my understanding tells me that the war will not be over for at least one year more and maybe two years

Yes it is Gods will that such things should be and we must submit

The calamity by flood is not so great as was expected   The crops are turning out as large and larger than ever which compensates the general community in part for the losses

Sacremento City is still nearly one half under water but they are now about stopping the water out of the city

I am now engaged in a political campaign besides attending to my Office and cannot now give you historys of matters and things as I would like too but should I write again which I hope to do I will give you a description of my trip to the Big Trees and an idea of how the Birds live which is entirely different from anything I have before seen

Hoping that you will excuse me this time and that you may again write me

I remain
Your friend
though unseen
John

P. S.   excuse errors etc. as I have to write in haste   I would have waited till I could do better but I will be travelling over the county for the next month and I want to answer punctual when I can

Lyndon Station (Ohio) Aug 25 1862

Mr Doble

Your kind favor of July 19th reached me a few days ago and I have now purposed to pen a reply in whatever words may come to my mind as I write. I am sorry I misunderstood your meaning in regard to "sympathy" exhibited on the part of the people of your part of the world. However understand you now, I think.

Maggie accompanied by her Mother spent near two weeks with us here. I dont see that Maggie is the least changed since I last saw her either in manners or apperance. It was quite a treat indeed to see them. Mr. D. only paid us a flying visit and we scarce had time to get acquainted untill he was gone. I am sorry he could not spend longer time with us. M. was not well neither was Lizzie when they left here for Ind. two weeks ago, but I hope they would soon be better, though we heard from them at Shelbyville and they feared Lizzie would have a sick spell

Mr. Doble intended starting for California again about this time and I presume you will see him as I understand Volcano is on the rout he intends going.

It was harvest time when they were here and I am sorry we did not have as much time for talking as I wished, but I hope to see Maggie again as she thought she would return this way again, however she told me something of her visit to Volcano which was interesting. And she *has told me* some things "of you" that I was *indeed sorry* and disappointed to hear. She also told me some things which I think are highly commendable in your character, and as you seem to know or think there was something "bad" she might tell I sincerely hope you will see and feel, (if you have not already done so) the evil of the things in which you are wrong and make every effort to over come that evil, and endeavor to live for the end designed by our Creator. But I am fully aware of my own incompetency for giving advice and hope you may excuse this, or at least not think me too presuming in giving it. And hoping the good may overcome the evil and that no ill may result from our correspondence I take pleasure in answering you again.

I was not aware that you had ever been in an army please give me some of the particulars in your next. Since you have witnessed the horrors of battle you can certainly appreciate what is going on much better than those who only hear of it. The war excitement here has been very high for the last few weeks. A number of young men of my acquaintance have volunteered under the last call. Some are badly frightened for fear of being drafted. Others say they will wait untill they are drafted. War meetings have been held nearly every day or night for a week or two. I attended one on Friday (the last for volunteers they said). It was largely attended by men women and children. The performances were music cannonading and several interesting addresses some of which I was not fortunate enough to get near enough to hear the crowd was so great. We have heard of the death of one of my cousins who was in the army near Richmond, another has not been heard of for several months supposed to be taken prisoner. Some were guessing here some time ago that the war would soon close but I see no indications at present. Would it were so.

As I know of nothing to write about that would be likely to be interesting to you I shall soon close this sheet. A description of the things you mention will be highly interesting to me, in your next letter. Hoping you may excuse whatever imperfections you may see in this,

I am, Yours respectfully
Lizzie

Volcano   Nov 9th 1862

Miss Lizzie

Your verry welcome letter of the 25th of August reached me about the 10th of October just as I was on the point of starting up into the mountains for a time I just returned last evening and as soon as possible begin an answer   I was much pleased with the matter and manner of your letter and hope I may be able to follow your advice however I will answer that more fully when I come to it in the letter I am sorry to hear that Maggie and Lizzie were not well   My Brother has not written me about that at all but I expect to be with him in San Francisco about the last of this week when he may tell me

He came by the steamer so that he was nearer Volcano at the Bay than anywhere on his route   I have been trying to get him to come up here but he thinks his business too important to leave at the present time so I will have to go down and see him   As Maggie has stayed behind her husband for a time, I have no doubt you will have another opportunity to see and talk with her and learn more fully her experience of life in California

Your advice I do not deem presumptious at all on the contrary I think I can see in it a real desire to benefit a fellow being that you may have reason to think is taking a course to his or her own injury   I thank you sincerely for the "hopes" and "advice" and too hope (sometimes almost against hope) that I may fit myself for the purpose designed by our creator in placing me here on this terrestrial sphere Each and every individual has his or her destiny to reach and as we are not allowed to see the future we can not know it until its arrival   I am determined on one line of conduct and that is to do what good I can and as little bad as possible for and to those with and among whom I may be situated and lay hold of all that seems best while I may sojour here and use my best judgment in doing my masters behests hoping only that all is right

Frequently I have seen the truth of the passage that the moat is visible in anothers eye but not the beam in our own and have then looked inward to try and discover the beam and have sometimes been so successful that at times a partial if not all removal of the beam has been accomplished

You are situated where the real horrors of war can not easily reach you   it is indeed horrible to view the effect of a hard fought battle   Yet should I get a chance to be in the Atlantic States i would undoubtedly volunteer again as I believe it a duty to my country but we are so far removed from the scene of action that we hardly feel the effects of the war only in taxation

I volunteered in 1846 and was in Mexico one year. I was at the battle of Buena Vista and got through without a scratch from an enemy though for many hours during two days the ball were flying so thickly around me that I could compare it to nothing I now think of than being immediately under a swarm of bees at that battle 765 Americans and about 2500 Mexicans were killed and wounded   I belonged to the 3 Regiment Indiana Volunteers under the command of James H. Lane

On the morning of the 23 of February 1847 after we had lain on the field all night without fire or blankets we were called into line at day break expecting to renew the combat when we found the enemy had fled during the night   We then spread out over the field occupied by both Armies during the preceding two days for the purpose of succoring the wounded and I sincerely wish never to see the like again

Many were the wounded we carried in who had lain on the field all the night and part of the day previous (during the first night all the wounded were carried in but the second night it could not be done) and many of them died after reaching the hospital   You will find a good description of the Battle in Frosts History of the Mexican War   It would be useless for me to attempt to give you a correct idea of the horrors of a Battle field and hope you will excuse from making the attempt as it can only be fully appreciated when seen or felt   I sometimes when reading the details of the battles now being fought seem too see the condition of the poor sufferers there immolated on the altar of the ambition of man and strongly wish and ardently hope our country may not ever see or experience the like again   If your speakers were eloquent I have no doubt you witnessed some of the enthusiasm and ardor that characterize the appearance of men going to fight the battles of their country   An ardor and enthusiasm that has carried untold Millions to an early Tomb

There must be a great many who are afraid of the draft and that fear is a draw back on the success of our Cause. The ways of Providence are inscrutible and we must abide the issue as his will may dictate but I sincerely hope it may soon end   Your information is the first I had that any of your relatives had gone into the army   Maggie never told me of it though I knew that T. A. McFarland had gone for time which was now ended

I fear much that the beginning of the end has not yet come   Civil internecine wars have always been the longest so far back as we have History of wars and there is no indications as yet that this one is an exception the rule   But let us hope on even if such is the case

I cannot conceive any ill that might arrise from our correspondence against which you hope should there be any danger of even the slightest ill arising from it   I for one am willing to drop all at once although I should always regret the unfortunate occurrence   A Correspondence such as ours can certainly bring ill to none as all we do is to spread a few harmless thoughts on paper for our mutual amusement and past time and to give if such may be information to each other   I earnestly hope and trust that this is not an indication that you are dissatisfied with the matter and manner of my letters however I should not be surprised knowing as I do that I have not the ability to interest for a length of time a calm thinking mind such as I conceive yours to be from the indications I see in your letters   As You have graciously consented and corresponded with me so long at my request and as I am no doubt the greatest gainer by your condiscention I should not grieve when you exercise your prerogative and cease when you think best   should you do so at any time I shall always feel grateful to you for what has passed

I hope your Brother may get safely through though he has indeed gone on a dangerous Road so far as bodily comfort is included   But we are creatures of the Circumstances surrounding us and have to lean continually on the guiding and protecting hand of Divinity to shape our Course and carry us through safely

The Secesh here have scared us several times a little but have made no actual demonstrations yet   Should the war continue for a year or two longer we will have some fighting to do in this State   All who have any real interest in the welfare of the country in which they live must feel some of the troubles of such a time and I sometimes think it an enviable condition of mind that can pass over such troubles without feeling the scathing that all thinking persons feel from their effects or

influences   And yet I would not have such a mind but would rather feel it than be
so cold as not to take some interest in the conditions of those around me

The following lines from Byron are applicable

> "There is nought in this bad world like sympathy
> Tis so becoming to the soul and face
> Sets to soft music the harmonious sigh
> And robes sweet friendship in Brussels lace."

My trip up the mountains was reasonably pleasant the weather has been verry
fine and is so still not by any means as it was this time last year   Through the
whole route I traveled it is nothing but a sucession of Mountains and hollows the
most of which are filled and covered with dense growth of Pine Fir Cedar Juniper
and Hemlock timber   In every locality nature seems to instruct all living things
how to live   The squrrels Coon Bears and Wild Cats all live in the ground or rather
in caves either in the rocks or in the clay made by themselves while the birds stow
their winters provisions in the bark of the Pines   to do this they bore or peck little
holes in the Pine bark just large enough to hold an acorn and in each hole stow an
acorn with the white stem end out   Wherever I was all the large Pine trees were
stowd full of acorns from about four feet from the ground and up for 50 and 60 feet
During the winter the Indians verry frequently rob the birds of their stores   I have
seen them take as much as one bushel of acorns from a single tree that had been
thus stored   Throughout the country where I have been evidences of the severity
of the last winter exist   Slides of land are visible everywhere   A small tributary
of the Mokelumne River shows the strongest signs I saw on every point of hill along
it land slides appear   one place about 4 acres of ground started down the hill
and moved in a body for about 12 feet and was stopped by some means when
numerous places around its edges run down into the creek   Some places as much
as 100 feet across and 10 to 15 feet deep along the whole course of the creek   The
timber brush and soil is all carried away   many trees 3 feet in diameter are washed
down and lay along the stream entirely stripped clear of bark and limbs showing
the immense force of the water   Near the head of this stream a Cabin is situate
in which two men were stopping when one dark night in the winter a terrible
crashing and roaring aroused them when they run out into the dark some 100 yards
down the creek when the noise ceased and they returned to the cabin verry wet as
it was raining hard   Next morning they saw that about a half an acre of ground
had started some 75 yards above the cabin which had many large trees on it and it
came down in a body to within 60 feet of the cabin and there divided by a cluster
of stumps passed each side of the cabin   The broken trees brush and earth being
piled up on each side and below the cabin for several yards   One of the men an
old mountaineer said that it was the most narrow escape he ever made

During my stay on a Ranch about 10 miles East of here a slight Earthquake
occured strong enough to make the dishes rattle and scare sleepers and make a
noise like distant thunder and lasted about 5 seconds and extended for some 10
miles North and South   Such things are so common on this coast that there is but
little attention paid to them nowadays

I was at the big tree Valley which is about 30 miles south East of here   The
Valley is about 100 yards wide flat ground and a fourth of a mile wide with the flat
hill sides on one side and is about one mile long   It is covered with a dense growth
of heavy timber and underbrush   They had cut good roads through and around it

so that a person could see all by walking around   There is 95 Cedar trees standing on it that are over 20 feet diameter and 10 or 12 of them are 30 feet through and there is some 10 or 12 that have fallen that are as large   One of them is hollow for about 100 feet where it is broken off through which a man can ride on horseback without stooping   One of them was cut down which took 3 men 6 weeks to get down   it was 25 feet solid wood 3 feet from the ground the stump was plained off and several balls were held on it   There was room enough for 3 cotillions to dance at a time on the stump   The bark was about 18 inches thick   I have a piece now that I trimmed down to 8 inches thick in order to get it all solid I brought home some of the timber of which I made a picture frame   They have a fine Hotel near the stump to accomodate visitors which are many

Now hoping that you may deem this scrawl worthy of an answer that is if you have patience to read it through and that you will excuse errors and omissions

I still am

As ever Most

Respectfully and

Obediently yours

John Doble

[LIZZIE'S LETTER OF FEBRUARY 5, HAS NOT BEEN FOUND]

San Francisco   Mar 5th 1863

Miss Lizzie E. Lucas

Your welcome well written letter of the 5th ult reached me today and as opportunity serves I write again   I had indeed begun to fear that I had entirely failed to interest you in my attempted descriptions of matters and things here but on receiving information from my Brother of your sickness that incipient fear became real and more serious for your safety which now by the receipt of your letter is happily discipated And I trust you may never again be visited by such a serious malady   This is however one of the ills that flesh is heir to and I suppose sooner or later all persons must suffer their share   I can easily see the almost impossibility of writing a letter on the wing as we say here when a person is traveling and so think your delay in answering aside from illness verry reasonable

Your journey I have no doubt has been a verry pleasant one as the greater part of it has been in one of the most beautiful sections of the American Continent and now that Railroads and Steamboats are on every line a person can travel nearly as comfortable as being at home and a storm or rain makes but little difference only when changing   Soon after I wrote you last I arranged my business in Volcano and came down here where I have been since assisting my Brother in his business and have some idea now of remaining here   that however I will not know certain until two or three months yet and maybe not then in consequence I have nothing to write about except that I may recollect something in the past

Now that Maggie has been with you so long I have no doubt that you are verry well posted in the appearance of matters in the country where I have been and my Bachelor arrangements there   So that with what I have written you can give a correct idea how we look and live in the Mines   If I remain here I intend to sell out there entirely and live here for the time only that I can be content believing that content is true happiness I will never live long in a place that I cant enjoy at least a reasonable share of it

The city as far as I now see is in a thriving condition and will in a few years be equal in business to any city in the world and in the course of the next decade will undoubtedly have all the trade between India and New York   I dont suppose you care about hearing of the trade so I will turn to something else

Of society here I can not speak advisedly as I am not yet acquainted but verry little but I see in every direction people of all grades and appearances and I suppose that we have here all classes from the highest to the lowest

I may have told you before but if I have I will repeat   Once in Volcano a lot of idlers were in my Office when the question of Nationality came up and after considerable talk we stepped out in the streets and in five minutes time we saw the following different people or representatives of them   I will give the color as I name them African and American Negro — Black White Bronze Yellow and Tawny (there happened to be a number of them on the street at the time) American Indians Cherokee a shade darker than ¼ negro — Walla a shade lighter than Negro redish color — Snake Indian Black but straight hair — American White — English Scotch Dutch Jew French & Spanish — Different shades called white — Kanaka (Sandwich Islander) light bronze color — Chinese Olive colored and a Turk swarthy colored After these were counted the parties who had argued that Nationalities were few among us gave up that there were many more than they had supposed and it is a notable feature throughout California that wherever you go you will see people from all parts of the world   I suppose that there is no place on Earth where so many different people work live and move together in peace and harmony except in *Cal.* And by the way now would be a first rate chance for you to see some of the world   Maggie will be coming back during the summer and will want some company and nobody would suit her better than you   She told me you was her favorite of all persons at home and I am sure she would most gladly have you with her here Come to this country and in the one trip you would see all modes of traveling all kinds and nations of people   All kinds of climate and soil all the different modes of dress life and living all kinds of fruits flowers and vegitations all most all kinds of birds and animals and in fact see and hear more that is strange to you than you could see by going three times the same distance on any other travelled routes in the world   Then in a year or so you could return home with a fund of knowledge sufficient to amuse all the Neighbors and friends of your acquaintance for the ballance of your life even if you should live to an exceeding old age

When if you come and it is possible to do so I will take you and Maggie up into the Mines for 2 or 3 weeks and see the Big tree Grove   The Big Cave near there and then any other place you may desire to visit   I will not promise more for the present lest you might think I was only joking when I am in good earnest   Well I almost forgot to tell you how I was now living   Since I came here my Brother has built a cabin across the back end of his lot and 18 feet of one end we live in and the other end is the Pick Shop   one corner 6 feet square is taken up by the big shop chimney (Maggie can tell you how that stands) one corner is occupied by sink looking glass etcetera and two corners by 2 3x7 beds while the sides are occupied by rough Book shelves and other traps that I brought with me and that we have gathered up since moving in here   We spend our evenings in talking writing reading etc and feel at home   At least I do   Abner is sometimes verry uneasy because Maggie is not around but I encourage him all I can by telling him the time is short and she will be along after awhile   He misses Lizzie verry much as of an evening he feels that he would like to hear her voice and have a play with her   To us in California time flies swiftly and twill be but a short time til the bright summer will be here and Maggie and Lizzie here again to cheer him

We have had a verry pleasant Winter so far there has been but verry little cold weather and but little rain as compared to *Cal* winters generally though I hear that up in the mountains they are having the usual amount of snow mud and rain

We are deeply interested here in the progress of the war although we do not see it as you do there   Our State has now commenced to arm and several Regiments of Soldiers are forming some to go East and some to go out on the Plains while others are intended for the Posts and Garrisons on this coast   God send they may get safely through the campaigns

I would apologise for the prosy character of what I have written if I did not think that in making the apology I would make matters worse so will send it along and trust to luck for an apology   I will however promise to try and do better in the future if opportunity should offer   So hoping and trusting that this may at least partially pay the perusal and that it may find you in the enjoyment of all the happiness possible for Mortal to enjoy and that you will confer on me the favor of again answering

I will remain a Friend

Miss Lizzie E. Lucas   John Doble

Dallas (Pa.)   April 15th 1863

Mr John Doble

A few days ago I was greeted by another letter from my California correspondent dated March 5th. Was greatly interested in the perusal of what it contained. And I shall take advantage of the present opportunity to respond once again. . . .

Maggie came up here with me in Feb. remained only a few days when she returned to Short Creek, since then I have not seen her though I hear from her frequently. I thought to have gone to see her again before returning home but fear it will be impossible for me to do so owing to the condition of the roads and some other inconveniences.

Thank you kindly for the invitation to accompany Maggie to Cal. and also for your kind offer to take us around to see the curiosities and wonders the place is noted for. I have often thought and wished to visit Cal. some day and have no doubt would see much that would be strange to me as well as usefull to myself and perhaps to others with whom I am acquainted (although I am not habitually very communicative). Maggie has insisted that I should accompany her and I should with the greatest of pleasure were there no hinderances to prevent it but owing to various circumstances beyond my controll at present I think duty bids me stay and more particularly since My Father is afflicted as he is I would feel loth to leave him to go such a distance not knowing at what time he may be called to leave us here and go to a long Eternity, but God forbid that he may not long yet remain with us, he is our only parent now and the thought that he may soon be taken from us is more than I can bear.

I fancy you and your Brother live quite cozy in your cabin and no dout enjoy many a good laugh when not otherwise too busily engaged or laboring under a *fit of the Blues* on account of feeling so lonely. But the months will soon pass around when — all well — Maggie and Lizzie will return to Cal. and all be all the happier after the few months of separation.

I see and know but little here that would be interesting to write about, there is a great deal of Political excitement as well as war excitement which is very much feared will cause trouble at home, worse for us in the North than the war where it is. Many Churches here are nearly broken up and I believe not one that has not had more or less disturbance among the members and with the preachers all on account of their political views. Neighbors and those who were friends are now at the bitterest enmity. What a change since we left this place two years ago. But I suppose you are better posted as to war and politics than I am and will say no more on that subject. . . .

Ever wishing you well in return for your kind regards in my favor, I am

Your Friend
Lizzie

San Francisco   May 12th 1863

Miss L. E. L.

Your verry welcome letter of the 13th ult came to hand today which I think was a quick trip to make across the continent though sometimes they may come quicker I perused your letter with much pleasure because you seemed to be enjoying good health and spirits and I truly hope you may ever enjoy them   And I feel much gratified by your flattering notice of my efforts to scribble something that will fill up the time for the passing moment for you and can fully assure you that your kind sensible and well written letters to me are more than sufficient for me to try to put something on paper that may please you as well   I have read every letter of yours over as many as 5 times and some of them more and always wish that I could put my ideas on paper in as clear and elegant a manner as you do but then as I cant I will do the best I can and write you of whatever I may think as I go along taking your letter as a guide to subjects first and then somethings else afterwards

You say truly Health is the greatest blessing mortals can enjoy and yet we can never fully appreciate it until we are made to feel it by experience   I am glad you escaped so well as not to again be affected with the same disease you had in the winter as I feared that the effects of the disease might appear again on the taking of cold

We should indeed feel grateful to the Giver for the blessing we receive yet seldom ever looks the giver when receiving or enjoying but only looks to the momentary enjoyment of whatever is to be received or enjoyed and seldom ever stop to think that all this comes from some power or source in which self has no say or power

Like you say "We should not complain" but think to ourselves "all is for the best" and bear whatever comes with the fortitude we are possessed of until "the cup of bitterness passes away" when we can look to the future with happier anticipations of the good to come

How dearly I should like to return to where I grew up like you are now   to go from farm to farm to see the old familiar faces and places of my childhood   To climb the same apple cherry and mulberry trees and look around upon the old familiar places that were wont to please my Boyish fancies   And fill up the happy days of childhood   To run along the pebbly brook and over the grassy hillsides that was always the holiday resorts of the children of the neighborhood and to move

around and about the creek and woods through and along which I have wandered
with girls and boys when manhood began to come upon me   Oh I should most
dearly love to visit these scenes once more before I come to that bourne from
whence no traveller returns

I can imagine you visiting some of your relatives   You first go into the house
shake hands of the men Kiss the women and children chat gaily with all for a brief
time then feel a something steal over you that indisposes you for talking   You
walk out in the yard look around perhaps all the time half absently answering some
questions that you may be asked   Soon your eye catches some old familiar object
you gaze at it the mind runs down the long vista of the past you soon loose sight
of the object that attracted your attention you see only yourself and others there
before you playing in childish glee around that stump or tree and then follow the
line of your life up towards the present moment until you are awakened from your
reverie by some question or remark by some one near you only to answer and then
wander again into the same train of thought   Happy memories of childish days
no changes or troubles can ever drive them entirely from us

I heard through Maggie of the severe affliction of your Father   I hope and
trust that ere this he has entirely recovered   It is a severe disease and is usually
slow of recovery but your Father being healthy and strong usually may sooner
recover from it

We are but sojourners here on earth and should always be prepared to go at the
call of that power infinate that governs us here   It is indeed a sad thought that
from parents and Brothers and Sisters we must at some time or other part   Yet is
it not a partial compensation at least to feel and know that they are only exchanging
his life of sorrow and trouble for a life eternal of happiness and unalloyed rest
That they are no longer suffering the pains and crosses of this world but are
enjoying that serene happiness that always accompanies undisturbed rest

Maggie I expect enjoys her trip home verry well   My Brother feels somewhat
lost without her   He is talking about going after her in the summer but I expect
his business is such that he will find it verry unsafe to leave here even for a short
time and if so Maggie will have to come back without him   But then she has been
over the road and can come along verry well as it is no great trouble to travel over
the Ocean Steam lines in fact a great part of the time a person is in better condition
and is better situated than when at home and have around them always something
new and strange to them

The present lines of steamers are the safest that have ever been on the California
line as they have had a long experience and have improved everything as they have
learned its necessity and therefore now every convenience that can be had for use
is to be found on the Ocean Palaces that pass between New York and San Francisco
I believe they are as well arranged as any of the River Steamers are and those
you know are as comfortable to be on as to be on land almost   You of course know
best what circumstances would govern or should govern you in your inclination   I
hope however that everything may turn round so as to permit you to come to this
country along with Maggie as I have no doubt she will have to come alone unless
you come with her and I believe you are the only person she would care to have
along with her   Not knowing anything about the circumstances I can not say
what is best to be done but will say this   If you come with her and I am able to
get off I will be your escort and go with you to many of the most noted places in

the State any one of which would most likely repay you for your trip to the country Maggie I have no doubt has told you what she saw while in the mountains and she only saw a verry small part of the Mining regions of the State   Yo Semite Valley the Big Trees and Cave City are among the most noted places in the State and the easiest of access but there are many others for instance the Geysers or boiling springs and the Mountain Lakes but then I would not agree at present to visit all but only part and I think you and Maggie togather would enjoy such a trip verry much

Yes I believe you are correct in your conclusions   We do get along verry well considering I have all my books with me here and find company in them when no better is around   If Maggie and Lizzie was here now we would be a lively family I would have Lizzie to play with while Abner would keep Maggie Company   I look forward with pleasure to the time that Maggie will be here again as then my Brother will not be so lonesome as now appears to be

It is a matter to be regretted that Political questions will estrange the best of Friends sometimes even the best of churches are not proof against this all prevading influence of interest in political questions of the present time Yet such always has been the case and I suppose always will be so long as Mortals exist to Act   Even here where we are almost out of the hearing of the Wars effect the churches have divided on politics and actually divided the association itself   All we can do so far as I can see is to take the world as we find it and try to do what good we can to those around us and let everyone enjoy their own views and follow the Golden Rule "Do unto others etc." as near as we can

I intended to have told you about a trip I took the other day out on the beach to Seal Rock and the Ocean House but as I have got so far I will leave that for another time if circumstances should allow me to again write to you

Hoping and trusting that you have found your Father again in good health and that you are enjoying all the happiness possible and that you will find sufficient in this to induce an answer   I will close by

Subscribing Myself
In Spirit and Truth

Miss L. E. Lucas   Your Friend Truly
                                        John Doble

Lydon Ohio   June 20th '63

Mr John Doble

Your kind favor of May 12th reached me on the 8 inst. rather a faster trip too than letters sometimes make across the Continent. Was perused with a good degree of pleasure as well as all the preceeding ones from the *same author*. You complain that you can not put your ideas on paper "in as clear and elegant a manner as I do" while I just think the reverse, and often wish I could write as well as you do and with as much ease as is apparent in yours, although I take pleasure in writing to my friends I am never pleased with what I have written after it is finished and would often cast it aside if I thought I could do any better in a second attempt. . . .

There is not so much political or war excitement here as was in Pa. and Va. while was stopping there and appears to be yet from the letters we receive — here things are as quiet as we could expect considering the condition of the country.

We see that there is a call from the President for 30000 more soldiers from this state. Several have lately volunteered. Brother Isaac was about to enlist with some of his classmates at the Academy where he has been in attendance but was persuaded to remain on account of his ill health, which entirely unfits him for Military duty. Quite a number of the colored population here have lately enlisted and have gone east I think.

We have a Soldiers Aid Society lately formed composed of nearly all the ladies both old and young for some distance around have already performed a considerable amount of work and forwarded to the Sanitary Commition and are still working hoping to be the means of comforting many a poor wounded or sick soldier. I attended church a week ago at a place a few miles West of us and where I had never before visited was very much pleased with the appearance of the country around and the people also. It was a country church and situated in a beautiful grove of forrest trees. I always was a lover of the woods hence thought it a delightfull place particularly in a hot summer day such as the one on which I was there. The country is not so much broken as where we live, is nearly level, and though it appears to be thickly settled and by wealthy people there is not so much cleared land thus leaving some of the most beautiful groves I have seen and a delightfull shady road to travel on. The exhibition of the Literary institute of Salem Academy come of Thursday last   exercises were tollerably good considering the times and number of students that have volunteered at different times and have gone to the army.

Now thinking I have written at sufficient length and perhaps more than is interesting or neatly performed I close thanking you for your kind wishes and hoping that health and happiness may ever be yours,

I Remain Your Friend
Lizzie

San Francisco   July 22 1863

Miss L. F. L.

Your sprightly pleasing and Friendly letter of the 20th *ult* reached me today and having opportunity I commence an answer to be completed as soon as possible . . .

I expect youre having verry warm weather now   Maggie has no doubt told you how cold our summers are here so it would be usless for me to tell you now how cool and sometimes disagreeable it is here   I have just returned from a walk through the City to North Point on the Bay and the wind is blowing strong from the North west bringing in a heavy bank of fog from the Sea which feels cool and chilly and makes a persons face feel as if they had been out in a frosty wind thought it is not so all the time yet enough so to make the winter the most agreeable part of the year here on the Bay . . .

By the way did you ever see any treatise on psychology which is the art principal or medium of sympathetic Communication   I saw one treatise on that principle and was made a believer in it too in part   That treatise held out the idea that writing would not only communicate ideas but would also between persons of congenial dispositions communicate feelings too   I became a believer in it thus far that between persons of sympathetic tempterments the one holding in the hand and reading the writing of the other would feel while reading nearly the same as the writer felt when penning the matter written and this is as near as I ever came to believing in Mesmerism or spiritualism   Perhaps I might have been lead to believe more had I studied the matter more but I could never think I had time to look into a matter that I could see no practical advantage in

I did think   no   I mean I might have thought that a kiss from the man would have been equally as pleasant if not a little more so but then I would not say so by any means   Since you reminded me I will try to give you my idea of kissing generally   It is a beautiful way of showing good feeling and an exceedingly pleasant way of greeting a friend   Not being accustomed to it I can not say how the feeling is now but on looking back through the long vista of memory I can see a time when a kiss sent a thrill of pleasure throughout myself that passed almost as soon as felt but left an impression that even now I can almost imagine myself again returning to my friends at home and receiving the same intense thrills of pleasure on greeting my near and dear relatives

I have never tried kissing a Man But I have thought that kissing should never be practiced only between the sexes thinking that it is a cold way to express affection between two of the same sex and a lively pleasant way between two of different sexes   I would like to know your opinion of the two   As I said before it is a pleasant way of greeting and I would dearly love to see it more generally practised between man and woman and not so much between women alone   This may be selfish but it is only an idea   Say! didnt you wish the men were there? You I hope will tell me the name of your Cousin in California as I might come across him sometime in my perambulations over the country

Your question is verry naturally put but it is not so easy to answer   Yet I will try to answer correctly   I have several times thought of going home when I was in a condition to go but then everybody around me was earnestly chasing the fickle Goddess fortune and each and everyone thought in the near future they would have a sure thing of receiving her most favorable smiles and wanted me to join in the chase and see if we could not be successful in winning her favors And I being already half won to their way of thinking was induced to put in my best attempts and after a long chase find we had all lost sight of what we were so earnestly seeking and that the Minx after leading us a long way with cunning glances and winning promises had suddenly taken wings and disappeared leaving us in a tangled maze exceedingly difficult to extricate ourselves from and only after many days travel and receiving many scratches from the brambles of envy and disappointment did we again find ourselves back at the starting point

I like this country so well that I intend to end my life here and I have not been in a situation for the last six years that I could go to the states and return here as I would wish although I could have went home any time since I have been here I am still waiting to get into a position that I can go and return in a way that my fancy has painted that I would like to go and come . . .

I am glad you are so well situated as to excitement of the war and hope its troubles may not reach you though I expect from the news we have here now that the excitement has been verry great in your neighborhood   We have just got the news of Morgans forces being dispersed up in Ohio and of the commencement of the assault on the city of Charlstown   I do most earnestly hope that this may be the last raid the rebels will ever be able to make into a Union State   From the news we have here we begin to believe that Peace is not verry far in the future   Oh what a blessing it would be to the whole country to have everything settled down again into a peaceful happy Government such as it was before the war commenced   The 300,000 called for will take many of the men from the country that are left but they had better all go than to allow any part of the country to seperate itself from the rest

July 23   7 oc P M

After another days attendance to my business I am seated in my cabin which I believe I have told you about to try to finish my answer to your verry kind and acceptable letter   On reading what I have written I am almost tempted to tear it up and try again but fearing I might not write even so well again I will let you have it all and you then will see the bad as well as what I might happen to consider the best and then to knowing that what pleases one will sometimes displease another I am flattered with the hope that what looks so poor to me may look somewhat better to you

I would dearly love once more to travel the country roads to a country meeting house situated on the border of some shady woods and hear a good sermon some pious minister suited to his calling and you describe your trip so clearly that I can almost fancy myself in the Company and passing through those pleasant shady roads and feel a Forrest summer breeze fan my cheek   But such I fear me such are for me passed forever   I suppose that the war has taken most of the young men of the country away from their homes but then I hope that they will soon be allowed to return to their friends and settle down in peaceful life

I see by the Telegraph tonight that the Rebel Morgan had got pretty well up into your part of the state with a part of his men   The telegraph says that he was about the middle of the state yesterday with 500 men so that you must begin to see some of the excitement of the war   I hope they may capture him with his entire force so that he can never make such another move into a quiet and peaceful state

No indeed not one particle more than is interesting on the contrary if you had written for the length of a Dozen more letters as long as this one I would still have been interested and feel when I got through reading it as if I could scarce allow that it was the end   You need not fear to write too much and in return for your kindness I will write of whatever I can think of that might possibly interest you

As I have now said all that your letter seemed to suggest as answer I will endeavor to fullfill my promise to you in my last letter

Some 8 or 9 weeks ago while visiting a young Lady acquaintance from the Mountains who was on a visit to another of my Mountain acquaintances we concluded to have a family ride and picnic on the sea shore so on the following Sunday one of the Men took us into his Spring waggon and took us out to the Beach

The waggon was a very large one and contained when we were all in two married men their wives and four children 2 unmarried Ladies and your humble servant with another Crusty old Bachelor   We had plenty of room and as we were bound to enjoy the trip we made the most of everything   We started about 8 o clock in the morning went directly west from the city of a barren hilly sandy country for about 5 miles when we came to a high rocky bluff or rather a stone bluff that juts out over the ocean about 75 feet high and nearly perpendicular   from the city a fine road is made out and around the face of this bluff over the water down to as fine a sandy beach as I ever saw   just at the bluff a house is built on the outside of the road and over the water about 70 feet from the water so that you can stand in the back veranda and look down on the water almost perpendicularly   About one hundred yards out from this point is a high rock that stands some forty feet above the water and is some 200 feet or more across with several smaller rocks around it   on these rocks there was some 200 or 300 seals or sea lions crawling about over the rock roaring at and playing with each other making a noise something between the roar of a bull and the bark of a dog and every once in a while plunging off into the water and swimming about and around the rocks   Some of them are verry large weighing as much as 2000 pounds and they are of a dark color and covered with a short crisp hair   We had a good opera Glass to look at them with so we could see them plain enough to see their teeth and eyes   I can not justly describe them to you but if you have a history of the seal it will give you a better idea than I can of their shape After looking at the sea lions for about an hour we went down on to the beach and drove south along the waters edge for about 3 miles over a level sand bed as smooth almost as a floor til we came to a little creek that runs into the sea from a small lake about a mile inland   We drove up this creek til we came to a beautiful spring at the side of the road where we stopped and had our Lunch   The earth was covered with flowers of the brightest hues and of all the colors of the rainbow   We each gathered a boquet and brought home with us besides several beautiful specimens of sea weed and also a large number of shells   We had a bright clear day and every one was highly pleased with the trip even the Old Bachelors   The young lady has now returned to her mountain home and I expect will never forget her family picnic on the sea shore

As we came home we came through one half the length of the City and many was the face turned to gaze at us seeing so many of us in one waggon was something unusual

I did not get my satisfaction looking at the sea lions and intend to repeat the trip just as soon as I conveniently can

I took a trip a short time ago across the Bay and down the Valley some 25 miles The Valley on the East side of the Bay is from 4 to 10 miles wide and is verry rich When I was over there the grain was ripe and was being cut   As far as the eye could reach was one sheet of Green and Golden grain with here and there a small bunch of men and horses with reaping machines cutting and binding the Grain Corn will not grow good in this Valley so that two thirds of it is small grain and the rest low vegetables and Hay

Some of the finest Gardens and Orchards that I ever saw are located in that Valley and around this Bay   I am afraid if I rambel on any farther you will get tired of following so Excuse all errors and you will do me a favor as I can not think of reading this over to correct errors for fear what was only a notion when I read the first part of my letter might become a will and I would then tear it up sure and try again

With my kindest regards to you my friend and hoping you may ever be blessed with all the happiness heart can wish   Hoping too that you may think this worthy of an answer and that our friendship thus begun may never change for the worse

I will remain

To Lizzie
Your friend
John

San Francisco   Aug 6th 1863

Dear Friend Lizzie

I feel that I am entitled to thus address you for the pleasure you have given me in your several letters   I am ventureing to write again before you have given your permission by an answer for reasons which you will see as you read this   We started out three years ago to write for each others amusement   I have tried to amuse you in my letters and you have not only amused me but have afforded me much gratification and unalloyed pleasure in your pleasing well written intelligent letters   I can only now hope that nothing may ever transpire to break our Friendship thus begun Although we may never have seen each other we can still feel the same towards one another that we could had we been conversing together and through life we may give each other pleasure by occasionally coresponding should other cares than those now demanding our attention engage our time

I have a hope and I will utter it now that our correspondence should last as long as we are able to write and we are situated at such distance   I have been expecting every letter that I have received from you to read in its pages Married Mr. – – – to Miss L. E. L. etc but even then I do not wish you to discontinue the correspondence but on the contrary then continue to write me so that I might have some profit from your extended experience and perhaps by your example I might be bettered in this world if not in the world to come

I am now an old Bachelor with no hope of ever being able to change my condition but only remain in single Blessedness and do what little good I may to those around me and go on through life a living example and warning to the rising generation to take care and marry when they are young and not wait til it is too late like the man who went into the canebrake to cut a cane and passed by all the beautiful ones to find a better and then had to take a poor one or none

Supposing then that you will be settled down living happily with the most favored one the one of your choice and enjoying life as much as it is possible for Mortal to enjoy   You could then give me your view of life from a more favored position than it is possible for me to attain and in return I would give you the view I have from what ever position I might be placed in   but I am forgetting the purpose of my extra letter

As I said before we have been corresponding for three years and do not know as yet how we look to each other personally   As I would dearly love to see you and feeling so strongly the inclination to have a view of you I thought you might at least have the curiosity if not the desire to see how I would look   Although my face is homely and my general appearance not prepossessing it is still the face and appearance of your correspondent and is the best I have   Hoping you will receive it favorably and send me yours in return I send it with some misgivings as to how it will be received   but good or ill I send it   As I said of the letter it is only paper and if I am presuming too much on the pleasures I have received from your kind and generous answers put it in the stove and there will be no more of it   You are the first one I ever ventured to send my *Carte* to and probably may be the only one And I shall live in hope until I receive the answer that will tell me that I am wrong or right in the matter   I think if I had your picture I could write in a conversational style altogether   I think I could do better if the picture was before me Then too we now only write a letter once in three months and if you have the time we can write oftener as I have plenty of time if I am a mind to use it and I will try to do better than I have done at least for a part of the time   And when you are married and settled down on the farm for life you can tell me all about the little parties and plays and the soldiers return meetings and the Barbacues and picnics that are sure to follow the close of this unhappy war   While I will try to tell you of the doing here and the general appearance of things as I see them in this great and growing city and rich and unparalleled strange state and country

I have already spoiled more paper than I intended to when I begun but when I get to writing to you it seems that I cant quit as I usually do when writing my letters generally

If you will only accept the enclosed and send me yours in return I will be (I wont say the happiest man alive but as near that as may be) verry much gratified indeed and shall be ever grateful

We are having now an unusual amount of shows excursions and parades in the city   The war times seem to stir up everybody to action   I am glad to see by the news that they have finally captured the Rebel Morgan   I hope his raid did not injure you or any of your friends

So with my Kindest regards for Your welfare and happiness

> I Remain
> Expectantly
> Your Friend
> John

Friend J. D.   Home (Lyndon, Ohio)   Sept 11th 1863

Some weeks have passed since your favor of July 22nd reached me and if I have too long neglected to reply, Believing you may excuse — shall only now take time to say by way of excuse that my time has been so occupied that I could not sooner write. I also was surprised though quite agreably — a short time since by receiving another, August 6th and since I have at length determined on attempting an answer shall try to serve up something that may do for a response to both yours in one though I shall not promise a very lengthy epistle, ...

Now I will return to your letter and endeavor to reply briefly as possible. Have never read any "treties on psycology" though what you say appears to me to be quite reasonable and agrees with the idea I have often entertained, that two persons of "sympathetic temperment" feel much the same while writing and reading the writing of the other. I was only quizzing, when I mentioned "kissing the men" but since you ask my opinion on the subject will here say that it is a habit that I have never been much addicted to, though when in society where it is customary as it is here a person is led to conform, (at least to some extent) and I own I like it *sometimes*. Think it a pleasant way of showing the warmest friendship between two of either the same or different sexes. Although it is often used deceptively, particularly among the ladies (I dont know so much about the men, perhaps you can tell me) for I have seen it practiced among ladies where I knew there was no friendship really felt at heart. Like you, would like to see it more generally practiced but differ with you a little in thinking it pleasant among women alone provided the feelings correspond, have seen boys kissing here in play, it looked rather rediculous though dont know why it should was it customary.

Of course I should have been happy to have met all that I used to meet then, men and all. The one I spoke of being in the army was killed in the battle of Gettysburg.

The name of the one in California is Wm. B. Lucas should you ever come across him you will please tell me. Would certainly have enjoyed the trip much more had some friend been with me to have enjoyed the pleasures for to me a true friend is the *dearest* boon this earth affords.

Excitement was wrought up to the highest pitch here during the Morgan raid though he passed several miles distant from and evry one expected him right here with all his forces. The malitia were called out and for a time scarce a man was left at home but all this was nothing compared with Quantrills raid in Kansas. When will the end of such things be? I long for the day when peace will again be restored, and all such men will meet their reward. . . .

As you express the wish I am willing and hope too that our friendship so strongly begun may prove lasting as our lives, and our correspondence untill some event would demand a close, in the event of my marriage as you sudjist, I dont know that it would be profitable to continue the correspondence particularly if I had a jealous husband, but we can arrange that after the occurence, and I shouldent wonder you are fancying now I am preparing for the *Catastrophe* as a reason for my long silence. And if you expect to see in this sheet "Married Mr - - - - to Miss - - - - you will be disappointed for I am yet an *Old Maid,* that despised name — although I have taken it from choice so far. And no doubt I am and have been doing like the "man in the cane brake" but thank fortune I have many good friends yet and several Bachelors are included. But why are you so disconsolate, without a "hope of changing your condition" if you wish it when the world is full of *pretty girls* if not in Cal. they are evry where else, and many of them I venture to say might be willing to launch their barque on the stormy sea of Matrimony were a good opportunity presented. But I remember you have in former letters told me your reasons which I think reasonable and good ones, and will now turn to something else.

I have often felt a desire to see at least your *photograph* and now allow me the pleasure of thanking you for it. It very nearly corresponds with *my fancied picture* of your personal appearance drawn from Maggies discription of you connected with what you have told me of it yourself. And instead of "putting it in the stove" have already introduced it to quite a number of other pictures I have, all of which I intend keeping long as I am able to keep them, as *Mementos of the friends they represent.* And shall grant your request by enclosing mine in return for this one, had a number of them but they have nearly all been disposed of or taken from me and the best ones picked out, however this one may afford you a faint idea of how I look, some tell me they are flattering others say not, I shall not say which is correct, only I would have you know that *my hair is not so grey on the top of my head* as is represented in the picture. . . .

Now hoping you will excuse all errors in this and my tardiness in answering

I remain Your friend

Lizzie

Friend Lizzie   San Francisco   Oct 9th 1863

Your most welcome and verry interesting letter of the 11th of Sept this day received and read with unalloyed pleasure and my partial anticipations were verry agreeably fullfilled by finding in your letter your "Carte" for which you will please accept all the thanks I am capable of feeling

I shall always be thankful for any kind of a letter you may choose to favor me with particularly if they always are written in the intelligent manner that has characterized all your letters to me so far so you need not be afraid of tiring me by writing too much as I can read tolerably well and have never tired yet in reading a letter from a friend or one whom I considered as such

I congratulate you on your good health and sympathise with you in the loss of relatives — such is life — I have lost since I came to this country two of my nearest and dearest relatives and felt deeply the loss and can thus therefore I think appreciate your solicitude for the dear one still lingering in the way that indicates the approach to the valley of the shadow of eternity   may your hope be fullfilled is my earnest wish

I supposed you were only quizzing but thought there might be some reality in a quizzical joke and as you frankly acknowledge that you like it I have no more to say in the way of doubt

I am glad to find our ideas agree on the custom in the main features   I can not tell you how kissing goes among Men because I have never been so kissed   I have seen men do so who came from France and I believe that is the only civilized country in the world where the custom of saluting with a kiss among the men is practiced and so the information you ask for is out of reach or I would most cheerfully give it to you   I remember well when I attended plays the large amount of kissing among the young folks and how intensely I then enjoyed the fun   I believe I would even enjoy the same now though I have no means of testing the matter I have no doubt if you sat by and looked at a play without taking part that you thought it ridiculous but if you had entered into the sport in spirit and feeling how different would probably have been your ideas   I am most to old to take part with children in a play but I do believe I could enjoy it for an hour or two yet

I will look out for T. B. Lucas and if I find him will let you know   I have not met him so far   I have known some five or six of the name of Lucas but not that name

I agree with you fully that "A true friend is the dearest boon on Earth" and therefore have always endeavored to cherish friendship wherever I have found it Often and often have I wished for one whome I could trust entirely as myself one who would be interested in all matters that I was interested who would keep for me what I would keep and guard my feelings as their own but to this time that one I have not found although life is fleeting and the best half of mine is gone I yet hope I will meet that one before my journey through life is ended   I have many friends in this country many whom I can trust thoroughly as men and a verry few I can trust as women but our circumstances are such that we can only be friends as this world goes on as interest may dictate in fact interest is the great leaver by which almost all actions are governed and which sometimes makes the best of friends enemies   It is hard school for a confiding person to be cast loose in the world among so many conflicting interests and passions but it is a school that makes the learning lasting   This is only my notion from what I have been able to observe as I passed along and what experience has taught me

I sincerely join you in your wish for peace once more but can not answer your question when will we have peace again   I wish I could   Our country is now passing through the most terrible ordeal that nations have to go through and I sometimes hope that it will come out all the better for the trial yet to me the future looks dark   I wish I could see matters in a clearer brighter light   I fear we may have peace to soon a peace that will only last for a short time to be broken by a still more devastating war but I will with you hope for the best and help my country what I can and leave the solution of all the troubles to him who does all things for the best   As far as we poor Mortals are able to see some will have a terrible Record to answer for   Yet I believe that no sin on this Earth ever goes unpunished and that all will meet with their just rewards   Tis a terrible time in some parts of the country and I am glad that you are so happily situated as to be out of the danger of any raids such as were made in Kansas

The season for Wild flowers is now over for the present but another one is coming and if you come out here with Maggie I will promise you at least one chance to see flowers to your hearts content   there is a great variety and abundance of wild flowers all over this country and you shall have a chance to see them if I am here when you come   I once was talking about the variety of flowers while sitting by a camp fire where a prospecting company were camped away up in the mountains when a dispute arose as to the variety   I started from my seat and stepped 25 paces in a straight line and picked one of each kind of flower that I could reach without stepping aside and on counting them I had twenty two different kinds this was on a little valley near a mountain stream where the ground was rich   the flowers are not so various on the hills though fully as abundant

There are some beautiful flower gardens around the City here but nothing that seems to me so pleasant as the mountain flowers   There is one peculiarity that is against the wild flowers here I have never seen but two or three kinds that have any smell at all   for fragrance they are nothing but for beauty of appearance they exceed all   So for looks I choose the wild ones and for fragrance the cultivated ones

This I think is a good comparison for the people of this world for beauty of appearance we choose the wild dashing ones while for real fragrance for solid value and worth of being we must take the more homely and cultivated ones

Again I must thank you for your willingness to continue our (shall I say Romantic) Friendship   No I will not now call it Romantic although that was the beginning   I think it real now and I too hope it may end only with our stay on this earth   the correspondence too might be kept up even though it should occasionally be stopped for a while by circumstances   One circumstance which I hope will not occur is your getting that Jealous husband for then I fear that we would indeed have to stop but I hope that he will be kind indulgent and generous and allow you to correspond as you may choose without consulting him

I did half way suspicion something of the kind was on hand but could not tell why I thought so but your ingeneous way of telling it has entirely scattered all my suspicions in that matter but I have no doubt that ere many more letters reach me I will see what you call a catastrope set forth in full in the paper as a verry happy circumstance   Well when it does happen I shall prepare myself to wish you much happiness   I propose that we adopt a plan to start our correspondence again if it should get stopped without our causing it   I suggest this mode

It takes 1 month for the mail to go sometimes one month to get ready to answer now allow 2 weeks more then hereafter should either of us not get an answer in two and one half of three months let that one write a note of enquiry which will answer the same purpose that I had partly in view by writing again before receiving an answer   If any of those *Bachelor Friends* should lie in the way just send me a Blank envelope (like the Irishmans) with a word or two in it and I will understand it and wait a few weeks longer and I will agree to do the same if I should find some disconsolate person of the female pursuasion who liked to take my arm for a walk down the journey of life

You I have no doubt are right in saying "There are many of them who are willing to launch their bark if a good opportunity offers" But who is going to take me for a good opportunity that is the question

I am verry much pleased with the picture   you are if any difference better looking than I anticipated   I rather thought you were plain looking because you wrote such splendid letters as it is an unusual thing for a pretty girl to write anything solid and sensible   The picture is before me and I almost fancy myself speaking to you and that I can see your eyes sparkling with merry humor   I don't intend to flatter you but I do think you have a noble form and features   The mind of that well formed head as appears from the outlines of the picture can not be anything else but pure and of the noblest stamp   I had not formed any definate idea of what your appearance was but have an inclination to believe that you were not so good looking as you are from the fact that you seldom see a pretty girl who can write a sensible letter and from your letters only I guessed that you might be rather homely   Now I can say you are verry good looking and that your features indicate a mild congenial disposition with a fund of benevolence and mirth just such a form and features as is fit to adorn the highest stations in life and will always be beloved by those around who may have much communication with you   I would not have mistaken the white spots for gray as they indicate that your hair is a glossy black I shall keep the picture with those I prize most and until I leave this world if Providence permits I can not be accountable for unavoidable accident   I have placed it on the first page of my Album where I intend it to remain until it shall be necessary to remove it to a better locality   You need not fear to tire me however much you may write nor displease me however little you may write but can only displease or tire me by not writing at all which I hope may not be the case while we are able to write   I hope that the event that would demand its close may not occur while we are so distant from each other and that if that jealous husband should happen in the way you will steal a few minutes while he is away to let your distant friend know you are still among the denizens of earth

We have had no political camp meetings here but have small meetings to most any extent   The Military camp for this part of the state is now in camp near the City and every day almost there is some parade in the streets   for the last few days there has been a great deal of parade in the Military line

I see a great deal of city life now here   I see on the streets all manner of dress color and appearances from the youngest to the oldest the prettiest and fairest to the most homely   The rich 1000 dollar silk dress and the dirtiest rags all passing and repassing in and out around and about all seeming anxious to hurry along and all probably seeking some object of their own interest   I have now written too much to attempt to describe the dress and modes at present nor do I believe that I could describe them understandingly if I was to try to do so   I certainly could not tell the names of the different kinds of dresses and varieties are so great that it would not pay to do so if I could

A friend from up country was here a short time ago and we went out on the beach and took another look at the seals or Sea Dogs as they are called   My friend was highly pleased with the trip and if you happen to reach these shores that will be the first excursion for you to make   I have been so closely confined to business since I last wrote you that I have no trip into the country to write about so that this letter will be more prosey than usual   I hope however it will repay perusal We are having most delightful weather they say this is the best season of the year here   The wind blows but verry little and the nights are clear and lovely   Hoping to hear from you soon again and that you are enjoying all the pleasures alloted to mortals

I am most Truly
Your Friend
John

I have read over and corrected my letter for once and am strongly tempted to tear it up and try again but as it is now 12 oc and I will not have time again this week to write I send it along hoping it may answer until next time and that you will excuse all errors as errors of the hand and not of the heart   I send you a paper with this that has some true pictures of the modes of life here and in other parts of California

Lyndon Station (Ohio)   Nov 20th '63

Friend Doble

Yours of Oct. 9th was received a few days ago and I embrace the present as the first opportunity to answer. . . .

I have been reading Bayard Taylors travels and adventures to and through California in the year of 1849, find it interesting, some places and things described it must be enchanting to visit. If I saw some one near who was acquainted with the places mentioned it would add much to the interest of the book. Am sorry I did not have it when Maggie was here. I presume most of the scenery mentioned in it has undergone considerable change since then so that the same traveller would scarce recognize the places now.

When any of those *Bachelor Friends* of mine have any *very particular* claims on my attention I shall probably let you know,—at present I know of no one who need hinder me writing this letter even if he knew anything of it—and when that event of which you speak does happen I shall certainly inform you of it. To me it is so far in the future I can't say whether it will be a happy one or not, or whether *he* will be jealous or what.

You ask who is going to take *you* for a "good opportunity" well I can't say, but perhaps you are underating yourself and lack selfesteem. A good supply of *that article* will sometimes fit a man for most any immergency of the kind in question at least I have known it to be the case on one or two occasions. At all events I sincerely hope you will ere long find that *one* friend who you so much long to meet and with whom you can trust the keeping of your all and may *she* prove worthy of your trust is my wish.

I am flattered that you are so pleased with the picture as you seem but do not know that the original deserves all the praise you bestow. Pictures are generally flattering you know. And perhaps if you saw the original might think this one was. I am only sorry I do not possess more of the traits of character you mention (say nothing of the *good looks*). Your idea that a pretty girl never writes a sensible letter I should not have thought of your judging of my appearance in that way. Was I left to judge of my own phiz from my letters would certainly fancy myself quite a beauty, but as it is have always thought my letters *very poor* and myself not at all handsome or possessing any attractions I see in some others around me. Had I placed the picture in your Album should have put it on the last page instead of the first—I am not so lucky as to have an Album in which to place my photographs yet although I have a number of them sufficient to fill one. And I hope fortune will favor me with one ere very long, when yours will occupy a conspicuous place no doubt.

Maggie spent a few weeks with us again and is now among the friends in Indiana as I suppose you are already aware, she did not know when she would return home when I saw her. I fear I shall not have the pleasure of accompanying her as I should like to do. . . .

Your Friend
Lizzie

San Francisco   Dec 29th 1863

Friend Lizzie

Amid the resounding din and excitement of the holidays your welcome letter of November 25th reached me and was indeed a welcome visitor come to cheer me in my comparative loneliness   I am under many obligations to you for your kind responses and shall endeavor on my part to do the best I can

Taylor is a verry good descriptive writer and an extremely interesting conversational writer   I have no doubt you were well pleased with his writings   I think he was not in the mountains just where I have been living but was near to it   the scenes are so similar that if Maggie had been with you you could no doubt have got a better understanding of what he describes so pleasantly

Many thanks for your kind wishes and should *that friend* be found I will certainly at the first opportunity cause her to make your acquaintance   Yet I am almost without hope as age is creeping on   the Span is nearly completed and if the next few years do not furnish the required opportunities I fear I shall have to complete the journey as I have begun it—alone   My opinion is that you verry much underrate your abilities and if I had nothing else in the world to judge from than this letter I would still say you verry much under rate your abilities to please This letter of yours is a *gem* written in an easy unassuming style ideas clearly expressed and withal a strong current of sly humor running through the whole of it I may have made erroneous calculations but true or false I am convinced of their truth and will maintain them until I see something else than I have yet seen to convince me that I am wrong and will therefore only reaffirm what my impressions

ELIZABETH E. LUCAS

JOHN DOBLE

were before   The picture shall keep the *first* place until some stronger will than mine places it somewhere else and the more I look at it now the more I am convinced that my first estimates of the pure and noble mind there enthroned were true You need never wish for more or better attractions than you now possess as they are sufficient for all purposes and if you were to now become possessed of the attractions you sigh for and then look back at what you now are you would soon wish to come back as you are

I expect Maggie can hardly get back here without you do come with her as her family will be more than she can take care of alone and I am satisfied if you were to come that when you returned home again as you would most likely do in a year or so you would be amply repaid for all the trouble you were put to by the new and strange scenes you would be constantly witnessing in your travels   In fact it would take more than a year before you could even have a good look round let alone seeing everything   Should you not come with Maggie I am inclined to think that you will regret it   Yet I cannot judge for you but am satisfied that whatever you do it will be all for the best   You could come out with Maggie and spend the winter and then return in the spring again all ready for the next summers duties

I will not attempt now to describe to you the celebrations and amusements that were and are going on here now as I have been at home busy all the time and will be throughout the holidays   I would speak of the services and celebrations in the churches were they not so much alike the world over that a description of one is a description of all and nothing only the country is new here   No I will take that back in part   The country is new to all   the people are new to some and Christmas festivals and plays are only new to the children

Since I have been here I have attended close to my business and have not the opportunities to look around me that I had while up in the mountains and this I hope will be a sufficient excuse for the shortness of my letter

If I promised you a description or an attempt at description of any of the places or things here that I have not given remind me of it and I will respond   I think some now of circulating through the mountains some this winter or early in the spring to look at some new mines and if I get off I will then have a chance to try my powers of description once more for your benefit

So hoping that you are enjoying all the pleasures possible during the holidays and that nought may ever mar the pleasures of your life I remain as ever

Your Friend Truly
John

Newspaper Clipping Attached to Letter

ABNER DOBLE

Our candidate for Mayor will be elected. That is a fore-gone conclusion; so palpable, indeed, that the purblind and fosilized regular Republican machine managers have become assured of it, have taken down their candidate, and, true to the only principle they recognize — to be on the winning side — have placed him on their ticket, not withstanding he refuses to endorse the Republican platform as such. Still we are willing all parties shall vote for our candidate but we can't help thinking what a strange sensation it will be for that crowd to vote for a true man for once. And what cause for general thanskgiving will the people of this city have when they have placed at the helm of the city government an honest, capable and earnest man.

In Abner Doble the people have a man whom the office has sought, as one eminently fitted for this emergency in public affairs. His life in our city has been above reproach in all his relations with his fellow citizens. His successful business career, in which he has risen from a wage-worker at the forge to be head of the heaviest business houses on this coast and the trusted agent and manager of one of the most extensive manufacturing interests in the world, is a sufficient guaranty of his ability. He will come into the office with no trains of political parasites to fatten at the public expense. He will go into the office with clean hands and will administer it in the interest of the people. He will enter upon his duties with a full under-standing of the needs of the people, and executive ability equal to the emergency, a determination to do the right thing with zeal; while all his acts will be directed by, and approved of, his own conscience. And we predict for him that when he shall retire at the close of his term it will only be to be promoted to a higher place by the votes of the people, who will say of him, as do his former employees, "He is the best and purest man in the State." Surely, the long-looked-for day of reform is at hand. The people are seeking men governed by a religious faith and accountability for places of public trust.

Lyndon, Ohio   Feb 5th 1864

Friend John

It is a great blessing when friends or acquaintances are far distant from each other to be able to converse through the medium of pen and ink, at least I have always found it so, and it is with pleasure that I now find myself with the necessary articles for communicating a few thoughts for your perusal in reply to your last which I received—and perused with pleasure just one week ago....

I have not heard from Maggie for sometime, then she did not expect to leave for home before Spring. So I could not go to spend the winter in Cal. as you so kindly sudjest, if I wished it. Thank you again for the invitation to accompany her dont know whether "I shall regret it" or not, But still think it my duty to remain at home although I should like the visit were circumstances more favorable.

I am not aware of anything to write you further now that would be likely to repay you the trouble of perusing and fear you may not be interested in what I have said so shall stop with a short letter also this time. I believe you have not promised a description of anything you have not given me, but shall be interested in the perusal of whatever you may think proper to tell me of. Now ever wishing you success in all your undertakings, I remain,

Your Friend
Lizzie

San Francisco   March 4th 1864

Dear Friend Lizzie

This morning at the usual hour I found myself wending my way to the Postoffice Two blocks of the distance is occupied by the City Markets and of a morning sometimes for 3 blocks of this distance the street is crowded with Market Waggons as close as they can stand side & side with the horses heads at the edge of the sidewalk each waggon filled with something for city folks to eat and the street and sidewalks crowded with Men women and children of all sizes nations colors tongues & Dresses some buying chattering or grumbling at the sellers while some like myself are looking on amused or disgusted as the case may be at what they see

There an old Woman at least sixty & I think an Italian is disposing of a load of Turkies chicks Ducks and Geese scolding first this one and then that and occasionally smiling like a flash of sunshine on a Glowering day as some verry fair young Maid comes up to buy a breakfast for her Mistress at home and see with what delight she drops the change in that capacious pocket at her side as she turns to wait on the next comer who is a fair boy who cant speak a word that I can understand but by motions makes the old lady understand that he wants a Turkey & Duck and demurs for a little time to the price the old Lady demands but finally pays as neither can understand what the other says there is no room for dispute No customer now being at hands she turns to her nearest neighbor and apparently enters into a friendly dispute as to who has made the most in their mornings sales and here I left them to go a little further when a dense crowd of all kinds of people Dogs Mules and horses are collected and seeming to be trying who can make the most noise   On coming up I find a team has become restive and there being no chance to run have so twisted round as to upset a small waggon with a large amount of Garden stuff in it that is now scattered among the feet and wheels in the street   I hurry on past these when I see what is the matter to find my way blocked up entirely by a vast amount of cabbage and cauliflower that is being transfered from a number of waggons into a store at hand and to get round which I push my way into the street and along through the crowd a space then into a cross street to the Office where I find your most Welcome and pleasant letter of the 5th of Feb. I open and glance over it then take from the box all our letters hastily stow them in pocket take another look at yours then with successions of pleasant feelings and gratification that I can not express in words I make my way back by another route   distribute the letters I have among the Men in the Shop then hasten to my Room to peruse your verry acceptable letter which done I return to shop and to the business of the day and when the day is oer and 7 o clock has come I commence trying to answer you in spirit and in truth as you have written that is in one way to fill up the measure as I have promised to keep up the correspondence and in another to use my best endeavors to please or gratify one who I believe will ever be a valued friend and if in the last I succeed I will be most fully rewarded and if I fail will be most deeply disappointed

Yes Leap year is here and fast gliding away and (I am forced to acknowledge the unpleasant truth) not a single Lady has dained to smile on me with that favor so necessary to fancied happiness

That fainting hope is I fear soon to be proved a reality   I wish some Lady would take compassion on my desolate condition and make herself happy by offering to convey my uncertain & wandering barque down the stream of time but vain is the

hope I fear   Women in this country are too much petted and praised by the sterner
sex to ever take advantage of the priveleges given them in the advent of Leap year
One woman is about as good as two men in the social Scale figuratively speaking
and being thus valuable there is but a poor chance for anyone to throw herself
away by even looking with favor even on one so poor and homely as your unworthy
friend   There is an old adage that I used to hear which is "every Jack has his Gill
etc" which I entirely disbelieve now though once when quite young I believed it
fully   My disbelief is not without foundation as you and I both well know are not
we in ourselves proof of its fallacy

Wouldnt I be happy to be called out by some fair one even if it was only to a
party would I put on my best collar and ruffles and step proudly onward to — to —
to — supper or somewhere else   I would that   and she wouldnt have to hint more
than once that anything was wanted to find a ready response

I expect those leap year parties are verry interesting though I never saw one yet I
would like to just for the novelty of the thing and to see how it would feel

I shouldnt wonder if you should overcome that natural timidity and before the
year was over find yourself acting the gallant to some spruce Bach that may happen
to secure your fancy and perhaps before the year is out instead of me it will be you
that will be having your measure of this worlds joys filled to repletion

Well if you do all I can say at present is Success attend you and may you never
know want or trouble but May your life glide smothly onward with all the attendant happiness for mortal to enjoy ready spread out to your hand so that possess and
enjoy it will only be necessary to think the wish and I hope that when such happiness does fall to your lot you will not forget your far distant sympathising friend
who will still be wandering on alone and uncared for only by the eye that never
sleeps   And that you will still occasionally let him have a word from you and a
glimpse at the real happiness it is sometimes allowed Mortals to enjoy on this earth

From your account and from all others I have received your winter has been a
verry severe one while in contrast to it our winter has been almost a continual
summer   We have had no cold weather nor but little rain this winter and the
people seem to enjoy it too   I have been out to the various places of resort here
and always find them crowded with people

Though the winter is so fine we still have suffering among us   three suicides and
two murders have occured here in the last week and today the most Eloquent Man
in the State died   All business will be closed tomorrow on account of his death
He was a Unitarian Minister and the greatest orator we have ever had in the State
The papers tonight speak of his death as a national calamity and mourn him as a
dear friend gone[33]   such is life the brightest and the dullest the high and low rich
and poor all must go the same way so far as mortal can see and happy are those
who like the great man who died today are ready when the time comes   He died
contented and happy believing that he had done his whole duty while living

I grieve deeply for the suffering of our poor soldiers in the field with all that the
Government can do to keep them comfortable there must be a great deal of suffering among them   But if they can only have kind friends at home to keep up a
continual correspondence they will have some little relief from the trials and priva-
tions of a soldiers life   Speaking of correspondence I read some notices in a New
York paper the other day that goes to show there are many who would like a

correspondence and that you may see how it seems I cut out the slip of advertisements and send it to you enclosed   I have seen several such lists of notices lately but one will be enough to show how they advertise

I would dearly love to have a good sleigh ride once more it has now been twelve years since I was in a sleigh so long that it seems like a dream almost forgotten I have no doubt you enjoyed it verry much   Maggie I understand will leave New York about the first of April probably before you get this letter   I am sorry that circumstances are so unfavorable as I know you are capable of much enjoyment of the varieties of life and would be more pleased with a trip to this country than you could possibly imagine   If you don't come Maggie will have to hire a girl to come with her but then I suppose it is no use to multiply words as you will do what is for the best   whatever you do I am satified it will be for the best because every person must act from the circumstances surrounding them and these circumstances will no doubt guide you rightly

You need not be afraid of writing too much as it is a pleasure to me to read your writing on any and all subjects and everything is interesting when written by a far distant friend in a good spirit so write long as you please I will never tire of reading what you may write

Valentines Day came and passed and if it had not been leap year I should certainly have sent you one but every time I thought of it I came to the conclusion that it would not be right to take the prerogative from any of the fair sex by being the first to send or make advances but I suppose that natural timidity prevented some from using their privileges   Well I must be content but I am somewhat consoled with the reflection that another leap year is four years off and several valentines days come around between now and then

Since I have been down here as I before wrote you I have been so constantly busy that I have not traveled round much so that the variety of scenery I had to write about among the mountains is taken away from me and consequently I can not flatter myself that my letters would be so interesting because of the want of variety but I hope however that you will still find them worthy of notice and reply and what they may lack in interest I hope will ascribe to circumstances and not to my earnest desire to interest as well as to be interested

Hoping and trusting that the alwise Ruler of all things will grant you the full enjoyment of all the pleasures mortals are capable of enjoying and that your every wish may be gratified

I remain as ever

Most Truly & Sincerely

Your Friend

John

Lyndon, Ohio   April 16th 1864

Friend Doble

Several days have passed since your friendly and interesting letter of March 4th was handed me but from some causes beyond my controll I have this far delayed an answer. Now trusting this will be none the less welcome on its arrival I shall proceed to pen you something in return for yours. . . .

Maggie I suppose is now far out on the waves of the Ocean, ere this sheet reaches you, you will have met her and perhaps she will have told you more of me than I could write—Wish I was with her, and to view some of the wonders of the world, I know I should enjoy it very much but it seems I was destined for a narrower sphere to wear away my few allotted days in doing what duty seems to require, or perhaps after all no real good.

I do hope M. will have a safe and pleasant trip and a happy happy meeting with her husband and friends at San Francisco, when the society of each will be all the more appreciated from the long separation. But all this is not answering your letter and I will now turn to it.

Leap Year parties and all such, rather "played out" here, have not heard of one since I last wrote you, and I was not at any one, so guess there is not much danger of my "acting the gallant" to any one. And if *I should* be the happyone instead of *you* to find a companion to glide with me along the remainder of my days on earth, it will not be the result of my own proposal as I should much prefer the old ways (of the gents making all the advances). The success and happiness you so kindly wish me in that event, and the *event itself* is I fear more than I shall ever be so lucky as to *realize* however I thank you all the same for the wish. . . .

I often think of the suffering the soldiers must endure and "Wish the war were over" that all might again return to their homes in peace. I have not a single correspondent in the army now though I did have two for a short time. They are home again having served their time and did not reinlist. Those notices you sent me are interesting though all seem quite choice in regard to the correspondents. One wishes "blue eyes" another "something of a tease" some beauty and intelligent communications and so on and from the ages of sweet sixteen to twenty or twenty two— as *your* correspondent does not claim to possess any of these desirable qualities she shall not answer any of the Notices, leaving that for others who it may interest i will turn my attention to your letter again.

Valentines Day passed without scarce a thought from me. I neither sent nor received any and believe I did not see one. I am sorry that the fact of its being leap year prevented you from sending one to me as I think I should have been quite pleased with it. You were only too considerate of the advantages of the Ladies while they were perhaps too timid or negligent to improve the opportunity afforded to them. I have come to the end of my sheet and I believe the end of my letter as I know of nothing interesting to write you further.

So ever wishing you Success and happiness,

I Remain as ever Your Friend,

Lizzie

Friend Lizzie   San Francisco   May 20th 1864

Your welcome and verry interesting letter of the 16th April was read yesterday and the contents perused as always theretofore with a great deal of pleasure together with some sadness and sympathy with you in your bereavment   Tis sad to see our near and dear friends passing away one by one and yet tis some consolation to believe they are only leaving us for a brief season when we will again all be united within that house not made by hands   I have sometimes thought that instead of mourning the absence of departed dear ones we should rather rejoice that they were now relieved from the cares sorrows and anxieties of this life and that they are enjoying for a time before us the celestial joys of Eternal rest   Our time on this earth is but brief at best a few days or at most a few years and we will go too through that bourne from which no traveler returns and I can earnestly join you in the prayer that all may be prepared when the last trumpet shall sound and we are called to the presence of the Omnicient one who I believe does all things for the best

Your brothers family will for a time feel severely the sad bereavement but let us hope there is a balm of Gilead for every wound and that he who has taken the father to himself will provide for the tender flock left behind

Maggie arrived safe and all the family in good health or nearly so on Saturday three weeks ago and have been boarding since at one of the hotels here well satisfied I suppose that she got through so well   She is waiting for her house to be fixed to move into while at the hotel   I have but little chance to talk with her but will after she gets home in her own house see if she will talk more though she does not seem to be verry communicative when talking of home   All I can learn from her is that you are the best one in the family and that she is verry sorry you are not now with her and that you are in truth the best girl she ever knew in her life   She thinks she had a verry hard trip while on the steamers because the weather was so rough that she was sick nearly all the way across but then she is all right now and I expect will want to try the same trip again before many years

I wish too you had come with her as you could have seen a little of the world and would have found out that all people in this world are nearly alike though all have different ways of acting through life   All are fullfilling their destiny and let me hope that while you are passing your time in doing your duty that it is only leading on to something better in the future and that you will yet find a chance to see something more of the world as it is   Would I be highly gratified if perchance I should have an invitation with proper thankfulness   But then leap year is fast gliding away and I have seen no prospect as yet for any Lady to pay her addresses to me so much so that I almost begin to feel as if I should reject any advances that might be made now because they did not come sooner   You I have no doubt will be the happy one in place of me as there is not the Ghost of a chance for me that I know of while you are among many chances   And the reason why I have not chances I will tell you in this country women are so few in proportion to the men that they are flattered and petted until they value themselves clear above the market rates   So that a common everyday article like myself cant even get a bid and they only go off when something offers that appears as valuable as themselves offers and the consequence is that many of them get sold for a song or what is worse only get a part of the song and have to sing the balance themselves and then they frequently end the bargain in a Divorce Court which brings them on the market again in a damaged condition so that everyday articles are worth more and cant think of making so disadvantageous a bargain   Now the case being different with you the sexes being nearly equal each one values themselves at about a fair rate and when a fair bargain is offered it is taken and being nearly equal proves lasting   For these reasons I am with you in the opinion that you should be the happy one in place of me and may you ever be as happy and contented as heart could wish or mind capable to enjoy is the wish of your distant though sincere Friend and Correspondent

The advertisements for correspondents did require a great many things tis true but I do not agree with you when you say you had none of the qualifications to make a good correspondent   Although you are not "sweet 16" or have not "blue eye" or are not "something of a tease" You have what some of them wish more than any of these   You are of riper years and still young with a warm sympathising heart a true honest steady and steadfast mind a handsome form and comely features a brilliant dark and liquid eye and possessed of a love for fun and mischief just sufficient to make yourself interesting in any position you may occupy   And if these are not of more value than the other accomplishments named then I am no judge of what is valuable in a woman or of what it takes to make a woman lovely in the eyes of man   You may think I am saying more than I am justified in saying having never seen you personally but you know I have seen your picture and looking at it now while I am writing I would again repeat that I believe you possess every qualification that I have ascribed to you and that you would have enjoyed amazingly a trip to this country because your mind is large and would expand as you comprehended more as you saw the world passing before you and you would see everything in its true light and profit accordingly   If I could have met since I have been here in this country with such a mind as I conceive yours to be then I have faith to believe that I should have been the happy one but not meeting with such a one I am still enjoying the miseries of single blessedness with a fair prospect of continuing so to the end of the chapter   But whatever fate may befall me I shall never forget while life lasts the many kind gentle sensible and intelligent letters I have been honored with from you and I sincerely trust that nothing may happen to mar our young friendship or that may tend to interrupt our correspondence   Nothing on my part shall be lacking so far as my power can prevent it though I can not write so much as I have formerly because I am always in one place now and cannot find new always to write about like I could while I was up in the mountains   I have thought I would take several trips up in the country this spring but business has fell off dull and we have taken the dull time to fix up the Ranch in place of going to the country

I went down the Valley some thirty miles a short time ago and a season when all the earth is usually covered with a thick dress of verdure and found that the dress this time was verry scant   We have had an unusually dry winter and the consequence is that farmers will not reap half a crop this year at no place in the state and times promise to be hard in proportion this summer   The wild vegitation feels the effects of the dry winter as well as that which is cultivated and so the mountains look barren and yellow in place of green and bright as usual at this season

I may have been too considerate of the privileges of the Ladies this year and really I am beginning to wish I had not held back so long but what is done can not be helped so I will have to let it pass this time and make up for it next year when it will be in order for me to make advances to the Ladies in place of waiting for them to come to me

I am still living near the shop in the City but I have made a great improvement in my Cabin I have got it all papered nicely with pictures cut out of the pictorial newspapers and you may depend it makes the room look verry nice and cheerful and affords me amusement to look at the pictures when I have got tired of reading or have nothing else to do   I dont know but I told you about it in my last but if I did I forgot it so I put it in now   Maggie laughed at it when she came in to see me after she got here but I told her it was only for old Bachelors to live in and not for Ladies

We have had a continual string of picnics Railroad & Steamboat excursions Balls and Plays going on all the time here but I have been to none of them because I have been too busy to loose the time   I see the long processions pass through the streets but do not feel inclined to take part in them   I would go out more if I was acquainted in the City but being a stranger I could not take part and enjoy myself so well as to stay away   In another while I hope to have been around a little so that I can tell how matters are carried on here as well as up the Mountains where I have been

I had these two sheets of light paper left and thought I would write to you on them if the ink show through you will be able no doubt to read them over and if they pay you for the trouble I will be satisfied so that I get a reply in the course of time

Hoping that this may find you and all your relatives in good health and enoying all the blessings possible and that you will write me again as soon as you can make it convenient

I remain most truly
and sincererly Your Friend
John

To Lizzie

Please excuse all errors as I can not take the time to look over the letter to correct them   I seldom do read over what I have written but on this paper I am apprehensive I have made many mistakes but will trust to your kindness and forbearance to correct any errors

Lyndon (Ohio)   June 24th 1864

Friend John

It has been several days since I received your last favor a letter that I was much pleased with by the way as usual, but I have been too busily engaged to sooner reply or I should have done so. . . .

I had long entertained the hope that maybe *some day* I should see California but have now given up the idea entirely though I should still be happy to go and see some of the sights and doings of the world as well as visit my friends there—nor would it be the least part of my pleasure to see my unseen correspondent who if I *should never* meet shall ever think of as a true and valued friend and I hope ere long you may meet with *that one* whose every trait of mind may be congenial to your own and even prove better than you *now concieve mine to be*—and may you be the happy one, long as life is yours. And should the correspondence between us become nessarily inturupted or cease altogether the friendship need not cease to exist— You still talk so discouraging—you expect to enjoy the "miseries of single blessedness to the end of the chapter" but as I have said I only hope you may be dissappointed in this, and that you will soon meet the *one* just intended to make you happy through all your future life.

I presume Maggie has by this time told you something of what I wrote her in my last about a month ago, concerning my future intentions. If so you will not be surprised when I tell you that a lonely Bachelor here has taken it into his head that your correspondent is the only person suited to his case and that I have at length consented to try the realities of the married state and settle down for life within half a mile of my present home. The time for the consummation of the event is not yet dessignated but it will be in a few months at most, unless something prevents.

Casting the barque on the sea of matrimony has always appeared to me like a *"leap in the dark* and whether I shall prove to be "the happy one" the future only will decide.

I am not in possession of anything that is going on here worth while writing about. Weather has been very dry although we had a nice rain this week that has greatly relieved vegetation of its drooping appearance, prospects for grain crops the coming harvest are but very poor, particularly the wheat and laborers are become so few on account of the war, that were the crops abundant they could scarce be saved. We have no picnics or any thing of the kind going on this summer, young men are so scarce I suppose is the principal reason and those who are at home are too much employed otherwise to attend to such things as they used to do here.

How I should like to take a peep into your cabin. I imagine it looks quite *Picturesque* and I can almost see Maggie laughing at it. You did not tell me of it in another letter. If you will excuse a shorter letter than usual I will soon close this one, my time is limited and news uninteresting perhaps to you. Atmosphere most uncomfortably warm — I shall be obliged to seek a cooler situation than my room in the second story where I am writing.

Now hoping you may pardon all my errors and ever wishing you all the good you are capable of enjoying.

I shall remain ever
Your True Friend
Lizzie.

San Francisco   July 22 1864

Friend Lizzie

Your unusually interesting letter of the 24th ult came duly to hand and was read with much pleasure and I would say joy if I was not afraid of stretching the truth too much   But indeed I was highly gratified to learn that one so Noble and just in sentiment as you are should have found a congenial Spirit with whom she could travel down lifes varried course with a fair prospect ahead of that unbroken stream of happiness that is sometimes alloted to Mortals that others may view and be admonished to go and do likewise

I shall ever cherish in my inmost soul a warm feeling of thankfulness to one whom I deem so good for her kind and friendly wishes towards one so unworthy as myself and it is my earnest wish that you will find in your expected husband all that heart or mind can desire and that you will ever have it to say that it was a happy day when you first met to part no more in life   You indeed are the *happy one* to be so fortunate and I hope that you may be able and willing to impart in your letters (which I hope may never grow less frequent) a little of the serene joy that will necessarily at such a glorious consumation of your wishes be your share in life to your old Bachelor Correspondent in his lonely walk through life

On my part the friendship I feel *will never cease* and should I be so unfortunate as to loose the occasional joy of perusing a friendly letter from you I shall deem it one of the most unlucky days of my life   Let what will happen I hope you will still condescend to impart a ray of pleasure occasionally to one who needs it so much On my part the promise I made before shall be kept and I will never keep a letter but a verry short time unanswered   I am not at all surprised at your giving up the idea of seeing California but at the same time you may yet take a notion after a few years spent in the married life to Emigrate to California and make it your permanent home   Should such be the case none will be more happy than your lonely correspondent to welcome you and yours to these blessed shores

Maggie had not tole me anything about it and the reason I suppose is that I have seen but verry little of her for the last month or two as she is now living on the Ranch and I am still enjoying the miseries of my lonely picture Gallery without a hope of ever bettering my condition   I believe I did describe the various modes of life in the Mountains to you in some of my former letters and to describe mine now all except the pictures would only be a repetition of what I have before written on the subject

My Brother having moved all his traps to the Ranch leaves me only about as I was in the Mountains   I still have my books to amuse and instruct me in my idle hours and if it were not for them I dont think I could stand it to stay here so alone

You say truly I think the step into the state of Matrimony is indeed a leap in the dark but the Ruler of all has so arranged matters that even the most unlucky marriages have their hours of happiness so that if you should not find all just as you could wish it you will still have some of the real pleasures of life and may those pleasures be uninterrupted is my earnest wish

I suppose the male population is verry scarce now throughout most of the Northern states and will be so for some time to come as there is no immediate hope that the war will soon cease   I would to God it were done it is so terrible for friends that should be to be fighting and all for such a poor object   Yet the Union must be preserved and until the south is willing to live in Peace in the Union the war must go on to the end and when that will be no mortal can tell   The season here has been a lively one so far   The 4th of July Celebration was the Grandest that has ever been in this state but for my part I have stayed about home all the time and have taken no part in any of the parties picnics or plays and therefore can not describe to you yet how they do in the city at such places   I was once in hopes I could tell you all about it before this time but so it is I cant do now so but will try and be able in the future to do so

I shall expect a kiss from the Bride when the happy times comes and are past and may you be as happy as a lark in early morn or a linnet in early spring and find every wish and expectation gratified so that every day and hour of wedded life to you may be an hour of blessed content

Hoping that nothing may ever transpire to interrupt our friendly communcations I shall still be

Most truly and faithfully
Your Friend
John

Friend John   Lyndon, Ohio   Aug. 19th 1864

This evening brought with it a friendly and welcome letter from you And as I expect to be very busily ocupied with other affairs for some time ahead I shall steal a few moments from my sleeping hours tonight in which to answer you and particularly because it may be my last opportunity of addressing you again ere I shall not feel my time so freely my own or my name may be no longer the same as it has long remained — but that I shall have to figure as Mrs. - - - - - instead of Miss - - - - -.

If I can really afford you *so much pleasure* (and to one who so much needs it as you say) by an occasional letter I shall promise to answer you often as circumstances are favorable for me so to do. As for me I shall ever be happy to hear of your well being and shall ever cherish your memory as that of a *true* and *worthy Friend* and it matters not whether the correspondence shall cease or be continued, know that my *frindship* shall ever remain the same for you.

It makes me feel sad for you to hear you talk so of being "alone" and "lonely" but come why dont you spruce up — go out in to company, attend those pic-nics and get acquainted with some fair one who perhaps may be an exception to the California fairs and is just the one suited to your fancy — and perhaps is just awaiting your acquaintance — be that as it may I hope you will one day find the true ideal of your heart and that the remainder of your life may be spent so pleasantly that you will forget all your past troubles or that they will only come before you in dim visions of the past — scarce worthy for ought except to be cast aside into the Ocean of forgetfulness.

The time for my departure from "single blessedness" is fixed for next Wednesday the 24th of August. We intend having the affair go off quietly as possible with none present except a few of the near friends.

A kiss from the bride you ask — You could have it most assuredly if I only knew how to send it to you.

It is now quite late and hoping you will excuse a short letter this time, I shall soon retire leaving you my most sincere thanks for your kind and good wishes, and hoping that you may one day realize all that you so kindly wish me — I shall ever remain,

                                                        Your True Friend
                                                              Lizzie

Friend Lizzie   San Francisco   October 9th 1864

Your verry pleasant and interesting letter of the 15th of August came safely to hand this week   I have not answered it before because I could not get time however it has only been on hand 4 days and as you no doubt are verry happy now and enjoying the ecstatic pleasures of the honeymoon you will not miss the occasional scribblings of your Cal correspondent   I am verry thankful to you for your verry kind wishes and sincerely hope and trust that there may never be a shadow across your path as you journey down the vale of life with the chosen one of your friends for your future companion   May you be blessed with all the happiness earth can afford and may your future life be a perpetual sunshine of continual bliss is the prayer of your humble correspondent

Enclosed I send you a blue flower from an evergreen Native California tree whose name I have now forgotten   It is an emblem of eternal regard and truth I send it that you may give it to your husband as a token and further as an emblem of my friendship   It is blue an emblem of truth   May the Love that exists between you ever be guarded by the shield of truth and fidelity   it is evergreen as an emblem of eternity   May that love ever be true and eternal so that when lifes fitful fever is past you may be enabled together to chant the praises of the giver of all good forever and ever

Again I thank you for your kind assurances of continued friendship and I assure you I do not regard it lightly but shall I hope always look with pleasure for the letters of my esteemed correspondent   Give my kindest regards to your honored husband and tell him for me that I hope he will not be jealous if his beloved wife does still occasionally honor her distant correspondent with a letter   Now that you are the *happy one* instead of me I shall expect you to give me good advice as to the beauties of the Married life and the course I shall pursue   I will take your advice now given and if I can find a good girl that wants to throw herself away on a poor superanuated Bachelor like me I will take her for better or worse and do the best I can to fullfill the destiny   I am told that the girls in the City are not the same they are in the Mountains but I am not enough acquainted with them yet to say anything about it but I will tell you when anything happens   I have got acquainted with several who do seem different but am not enough acquainted to see exactly what they are   Since I have been in the city I have been so constantly at my business that I have visited but verry little even with those I have been heretofore acquainted but will in the future endeavor to extend my acquaintance so as to follow out the advice you give me

I have been out to the ranch all day today and left Maggie and the children in good health and all getting along finely

The Political Campaign is now fairly opened here and the war news with it keep up quite an excitement   The news you have so I will not say anything of that I have been so constantly busy here that I have not got any trips to write you of but I hope to make some trips to the country this fall so that I can tell you how thinks look   The Dry Season has so affected the general business of the country that most everybody expects verry hard times here this fall though it will make but verry little difference with me as my occupation is such that a difference in the general business of the country does not affect it much

Again I thank you for your kind assurances of continued friendship and with my most hearty congratulations on your happy Union and hoping to hear at an early day that you are enjoying all the blessing possible

I remain still your
Friend as ever
John

Lattas (Ohio)   Nov. 30th 1864

Friend John

After some delay I now find myself ready to acknowledge the receipt of your kind favor of Oct. 8th. I should have written sooner but various hindrances in the way of domestic affairs have prevented me. Nothing in the way of a "jealous husband" however has prevented my writing, for he exhibits no feeling of that kind but often tells me that he has no objections to my continuing occasional friendly correspondence with any of my old friends if I wish it, and is kind and generous with me in evry way.

So you are right in supposing me in the enjoyment of the pleasures of the *honeymoon* for it is really so — I am married (although it seems odd to think it) and I now realize the pleasures of the new state of existence as all that I had formerly anticipated. And since you ask my advice as to whether you shall go and do likewise I shall say as before when you succeed in finding any one just (or may do) nearly suited to your fancy (which I sincerely hope you may ere long) Why get married and live happy and content the rest of your days. Yet think not, the married life entirely free from all ills troubles and disappointments for such things we can only look for with certainty mingled with our fleeting joys and pleasures while in this vale below.

Thank you for the sweet little flower enclosed in your letter, sweet not in itself alone but for its meening — and may your kind wishes accompanying it one day be all your own to enjoy as well as ours is my prayer. . . .

And wishing the same as ever to hear from all my old friends. I am expecting a letter from Maggie soon — tell her so.

Your friend

P.S.   My new address is   Lizzie

Mrs Joseph Henry
Lattas
Ross County
Ohio

[TWO LETTERS SEEM TO BE MISSING]

San Francisco   Aug 8th 1865

Friend Lizzie

Yours of the 23rd of May reached me or rather I reached here and met the letter about a Month ago   I was much pleased with your letter and gratified too to see by its tone that you are comparatively happy and contented and enjoying life as well as it is possible for any on earth   May your life still be the happiest possible for mortals to enjoy is my earnest wish and may the pathways of Matrimonial bliss ever be green and strewd with Heavans choisest blessing as you journey through life

I believe when I last wrote you I was just recovering from a severe spell of sickness   I got well and went on with my business there [arranging for cotton purchases in Mazatlan, Mexico] for several Months and finally sold out and came loosing largely by the trip   During the last two months I was sick all the time with the Ague Dysentery and Small pox and think myself lucky in escaping with my life I have been confined to the House for three weeks since I came home which may account for and must be my excuse for not answering your letter sooner   My health is now as good as ever as it was or will be in a short time and so is the health of

Maggie and her little family   The boy is growing fast and more pretty as he grows larger

Being so much occupied with sickness and business in Mazatlan and not understanding the language of the people I can not give you as good an idea as I would wish of their manners and customes though having all the time I was there some 8 or 10 of them men and women employed in handling cotton I did see some of their manners   The dress of the Richest Class is verry near the same of the American while the poorer classes dress but verry little   A Skirt shirt and Shawl being their entire dress except sandals on the feet   The climate is verry warm so that but little dress is necessary   in fact if it was fashionable to live as Adam did in the Garden it would be no serious inconveniance to go without any dress at all

The furniture of the houses is more scant and primitive than the dress and an Iron Vessel is seldom used and among the poorer classes not used at all   Corn and pulse or Vegetables is the principle food and meat sometimes   I was in several of the finest Houses in the City and will endeavor to describe one which will do as a description of all as the only difference in any is the fineness or cost of Material there being an uniform sameness in appearance of all   I was invited to dine at the home of one of the wealthy with whom I was dealing   at 5 of P M I presented myself at the door was met by the Host and Introduced into a large square Room brick floor white bare plastered walls and whitewashed timbers overhead heavy hardwood doors and window shutters 2 windows with an Iron grating on the outside something like a prison (all houses or rather windows in the City are so grated)   In one corner of the Room a Piano covered with Turkish plush (a Rare thing here) one side a long Japanese settee (another rarity) in one corner a dresser for bottles and glasses and some 5 or 6 chairs scattered around promiscuously   After talking a few minutes with mine host the Lady of the House a large square built Matronly appearing dame of about 50 years followed by one girl the picture of the mother and one a small fair looking bright eyed damsel of about 16 and a boy near the same age who looked more like a girl than a boy came into the Room and were formally introduced to Don Juan Doblay as the friend of Paterfamilias   I could talk but verry little spanish the Ladies could talk no English so all our conversation was carried on through the Father and son who talked English verry well   After conversing awhile we were summoned to dinner by the ringing of a little bell   We passed through two rooms into the corridor inside the yard where the table was set The first Room about 20 feet square with one bed consisting of an iron bedstead with Mosquito rack and curtains over it a mattress of corn husks with two tanned cow hides and one counterpane as bed and bedding   Beside the head of the bed a small dressing Case set up on a frame   Around the room 2 chairs two trunks and a writing desk which showed this was the parents Room   The next room being nearly similar I supposed was the Sons Room   each Room had one looking glass and no other ornament the walls all entirely bare and brick floors

The table was well supplied with Rich furniture which is common all over the world being only common English Queensware (the wealthy there use Queensware and the poor use altogether common Potteryware)   The table had no cloth and we sit on stools around the table the same as anywhere only we sit farther apart in order I suppose to keep cool more easily   We first had a slice of beef with bread and onions then a slice of Pork bread Garlic and Pepper then fruits such as orange lemons bananas and Mango apples nuts and raisins and then wine and coffee   Each and every course was entirely removed before the next course came on   Four servants waited on us   We remained at the table for full two hours and when I left I was more hungry than when I commenced if any difference as everything was what I call verry scant though was somewhat excused because I was so verry politely treated   They make up in politeness what they lack in provisions   After dinner I talked a few minutes and returned hoping I would never have another invitation out to dinner while there and so I felt the three or four times I was honored with an invitation.

The Girls were dressed verry rich and Gaudy the dresses being verry brilliant colored and of fine material and presented nothing unusual in their appearance more than the colors   The Father was a Spaniard and white the Mother was half indian and inclined strongly to a copper color   The oldest girl like the mother the other two children like the Father   It is nothing unusual here to see all shades of color from a tawney white to the darkest black in the same family   The kitchen furniture is more simple still consisting of a stone to grind the corn and a few pans and pots of Earthenware to cook in   Nearly all the bread used in the country is made of corn   they soak or boil the corn until it is thoroughly softened then wash off the hull and grind it between two small stones by rubbing them together and then bake on an earthenware pan placed over a hole in the ground or in a bank of brick and mortar made for the purpose with a little charcoal fire in it to execute the cooking

If my description is imperfect I must beg you to excuse me for I was so much sick the last few weeks there that I have forgotten a great deal of what I then thought I could write about so that my friends at home would be amused thereby

Everybody smokes in the country   The first thing offered a visitor is a cigar and men women and children smoke but I never saw a Mexican chew tobacco nor smoke a pipe yet   They smoke paper cigars all the time they can

Now that you are happily married and have much to attend to in the way of Domestic duties it will not do for your distant Bachelor friend still lonely and desolate as ever to bother you with his griefs and anxieties too much nor make his letters too long for fear you may tire of the correspondence and thereby deprive him of one of his greatest pleasures which is a letter from you and with my kindest regards to your husband who I am glad to learn is not likely to be jealous and hoping your pathway through life may be the smooth and unbroken and that fortunes fairest smiles may always greet you in every undertaking

> I Remain as ever
> Your Friend
> John

INDIAN NUMBERS

A flat sound

Luta	1	Ko-went-ta	8
Ote-co	2	Wo-aa	9
To-lo-co-se	3	Na-a-cha	10
O-e-sa	4	Lu-sac-a-na	11
Ma-su-ca	5	Ote-sac-a-na	12
Tem-o-ca	6	To-lo-ta-ga	13
Ken-a-kuc-a	7		

[Compare these numbers with those given in C. E. Grunsky's "Stockton Boyhood," Bancroft Library, 1959, p. 77. Probably both lists were taken from the Miwok Indians at Pleasant Springs, 8 miles east of Mokelumne Hill.]

THE MAP
AND ACKNOWLEDGEMENTS

The larger map of the central mines in this volume has been compiled from the following sources: U. S. Geological Survey quadrangles covering this area—Placerville and Jackson sheets used as base maps. Place names are largely those in use during the '50's and early '60's. Many of these have long since evaporated from the land, and some are now forgotten even by local residents. Most of the names in Amador County appear on J. M. Griffith's "Official Map" of that county, 1866. There is no comparable complete early map of Calaveras County. I have relied to some degree on George Goddard's "Map of a Survey of the Mokelumne Hill Canal," of which there is a copy in the Bancroft Library. This shows much of the surrounding area from a "reconnoissance" that leaves much to be desired for accuracy. This area is also covered by J. D. Whitney's "Topographical Map of California" 1873, from which a few names have been secured. Southern El Dorado County is well covered by the A. J. Doolittle "Township Map of Central California," 1868, which is by far the most detailed map of the district north of Yoemet and Fiddletown.

Information has also been obtained from the scrapbook of articles written for the San Andreas and other local papers by Judge James Alexander Smith of San Andreas, also from conversations with Judge Smith, and from the files of *Las Calaveras* the journal of the Calaveras Historical Society, from Mrs. Sadie Hunt the secretary of that Society, from the detailed diaries of Alfred Doten kindly lent by Mr. Warren Howell, and from the present journal of John Doble.

A file of the *Volcano Weekly Ledger* 1855-1859 in the possession of Mr. Abe Garbarini of Jackson has been of help in locating obscure and forgotten townsites and early stores, ranches and gold camps. A series of articles in that paper contributed by an unknown author who calls himself "Traveler" are of especial interest, as well as numerous letters from out-of-the-way mining centers. The *Amador Weekly Ledger,* a continuation of this file (1863-64), has been examined in the Bancroft Library.

John Doble's wanderings are chiefly confined to the area of this map. Places visited by him are reproduced in bold face. Places which have not been accurately located are preceded by a (?) mark. Quartz mines

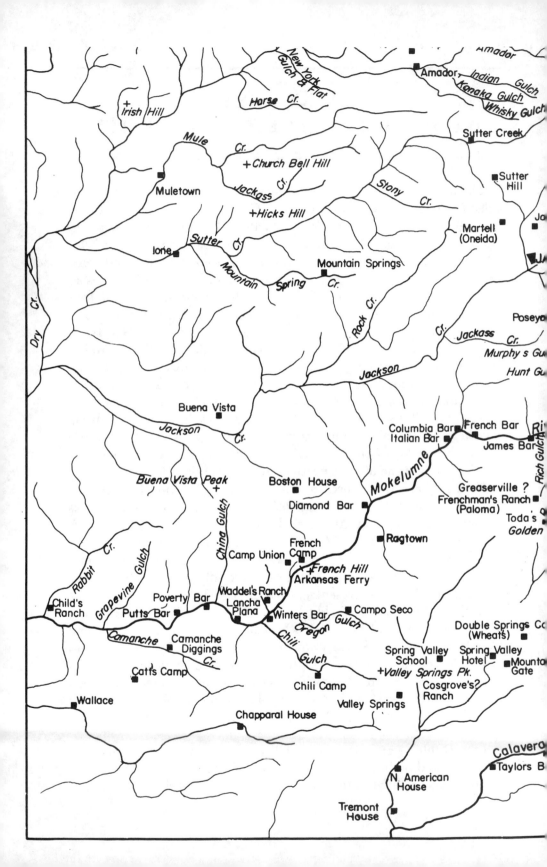

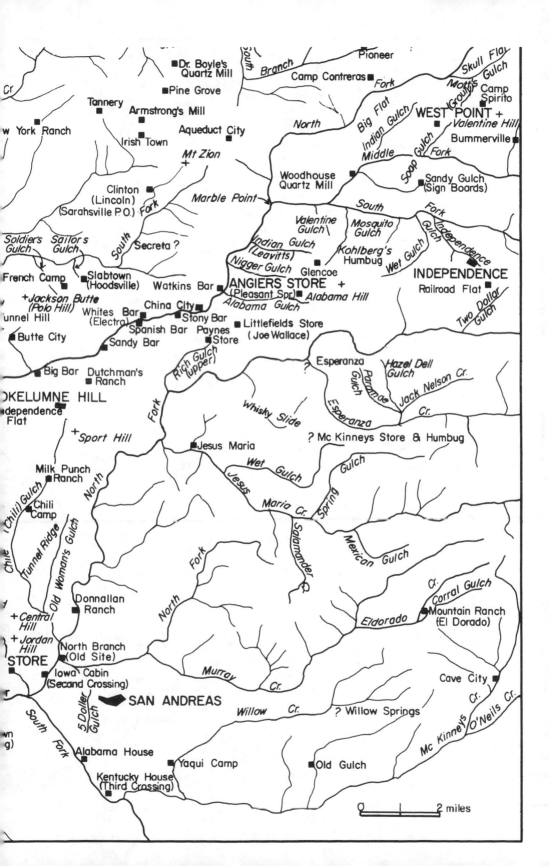

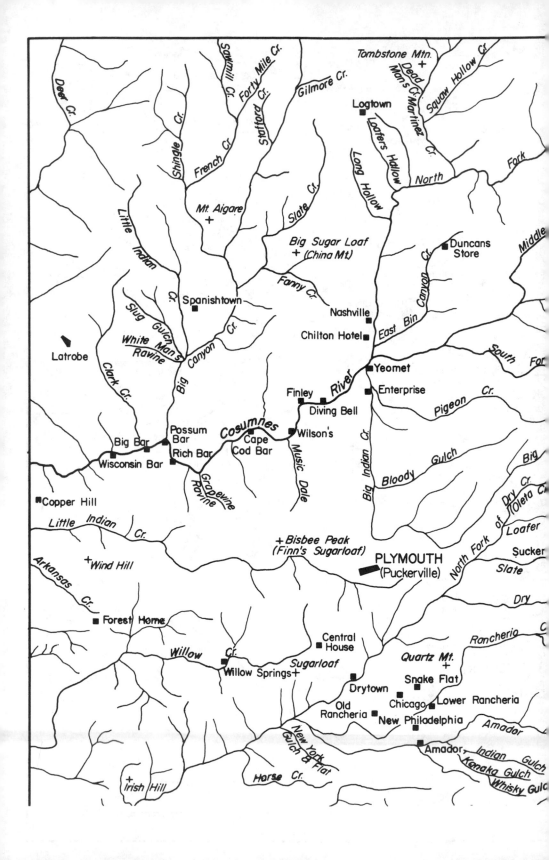

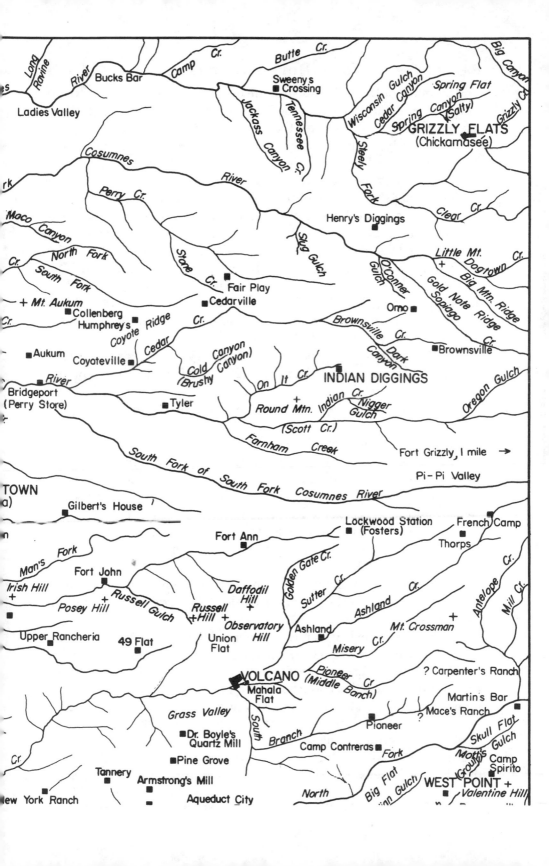

and sawmills of the '70's and later are omitted, as well as roads, towns and ranches established after the '60's. Alternate names, when known, are given in brackets beneath the selected name.

Fort Grizzly, mentioned by Alfred Doten, as "seven miles from Indian Diggings" has been located on the map by Owen C. Coy printed lately at Sacramento.

The smaller sketch maps of the Pleasant Springs area and of Volcano are largely based on Doble's descriptions. For assistance in gathering information, I am indebted to many persons, amongst whom are: Muriel and Jack Thebaut, Mrs. Joey Griffith, and Walter Blomquist of Volcano; N. Burt Randall, Jim Hibbard, John Bradigan, and Mrs. Betty Bose of Fiddletown, and Paul Lewis of San Andreas. The Mc-Kisson brothers, Robert F. and Harold, who were born and still live on the Pleasant Springs site, have been very helpful. Walter Hartgrove of Oakdale has assisted with the map.

Mr. Warren Howell, a good friend, has very generously permitted me to examine the extensive and useful Alfred Doten diary (now the property of the University of Nevada) and to gather from it some otherwise inaccessible data. I am also deeply indebted to Dr. George P. Hammond, Director of the Bancroft Library, for examination of the rich resources of that notable institution.

John Doble of Berkeley, a grandnephew of our "John," has been most generous in providing documents and photographs and gaining the consent of his family to the publication of these records. The Lizzie Lucas and Margaret Doble letters were long ago saved by the Doble family. They had never seen the journal. Another descendant of Abner Doble, Mrs. Victor H. Doyle (née Delphine Ferrier), has been most gracious. Mr. and Mrs. Doyle have recently visited members of the family still living in Indiana. I also want to thank my friend Mrs. Clotilde Grunsky Taylor for the records of her grandfather and his associates.

Finally, I acknowledge an exceptional obligation to Mr. James R. Little of Columbia, Missouri, who has saved and copied the John Doble letters to Lizzie Lucas, Mr. Little's grandmother. He has recently presented this correspondence to the Bancroft Library. My debt is large to the Bancroft Library and to the Huntington Library, for many courtesies, and to Miss Ruth Teiser for valuable help in reading the manuscript and page proofs.

Publication has gone forward under the encouragement and interest of Mr. Fred Rosenstock, the fortunate owner of the Doble Journal.

NOTES

1. Oscar Lewis: "Sea Routes to the Gold Fields," New York, 1949, provides a review of Cornelius Vanderbilt's enterprise in establishing the Nicaragua route, and quotes the experiences of travelers down to the time of Mark Twain in 1866. See also: Roger Baldwin: "Tarrying in Nicaragua, 1849," *Century Magazine,* October, 1891; Thomas E. Massie: "Diary of a Voyage" Ms. Bancroft Library, who describes in humorous detail a Nicaraguan crossing from west to east; O. P. Fitzgerald: "California Sketches," Nashville, 1879, remembers his crossing, 1851, as larded with whiskey, profanity and gunpowder; Samuel F. Holbrook: "Autobiography," 1857, mentions his eastward crossing in 1851 and the difficulties on the muddy trails as encountered by Doble; Joseph A. Stuart: "My roving Life," Auburn, Calif., 1895, went east by Nicaragua in November, 1851, returned in December on the *Daniel Webster* (Doble's ship, but a month later), crossed Nicaragua again and boarded the *North America* at San Juan on January 4, 1852, for San Francisco; the Rev. John Steele: "In Camp and Cabin," Lodi, Wis., 1901, records his eastward trip by way of Nicaragua in July, 1851; J. C. Buffum: "Diary, 1847-1855," Ms. Calif. State Library, and transcript in Bancroft, returned from the mines via Nicaragua in December, 1851. John M. Letts: "California Illustrated," New York, 1852, has interesting descriptions and sketches of various scenes in Nicaragua and Guatemala, on Doble's route. Doble's account is superior, more detailed.

2. The famous Castillo Viejo destroyed by the young Captain Horatio Nelson, in 1780.

3. "The Gault House was opened in 1850 by John B. Nye and Samuel Geddes on the southwest corner of Center and Market streets, in Stockton. It was a 2½ story wooden structure costing $12,000 ... destroyed by fire August 20, 1881." (Note by V. Covert Martin.)

4. This name, not readily decipherable, seems to read: "Semmins." Major John Stemmons is mentioned in the "Doten Diary" June 28, and July 1, 1853, as the proprietor of an inn on the Stockton-Mokelumne Hill road, presumably the Six Mile House where Doble stopped. Doten says that Stemmons had a young son and a blue-eyed, 'teen-aged daughter, Maria: "... dined at the Stemmons House and had a long chat with the Major. Saw his pretty daughter. ... I put up at old Major Stemmons for the night. After supper as there was a violin there I was pressed into service. I played a lot of my best tunes and a little boy of the Major's danced. I sang several of my best songs, and altogether we had a fine little time. *Miss Maria Stemmons looked on with all her big blue eyes and allmost made me fall in love again.*"

According to his obituary in the *San Francisco Chronicle,* May 27, 1856, Major John Stemmons came to California from Kentucky in 1849, "with his three sons. ... His comfortable cabin was the favorite resort of a few who knew him. He was a Representative from San Joaquin County in the California Assembly in 1854." He died of cancer in San Francisco, May 26, 1856, at the age of sixty.

Stemmons deserves attention as the reputed author of an undiscovered book on

California and the Plains: "The Journal of Maj. John Stemmons of Rocheport, Mo. ... Noted down in the shape of familiar letters to his friends, and embracing every incident connected with his trip to California, over the Plains last year [1849]." Published by Fisher & Bennett, St. Louis. A notice of this was published in the *Missouri Republican*, February 21, 1850; quoted by Dale Morgan in his "Pritchard Diary," Denver, 1959, p. 12.

Friederick Gerstaecker in his "Travels," London, 1854, says that nearly every mile between Stockton and Double Springs had a tent or log cabin. At least eleven of these were hostleries of varying degrees of luxury.

The Six Mile House, no trace of which remains, seems to have been located at a spring or sump now filled in, 100 yards south of Highway 8, and about ¼ mile southwest of the Glenwood Store at one time known as Enterprise, 6 miles east of Stockton.

5. Alfred Doten seemed to favor the Tremont House. In September, 1851, by his "Diary," he "partook of one of Mrs. Taylor's excellent dinners to which we did ample justice" and he witnessed a fight between a Frenchman and one of the proprietors, possibly Harris the bartender. The Frenchman had taken sides with a Negro who was being refused service in the dining room.

On October 30, 1852, Doten says that Dave Keller and another man had just bought out Taylor's Tremont House.

According to Rensch, Rensch and Hoover's "Historic spots in California — Valley and Sierra Counties," Stanford Press, 1933, there were seventeen public houses along the Linden Road in 1850. The Tremont House stood 1½ miles south of the North America House "on the North side of the road nearly half way from Jenny Lind to Valley Springs." It was built of lumber brought around the Horn. No trace remains today. "Linden grew up around the 15 Mile House, a tavern established by Dr. W. W. Treblecock in the fall of '49."

The site of the 15 Mile House is now said to be "Solari's" two miles east of Linden.

6. The first county seat of Calaveras County. The remains of the Court House are preserved in the yard of the Wheat home where seven generations of the Alexander Wheat family have lived, and/or are living. See: The *Calaveras Prospect* (San Andreas), July 15, 1899; E. A. Wiltsee in *Stamps*, June 29, 1935, and in *Calif. Hist. Soc. Quarterly*, vol. 11, 1932, pp. 176-183; J. A. Smith "Early Calaveras History," *Hist. Bulletin* (Calaveras Co. Hist. Soc.), vol. 1, no. 1, p. 1; Maud S. Washburn, "Iowa Log Cabins," *Las Calaveras*, vol. 6, no. 1, p. 3; Ida M. Wimer: "Alexander Reid Wheat," *Historical Bulletin* (Calaveras Co. Hist. Soc.), vol. 1, no. 4. R. C. Wood's "Calaveras the Land of Skulls," Sonora, Calif., 1955, pp. 41-45, and photo opp. p. 79.

7. An article in the *Stockton Record*, copied in part in *Las Calaveras*, vol. 5, no. 4, recalls some anecdotes of D. Latimer and his store. He was a good-natured Yankee. His daughter came out in the *Gold Hunter* on the same voyage as John Doble, and that may be the reason that Doble and his partners headed for Latimer's place upon arrival in California.

"David Lattimer" is listed in the "Directory of men in Calaveras County," in 1850, according to notes in "Diary of a 'used up' miner, Jacob Henry Bachman," *Calif. Hist. Soc. Quarterly*, vol. 22, 1943, p. 83. The *Calaveras Chronicle*, October 12, 1861, lists him as postmaster at "North Branch," the official name for his place in Latimer Gulch.

Latimer's Store seems to have been situated on an old excavated site just west of the old road near the junction of the North Branch of Calaveras River and Latimer Gulch. Mr. G. Macchianello had a store at or near this location in later years. In Latimer's time there was a cluster of some 50 tents, near his store. Even today, tourists stop nearby to pan gold, rarely retrieving more than a few flakes and experiencing the same kind of poor luck that Doble had at this place.

There seems to have been but little successful placering in Latimer Gulch. The quartz ledges above it were another story. Doten writes in his "Diary," June 22, 1851: "Took supper at Toaler's [Toda's?] house about a mile above Double Springs. There we saw some pretty girls and ate supper with much satisfaction. Arrived at Chinn's Ranch at 10 in the evening . . . There has been some very rich quartz found between the forks of this [Calaveras] river and today there was a meeting held at Mr. Lattimore's store to make regulations for it. Our quartz lead runs down one side of [Lower] Rich Gulch on the Moquelomne river and this gulch has been one of the richest in California."

8. A Frenchman operated the sawmill and Edwin Taylor was the storekeeper at Buckeye, east of Moke Hill. Taylor later became postmaster at Railroad Flat.

9. Angier's Store is indicated on the Goddard Map of the Mokelumne Hill Canal. It stood on the westward slope of Alabama Hill, above Alabama Gulch (which Doble sometimes calls Spring Gulch), where the Robert F. McKisson residence now stands. A sketch of the Angier cabins approximately as they appeared in Doble's time may be seen in C. E. Grunsky's reminiscences edited by his daughter Clotilde G. Taylor, and entitled: "Stockton Boyhood," Bancroft Library, 1959, p. 11. Carl E. Grunsky's father, Charles, had come to America from Germany in 1844, and in 1849 he joined the Eutaw party of Alabamans who reached the gold country by way of Panama. They mined very successfully at Upper Rich Gulch, they named Alabama Hill, and Grunsky built the store and boarding house at Pleasant Springs in the fall of 1849. They eventually operated a string of fifty or sixty pack-mules to transport supplies for that store. Charles returned to Württemberg in 1851 and brought out his bride early in 1852, by the Nicaragua route.

The Grunsky enterprises are much more fully described in the letters and diaries of Charles and Clotilde Grunsky translated and edited by Clotilde Grunsky Taylor and distributed in mimeographic form to present-day relatives. A copy is available in the Bancroft Library which also has the original manuscripts. Charles Grunsky had met the Angier family in Alabama and they all traveled together, along with the Hoerchner's, to San Francisco and into the mines, where the three heads of the families as well as Capt. Tobin and Dr. Angier the dentist, who may have been one of D. L. Angier's cousins, formed a partnership.

D. L. Angier and his wife Selina had at that time a son James and a daughter Betsy. They had lost an infant son, Cutler, on July 4, 1849, at sea, and the German doctor Hoerchner also lost a child on this voyage. The remains of both these children were brought to San Francisco where they were buried (*Daily Alta California,* Aug. 16, 1849).

D. L. Angier took charge of the store and boarding house at Pleasant Springs, late in 1850. It did well under his management. "Mr. Kohlberg" (Doble's Colburg?) was put in charge at Rich Gulch, Dr. Adolphe H. Hoerchner set up the wholesale end of the business at Stockton. D. L. Angier ran the pack trains until October, 1850, when he, with his family, took over the management of the Pleasant Springs store. Grunsky supervised the pack trains during the winter. He then had 35 mules with five Mexican muleteers, more were added later as well as a stock of live cattle for slaughter at the Springs. In January, 1851, business at the store on each of five or six Sundays had amounted to "more than $1000," but was falling off.

Charles Grunsky's return to Germany, his marriage to Clotilde, and their crossing of the Isthmus of Nicaragua are described in detail. George Angier, a cousin of D. L. Angier accompanied them. Charles heard that Dr. Hoerchner had built a brick warehouse and a hotel, the "Crescent City," in Stockton. This hotel was being managed by Herman Bomeisler and "Isel" (Joel?) Angier, another cousin of D. L. Angier. Early in 1852, a "large new building" had been erected by D. L. Angier at Pleasant Springs, where 100 miners were then working.

In May, 1852, Charles and Clotilde arrived in Stockton and stayed at their own hotel, then being managed by Dr. Hoerchner's brother. The partners had added a ranch and a quartz mill to their rapidly expanding enterprises. In July, 1853, the partnership broke up. Charles Grunsky took the run-down hotel and the ranch five miles east of Stockton, D. L. Angier accepted the Stockton warehouse, and Dr. Hoerchner took over the store at Pleasant Springs which was valued at $11,600. The Angier's were then planning to return to the States. Dr. Angier, the dentist, remained and did not return East until 1864.

Dr. Hoerchner, when the placers gave out, established a sanitarium for worn-out miners at Pleasant Springs. Every trace of this has vanished. It was located northeast of Robert McKisson's house. This house still has the remains of the rock-walled cellar of Angier's Store beneath it. The place boasted a schoolhouse until a few years ago, and old-timers still remember it as "Pleasant Springs."

Dr. A. H. Hoerchner was the first postmaster at Pleasant Springs; postoffice established March 16, 1855; moved to Rich Gulch in 1857, discontinued 1867, reestablished 1887, and discontinued in 1903, (Paul Lewis note). The postoffice records and other sources give his name as Hoerschner. The Grunsky letters consistently spell it Hoerchner and his gravestone in the Mokelumne Hill Protestant cemetery perpetuates it as "Hoerchner" and says he was a native of Eisenach, Saxony, and that he died on Sept. 23, 1870, aged 47 years, one month, and 5 days.

Dr. Hoerchner was said to have been a member of the spoofing Order of E. Clampus Vitus at Mokelumne Hill in 1850, but like so many Clamper yarns, this may be apocryphal.

10. Mr. Harold C. McKisson has shown me a small excavated flat with a pile of stones on it, about 200 yards west of his house at Pleasant Springs. This spot may well be the site of Doble's tent and stone fireplace. It is "on the side of the hill about 50 yards above the bottom of the [Alabama] Gulch."

11. A few of these mortar holes may still be seen in the bed rock along the bottom of Alabama Gulch just below the present road crossing. When the road was paved, most of the mortars were covered up and blasted away. One of these has been rescued by Mr. Harold McKisson.

The Indian Camp lay on the hillside just north of the road and east of Alabama Gulch. The shallow saucer-shaped excavation for the round house, about 30 feet in diameter, is still visible. The only round houses remaining today are those at Tuolumne and Ione.

Polo was a wild Miwok chief in this district, mentioned by Bayard Taylor ("Eldorado"), and Taylor named what is now Jackson Butte—"Polo's Peak." Polo was killed by a member of Stevenson's Regiment in 1851. A later head-man was "Chief McKenzie." See: "Indian History of Calaveras" by George Poore, Jr., *Historical Bulletin* (Calaveras Co. Hist. Soc.), vol. 1, no. 4; and Grace Lytle "Personal memories of Rich Gulch and Glencoe" *Las Calaveras,* vol. 7, no. 2, for recollections of the last Indians at Pleasant Springs.

Doten mentions what apparently were these Indians on Sunday, September 14, 1851: "Some went hunting, some played cards etc. while others went up to the head of [Rich] Gulch to the 'Indian Rancheria' to prospect some of the squaws."

12. J. D. Borthwick: "Three years in California," Edinburgh and London, 1857, has a memorable description of Mokelumne Hill. He gives a first-hand account of the bull-and-bear fight held on "March 15, 1852," with illustrations. The *Calaveras Chronicle,* published at Moke Hill, in its issue of February 14, 1852 (vol. 1, no. 18) runs an extended advertisement of this fight which was announced for the next day.

13. This was the miner's cat or ring-tailed cat *(Bassariscus),* belonging to the raccoon family. Cats were uncommon in the mines and these gentle little nocturnal beauties were the mouse-catching substitutes.

14. This seems to be the place described by the author of "Tracks of a Traveler" in: *Volcano Weekly Ledger,* vol. 2, no. 41, Aug. 1, 1857. "Traveler" calls it "French Camp" at the east base of Jackson Butte, half a mile from "Hoodsville" (Slabtown), a collection of canvas houses and other shanties to the number of a dozen, principally occupied by Frenchmen. "The chief production seems to be goats, of which I counted fifty-seven."

From this place "Traveler" hiked around the south side of Jackson Butte to Butte City where, as reported in the August 15 issue of the *Ledger,* he found some foreigners who couldn't speak English engaged in the erection of a large stone building. Possibly this was the "Ginocchio Store," an empty structure still standing on the site of Butte City.

The camp called Secreta is not mentioned by "Traveler." It was evidently somewhere near Slabtown. Clinton, in "Traveler's" time, is said to have had the post-office name: "Sarahsville."

15. Chickamasee seems to be an Indian place name, not previously recorded. The present Grizzly Flats postoffice building in El Dorado County, is one of the oldest in the state. It may well be that the early name, Indian Diggings, antecedes the present contracted form of that name. Very little remains there. Both places are described in Paoli Sioli: "Historical Souvenir of El Dorado County," Oakland, 1883.

A number of communications from obscure and forgotten camps near Volcano are to be found in the *Volcano Ledger,* which says (vol. 1, no. 5, Nov. 17, 1855) that 75 buildings were put up at Indian Diggings since July 15, 1855. This indicates a spurt of activity in that year. Doten who visited the "Diggings" on October 30, 1854, says it was "not much of a place as yet, the town consists of some forty or fifty houses, the El Dorado and the St. Chalk [St. Charles?] included."

16. There is some question as to just where Esperanza was located. Some say it was a little distance up Esperanza Creek from its junction with the North Fork. Owen Coy puts it on the Mokelumne River, on his map. Doble's statement shows that this must be wrong.

Doble says he "went up the River," evidently meaning Esperanza Creek, to "McKinney's branch," another unlocated stream or gulch. The *Calaveras Chronicle* vol. 1, no. 1, Oct. 18, 1851, mentions "McKinnie's Humbug," between Moke Hill and San Andreas, and "some 6 miles from Moke Hill." This was evidently not the better-known McKinney's near Cave City.

On April 7, Doble mentions a "McKinney from Maine" who killed their dog Stingo. On June 22 he says that this McKinney had a brother Abe. John McKinney a miner, hunter and trapper of 1850, had his name given to a creek in Placer County and a bay where he had a resort on Lake Tahoe (E. G. Gudde, "California Place Names," Univ. Calif. Press, 1949).

17. Valentine Granados, well known Mexican prospector of Calaveras County. His name is commemorated in Valentine Hill north of Bummerville, and in Valentine Gulch, a branch of the Middle Fork of the Mokelumne.

18. This particular Greaserville, one of many, was at or near Butte City. A more polite name for the Mexican camps near or in the mining settlements was Sonoran-town.

19. Some early accounts of Jackson are not highly complimentary, for instance, the *Sacramento Union* quoted in the Amador *Weekly Ledger*, vol. 8, no. 39, Aug. 1, 1863, has this to say:

"Passed through Jackson an uninviting little town squeezed together on one short street which is entered through a sort of Mongolian vestibule, the first half of it being lined with the queer shanties of the Chinese and their jabbering inmates."

To which Tom Springer, editor of the *Ledger*, retorted: "We will bet that the author of the above was tight when he passed through this place."

Rivalry between Jackson and the neighboring town of Moke Hill was even more furious in the '50's. H. A. DeCourcey, editor of the *Calaveras Chronicle*, responds to scurrilous taunts from the *Jackson Sentinel*, with protestations on the cleanliness of Moke Hill in comparison with the nauseous fumes arising from the streets of its neighbor beyond the Mokelumne, where a grizzly bear was kept tied on a chain.

20. This spring was against the rock near the present Masonic Cave. Sluicing operations finally washed out the bed of North Branch so deeply as to destroy the spring.

21. This questionably felicitous name was reputed to have been a brainwave of the local wag, Doc. W. I. Morgan, whose house stood at the west side of Masonic Rock, opposite the famous "bend." Doble's description would place the "bend" along the west side of South Branch, to the south of the bridge crossing Sutter Creek near the entrance to its canyon. See entry of March 13, 1852.

22. It has been said that volcanoes existed only in the imaginations of the miners and the fancies of some of the journalists. That may be true of the journalists but not of the miners. Bayard Taylor in his "Eldorado," New York, 1850, gives a sketch of a cabin under the east face of Rocky Point (Masonic Rock—Doble's "pile of rocks"), as well as a description of Volcano in 1849. Taylor seemed to think that the blackened cave entrances at Rocky Point were exits of volcanic fires.

Taylor's fancy led him astray, and the early miners who named the town perceived and interpreted the evidence correctly when they declared, from the nature of certain rocks, that there had been a volcano in the vicinity. Doble's statement is one of the earliest on record. He says that the peculiar "fused" rocks lying over some of the limestone ledges had the appearance of lava. Similar remarks come from the [San Francisco] *Daily Evening Bulletin*, October 7, 1857: "the miners called the light, grey, yellow and reddish colored stone above the limestone, lava."

This very rock is now being quarried for building stone and ornamental "picture rock." It is a tough, heavy, siliceous material (welded tuff) formed by the fusion of volcanic ash and pumice during explosive eruptions from an open vent such as a fissure or a volcano. The peculiar rock disintegrates upon prolonged exposure, and examples of such weathering, well known to the miners and mentioned by Doble, may be seen near the Catholic cemetery in Volcano.

The second issue of the *Volcano Ledger*, November 3, 1855, contains two stories on the history and appearance of the town. One of these says that the name "was suggested by the evidences of volcanic action which were exhibited here in the immense ledges of granite rock which lie in normous piles all over the adjacent foothills, particularly those on the northern side." Change "granite" to "lava" and the reports tend to agree.

The idea that Volcano was situated in a "crater" seems to have arisen during the late 1850's, when the town was nicknamed "Crater City." None of the early records known to me say anything about this supposed crater. Doble, Doten and the early newspaper accounts do not mention it.

Another legend of Volcano revolves around the tale that two members of Stevenson's Regiment, who were said to have been the first to mine there, perished during the winter of 1848-49. Their bodies lying in their huts were purported to have been found the next spring by Mexican prospectors. The name Soldiers Gulch—first applied to Volcano—is reminiscent of this episode. The origin of that report seems to be obscure. Col. Stevenson who led a party from his ex-regiment into the Mokelumne River placers in the fall of '48, denied that he had lost any of his men that winter. The diaries of members of Stevenson's regiment do not mention the incident nor do Doble, and Doten, and the newspapers. The demise and final resting places of most of the members of the regiment are matters of record. Until further evidence is produced, one may remain skeptical.

Jesse D. Mason whose excellent account of Volcano appeared in the "History of Amador County, California," Oakland, 1881, is one of the first to recount the tale of the dead soldiers. This may be significant, as Mason came at least as early as 1853 and had a wide local acquaintance.

The earliest version of the soldier story seems to be that in the *Volcano Ledger*, vol. 2, no. 13, Jan. 17, 1857, where it is said that soldiers from Stevenson's Regiment discovered Volcano and *named it*. Evidently this version was being told before the death tale was circulated. The deceased could scarcely have transmitted the name unless they had written it down somewhere.

A fine enlargement made from Walter Blomquist's old tin types may be seen in the barroom of the St. George Hotel. This is a composite of three original photos, and shows the town as it was in Civil War days (or slightly later), crowded between the ravaging sluicing operations in Soldier Gulch and on Sutter Creek. A fair reproduction of this view is given in Mary E. Crosby's "California's Mother Lode," Universal City, 1959, p. 17.

Miss Crosby's pamphlet: "Volcano," Universal City, 1957, gives the history as well as photographs of the past and present appearance of the village—one of the most interesting relics of mining days to be found in the Mother Lode. She reproduces a curious old lithograph of the town as it was in 1856. Another view may be found in C. B. Glasscock's "A Golden Highway," Indianapolis, 1934, opp. page 260.

A survey by John Samuel Fox, "Volcano and Buildings, Registered Landmark No. 29" [California historical landmarks], Berkeley, 1936; 9 typed pp. and bibliog., gives a short history and the condition of the town at that time. Pearl E. Brown's thesis: "History of early mining in Amador County," may be consulted in the Bancroft Library.

Volcano's eruptive days are not yet over. Only recently, and perhaps even today, the place may be threatened with a watery grave, as it lies on a valuable dam site.

Stories of Volcano are told by Evelyn Wells and Harry C. Peterson in: "The '49ers," New York, 1949, pp. 105-110. Here is an account of the drowning of the town "under the waters of a great dam." Evelyn might be excused for this, but what about Harry?

Paradoxically, the immediate threat is not too much water but too little. The town's source supply has been cut into by mining operations. Survival now hangs on the availability of a meager supply of water.

23. A. M. Ballard was the proprietor of the National House, in Volcano in 1855. He was notorious for his coffee, "Ballard's coffee," which he was accused of having found growing in the woods! (*Volcano Ledger*, Oct. 3, 1857). His "Humbug" was evidently located in the gulch along the present road from Pine Grove to Volcano, just where the road makes its last plunge into the valley of Volcano (South Branch).

24. Dr. Thomas Flint of the firm of Flint and Bixby. Mason says that he built the National House at Volcano in 1851. His diaries, across Panama in 1851 and to Illinois and return with sheep in 1852-1855, were published in *Annual Pub'l's. Hist. Soc. Southern Calif.*, vol. 12, 1923, pp. 53-127; issued separately (1924), with notes by Sarah Bixby Smith.

Roderick Stowell, the hot-headed Texan gunman and knife fighter, evidently had some association with Flint who was a hardy Yankee but scarcely one to incite others to violence. The story of Rod's trial, in a slightly different and less detailed version, has been told by Mason (Hist. Amador County). Mason tells of another killing by the violent Rod. Tradition has accused the miners of impulsive "justice" in their *vigilante* trials and necktie parties. But here, as in other cases mentioned by Doble, there was an uncommonly charitable dispensation of "miner's law." Stowell finally came to trial at Mokelumne Hill in April, 1853, and he was set free "for lack of evidence," (entry for April 10, 1853).

Other cases of leniency or indifference may be recalled, nevertheless the lawyer, Leonard Kip, who visited Volcano in 1850, wrote a story "The Volcano Diggings; a tale of California Law," New York, 1851, in which the early crude state of society is described. The tale develops into a powerful critique of the unjust workings of "Lynch law" in the mines.

Kip's harrowing story may have had some influence. The "Green Horn Lyceum" at Ashland, a camp of not more than 40 cabins, situated on Sutter Creek, 3 miles above Volcano, had under discussion in 1856 the topic: "Resolved that it would be policy for the government of the U. S. to abolish Capital Punishment," antedating modern debates on this subject by more than one hundred years, (*Volcano Ledger*, vol. 1, no. 16).

25. James B. Troutman is listed as a member of Co. F., Stevenson's Regiment. This can hardly be the same man. Doble knew Jim Troutman and Doc. Carpenter very well as they were both his partners. His statement that they came across the Plains together can hardly be doubted. James A. Troutman died at Volcano in 1853. His gravestone preserves one of the oldest dates in the local cemetery. The stone itself looks remarkably fresh, as though it had been set up recently.

26. Samuel Elsie, a Scot, was drowned on December 31. He was probably the Elsie who ran a ranch in Grass Valley near Volcano. His daughter (?) Hannah was married to John James on May 15, 1853, at Volcano (see entry for that date).

These floods drowned some of the miners and starved out many more. Doten reports in his "Diary," January 3, 1853, at Spanish Gulch, that "The miners about the Mariposa were reduced by starvation to rob the teams on the road, and large bands of them are on their way from Angels, Vallecito, Murphy's Jesus Maria and many other places down to Stockton and San Francisco, being fairly starved out. There is a small quantity of flour at the [Mountain?] Gate for sale at a dollar a pound. Hard times indeed!!!"

27. Compare entries for October 24 and 25, 1852, and June 11, 1853. She was a sister of the Lewis brothers according to Mason. An obituary of James L. Halstead appeared in the *San Jose Pioneer,* vol. 12, no. 2, Feb., 1897, pp. 232-4. A native of New York State, he became a lumber merchant and later a distinguished lawyer in Santa Cruz County. Mason says that he took up a ranch on lower Volcano Flat next to town in 1851, raised potatoes and sold them to the miners. Doble's entry of November 13, 1853, shows that on that date J. L. Halstead married Miss Brown a recent overland emigrant.

28. Mason says the murderers were one Chris [Stevens] and Harry Fox, who were captured on board the steamer *Brother Jonathan* returning to Nicaragua from San Francisco. Chris threw himself overboard and was drowned. Harry was taken to Moke Hill, escaped from jail and was recaptured. See: entry of October 6, 1853, where Doble indicates that Chris's last name was Stevens.

29. This was evidently the larger part of Kit Carson's drove of 8,500 sheep in two separate flocks; *Calif. Hist. Soc. Quarterly,* vol. 1, no. 2, Oct. 1922, p. 149.

30. This was the first destructive fire in Volcano. The Empire Hotel, Frank Tarbell, proprietor, was completed on the site in December. This burned in the great fire of 1859 and was replaced by the first St. George Hotel which burned in October 1862. The present St. George Hotel, so named to 'thwart the demonic Fire Dragon,' was built on the spot in 1867 and now for nearly 100 years the charm has held; so goes the legend. Actually the owner of the first St. George was none other than B. F. George! Could he have been the "Mr. George" who with his "lady" lived with John Doble in Volcano? The old structure was competently renovated by Walter Blomquist in 1932, and it was purchased by Doctor and Mrs. Griffith. It is now owned and managed by Mrs. Joey Griffith.

31. Peter Y. Cool built the Methodist Church at Volcano, dedicated July 15, 1852. The next year he was replaced temporarily by J. L. Bennett. Rev. J. W. Brier, the Jayhawker of Death Valley fame, took over in July, 1857, and built a new church. Thomas Starr King is said to have spoken there during the Civil War — (C. V. Anthony: "Fifty Years of Methodism," San Francisco, 1901).

Cool and Father Rickey built the first church and school at Ft. John, and Cool was one of those for whom Ministers Gulch was named — (Coke Wood, "Calaveras," pp. 35 and 96). Cool's brief diary is in the Huntington Library. It mentions operations at Amador City, Dry Diggings and Ft. John.

32. The Calaveras Big Trees State Park on Highway 4. It was here that one of the great sequoias was "skinned" for the Crystal Palace Fair in London. Some of the local people thought that those who skinned the bark from the tree should have been skinned themselves.

33. Thomas Starr King. Doble may have heard him orate for the Union cause at Volcano.

34. Letter from Elizabeth Grey, assistant in the Genealogy Division, Indiana State Library, Indianapolis; and, "Atlas of Shelby County, Indiana," Chicago: J. H. Beers Co., 1880, p. 28.

35. *Alta California,* July 1, 1850.

36. "History of Humboldt County," San Francisco, 1882, p. 180.

37. Phelps: "Contemporary biography of California's representative men," San Francisco, 1881-82, vol. 2, p. 100. Murray: "The builders of a great city," San Francisco, 1891, vol. 1, p. 143 (and photo).

38. Clipping attached to letter of John Doble, December 29, 1863.

39. Information from Mr. John Doble of Berkeley, California.

INDEX